Edinburgh Companion to Twentieth-Century Scottish Literature

Edinburgh Companions to Scottish Literature

Series Editors: Ian Brown and Thomas Owen Clancy

Titles in the series include:

The Edinburgh Companion to Robert Burns
Edited by Gerard Carruthers
978 0 7486 3648 8 (hardback)
978 0 7486 3649 5 (paperback)

The Edinburgh Companion to Twentieth-Century Scottish Literature
Edited by Ian Brown and Alan Riach
978 0 7486 3693 8 (hardback)
978 0 7486 3694 5 (paperback)

The Edinburgh Companion to Contemporary Scottish Poetry
Edited by Matt McGuire and Colin Nicholson
978 0 7486 3625 9 (hardback)
978 0 7486 3626 6 (paperback)

Forthcoming titles include:

The Edinburgh Companion to Muriel Spark
Edited by Michael Gardiner and Willy Maley
978 0 7486 3768 3 (hardback)
978 0 7486 3769 0 (paperback)

The Edinburgh Companion to Robert Louis Stevenson
Edited by Penny Fielding
978 0 7486 3554 2 (hardback)
978 0 7486 3555 9 (paperback)

The Edinburgh Companion to Irvine Welsh
Edited by Berthold Schoene
978 0 7486 3917 5 (hardback)
978 0 7486 3918 2 (paperback)

The Edinburgh Companion to Scottish Romanticism
Edited by Murray Pittock
978 0 7486 3845 1 (hardback)
978 0 7486 3846 8 (paperback)

Edinburgh Companion to Twentieth-Century Scottish Literature

Edited by Ian Brown and Alan Riach

Edinburgh University Press

© in this edition Edinburgh University Press, 2009
© in the individual contributions is retained by the authors

Edinburgh University Press Ltd
22 George Square, Edinburgh

www.euppublishing.com

Typeset in 10.5 on 12.5pt Goudy
by Servis Filmsetting Limited, Stockport, Cheshire, and
printed and bound in Great Britain by
CPI Antony Rowe, Chippenham and Eastbourne

A CIP record for this book is available from the British Library

ISBN 978 0 7486 3693 8 (hardback)
ISBN 978 0 7486 3694 5 (paperback)

The right of the contributors
to be identified as authors of this work
has been asserted in accordance with
the Copyright, Designs and Patents Act 1988.

Contents

Series Editors' Preface   vii

Introduction   1
    Ian Brown and Alan Riach
1 Arcades – The Turning of the Nineteenth Century   15
    Cairns Craig
2 Scotland, Empire and Apocalypse – From Stevenson to Buchan   25
    Murray Pittock
3 Literature and World War One   37
    Trevor Royle
4 Arcades – The 1920s and 1930s   50
    Alan Riach
5 Twentieth-Century Scottish Drama   61
    Donald Smith and Ksenija Horvat
6 The Modern Scottish Literary Renaissance   75
    Roderick Watson
7 Literature and World War Two   88
    Douglas Gifford
8 Arcades – The 1940s and 1950s   103
    Moira Burgess
9 Language, Hugh MacDiarmid and W. S. Graham   112
    John Corbett
10 Post-War Scottish Fiction – Mac Colla, Linklater,   123
    Jenkins, Spark and Kennaway
    Bernard Sellin
11 Arcades – The 1960s and 1970s   133
    Ian Brown and Colin Nicholson
12 The (B)order in Modern Scottish Literature   145
    Carla Sassi
13 The Seven Poets Generation   156
    Robyn Marsack

14 Language and Identity in Modern Gaelic Verse   167
     Michelle Macleod
15 Arcades – The 1980s and 1990s   181
     Michael Gardiner
16 Scottish Contemporary Popular and Genre Fiction   193
     Marie Odile Pittin-Hédon
17 Poetry in the Age of Morgan   204
     Donny O'Rourke
18 Entering the Twenty-first Century   214
     Ian Brown

     Endnotes   223
     Further Reading   245
     Notes on Contributors   252
     Index   255

Series Editors' Preface

In 1919, T. S. Eliot (or perhaps a sub-editor) posed the provocative query, 'Was There a Scottish Literature?' and critical angst on this subject has ensued over the ninety years since. The view of the editors of this series – and a prime motivation for its production – is that however valid the question within one concept of literary tradition, it does not make sufficient room for the nature of literatures produced by multilingual and multivalent cultures. The question was always more complex than Eliot seemed to allow. Further, by their nature, certain Scottish literary works have also been subsumed into the corpora of other literary traditions – for instance, medieval Irish, Latin, or modern English. Such intercultural richness and hybridity, we argue, is not a weakness in a literature's history, but a token of international openness and cosmopolitan potential.

Study and research, not to mention creative writing, since 1919 and perhaps especially of the last twenty years, make Eliot's still historically interesting query redundant as a serious contemporary enquiry. To be fair, the political and educational structures are still in place that at times separated Scottish literature in Gaelic from that in English or Scots – and led sometimes to amnesia regarding that in other languages like Latin. But that Scottish literature was, and is, is clearly recognised. It glories in the resources of historic canons in at least four languages that each stand as internationally important, worthy of careful study and richly enjoyable, and it is now absorbing work in, or influenced by, languages from Scotland's newer vibrant language cultures.

Much new scholarship supports the authoritative, accessible, succinct and up-to-date studies comprising the various volumes of the *Edinburgh Companion to Scottish Literature*. These recognise that worldwide interest in Scottish literature, both in universities and among the reading public, calls for fresh insight into key authors, periods and topics within the corpus. Each of these three categories of *Companion* is represented in the 2009 publications. This first tranche of our new series marks the vigour and rigour of the study of Scottish literature and its enjoyment. It sets aside old questions, and gets on with the acts of studying and enjoying.

Ian Brown
Thomas Owen Clancy

Introduction

Ian Brown and Alan Riach

'Renaissance' may not be the key word in Scottish culture from the nineteenth until the twenty-first centuries, but it surely recurs. From Patrick Geddes's heralding a 'Renascence' in the 1890s, through the Scottish Literary Renaissance, however defined, in the 1920s, with Hugh MacDiarmid at its centre, through the late twentieth-century cliché of the Scottish theatrical renaissance, the concept of a Scotland, or rather many Scotlands, rediscovering, reshaping, redefining and remaking itself, and themselves, is a constant refrain. And at the end of the century, through democratic referendum, the nation was in another sense reborn, remaking a parliament.

Literature is an essential way in which people in communities convey to themselves and others their concerns and imaginings. In twentieth-century Scotland, perhaps its greatest achievement was to convey a diversity of different Scottish identities to each other. Scotland, in literature, can only be defined as a multi-faceted, complex identity, with many unfrequented areas and unexplored riches. It is described in this way in contrast to a linear, monolithic literature with imperial weight and the trajectory of a colonial empire, unified by a single language. When, in the early 1920s, MacDiarmid suggested that the Scottish literary movement might begin where the Irish movement had left off, he was recognising not only a spirit of artistic and literary awakening in a kindred nation but also a political dynamic setting itself against British imperialism and attempting to redefine its own variety without dependence on the imperial ideal. Only by recognising the diversity of silenced voices within that single identity might Ireland redefine her own potential. Similarly, if the nineteenth-century British empire, which in many ways as recent historians have observed was also a Scottish empire, had conferred the status of exaggerated Scottishness on the iconic images still globally recognised – tartan, kilt, bagpipes, whisky – it had simultaneously silenced the other voices – Gaelic voices, women, the brutalising ethos of industrial exploitation, the historical richness of Scotland's cultural production over centuries. It would be wrong, nonetheless, to sentimentalise this silencing as a simple victimisation of pristine innocence: some of

1

the Highlanders removed under the Clearances, for example, themselves became slave-owners.

For MacDiarmid, however, and for his immediate Scottish contemporaries reading the great Irish writers of their and the preceding generation and the international modernist writers from America, France, Germany, Italy and elsewhere, the need for literary reconfiguration in Scotland was pressing. Yeats had shown one way, by staying in Ireland while keeping one keen eye on London and an international readership. He had come from a quasi-mythic Celtic twilight world, emerged into a revolutionary twentieth century and found a way of dealing publicly in a new state with the priorities of civic life. Joyce had shown a different way, of aesthetic priorities and the pre-eminence of art above politics, while maintaining the political authority of a common humanity in his fiction, more subversive of the idea of imperial hierarchy than any bloody street fight. MacDiarmid saw strengths in them both, and in O'Casey's staunch, revisionary plays with their resources of comedy and sceptical patience. Hard politics and high art were MacDiarmid's intention. 'Scots steel,' he wrote, 'tempered wi' Irish fire / Is the weapon I desire.' And to 'Make it new' (in Ezra Pound's well-worn phrase) he needed both, on the one hand, Joyce's aesthetic priorities and socialist vision and, on the other, Yeats's bardic individualism and practical engagement with civic social politics. Hence what is so often seen as merely contradictoriness: acceptance of the need for powerful intervention that might be called fascist, and commitment to international communist revolution. MacDiarmid embraced more than even he could hold and, so, reinvented himself in many more than one corporeal presence. If the Irish writers set an example that might be freshly deployed in a Scotland where writers and artists were determined to re-imagine a nation, the writers and artists had to reinvent themselves to deliver their developing vision.

Renaissance, rebirth and reshaping has not only been a refrain in literature. It has been a motif for the makars of literature. Leslie Mitchell gave birth to Lewis Grassic Gibbon. John Hay Beith became Ian Hay. Christopher Grieve re-enlisted himself as Hugh MacDiarmid and a small battalion of others, most of whom fell nobly in battle. Tom MacDonald became Fionn Mac Colla. The last three made their nominal journey from one Scots language community, a Germanic one, to another, a Gaelic one. Osborne Henry Mavor avoided Gaelic, becoming James Bridie. Elizabeth (Betty) Clark became Joan Ure, thinking the latter surname sounded 'more Scottish'.[1] Meantime, Gaelic writers' names went, by the process of translation, in contrary directions. Somhairle MacGill-Eain both became Sam (and Sorley) MacLean and remained Somhairle MacGill-Eain, just as Ruaraidh MacThòmais/ Derick Thomson and Iain Mac a' Ghobhainn/Iain Crichton Smith oscillated between languages. This voyaging in words marks two other features of

Scottish literature in the twentieth century. One is love of, concern for and play with languages. The other is the transgressing of boundaries, borders and genres. It is as if Scotland – an understated nation, an imagined set of communities, an ancient nation never fully centralised governmentally, let alone linguistically – found itself/itselves in stravaiging between fixed identities. For Scottish literature, especially in this last century, when the imperial certainties were being broken, margins are doors to new perceptions and expression, liminality becomes a central ethos and 'Celtic fringes' Celtic centres.[2] Often the emphasis in considering MacDiarmid's Drunk Man's 'whaur / Extremes meet' is on extremes, but the meeting is at least as important. Borders are there to be crossed.

The twentieth was the century in which, as Cairns Craig has demonstrated clearly,[3] Scottish literature came to be seen in a new way. In 1919, it was possible for T. S. Eliot to review Gregory Smith's *Scottish Literature: Character and Influence* under the heading: 'Was There a Scottish Literature?', as the series editors note in their Preface. What Craig has shown is the way in which for much of the nineteenth century and into the twentieth, 'Scottish Literature' was seen as a sub-category of 'English Literature'. The impact of such a process, a consequence of the Scottish invention of English Literature – itself a function of the Scottish post-Union and imperial role – was that even into the twenty-first century some critics have difficulty accepting Scottish traditions. The 'Great Tradition' vision of Eliot and, after him, Leavis sidelines key figures like Scott, leaving a perception only recently addressed of Scottish literature as somehow discontinuous and fragmented. Such a perception can only arise when some key Scottish literary figures are appropriated to an exclusively-delineated 'English' literature, while the conception of Scottish literature has often been narrowed to literature in one language, usually, in this flawed vision – where Barbour's *Bruce* is seen as the wellspring – Scots. This was compounded by the fact that the critical study of Scottish literature in Gaelic was subsectioned for many scholars by its inclusion within the remit of Departments of Celtic at great universities, beginning with Edinburgh in 1882 and Glasgow in 1901. Recent histories, in most detail *The Edinburgh History of Scottish Literature* (2007), have exposed the flaws in this argument. They have done so on the basis of the long-term impact of twentieth-century scholarship. This *Edinburgh Companion to Twentieth-Century Scottish Literature*, then, takes as a given that Scottish literature expresses itself in several languages, arises from several communities, has different canonical structures from the 'Great Tradition' of English literature and includes diasporic Scots. An older view, often Scots-language focused, could see Norman MacCaig as quisling for writing in English and narrowly exclude, say, Muriel Spark from 'Scottish' literature. In effect, this responded to an appropriative model of English literature that sought to embrace a canon and define only writers not in 'its' canon as of other literatures. Perforce, Scottish literature must be more flexible, subtle and interlingual. Scotland's literature grows out of more than three languages and a nation of voyagers. If, at times, we all need canonical orthodoxies and the virtue of vertebrae, we also need openness of mind.

It is, of course, not simply a matter of openness. Often the choice of language in which an author writes has specific politico-cultural meanings both for the writer and the recipient. Katja Lenz has observed of Robert McLellan's drama:

> The decision to write a play in Scots is still a political step. With some authors, the choice of Scots is clearly a statement of national and cultural politics. In less radical cases, Scots serves to transmit a feeling of specifically Scottish identity.[4]

Clearly what Lenz has to say might be applied to many writers from John Buchan through Bill Bryden, Tom Leonard and Liz Lochhead to Matthew Fitt. Each has her or his own explicit reasons for language choice and these may even be economic: in the case of drama it has been long recognised that a new play in Scots usually does 10 per cent better at box office than a new non-Scots play.[5] Joyce McMillan illuminates this point, talking of Chris Parr's changing of the Traverse Theatre policy towards new Scottish writing:

> At the Club AGM in June 1976, [Parr] produced a series of audience figures for 1974–75 and 1975–76 which showed quite clearly that Traverse productions did better than visiting shows, and Traverse productions of new Scottish plays did best of all.[6]

Yet, while such economic arguments may apply for Scots-language writing, it is hard to see how they might apply to Gaelic-language literature. It is surely the case that box-office interest arises from a more fundamental source, one uniting writing in both Gaelic and Scots. That is the urge to hear or read a mother tongue, one in which writer and audience/readers feel most comfortable. An added factor, for Scots at least, may be a desire to assert the acceptability and expressiveness of a language for many years marginalised, even stigmatised.

Both Gaelic and Scots were explicitly stigmatised in the Scottish education system under the 1872 Education (Scotland) Act's influence. This privileged the position of English, arguably in support of the British imperial project. The creative choice to write in any of Scotland's languages has since then not only been cultural, but at some level political. It is a mark of Scottish literature's developing inclusiveness that, rather than a decline in Scots and Gaelic writing, the twentieth century arguably saw steady increase in both languages' creative potential alongside that of English, perhaps in reaction against the implications of the 1872 Act. Recent years have seen the foundation of publishers like Itchy Coo (2002) for Scots writing and the Ùr-sgeul imprint at CLÀR (2003) for Gaelic. A century of attrition in Gaelic is summarised by Michelle Macleod and Moray Watson:

> The twentieth century has seen a dramatic decrease in Gaelic speakers in Scotland: the 1901 census recorded 202,700 speakers; the 2001 census only 58,652. In 1901, although only a minority of Scotland's population spoke Gaelic (4.5 per cent of the total population), the Gaelic community was stable; by 2001, the language community was in flux and facing its language's death,[7]

Despite this, the Gaelic Language (Scotland) Act 2005 was implemented in 2006 and established Bòrd na Gàidhlig. This body is responsible for the preservation of Gaelic as an official language enjoying the same respect as English in Scotland.[8] Such developments reflect a century-long interest in matters of linguistic choice. While this interest is not only literary, literature has been a key ground of contestation of the meaning and potential of their languages for the communities of Scotland. Resistance to monolingualism is a key creative strand in Scottish literature.

One of the literary implications for communities that are at the least bilingual is considerable sensitivity to linguistic inflection, such factors as register shift, for example, or moving between language communities in everyday usage: A. J. Aitken's 'covert' and 'overt' scotticisms. Ian Brown and Katja Lenz, discussing the specific case of Alan Cummings and Forbes Masson's comedy writing for the television series *The High Life* (1995) have talked of the writer/performers' 'linguistic awareness' and 'their concern to exploit the creative potential of the interaction of English and Scots in dialogue, and their use of Scots words and forms, particularly those incomprehensible to English-only speakers, to achieve a subversive comic effect'[9]. They suggest that this subversive effect undermines the authority of a monolingual English-speaking hegemony that cannot understand the implications of what is addressed to its members in Scots. They cite, for example, how this subversion could extend beyond the television drama to the authors' relationship to the BBC itself. The word 'fud' was used freely on several occasions, presumably because monolingual English producers did not understand what was being said, when its English equivalent would simply be banned. In other words, creative choice of language carries a wide variety of potential associations, not the least of which is assertion of the vitality and identity of any specific language-community. Within such a framework, writers do not make once-and-for-all linguistic choices. While some writers do in effect write in one language, Muriel Spark or Norman MacCaig in English or Robert McLellan or Sydney Goodsir Smith in Scots, others have adopted

one language predominantly at specific periods of their creative life in the
way Hugh MacDiarmid did. Others still move back and forth between languages according to the need of the creative moment: Iain Crichton Smith
did between English and Gaelic. Meantime, Aonghas MacNeacail provides
translations of his poems that are themselves arguably original creations.
Others, working across genres, may write in different languages in each genre:
Stewart Conn's poetry is mainly in English, while much of his drama uses
Scots; Christopher Whyte's novels are in English and his poetry in Gaelic,
for him a learned, chosen language of creative expression. While the example
of Cummings and Masson marks the phenomenon of self-conscious shifting
between languages for comic subversive effect, it is clear that there are many
more complex interactions creatively possible between the languages of
Scottish literature. Individual choices are made at every point, to be decoded
and understood individually in the contexts of the time. There is no single or
hegemonic Scottish literary language. Even intermittent attempts to stand-
ardise the forms of spelling used for writing in Scots have failed. Varieties
of Scottish Gaelic are numerous. And the Scottish idiom of the English
language (Scottish Standard English as opposed to Scots) is as distinct in
its own way as New Zealand English or Australian English (each legitimised
by an Oxford dictionary). It is as if the vitality, flexibility and slipperiness
of language-use in Scottish literature is a key creative function that writers
exploit in every way they can. The centrality of language itself (considered
both as subject matter and in terms of the different languages he has translated) in the work of Edwin Morgan is powerful evidence of this. For Morgan,
following the example of MacDiarmid in key respects, language becomes the
essential, uniquely human, liberating phenomenon.

However, it would be wrong to suggest that liminality, border-crossing and
linguistic flexibility were the only major characteristics of Scottish artists
redefining their nation in the twentieth century. The Scottish Literary
Renaissance of the 1920s and 1930s may be characterised as a radical reinter-
pretation of Scotland's cultural history and an application of that past to
the possibilities of Scotland's future, understood from the position of living
within Scotland. Throughout the trajectory of the British empire, Scotland
had never been central to anglophone internationalism. In the 1920s,
writers, artists, intellectuals, people of all kinds, were questioning the value
of the sacrifice of independent identity. The archaeological excavation of
Scottish literature and the rediscovery of long traditions hitherto maintained
only by specialists began to be the provenance of writers and journalists such
as William Power, George Malcolm Thomson and MacDiarmid himself.
Looking over the work of Neil Gunn in the Highlands, it is not only the panoramic series of novels, each building uniquely into a comprehensive vision of
Scotland from the fishing communities of Caithness and the cleared straths of

Sutherland to industrial Glasgow and the pubs of Edinburgh, that impresses, but also Gunn's engagement with practical, day-to-day politics in his home area. The burden of social responsibility and the commitment to artistic prac-tice were not foreign activities to men like Gunn and MacDiarmid. Similarly, Catherine Carswell, writing her revisionary biography of Burns, risked public opprobrium and her job as a reviewer for *The Glasgow Herald* when she dared reclaim Burns as both poet and vulnerable man from the hagiography of the clubs and associations who kept him as an icon.

Throughout the twentieth century, and especially after World War Two, disparate people formally co-ordinated themselves in organisations as part of a general recognition of the responsibility of rediscovering and revitalising Scotland's cultural history: the Saltire Society (1936–), the Association for Scottish Literary Studies (1970–) and others built on the example set by the writers of the 1920s and those that followed. Norman MacCaig and Edwin Morgan, as teachers in schools and universities, Robert Garioch in his work – as described in conversation with Alan Riach – as 'the *Scottish National Dictionary*'s orraman', Sydney Goodsir Smith in his scholarly work on Burns and Fergusson, numerous other poets in their editing of the work of earlier Scottish writers – almost everyone involved in creative work in the Scottish Literary Renaissance was also involved in helping to make more widely avail-able the work of Scotland's past writers. A similar or at least related story is still to be explored in terms of Scottish art and music.

Therefore it seems appropriate to remind ourselves that the word 'Renaissance' in this context is probably less an excessive hyperbole than a literal description of the rebirth of a nation's cultural vitality. If this rebirth established the variety of voices, the flexibility of linguistic identity, the dynamic diversity of geographical and political lexicons, as essential to any sense of what Scotland might be – that is, if it confirmed the idea that the word 'Scotland' could no longer signify a single set of clichéd and familiar images and stock responses – then at the same time it established a vertebrate cultural identity that stretched back in Scots before James I and Barbour and in Gaelic to a bardic tradition in Scotland, co-aligned with bardic practice in Ireland. Both determined openness and a real sense of spine were deeply embedded in the Scottish Renaissance's work.

Later in the twentieth century a less formally titled renaissance took place in theatre. Somewhere in the decade between the Traverse's foundation in 1963 and the Scottish Society of Playwrights' in 1973 a substantial sea-change took place in Scottish drama. Yet it is also fair to say that, throughout the twentieth century, the nature of Scottish drama was constantly transform-ing. A nineteenth-century National Drama flourished, often around adapta-tions of Scott's novels and derived mainly from the work of the Edinburgh Theatre Royal. By the end of the century, that tradition had chiefly migrated to popular penny geggies, temporary theatres often in markets or fairs. Meantime, the railway's arrival had created the quasi-industrial system of UK-wide touring of both variety artists and productions based in London's West End. Whereas, before the railways, there had been a number of key UK theatre centres including Edinburgh, Glasgow, Bristol, Norwich and York operating tours from major regional centres, the West End system prevailed by the end of the nineteenth century and much Scottish dramatic provision was through UK-wide touring. While there were Scottish playwrights like J. M. Barrie able to work within this system, they were few.

The cultural movements that stirred at the beginning of the twentieth century (heralded by Geddes's 'Renascence') had, however, a broader cultural impact. In drama, this was complemented by the rise in social consciousness linked often with Ibsen and Shaw and initially fostered in London by J. T. Grein's Independent Theatre. The twentieth-century repertory movement came from these developments. It is easy to sentimentalise this movement and exaggerate its moral and artistic seriousness, but at its best it was committed to locally-rooted writing of a high order. In 1909, following original plans outlined in 1900 for a Glasgow-based repertory company,[10] Alfred Wareing and others founded the Glasgow Rep (also called the Scottish Playgoers and 'The First Citizens' Theatre in the English Speaking World'[11]). By 1912, similar ideas arose in Edinburgh where Pittendrigh MacGillivray and his playwright daughter, Ina, founded the Scottish National Repertory Theatre. Both companies were interested in the encouragement of Scottish drama and both halted operation in 1914 when war broke out. The Edinburgh company folded on Ina MacGillivray's death in 1917, while the Glasgow one wound up in 1920. In 1921, the Scottish National Players, first conceived of in 1914, were launched with ambitions to become a national theatre, but remained locked in amateur activity until they in turn ceased operation in 1953.

These apparently false dawns can now be seen to foreshadow Scotland's current theatre provision. Touring repertory theatre developed from the 1920s in Glasgow and Edinburgh, Glasgow hosted in the 1930s a number of Little Theatres, while Perth Theatre became in 1935 the first modern building-based 'Rep'. After similarly building-based initiatives in St Andrews and Dundee, the Wilson Barrett Players played repertory, touring to Edinburgh and Glasgow between 1941 and 1955. The major influence on the future of Scottish drama in this period, though, was James Bridie's 1943 Citizens Theatre. In 1951 Pitlochry Festival Theatre was launched and in 1953 the Gateway Theatre Company (later in 1965 morphing into the Royal Lyceum Theatre Company). By now, a framework supporting the development of Scottish drama existed within the context of the presentation of classic and international plays. Repertory developments through the late 1930s into the early 1950s was paralleled by Glasgow Unity Theatre's establishment, amalgamating several leading amateur Glasgow theatre companies and creating a professional company dedicated to socially conscious drama on Scottish working-class themes. Arguably, Bridie's suspicion, even jealousy, of Unity caused its early demise in 1951 at the hands of his chairmanship of the Arts Council's Scottish Committee. Unity's work nonetheless continues to influence Scottish playwriting and directorial practice: the language, methodology and vitality of John Tiffany's production of Gregory Burke's *Black Watch* (2006) is a modern embodiment of many Unity values.

Certainly, then, the Traverse's foundation can be seen as beginning a revitalisation of Scottish drama, but it cannot be seen simply as a renaissance's beginning. There were strong earlier foundations in twentieth-century Scottish drama that underpinned the reshaping of theatre since 1963–73. What that period did provide without question, however, was a sense that Scottish drama could sustain itself creatively and be highly varied, and that Scotland's languages, in the 1970s surely pre-eminently Scots, are vital theatre languages. This sense was strengthened by the creative productions of BBC Scotland's Radio Drama Department during this period, led by Stewart Conn and Gordon Emslie. In this often fraught, but fundamentally encouraging, environment new dramatic talent grew. By the time the Scottish Theatre Company for a time in the 1980s sought to establish a national theatre, there was no doubt that Scottish drama was renewed, a key element in Scottish culture's re-imagining itself. The complex story of developments in Scottish theatres, playwriting and audience expectations seems to represent a rich variety of experimentation and achievement from the perspective of the twenty-first century. Yet it is also a story about a literary genre working in the absence of a political capital city with a nineteenth-century ideal of a national theatre locked into it, a potentially conservative establishment. Such an absence may be a strength in the twenty-first century, when a national theatre might function better without such a concrete fixture as a single theatre building in a single city. This remains a controversial issue, both energising and bedevilling contemporary Scottish theatre, with funding cuts and the collapse of some companies accompanying the unpredicted successes of some others. Nevertheless, by the time, following a Federation of Scottish Theatre initiative after years of earlier campaigning, the National Theatre of Scotland was launched in 2006, the various attempts to develop a twentieth-century drama for Scotland had borne wide-ranging twenty-first-century fruit. A major literary form, drama, which in Scotland at the beginning of the twentieth century might have been in danger of becoming simply a branch of West End industrial theatre had reformed itself as an internationally cutting-edge element of Scottish literature.

In the 1930s, in poetry the major controversy was less over centralism in publishing houses or poetic forms than over the matter of language.

Famously, MacDiarmid and Grassic Gibbon, having achieved masterworks in Scots in poetry and prose, commissioned Edwin Muir to write a book about Walter Scott in which Muir said the only way forward for Scottish literature was for writers to use the English language – exclusively. Perhaps Muir was only following MacDiarmid's indication that the Irish writers were the precedents Scots could learn from, and indeed, in the early twenty-first century, Yeats and Joyce have an international cachet in the anglophone literary world denied MacDiarmid and Gibbon (or Burns, Fergusson, Dunbar and Henryson). So maybe Muir had a point. But MacDiarmid's response was explosive. He had demonstrated the literary validity of different languages, different voices, different kinds of speech, and extended this affirmation by editing *The Golden Treasury of Scottish Poetry* (1940), including for the first time translations from Latin and Gaelic alongside poems in Scots and English. There was nothing by Muir. He sought to demonstrate the literary quality of a tradition encompassing more than one language, more than one centre, but strong enough in both diversity and direction, not to be merely dissipated by pluralism.

In a way, MacDiarmid has won this battle. In the twenty-first century, few would dispute the validity of a multivocal literature. Yet there may seem something wilful and determined about his insistence. That is because of the struggle he was required to make to bring into contact the exaggerated aspects of Scottishness and the silenced voices which had been so characteristic of the nineteenth century. That is why Gregory Smith's theory of Scottish identity appealed to him so strongly. Smith, in a historico-critical study entitled *Scottish Literature: Character and Influence* (1919) affirmed the appropriateness of the grinning gargoyle sitting by the saint on the cathedral wall, the need to accommodate the gruesome with the beautiful, the human capacity to comprehend the virtues of the saved with the tortures of the damned. He decided this was the major characteristic not only of Scottish literature, but of the Scots people from medieval times to the early twentieth century, and he gave this characteristic the term, the 'Caledonian Antisyzygy'. The term has been defined over the years in a variety of ways, but one function it had was to encapsulate the idea of a split between heart and head. This conception has become such a cliché of Scottish critical discourse it is surely due for abandonment. A truth it does embody, however, is the protean, multivalent, multilingual and multiform nature of Scottish culture, most evident in its literature. Nowhere is this clearer in the last century than in the novel. And the novel does not stand alone in its impact. One of the major influences on the representation of Scotland on screen has been through the means of novel adaptation. While this discussion will not attempt to cover the field of film and television, it will be clear from time to time that what is said about the novel has implications for the understanding of film and television representations, both Scottish and about Scotland. This close link has been most recently and comprehensively discussed by Richard Butt.[12] Butt demonstrates the powerful impact for most of the twentieth century of the triumvirate of Scott, Stevenson and Barrie as the prime sources for Scottish literary screen adaptation and, of course, Stevenson's much-filmed Jekyll and Hyde offers a prime paradigm of antisyzygetical personalities. But many of the adaptations of these and other Scottish authors also offer evidence of what has been one major element of the twentieth-century Scottish novel, its commodification of versions of Scotland.

This commodification packages Scotland's potential. So there is a strand in the twentieth-century novel, no doubt following nineteenth-century initiators, that represents a 'Scotland', often a 'Highland Scotland', a wilderness in which a person may find a true self, a higher or purer truth. This Scotland appears again and again in popular fiction, from Compton Mackenzie's comic Highland novels to the popular Hamish Macbeth 'police procedural' novels of M. C. Beaton, one of the several pseudonyms of Marion Chesney. Mackenzie's *Monarch of the Glen* (1941) inspired the long-running television series of the same title (2000–5), while Beaton inspired the *Hamish Macbeth* television series (1995–7). Such novels have been inaccurately labelled from time to time as 'Kailyard', a term often used loosely and pejoratively. Despite deserving closer and more precise consideration, it is generally taken to imply sentimentality, cosiness and 'down-home' conservative values. However they are labelled, such novels certainly embody a version of Scotland and its society that is presented as an attractive 'brand' to an international public, eager for both books and television programmes. This strand of twentieth-century Scottish fiction is extensive, ranging from A. J. Cronin's Dr Finlay stories to, by extension, the Mma Ramotswe novels of Alexander McCall Smith; from the adventure novels of Ian Fleming and Alistair MacLean to the genre fiction of Ian Rankin. Yet, it should be clear from this summary that these novels are not in any sense necessarily unworthy of critical attention. Rankin's work alone is evidence that within this strand, writing can embody both seedy popularity and high seriousness. The point is that the strand works through generic representation to present a variety of constructs that purport to stand for Scottish society. It may include a strong component of sentimentalisation and sensationalisation of working-class life, especially of the West Coast, and of violence found in such clearly commercial work as *No Mean City* (1935) or later work often described as embodying Clydesideism, a sentimentalisation of the urban working class.

The efflorescence of generic or commodified novels in the twentieth and twenty-first centuries is matched by another development: novels that in one way or another seek an encompassing and essentialist – or at least ontological – vision of Scotland and its life. These novels often reconfigure the aesthetic form of the genre itself. Such novels are concerned with the very nature of being, both in art and life. They question established conventions, seek to establish counter-conventions and often explore the potential of language. George Douglas Brown's *The House with the Green Shutters* (1901) with its remorseless invocation – and undermining – of the cosy Kailyard novel's conventions is a striking early example of this strand. Later examples include Lewis Grassic Gibbon's trilogy *A Scots Quair* (1932–4). There, in exploring anew conventions of rural fiction, Gibbon creates a new version of language, apparently an anglicised Scots, or perhaps, a scotticisation of English, that allows him to move freely between the expressiveness and registers of both Scots and English. He himself in his *Note* at the beginning of the first novel in the trilogy, *Sunset Song*, uses this analogy for the relation of Scots and English:

> If the great Dutch language disappeared from literary usage and a Dutchman wrote in German a story of Lekside peasants, one may hazard he would ask and receive a certain latitude and forbearance in his usage of German. He might import into his pages some score or so untranslatable words and idioms – untranslatable except in their context and setting; he might mould in some fashion his German to the rhythms and cadence of the kindred speech that his peasants speak.

This is perhaps disingenuous. The idiom of the *Quair* is Scots, not English. The narrative voices arise from the place and the characters where the novels are located. This is a strong contrast to the great novels of Scott and Stevenson, where predominantly the narrative language is English, as opposed to the spoken Scots of the characters. The 'speak of the Mearns' in the *Quair* becomes not only the expression of Gibbon's Mearns novels and the life he seeks to embody in them; it becomes itself the main medium of the very being and meaning of the novels. His heroine, Chris Guthrie, is torn between two languages, that of home (Scots) and that of learning (English), although she also lives in and through both, achieving a certain hybridity, and in one way or another all the characters of the novels of *A Scots Quair* journey – or refuse to journey – between languages.

Sunset Song has been widely taught by choice in Scottish schools and remains a popular classic, memorably dramatised as a television serial (though only once, in 1971) and for theatre production (more than once, including within Alastair Cording's 1991 *Scots Quair* trilogy). It has been voted 'Scotland's favourite novel' in newspaper polls. Of course, the danger is that it propagates imitation, exaggeration and caricature. Yet it would be wrong to stigmatise Gibbon as limited to the depiction of country life, when the trilogy was deliberately planned to take us from farm to small town to industrial city in the last novel, *Grey Granite*. Gibbon's first novel, *Stained Radiance* (again with a young woman as the central character) is also city-based. His vision is panoptic, as is that of Neil Gunn. The city settings and linguistic idiom of Alasdair Gray, James Kelman and Liz Lochhead at the turn of the twentieth century are not unconnected to the reconfigurations in the work of Gibbon and Gunn in the 1920s and 1930s.

The paradox of a commodified essentialism, the attempt to establish a new insight that in turn is appropriated, represents a fundamental bipolarity. And at every point, when the danger of new commodification has emerged, some novelists have sought to escape it and enter new territories of experience and expression. It is a feature of their work that many sought to develop their experiment by seeking to enter different dimensions of mental experience or investigate the potential for linguistic exploration. The phantasmagoric sequences towards the end of George Friel's *Mr Alfred M.A.* (1972) represent one example of the former, while Iain Crichton Smith's Murdo stories explore both mental dislocation and linguistic legerdemain, each in a sense embodying the other. The remarkable pejorative reaction of some 1994 Booker judges to James Kelman's prize-winning *How late it was, how late* can be understood not only as a metropolitan clique's parochial obscurantism, pained at being stretched beyond its comfort zones. It can also be understood as an honest failure to comprehend the profound nature of Kelman's reconstruction of both language, based on Glaswegian Scots, and novelistic form. Kelman himself may be seen to take the tired convention of Clydesideism in some of his work and reshape and reform its conventions into new understandings of the angst of existence and the potential of language simultaneously to explore, expose and hide experience. In short, such novelists are at work 'whaur Extremes meet'. Their contemporaries in other forms are similarly engaged: Anthony Neilson's plays *The Wonderful World of Dissocia* (2004) and *Realism* (2006), as confusing to metropolitan critics as some of Kelman's novels, spring to mind, as do many of the poems of Edwin Morgan and Tom Leonard. The topic of much of twentieth- and twenty-first-century Scottish literature is bound up not only with the varieties of language, but the very nature of what is possible in Scottish languages and literature. Matthew Fitt's *But n Ben A-Go-Go* (2000), a futuristic dystopian science fiction novel in Scots, is only one example of the ways in which the bipolarity between what are here called commodification and ontology is expressed and denied, explored, revisited and revised transgressively, across genre and language boundaries.

The meeting, melding and reshaping of extremes forms a key trope and a major theme of Scottish literature throughout the twentieth century. That such questing and questioning should be so clearly a central factor in the literature of Scottish communities that have spent the last century revisiting and revising their own nature and relationship to the rest of world is hardly surprising. The crises of that century demanded response. Twentieth-century Scottish literature's reply is vigorous and healthy. It is one of the most vibrant, multi-faceted, rich and under-researched cultural and artistic responses to, and accounts of, its era. The answer to Eliot's 1919 review title, 'Was There a Scottish Literature?' is surely 'Was there ever!' But not even as astute a mind as Eliot's could then have predicted what it would become.

CHAPTER ONE

Arcades – The Turning of the Nineteenth Century

Cairns Craig

Few periods of Scottish literature are less well understood than the fifty years between the 1870s and the 1920s. They are regularly presented as the terminus of a long decline of Scottish culture from the significance of the Enlightenment and the achievements of Burns and Scott, or, alternatively, as the pale foreshadowing, in Patrick Geddes's 'Scottish Renascence' of the 1890s and in the Scots poetry of Charles Murray and Violet Jacob, of Hugh MacDiarmid's 1920s 'Scottish Renaissance'. They are also recalled as blighted by the early deaths of major writers such as Robert Louis Stevenson (forty-four in 1894), or potentially significant writers such as George Douglas Brown (thirty-three in 1902) or John MacDougall Hay (thirty-nine in 1919), and by the World War One death of promising writers like Charles Hamilton Sorley (twenty in 1915). Those who were then regarded as the most prominent Scottish writers, like J. M. Barrie, have become so associated with 'Kailyard' literature – 'characterised by the sentimental and nostalgic treatment of parochial Scottish scenes, often centred on the church community'[1] – that they are rarely given serious attention. Indeed, in so far as the period has acquired critical focus it is through the confrontation of Kailyard and anti-Kailyard presentations of Scottish small-town life, the former represented by Barrie's *Auld Licht Idylls* (1888), the latter by George Douglas Brown's *House with the Green Shutters* (1901). Even the efforts to recuperate women writers, which have enhanced other periods of Scottish writing, have not raised the Findlater sisters from critical neglect, despite Virago's 1986 republication of *Crossriggs* (1908). This period is trapped between the decline of native Scottish traditions – the erosion of that 'democratic intellectualism' George Davie described as ending in the 1870s – and the dominance of a British imperial ethos in which Scottish culture had only a ceremonial significance.

Yet in this period the infrastructure of Scottish culture was transformed by resurgent cultural nationalism: the Scottish Text Society was founded in 1882 to 'publish in each year about 400 pages of printed matter [. . .] illustrative of Scottish Language and Literature before the Union';[2] the Scottish National Portrait Gallery was founded in 1885; the Scottish History Society

15

was formed in 1886 to 'raise a national monument, even more consistent and durable than those spectral and embarrassed columns which perplex the tourist on Calton Hill'.[3] Professors of literature such as David Masson in Edinburgh were writing appreciations of 'The Scottish Contribution to British Literature',[4] while John Nichol, in Glasgow, was illustrating the equal status of Scottish and English poets by the fact that 'Shakespeare and Burns are this day read from the banks of the Connecticut and the Columbia river to the sands of Sydney and the Yellow Sea'.[5] Book-length studies of Scottish thinkers, writers and explorers appeared in the *Famous Scots* series, including influential works on Thomas Reid and David Hume, and the first major histories of Scottish literature – John Merry Ross's *Scottish History and Literature to the Period of the Reformation* (1884), Hugh Walker's *Three Centuries of Scottish Literature* (1893) and James Hepburn Millar's *History of Scottish Literature* (1903) – underlined Masson's view that 'the rise and growth of Scottish literature is as notable a historical phenomenon as the rise and growth of the Scottish philosophy'.[6] Scottish philosophy was just as vigorously transformed: Andrew Seth's *Scottish Philosophy: A Comparison of the Scottish and German Answers to Hume* (1890) established that Kant and Hegel had failed, just as [Reid] had done, to answer Hume's scepticism; W. R. Scott's *Francis Hutcheson* (1900) for the first time described an eighteenth-century 'Scottish Enlightenment'; Norman Kemp Smith's interpretation of Hume not as 'sceptic' but as 'realist' set the pattern for modern views of Hume.[7]

Late nineteenth-century Scotland also accommodated some of contemporary science's most dramatic developments. William Thomson (later Lord Kelvin) and Peter Guthrie Tait's *Treatise on Natural Philosophy* (1867) had set out to overturn Newtonian physics, replacing 'Newton's *Principia* of force with a new *Principia* of energy',[8] a task actually fulfilled by their close collaborator, James Clerk Maxwell, in his *Treatise on Electricity and Magnetism* (1873). As Einstein himself acknowledged, Maxwell's conception of 'Physical Reality [. . .] as represented by continuous fields' was 'the most profound and fruitful that physics has experienced since the time of Newton'.[9] As Kelvin and Maxwell's biographers have made clear,[10] these revolutionary scientific breakthroughs depended on the specific context of Scottish education and industry. The significance of such achievements hardly suggests a culture in steep decline.

Part of the problem for literary understanding of this period has been the narrowing of what is considered as 'literature' from the broad range of the 'written' to a narrowly defined 'creative writing'. That narrowing had not taken place before 1920; critics continued to regard writing in history, philosophy and theology as part of 'literature': the article on 'English Literature' in the ground-breaking ninth edition of the *Encyclopaedia Britannica* (1875–89) could list David Hume and Adam Smith as the great eighteenth-century writers. The questions now asked of the late nineteenth century, however, are narrowly literary: where are the Scottish equivalents of the great realist novelists? Why did Scottish writers, living in one of the most industrialised countries in the world, fail to describe Scottish urban reality? If we look at literature through the lens of the period's Scottish science, however, we can see a different relationship between literature and 'reality', because the new energy science had demolished traditional conceptions of material reality. Instead of a world of atomic particles, the new science proposed a world consisting only of an energy, 'constantly changing the form in which it presents itself' and like 'Proteus himself in the variety and rapidity of its transformations'.[11] This world's atoms are fluid vortices rather than material particles: the 'real' is constituted not by fixities encountered in our supposedly material world but by transformative energy that continually flows through it.

To represent in fictional terms this new 'reality' required radical displacement of the 'realism' of classic nineteenth-century fiction. It was such a displacement that Robert Louis Stevenson advocated in his 'Humble Remonstrance' of 1884: 'A proposition of geometry does not compete with life; and a proposition of geometry is a fair and luminous parallel for a work of art. Both are reasonable, both untrue to the crude fact; both inhere in nature, neither represents it.'[12] For Stevenson, realists mistake the nature of art but, for energy scientists, they mistake the nature of the 'real', since material reality is an illusion concealing rather than revealing truth. Representing this new reality requires a different kind of fiction, one that first appears in George MacDonald's *Phantastes* (1858), which, according to Colin Manlove, 'could fairly be said to be the founder of much modern fantasy'.[13] MacDonald, who studied mathematics and natural philosophy besides divinity at Aberdeen in the 1840s, used the literary tradition of the German fairy tale to present this new world of transformative energy:

[L]ooking out of bed, I saw that a large green marble basin, in which I was wont to wash [. . .] was overflowing like a spring; and that a stream of clear water was running over the carpet, all the length of the room [. . .]. And, stranger still, where this carpet, which I had myself designed to imitate a field of grass and daisies, bordered the course of the little stream, the grass-blades and daisies seemed to wave in a tiny breeze that followed the water's flow [. . .] as if they were about to dissolve with it, and, forsaking their fixed form, become fluent as the waters.[14]

MacDonald confronts his readers with a world where substantial 'form' becomes as 'fluent as the waters' and artificial forms (patterns in carpets) can be conduits for their biological equivalents' emergence. Here physical forms are simply the ephemeral structures of a dynamically changing pool of energy.

MacDonald's work, first published in 1858, inaugurated a period when Scottish writers produced some of the modern world's most powerful 'myths', each inspired by the consequences of the new physics. Robert Louis Stevenson's *Strange Case of Jekyll and Hyde* (1886), for instance, has been read in terms of Victorian puritanism's repression, but the 'dissipation' Jekyll succumbs to when transformed into Hyde mirrors one of the most disturbing of the new science's outcomes – the 'dissipation' of energy that will result, eventually, in a universe without any differential in temperature where no activity will be possible. This entropic universe Jekyll inhabits is vividly presented by the cityscapes through which the characters move:

> Mr Utterson beheld a marvellous number of degrees and hues of twilight; for here it would be a glow of a rich, lurid brown, like the light of some strange conflagration; and here, for a moment, the fog would be quite broken up, and a haggard shaft of daylight would glance between the swirling wreaths. The dismal quarter of Soho seen under these changing glimpses [. . .] and its lamps, which had never been extinguished or had been rekindled afresh to combat this mournful reinvasion of darkness, seemed, in the lawyer's eyes, like a district of some city in nightmare.[15]

The city is decaying towards entropy's 'indistinguishable equilibrium of ruin' (as David Masson had described it);[16] the energy it expends on lamps will only hasten the 'reinvasion of darkness'. Stevenson's story involves apparent defiance of the irreversibility of energy transformations proposed by the new science, since Jekyll can undo his transformation into Hyde and escape the consequences of Hyde's crimes. Such reversibility, however, is illusive and those who break into his locked chamber on the final night hear that 'the kettle with a startling noise boiled over',[17] symbolically announcing energy's dissipation. Transformed into Hyde, Jekyll provides himself access to immediate energy greater than his own, but each expenditure of Hyde's energy consumes Jekyll's future energy resources. Hence, towards his end, Jekyll comes to think of 'Hyde, for all his energy of life, as of something not only hellish but inorganic', as though 'the slime of the pit seemed to utter cries and voices [. . .] that what was dead, and had no shape, should usurp the offices of life'.[18] To resist involuntary transformation back into Hyde, Jekyll requires not only 'a double dose' of his potion but 'a great effort as of gymnastics'.[19] The energy Hyde expends leaves Jekyll 'a creature eaten up and emptied by fever, languidly weak in both body and mind',[20] because he has reached an entropic state in which he cannot sustain himself.[21]

The irreversibility of Thomson and Tait's theories had, however, been challenged by one of the most radical thought experiments of modern science, an experiment coming to be known, thanks to Thomson, as 'Maxwell's Demon'. The 'demon' has lived an extraordinary life in modern science, migrating from physics to information theory,[22] but began – like Jekyll – as an attempt to outwit the inevitability of entropy. What Maxwell's demon claimed to show is that the second law of thermodynamics, requiring that heat flow from hotter to colder substances, is not, as Kelvin believed, a necessary outcome of the nature of the universe but simply a statistical probability. Maxwell's demon is a molecule-sized creature who sits between two containers of gases, one hotter than the other. The temperature of the gases is a function of the velocity of the particles of which it consists, but in any gas there will be particles which are faster (hotter) or slower (colder) than the overall average. The demon operates a shutter which allows particles to pass between the two containers but only allows the fastest from the cooler container and the slowest from the warmer container to be exchanged. As a consequence, heat (the average speed of particles) 'flows' from the cooler to the warmer chamber, reversing the second law's apparent necessity. Maxwell's 'demon' is a fiction but reshapes our conception of reality even more radically than Thomson and Tait's original conception of protean energy, since it initiates what we now call 'chaos theory'.

In Maxwell's demon a fairy tale announces new scientific truth; the boundary between the two, in late nineteenth-century Scotland, was dissolving. Maxwell's experiment can be seen repeated in fictional terms in J. M. Barrie's *Peter Pan* (1904). Like the demon, Peter guards the shutter that keeps two spheres – the sphere of Edwardian London and the sphere of Neverland – separate. At Peter's invitation certain particles – certain children – may cross from one sphere into the other, thus renewing the energy of the Neverland at the expense of the domestic sphere: 'She dreamt that the Neverland had come too near and that a strange boy had broken through from it. He did not alarm her, for she thought she had seen him before [. . .] But in her dream he had rent the film that obscures the Neverland, and she saw Wendy and John and Michael peeping through the gap.'[23] This continual transfer of new energy safeguards Peter's experience of the Neverland from the entropy which haunts his adversary, Captain Hook:

Smee: I have often noticed your strange dread of crocodiles.
Hook: (*pettishly*) Not of crocodiles but of that one crocodile. (*He lays bare a lacerated heart.*) The brute liked my arm so much, Smee, that he has followed me ever since, from sea to sea, from land to land, licking his lips for the rest of me.
Smee: (*looking for the bright side*) In a way it is a sort of compliment.
Hook: (*with dignity*) I want no such compliments; I want Peter Pan, who first gave the brute his taste for me. Smee, that crocodile would have had me before now, but by a lucky chance he swallowed a clock, and it goes tick, tick, tick, tick inside him; and so before he can reach me I hear the tick and bolt. (*He emits a hollow rumble.*) Once I heard it strike six within him.
Smee: (*sombrely*) Some day the clock will run down, and then he'll get you.[24]

The crocodile that has already begun to consume Hook, like the Hyde who consumes Jekyll, is indicative of the irreversibility of energy dissipation which Peter, like Maxwell's demon, is able to defy.

The implication of Maxwell's demon is that only through the imaginary can one begin to grasp this new universe. That possibility produced one of the period's most successful works of popular science, *The Unseen Universe* (1875), written by P. G. Tait and another Scottish scientist, Balfour Stewart. Tait and Stewart used Maxwell's theory to suggest that, if the universe consisted only of energy in transformation, then that energy could be psychic as well as 'physical': just as the 'law of gravitation assures us that any displacement which takes place in the very heart of the earth will be felt throughout the universe', they argued, so 'we may even imagine that the same thing will hold true of those molecular motions which accompany thought'.[25] Hence, all past mental acts are somehow stored as spiritual energy in another, unseen, dimension of the universe. Myths are among the forms by which human beings have figured to themselves this unseen universe; the study of myth becomes, therefore, one way in which we can chart the universe's spiritual evolution and project the new energy science's spiritual implications. This intersection of energy physics and myth was exploited in the work of Scotland's leading theologian of the period, William Robertson Smith, who had studied natural philosophy in Aberdeen and then theology at Edinburgh's Free Church College. By scientific comparison of the myths of ancient peoples he sought to demonstrate the superior spiritual content of the Judaic tradition and thereby provide an evolutionary account of the development of 'spirit' to match Darwin's evolutionary account of biology. This required him to argue, however, that the Word of God was itself historical, to be understood only in relation to the psychological development of the human beings who were its recipients. As a consequence of the publication of these views in articles in the ninth edition of the *Encyclopaedia Britannica* (of which he was later to become editor), Robertson Smith was dismissed from his post at the Free Church College in Aberdeen. He was subsequently appointed to a professorship in Arabic in Cambridge where his closest colleague was a young classicist, J. G. Frazer, who, inspired by Smith's comparative study of early myth and religion, started on what would be a life's work, *The Golden Bough*. This first appeared in two volumes in 1890, was revised in three volumes in 1900 and became twelve volumes in the third edition, completed in 1915. *The Golden Bough* was written as a work of science; by the 1920s and 1930s its scientific standing had already begun to be challenged, leaving its impact to rest on what had all along been the real source of its power – the perfection of its literary style.

The Golden Bough opens as a kind of detective novel, a search for the explanation for 'a strange and recurring tragedy' by the woodland Lake of Nemi in Roman antiquity:

In this sacred grove there grew a certain tree round which at any time of the day and probably far into the night a strange figure might be seen to prowl. In his hand he carried a drawn sword, and he kept peering warily about him as if every instant he expected to be set upon by an enemy. He was a priest and a murderer; and the man for whom he looked was sooner or later to murder him and hold the priesthood in his stead.[26]

To explain that murder, Frazer roves through mythologies and folk customs from ancient Egypt to Australian Aborigines, linking ritual sacrifices to the fear that the gods and goddesses of fertility will abandon the earth. Frazer concludes that 'the hope of progress – moral and intellectual as well as material – in the future is bound up with the fortunes of science'.[27] It was not, however, this belief in scientific progress which caught the imagination of his readers but his belief in 'the permanent existence of such a solid layer of savagery beneath the surface of society, and unaffected by the superficial changes of religion and culture', such that 'we seem to move on a thin crust which may at any moment be rent by the subterranean forces slumbering below'.[28] The savage myths Robertson Smith believed we could reconstitute from the past, Frazer discovered were the very foundations upon which modern society was built: 'Now and then the polite world is startled by a paragraph in a newspaper which tells how in Scotland an image had been found stuck full of pins for the purpose of killing an obnoxious laird or minister.'[29] Scotland is the epicentre of the collision between ancient myth and modern progress, where modern progress turns back into myth.

The Golden Bough is one of the early twentieth century's most influential books and it must count as the outstanding achievement of Scottish writing between 1870 and 1920. It brings into focus the dominance of myth in the period's Scottish writing, not – as often suggested – an evasion of the modern world, but an attempt to grapple with what is truly *modern* in the world. We see this, for instance, in Arthur Conan Doyle's work. The first Sherlock Holmes story, *A Study in Scarlet* (1888), presents Holmes as representing 'the science of deduction',[30] but what this ultra-rationalist must encounter in Doyle's most famous story, *The Hound of the Baskervilles* (1902), is a 'supernatural' hound, returning from a primitive past as a 'demon' that 'could not possibly be any animal known to science'.[31] When finally confronted, 'never in the delirious dream of a disordered brain could anything more savage, more appalling, more hellish, be conceived than that dark form and savage face which broke upon us out of the wall of fog'.[32] Modern science continually calls up its apparent opposite.

It is a confrontation Scottish writing repeats in a variety of locations throughout the period: it takes place in the American wilderness in Stevenson's *The Master of Ballantrae* (1888); it takes place in Africa in John Buchan's *Prester*

John (1910); it takes place in Scotland in George Douglas Brown's *House with the Green Shutters*, when a contemporary drama of progress's destructive power encounters, in its formal structure, ancient Greek tragedy's outlines. It is also reflected in the period's Celticism: indeed, it might be embodied in the works of Fiona Macleod, the female Celtic bard whose characters are trapped in an ancient, expiring culture, but who was herself the fictional creation of William Sharp, professional biographer of nineteenth-century British and German writers. Sharp's transformation of himself into a female Celt was confirmation that if 'the form changes; the essential abides':[33] if Celtic culture is apparently passing, nonetheless its energy can be transfused into the modern world. Macleod's characters, like Alastair in *Pharais* (1894), move in a doom-laden world, but one in which decay and defeat, both cultural and psychological, are the gateway to alternative reality:

> If, months ago, God had filled with dusk the house of the brain, it was now not the dusk of coming night but of advancing day. Fantasies beset him often, as of yore, but never with terror or dismay. The moorland tarn held no watching kelpie: instead, he heard the laughter of the fairies as they swung in the bells of the foxglove [. . .][34]

Patrick Geddes published Macleod's work in the influential journal *The Evergreen* (1894–5) and Geddes, a biologist as well as a publisher and town-planner, provides another link between Scottish science and Scottish writing, since his promotion of Celticism was part of his effort to overturn Darwinian conceptions of evolution by establishing that what biological science revealed was not the 'survival of the fittest' but 'how love, not egoism, is the motive which the final history of every species justifies; how fostering, not ravening, is the pioneer process in the ascent of life'.[35] Celticism provided a possible alternative model to a modern world warped by the acceptance of the 'truth' that life is a Darwinian struggle.

It was in this period, meantime, that substantial prose writing in Gaelic began. The first Gaelic novel, Iain MacCormaic's (John MacCormick's) *Dùn Aluinn no An t-Oighre 'na Dhìobarach* (*Dunaline or the Banished Heir*, 1912), is set during the Clearances. This marks a feature of those early Gaelic novels, the use of historical contexts to address current issues, not an evasion of the contemporary, but its contextualisation and a reclamation of an appropriated past. The next novel, Aonghas MacDhonnchaidh's (Angus Robertson's) *An t-Ogha Mór* (*The Great Grandchild*, 1913), set during the Jacobite Risings, continues this methodology, as does Seumas MacLeòid's (James Macleod's) *Cailin Sgiathanach* (*Skye Girl*, 1923), set in eighteenth-century Skye. These mark the first, somewhat faltering start of written Gaelic fiction, to be taken further only in the 1970s.

In their resistance to realism's conventions, many Scottish authors adopted – or, indeed, were inventors of – forms of 'popular' literature which twentieth-century criticism tended to consider irrelevant to 'serious' literature's history. Andrew Lang's fairy tales and romances, for instance, like *The Blue Fairy Book* (1889), *The Green Fairy Book* (1892) and *The Red Book of Romance* (1902) were written for adults, though are often now subsumed within children's literature. John Buchan's thrillers, like *The Thirty-Nine Steps* (1915), provided the model for many later heroes of the genre (including Ian Fleming's James Bond) but Buchan's place in accounts of Scottish literature rests largely on his 'serious' historical fiction – for example, *Witch Wood* (1927) – and his contribution to the revival of poetry in Scots through the influential anthology *The Northern Muse* (1924). His sister Anna, on the other hand, whose sales were greater than his, is rarely mentioned.[36] Even in *A History of Scottish Women's Writing* she is treated alongside Annie S. Swan as though she were a nineteenth-century writer,[37] when, in fact, only one of her books was published before World War One. Writing under the pseudonym of 'O. Douglas', her romances are set in a social world so apparently conventional that Beth Dickson asks, 'Does the "O" in O. Douglas [. . .] stand for "nothing" – nothing to do, nothing to say, woman degree zero?'[38] Buchan, however, uses her 'fictional' authorial self to set her romances of middle-class life in ironic juxtaposition with literary expectations of fiction. *Pink Sugar* (1928), for instance, takes place in a house called 'Little Phantasy', near to 'Merlin's Haugh', and has a heroine quoting Tennyson's 'Lady of Shalott' to explain her lack of a husband and a maiden aunt who has as one of her friends a 'Christian Johnstone' – who cannot be the Scottish woman writer of that name who died in 1857. It also has, as one of its characters, an author of 'mild domestic fiction' who is neither mild nor domestic. This texture of artifice emphasises the deliberate artificiality of the narrative itself in producing a safe place for its characters – and its readers – to escape to, while ironically subverting that very desire. Such subversions of artifice by artifice are typical, too, of Barrie, in novels such as *Sentimental Tommy* (1896) and plays like *Mary Rose* (1920). Barrie had been a student of David Masson's at Edinburgh University and, as R. D. S. Jack has shown, Masson's theory of literature was one which emphasised the superiority of romance, and of the power of imaginative transformation, over the powers of realism. That Masson had also been one of the first to appreciate the consequences of the new physics of energy is suggestive of how closely related is the anti-materialism of the new physics to the anti-realism of the period's Scottish literature. As Robert Louis Stevenson put it:

> The immediate danger of the realist is to sacrifice the beauty and significance of the whole to local dexterity, or, in the insane pursuit of completion, to

immolate his readers under facts: but he comes in the last resort, as his energy declines, to discard all design, abjure all choice, and with scientific thoroughness, steadily to communicate matter which is not worth learning.[39]

Scottish writers' refusal to commit themselves to the declining energy of 'matter' was thus an 'evasion' of reality only if one assumes that the only reality was a social world defined by material circumstance and evolutionary conflict – and, like the nation's scientists, that is precisely what they set out to question.

CHAPTER TWO

Scotland, Empire and Apocalypse – From Stevenson to Buchan

Murray Pittock

Stevenson [. . .] was a most potent influence [. . .] He had the same antecedents that we had, and he thrilled as we did to those antecedents – the lights and glooms of Scottish history; the mixed heritage we drew from Covenanter and Cavalier; that strange compost of contradictions, the Scottish character; the bleakness and the beauty of the Scottish landscape.
(John Buchan, *Memory Hold-The-Door* (1940))[1]

Stevenson's death in 1894 took place far from Scotland. The literary values he represented, which Buchan celebrates – those of Scott in *The Master of Ballantrae* and *Weir of Hermiston*, Hogg in 'Thrawn Janet' and *Jekyll and Hyde* and the contemporary 'Book for Boys' of his friend W. E. Henley in *Kidnapped* and *Treasure Island* – were being challenged by a new generation which showed signs of departing from them altogether. Patrick Geddes' (1854–1932) *The Evergreen* (1895–6) was a journal for the new group of programmatic 'little magazines' which flourished in the sometimes intense atmosphere of the 1890s. *The Evergreen*, which in some respects was a respectable counterpart to *The Yellow Book* (as the contemporary notices were not slow to point out), was in others close to the literary magazines of the Celtic Revival in Ireland. It posited a 'Celtic Renascence', a 'cultural rebirth' in Scotland, as part of a pan-Celtic movement which saw the development of international Celtic congresses at Dublin (1901), Caernarfon (1904) and Edinburgh (1907) and of Celtic games such as hurling, shinty and Gaelic football, which developed quite rapidly in Scotland as well as in Ireland. From 1887, Geddes 'organised annual summer schools' which brought international artists to Scotland, and in 1891 asked John Duncan the painter, 'to oversee a Celtic Arts and Crafts School'. Just as *The Evergreen* borrowed the title of Allan Ramsay's 1724 publication (which aimed 'at a return to local tradition and living nature'), so, like Ramsay, Geddes sought to develop Edinburgh's status as a cultural capital by all the means at his disposal: the building of Ramsay Garden round Ramsay's original 'Goosepie' house in 1892–3 was an indication of Geddes' homage to his predecessor, as well as his own plans for the future of the city. Others were also active in this movement, both in Scotland and Ireland.

David McGibbon argued for a Scottish national architecture, while in 1897, Douglas Hyde established 'a Scottish branch of his Gaelic League'. The idea of a national culture and national traditions of architecture, art and design began to develop in Scotland as a consequence of these still underestimated developments, which set up Irish and Scottish cultural links, both at élite (the Countess of Aberdeen's supply of Irish material to the 1886 Edinburgh Exhibition) and cultural nationalist levels. Among other important points of engagement, Elizabeth Corbet (Lillie) Yeats 'studied watercolour with Nina Borthwick, an artistic Scots mentor with strong Gaelic League affiliations', while Phoebe Traquair was another key figure in ensuring cultural contacts over the Irish Sea.[2]

Neither Geddes nor his friend William Sharp (1855–1905), who wrote a number of dreamy Celtic romances as 'Fiona Macleod' had any interest in the strongly political implications of the contemporary Irish Celtic Revival, however, a fact which probably contributed to the split between Sharp and Yeats. Geddes and Sharp were more interested in rehabilitating the importance and centrality of a supposed Celtic worldview which had been marginalised by generations of historians who had disseminated the myth, developed for political purposes during the Scottish Enlightenment, that Scotland was divided ethnically between Germanic Lowlanders, who were amenable to English civilisation and might even contribute to it, and Celtic Gaels, who were a doomed and rather fey race – on a good day the source of imagination to ameliorate Teutonic rationality, on a bad, the hysteria which undermined Teutonic judgement. The association of Celtic qualities with those attributed to women in the Victorian period was no accident. This stereotyping almost certainly led to the implicit – and sometimes explicit – racism of some nineteenth-century thought. British attitudes to the west Highlands during the potato famine of the 1840s did not differ greatly from those towards Ireland, and the Highlands only began to emerge from the era of Clearances by virtue of the Napier Commission of 1885, which in its turn depended to a degree on the revisionist pro-Celtic history of W. F. Skene's *Celtic Scotland* (1879–80). However, the literary rehabilitation of the Gael as part of a new revaluation of Celticism did not match up to the practical benefits of the 1886 Crofting Act. Sharp's own (published under 'Fiona Macleod's' name) *Pharais* (1894) presented Celtic Scotland as dreamy, feminine and prone to the 'mind-dark' of hereditary madness, an image not really removed from that of contemporary images of the hysterical (female) Celt as providing imagination for the rational (male) Anglo-Saxon within Britain.

Sharp's work was influential, though, on subsequent Scottish writers. While the parish pump – so-called Kailyard – fiction of Ian Maclaren and S. R. Crockett, celebrating the small-town Lowlands, was rebuffed by George Douglas Brown's magnificent synergy of Hardy, Zola and Aeschylus in *The House with the Green Shutters* (1901), the sentimentalisation of the Gàidhealtachd which Sharp celebrated was received with much less criticism. In part this was almost certainly due to the politicisation of the Gael in Ireland which Sharp's brand of Scottish Celticism denied. When a statesman of the calibre of Eamonn de Valera (1881–1973) could purvey the fantasy of an idealised peasant Ireland as serious politics, it was perhaps no surprise that Scottish nationalists sympathetic to the Irish experience such as Neil Gunn (1891–1973) received Sharp's brand of fey, feminised and foredoomed Celticism relatively uncritically. In *Butcher's Broom* (1934), Gunn linked the traditional Scottian historical novel with its 'old vs new world' plot to an idealised and feminised Gàidhealtachd, where the wisdom of Dark Mairi of the Shore is more than a little reminiscent of Sharp's 'wise woman' theme; similarly, *Highland River* (1937) and *The Serpent* (1943) did little to dispel the notion of the Highlands as a place where immemorial autochthonous value withstood the assaults of rationality and Presbyterianism alike. Like the House of Peace in Gunn's *The Silver Darlings* (1941), Sharp's Highlanders also seem given to a mildly catholicised non-denominational 'Celtic Christianity' of a kind still popular in New Age fantasising about the early religion of the Celts. Surely the 1900 publication of Alexander Carmichael's (1832–1912) *Carmina Gadelica*, with translations and lovely neo-Celtic typesetting, helped create, or at least reinforce, aspects of these views, especially the notion of the incipient Catholicism of a mostly Protestant Gàidhealtachd.[3]

Gunn is a more defined and vertebrate writer than Sharp, and it would be wrong to engage in too much criticism of his highly atmospheric and evocative work, which, when combined with sufficient background information, provides a powerful new impetus to the historical novel, and shows itself capable of making the ordinary man – Roddie or Finn for example – into a hero. However, Gunn, Lewis Grassic Gibbon (1901–35), Fionn Mac Colla (1906–75) and others belong to the 'Scottish Renaissance' which descended from Geddes' call of 1895, and which in prose fiction was heavily laced, in its 1930s as in its 1890s variant, with a spiritualised and idealised Celticism which was seldom interrogated. The Lowland Kailyard of Crockett and Maclaren (and, most unfairly, Barrie) was savagely attacked, the Highland one received an altogether easier ride. Even Gibbon, otherwise a sophisticated writer, indulges (again in Hardyean vein) in elegiac ruralism, if not a Celticism, at the end of *Sunset Song*, and, more crucially, avoids the impending denouement of a clash between abstract politics and human values in *Grey Granite* by having Chris Guthrie die back into the land on Bennachie, the traditional border between Lowland and Highland for north-east Scots.

There is a strong case to be made that much of Scottish literary history and criticism has overstated the importance of writers whose class or nationalist

politics fit comfortably into a national(ist) narrative of an evolving literature, and has downplayed the significance of figures such as Sir James Barrie
(1860–1937) and John Buchan, Lord Tweedsmuir (1875–1940) whose lives
were largely spent outwith Scotland, and who are not credited with radical
political positions: though Barrie's support for women's suffrage, reflected in
What Every Woman Knows (1908), makes an interesting contrast with the
traditional symbolic freight of the gendered nation borne by Dark Mairi – and
even Chris Guthrie.

The same is true to a lesser extent with Arthur Conan Doyle (1859–1930):
just as Buchan effectively invented the spy thriller and made Ian Fleming
and Frederick Forsyth possible, so Conan Doyle gave shape and enormous
impetus to the modern detective story. Sherlock Holmes is outsider, scientist,
vigilante, intellectual and bourgeois all in one: a powerful combination to be
deconstructed into characters such as Poirot, Morse, Taggart, Maigret, Dirty
Harry and Kay Scarpetta by future novelists. Meanwhile, *The Lost World*
(1908) provided the basis for a whole series of creature features throughout
the history of cinema: even the location of *Jurassic Park* is very close to that
chosen by Doyle for his 'lost world', while the title of his book is of course
given to the second film of that franchise. His Professor Challenger short
story, 'When the World Screamed' (1928), similarly offers an early variant of
the Gaia hypothesis. Conan Doyle is, in many respects, a Scottish writer of
global influence and reputation, largely ignored for study in his own country.
Moreover, he, like Buchan, stands to an extent in the tradition of Stevenson,
inflected by *fin-de-siècle* concerns – though *Jekyll and Hyde* more than touched
on these. Arguably, Stevenson's work itself is more difficult to evaluate unless
his relationship to Conan Doyle and Buchan – and their importance – is
critically exchanged at its full rate. All arguably still suffer from the academic
suspicion that readability is inversely proportional to complexity: the ghost
of Modernist élitism still dogs its contemporaries.

The literary-critical narrative of Scottish poetry might also benefit from
a little reorientation. Despite Trevor Royle's anthology *In Flanders Fields*
(1990), more attention could be paid to specifically Scottish responses to the
reality – rather than a fictional construct of the effects – of World War One,
while the vernacular poetry of Charles Murray (1864–1941) and Violet Jacob
(1863–1946) exists critically, if at all, as a branch line of inquiry, well away
from the MacDiarmid Express. Experimental poetry and fiction like that of
Canon John Gray (1866–1934), for many years parish priest in Edinburgh's
Morningside, is also almost completely absent from consideration as Scottish
literature: though Gray's complete poems were edited in 1988, and considerable critical work continues to be published on him, he is not evaluated in
the context in which some of his best work was written, though his literary
papers are in the National Library of Scotland.

Barrie's extraordinary and wily complexity is covered elsewhere in this *Companion*: the remainder of discussion here is devoted to the almost equally complex figure of John Buchan, the Zionist frequently cast as an anti-Semite, the Scottish patriot sometimes thought of as a mindless British imperialist. Such views are notably unjust.[4] Buchan was a strong supporter of the Scots language (his own *Poems in Scots and English* appeared in 1917) and an early publisher of Hugh MacDiarmid, who was anthologised in his *The Northern Muse* of 1924.[5] In 1932, Buchan spoke to the House of Commons in strongly patriotic terms, stating that 'every Scotsman should be a Scottish nationalist'. In 1923, he 'was elected Chairman of the Parliamentary pro-Palestine Committee, and later spoke so widely for the Jewish National Fund that his name was inscribed in the Golden Book'; in 1940, he was on the SS British arrest list, as a Jewish sympathiser.[6] Buchan's politics and the institutional politics of Scottish literature are not always congruent, it is true; but Dickens's and Tennyson's support for the massacre of blacks in Jamaica by Governor Eyre hardly removes them from the English canon, and there is nothing remotely to compare with these sentiments in Buchan. On the contrary, his slipperiness and polyvalence as a writer seems to derive from his discomfort with the part he played as a great imperial servant: his mask-like face and suppressed accent find verbal expression in his fiction, where repeatedly a successful – often Scottish – figure of status, wealth and power comes face to face with the emptiness of his own life, a suppressed past or is displaced, harried and pursued by enemies.[7] Buchan writes par excellence of the experience of the Scot in the British empire – outward conformity, inner longing, nostalgia, rebellion, fear or simply the existential void of *mauvais foi*, the Sartrean bad faith which indicates that an outward role is compromising an inner authenticity. It is not the old Scottish literary duality of sentiment and reason, repression and desire, nature and supernature, that Buchan explores, but the new one of self and career, integrity and success, Scottish identity and public role as a Briton. This is not his only major theme, but it is a recurrent concern throughout his fiction, together with a sometimes extraordinarily prescient view of the condition and state of global civilisation: the jihad theme in *Greenmantle* (1916) (a novel poorly imitated by Agatha Christie in *Passenger to Frankfurt* (1967)) is one example of how Buchan's fiction continues to be relevant today.

John Buchan's first novel, *Sir Quixote of the Moors* (1895) was written while he was still a student at Glasgow, and a number of his best short stories were published early in his career: his first main collection, *Grey Weather: Moorland Tales of My Own People* (1899) reflects the intensity of interest in locality and its consequences for identity and belief that is to be found throughout his fiction, and which can be related both to Hogg and to more recent Scottish writers. In *The Watcher by the Threshold* collection (1902), the novella *No-Man's-Land* (1898) portrays an Oxford Scot returning to Scotland to discover a lost race in the hills, the originals of the Picts or Brownies, in a world which is not unlike Hogg's Brownie stories, but charged with a greater menace of suppressed history. The story is powerful, threatening and evokes the Southern Uplands landscape with vigour; it also seems to portray a hidden and repressed identity still lurking within a Scotland apparently integrated into modernity. 'Fountainblue', in the same collection, introduces what was to become a favourite theme of Buchan's: a great man whose worldly success in the British empire is ultimately no compensation for the loss of a childhood home and the integrity of community it represents:

> Fountainblue, the last home of the Good Folk, the last hold of the vanished kings, where the last wolf in Scotland was slain [. . .] the last saint of the Great Ages taught the people, – what had Fountainblue to do with his hard world of facts and figures? [. . .] He had left it long ago [. . .] He was rich, very rich and famous. Few men of forty had his power [. . .] suddenly in this outlandish place the past swept over him, and he had a vision of a long avenue of vanished hopes.[8]

This *locus amoenus*, the special or favourable place, with a character distinct from the universalisable premises of modernity, where a person might encounter the existential reality of self, was to remain a major concern of Buchan's, as it was in Barrie and Gunn. In a sense all Scotland is both the familiar and the 'outlandish' place in Buchan's fiction, and all Scots are outlanders, pretending to be insiders in an imperial world they have done so much to create, but to which they can never ultimately belong. Frequently the worlds of politics, ideology and empire itself can seem – in Walter Bullivant's phrase from *Greenmantle* – a 'great game', where the onlooker, Buchan's narrator, is almost detached from that in which he participates.

For example, in 'A Lucid Interval', first published in *Blackwood's* in 1910, liberal and reactionary politicians eat a curry with a potion in it and reverse their beliefs, threatening the political equilibrium of government. The dangerous doubling of *Jekyll and Hyde* is dissolved into the arbitrary world of farce, where political views are formed by one's last meal, rather than by experience, judgement or passionate commitment. To some extent, this is because there is the suggestion that success is an act, if not a lie. Many of those involved are Scots: tellingly, when Cargill stops being a smooth politician and starts to argue and speak directly, his Scots accent – sign of authenticity from Jeanie Deans on – deepens and broadens, while the man himself looks healthier. When he eats the reverse potion at the end of the story by contrast, he becomes 'an older and more commonplace man, and harmless, quite harmless'.[9]

Prester John, perhaps Buchan's first important novel, appeared in 1910. The themes of the fragility of empire, the power and autonomy of the Scots diaspora, 'us far-wandering Scots', and the partial alienation of Scots from the external world of the British empire to which they have to conform to succeed, are all present. At the opening in Kirkcaple in Scotland, the hero's free life as a boy by the shore, where he 'made believe that I was a smuggler or a Jacobite new landed from France' is contrasted with 'the fashion of the genteel in Kirkcaple to put their boys into what were known as Eton suits [. . .] I had been one of the earliest victims [. . .] [of] the bondage of fashion'. The confining world of Anglicising class values contrasts with the free life of the boys by the shore, where the hero, David Crawfurd, first comes across the secret life of John Laputa, the African freedom-fighter with whom he will contend as an adult in South Africa. Laputa's prospective rising is compared to that of the Jacobites (thus identifying his secret activities by the shore with the hero's), and the hero, in conversation with Laputa, hopes 'to see the day when Africa would belong once more to its rightful masters', black Africans. This sentiment is disowned, but it is clear that the Scot knows what it is to be a rebel, knows the mentality of the oppressed. Both Boer and Scot also have much in common, displaying their kinship over 'a bowl of toddy'; meanwhile, Japp, the repellently drunken racist storekeeper, serves as a poor representative of the 'nation of shopkeepers' in contrast to the Napoleon-like nobility of Laputa. A Scot saves the British empire; but Crawfurd seems to prefer those he saves it from to those he saves it for, unless they are Scots: '[T]he Scotch tongue worked a spell on me. It cleared my wits [. . .] At last I knew I was among my own folk.' There is relatively little Britishness in *Prester John* that is not Scottish first, last and foremost.[10]

The Power-House (1913) is Buchan's first major venture into spy fiction. It is essentially a simple tale, told with a directness and speed which are evidence enough of the fact that while he was departing from Stevenson in terms of subject-matter, Buchan had learnt much from his master in terms of direct and pacey narrative. The darkness of mood in *The Power-House* is, however, palpable in comparison with Stevenson. Its most famous line, 'You think that a wall as solid as the earth separates civilisation from barbarism. I tell you the division is a thread, a sheet of glass', spoken by the villain to Edward Leithen, the hero, could serve as a prescient characterisation of the twentieth century.[11] The British empire is presented as an unstable and fragile entity and, although evil is defeated, there is a sense that things could easily have gone the other way.

Buchan's most famous novel – undeservedly and in no small part due to the outstanding 1935 film – *The Thirty-Nine Steps* (1915) has a plot of quest, pursuit and flight which was repeated many times in his subsequent fiction, while its secret conspiracy to take over the world is the clear ancestor of SPECTRE and other international criminal organisations tackled by James Bond. It is noteworthy that the strong anti-Semitism shown by Scudder at the beginning – sometimes quoted against Buchan – is condemned by Sir Walter Bullivant at the end. The hero – typically – is a Scot with extensive experience furth of Scotland (in this case Richard Hannay), and the sense of imperial fragility is if anything intensified by Hannay's own feelings of displacement in England. 'England was a sort of Arabian Nights to me [. . .] But from the first I was disappointed with it,' Hannay remarks, simultaneously orientalising the occidental imperial heartland and distancing himself from it. When he flies from danger, it is to Scotland that he runs to hide, where he camouflages himself back into the culture he has long since left: 'I was the living image of the kind of Scotsman you see in the illustrations to Burns's poems.'[12] Hannay's espionage work, both in *The Thirty-Nine Steps* and *Greenmantle*, dangerous though it is, is 'a great game', to recollect Bullivant in the first chapter of *Greenmantle*, in which 'the wandering Scot' – that recurrent image in Buchan – saves the war on its eastern front. In far-distant places, Scots recognise each other by the use of Scots speech and Scots songs, a freemasonry of private language which enables them to communicate to each other in terms fundamentally inaccessible to all the world beside. Once again in *Greenmantle*, Scots are needed to save the British empire, but in doing so they remain Scots. The Hannay and Leithen books continue to refer to this theme throughout Buchan's career.

In *John Macnab* (1925), Buchan offers a lighthearted version of the exile and displacement of the Scot as imperial servant, as Leithen and two of his friends take a sabbatical from the tedium of their high-achieving London lives to go poaching for a bet in the West Highland landscape round Haripol and the Machray deer forest first introduced in *The Three Hostages* (1924). The idea that there is a reiving, disobedient spirit at work under the surface of Scots respectability in the British empire is a disturbing, if humorous, presence in the text; moreover, Leithen's ability to communicate with the gipsy boy Benji is evidence of the depth and authenticity of his contact with the ordinary which Buchan was to revisit in *Sick Heart River*.

In *A Prince of the Captivity* (1933), Buchan's hero is Adam Melfort, who is sent to prison in England because he takes responsibility for a foolish forgery of his wife's. As a result of this disgrace, he can only serve the empire in secret, behind enemy lines as a spy. In his existential moments of crisis, he remembers the island of his youth, Eilean Ban, where 'good King Robert had once sat' in exile and where 'a young prince with yellow hair' had hidden in 1746 from 'English ships, his enemies'. Eilean Ban is the island which – rather like the islands of Barrie in *Mary Rose*, *The Admirable Crichton* and elsewhere – signifies the identity that cannot be colonised or lost, the last redoubt of self where the Scottish spirit thrives: Eilean Ban is real, but also Neverland, beyond space and time. Like the Jews, the disgraced Adam has no real home: in World War One he works for a Zionist spymaster, Meyer, who dies saving Adam's life; eventually, Adam himself is the victim of the Nazis. Both Adam and his Scots friend and helpmeet Amos bear Jewish names, and in no other book is Buchan's comparison between the 'far-wandered Scots' and the Jews without a homeland so clear. 'Dispers'd Israel' belongs both to Jerusalem and to Eilean Ban. 'Are we not both working for the peace and felicity of Jerusalem?' Meyer asks Adam on sending him on his mission; Meyer's last words to Adam as he goes to his death are: 'We will meet some day outside Jerusalem.' Adam's last vision is of the sun dazzling the water to gold on the shore at Eilean Ban; his own Jerusalem the Golden. The prescience of the book in its defence of small nations, cosmopolitans and displaced persons against Nazi race purity and tyranny is not generally appreciated. Adam Melfort becomes a Belgian, a Dane, a man of many nationalities – as a Scot must do, as a Jew must do without a country – he is the hero, the old and new Adam who becomes all things to all men so that they may be saved. His death – like Meyer's at German hands in World War One – is the death of humility, nobility and sacrifice at the hands of raw, brutal and latterly racist nationalism. In 1933, many quite respectable politicians and writers in Western Europe were still prepared to think well of the Nazis; but Buchan knew exactly what they were about. A *Prince of the Captivity* is a pro-Semitic, even a Zionist, novel.[13]

Buchan had in many respects diverged from Scott, who was his ultimate master, or Stevenson, from whom he assuredly learnt so much of the pace of narrative, but in the themes of the *locus amoenus* as a place where the universality of Enlightenment values is both enacted and challenged, he was very much Scott's heir. This was the case too in his historical fiction, which like Scott's (and Stevenson's) drew heavily on the period of Scottish history which can be characterised as the Fall of the House of Stuart: 1638–1788, the era which had seen Scotland's native dynasty and national independence lost, and the country riven by religious war, though Buchan also engaged with classical subjects (for example in 'The Lemnian' (1911), where a man from a small island country ends up fighting for the Greece he hates, yet another story where eventual success comes at the price of one's original sympathies).

It was, however, to be Scotland during those crucial hundred and fifty years which engrossed Buchan's deepest attention, as it had engrossed the attention of Scott and Stevenson before him. It was the subject of his earliest novels, *Sir Quixote* (1895), *John Burnet of Barns* (1898) and *A Lost Lady of Old Years* (1899). In 'The Earlier Affection', published in *Grey Weather* in 1899, a group of Scots Presbyterians help some Highlanders, hunted in the aftermath of the '45, to kill the redcoats pursuing them: Scottish national solidarity against the English coalesces once more at the moment of crisis, obliterating any internal divisions; all but one speak in Gaelic as a sign of autochthonous solidarity. In 'The Company of the Marjolaine' (1908), Buchan portrays

Charles Edward Stuart in later life in an episode where he is about to be
offered a crown in America, one of those historical events for which Scott
is the only clear source. Buchan returns to the Jacobite theme in *Midwinter*
(1923), another novel of identity, flight and pursuit, but one which ends
with the defeat of its Jacobite protagonist. *Witch Wood* (1927), which itself
has roots in the mysterious imperial tale 'The Grove of Ashtaroth', first published in 1910, stands at the apogee of Buchan's historical writing: indeed, he
thought it his best novel.

Witch Wood opens with a prologue which is a tour-de-force of the effect
of change not only on the landscape and the human mind, but on the very
interpretation of reality itself, a reality created by language: as Buchan puts
it in *The Island of Sheep* (1936), '[A] name can sometimes be like a scent or
a tune, a key to long-buried memories.'[14] How things are named, called and
identified is crucial throughout the novel, as is the differing nature of their
representation in the classics, scripture, orality and folk memory, the recollection of which restores the reality it once represented: 'My mouth shaped
the word "Melanudrigill", and I knew that I saw Woodilee as no eye had seen
it for three centuries, when, as its name tells, it still lay in the shadow of a
remnant of the Wood of Caledon.' The perversion of that wood to witchcraft
by Presbyterian fanatics and its eventual destruction in a more material age
symbolise the exhaustion of the native spirit of Scotland. The death and exile
respectively of its last hero and heroine, Montrose and Katrine Yester, lead to
the conclusion of the hero David Sempill, that 'all roads are the same for us
that lead forth of this waesome land': exile and displacement are the future of
Scotland. Montrose is a Year King of Frazerian kind, while Katrine Yester is,
like Adam Melfort, a Christ-figure. Sempill is a Scottian hero (loosely based
on the historical Robert Kirk of Aberfoyle) who in the end does not embrace
modernity, but exists to validate the loss of a valuable and beautiful past.
Nor is the world of Covenanting fanatics limited to the seventeenth century:
in his attack on the vicious – indeed genocidal – anti-Irish racism after
Philiphaugh (1645), Buchan is equally reflecting on anti-Irishness in the
Kirk of Scotland, as demonstrated in the infamous Church and Nation report
of 1923. Similarly, Montrose's statement, that 'I am on the side of the free
people of Scotland' reflects both on historical and contemporary enslavement
to ideology, not a little reminiscent of the poetry of Edwin Muir. Katrine's
innocent pre-Reformation Scottish identity lies far closer to the 'New
Jerusalem' than the ideological literalism of the 'muckle weans that play at
being ancient Israelites' of Covenanting bigotry, whose contribution to the
'guid cause' is to shoot 'the Irish in rows on the Yarrow haughs, ilk ane aside
his howkit grave' and torture their women ('Tam Porteous kittled her wi'
his sword point [. . .] Just in the way o' daffin') and children to death. *Witch
Wood* is a radical, powerful, historical novel, which finds Scottish society just

as wanting as any of its contemporary Renaissance texts, but which in its narrative complexity and the riches of its symbolism places Scott's historical novel and Hogg's 'mountain and fairy school' in the context of contemporary ideas of the Fisher King – all without losing a detailed and indignant historical specificity.[15]

Five of Buchan's major themes, Scottish experience of empire, exile and displacement, race and identity, doubling and Northernness, converge in *Sick Heart River* (1941), the last of the Leithen stories. One of Buchan's best novels, this builds on the existential powers of the North to rejuvenate and render experience authentic explored in *The Island of Sheep* (1936), the novel of the ageing Hannay as *Sick Heart* is the novel of the ageing Leithen.[16] A dying Leithen goes on a mission to recover the Quebecois Galliard, who has abandoned his adopted life in the United States to return to the Canadian wilderness. This part of the plot reprises Adam Melfort's quest to Greenland in the anti-Nazi novel *A Prince of the Captivity* (1933), but here the effects are more sombre. In Leithen, Buchan powerfully revisits the theme of the double life a careerist Scot must lead in the British empire: Leithen begins not to 'care a jot about the present or future of a great British dominion' (p. 47) and reflects that 'now his castles had been tumbled down' (p. 103), his career emptied of meaning by impending death, 'in retrospect his career seemed lonely, self-centred and barren [. . .] cheap bravado' (p. 66). Leaving no son behind him, Leithen's success and infertility can be read as a vision of Scotland's role in the British empire: success at the cost of life and integrity. Galliard, whom Leithen goes to recover, has likewise fled a society in which he has succeeded for the authenticity of his homeland.

Leithen's long journey into the frozen North is not a return physically to Scotland, but is a mental return there: as he journeys, the identity he begins by sinking into the generic 'English' (not an uncommon self-description by Scots abroad in the early twentieth century) is gradually restored to him. His guide to the North, Johnny Frizel, is half Native American and half Scots and speaks with a 'broad Scots accent' (pp. 34, 40), Leithen begins by telling him that 'I am an Englishman, as you see' (p. 43). As the book progresses, his answers change through 'I come from England. I'm Scots' to '"Scotch, aren't you ?" "Yes, but I live in England"' (pp. 108, 134). Johnny 'discovered that Leithen was Scots' (p. 64), and their search for Sick Heart River becomes, like that of Neil Gunn's *Highland River*, a search for origins, origins which are, in Buchan's more complex text, truly sick at heart. In the end, Leithen finds meaning by giving his life to save the Hare tribe of Native Americans from their version of the misery and ennui of a cultural displacement brought about by industrialisation, commerce and colonialism: '"We white folk [. . .] don't seem to be able to do anything for their minds"' (p. 149), Leithen comments; but he goes on to share their 'very ancient loyalty' (p. 151). In the

Hares, Leithen at last 'had found a clan and a family' (p. 187). Just as the Frizels are the result of a physical marriage of Scot and Native American, so Leithen finds a family of the mind among the same people. Sometime attorney-general and pillar of the British state, Leithen dies embracing a suffering Native American people with 'tenderness' (p. 182), true at last to the suppressed Scottish identity, authentic and autochthonous: "'the world [. . .] I [. . .] could no more reject than my own skin'" (p. 143). Heir of the great Scottish Native American chieftains such as MacGillivray of the Creeks or Ross of the Cherokee, Leithen dies not as an imperial servant but as a colonial subject, his Christ-like sacrifice for the suffering subaltern related to the world by a French Catholic priest. In the 'cathedral of the North' where Leithen confronts destiny for the lives of the Hares (pp. 172, 175, 185), 'the brotherhood of all men, white and red and brown' (p. 150) is again realised. *Sick Heart River* transcends the shoddy and narrow view of Buchan as a racist and imperialist even more powerfully and eloquently than *The Master of Ballantrae* transcends the cliché of Stevenson as a mere writer of adventure stories.

CHAPTER THREE

Literature and World War One

Trevor Royle

World War One changed Scotland in many profound ways. In May 1914 a Home Rule Bill passed its second reading in the House of Commons, mainly as a result of the promptings of the Scottish Home Rule Association and the Young Scots Society, a radical-minded grouping within the ruling Liberal Party who were in favour of free trade, social reform and what they called 'the unquenchable and indefinable spirit of nationalism'.[1] The outbreak of war three months later meant that the Bill was never enacted and the devolution debate would not be reopened until towards the end of the century. But there were other significant changes. War boosted the country's heavy industries, especially in the west. It encouraged women's employment: by 1918, 31,500 female workers were employed by Scotland's munitions industries. In the war's early months the proportion of men aged eighteen to forty-one enlisting voluntarily was higher than elsewhere in the United Kingdom. To expand Britain's small Regular Army Lord Kitchener, Secretary for War, called for the creation of a huge 'New Army' of volunteers; the response in Scotland, as elsewhere, was enthusiastic.

Despite initial doubts, the volunteer principle worked: by the end of 1915, the British total was 2,466,719 men, more than that achieved after the introduction of conscription in May 1916 and just under half the wartime total of 5.7 million men serving in the army during the war. Of this, 320,589 (13 per cent) were Scots. By the war's end, the number of Scots in the armed forces was 688,416: 71,707 in the Royal Navy, 584,098 in the Army (Regular, New and Territorial) and 32,611 in the Royal Flying Corps and Royal Air Force. Culture too was affected: although it would take time for the effects to be felt, literature in Scotland was transformed by experience of World War One.

At the outbreak of hostilities Scottish literature was largely in the doldrums. Robert Louis Stevenson (1850–94), Scotland's greatest writer of the late nineteenth century, was dead, and much poetry being published was either sentimental, historical verse or Celtic Twilight's mystical vapours. Fiction was generally stuck in the Kailyard, the catch-all phrase used by

J. H. Millar (1864–1929) in the *New Review* April 1895 issue to describe the novels of J. M. Barrie (1860–1937), S. R. Crockett (1859–1914) and Ian Maclaren, the pseudonym of John Watson (1850–1907). Here was a well-defined arcadia of village life, a school of rural sentimentality ignoring the ills of turn of the century Scotland, its faltering industrial development, poverty and high mortality rate. Critics like Millar regarded Scottish writing in an overall British context, doubting if Scots as literary language could survive in the twentieth century. As Cairns Craig has observed, it was a barren period in the country's literary affairs:

> When T. S. Eliot, in a review in 1919, asked 'Was There a Scottish Literature?' the past tense perspective seemed all too appropriate to the possibilities of Scottish literature surviving into the twentieth century as an independent cultural force. Scotland, politically more integrated into British society by the efforts of the First World War than it had ever been before, and seemingly culturally absorbed into English values by its participation in the previous century's imperial ambitions, had to look back to the period of Scott for a time when a writer's presentation of Scotland and the Scots had received international attention and literary recognition.[2]

Signs of hope were few and far between. In 1901 George Douglas Brown (1869–1902) exposed the limitations of the Kailyard school in his novel *The House with the Green Shutters*. Borrowing many Kailyard features and characteristics – the rural setting, the raised expectations and a familiar cast of characters – he then destroyed them by showing the impact of external social change. John MacDougall Hay (1881–1919) employed a similar structure in *Gillespie* (1914) including many themes explored by Brown. Although neither was destined to produce further great fiction, both *The House with the Green Shutters* and *Gillespie* indicated one direction taken by twentieth-century Scottish fiction.

The years before World War One also saw a revival of verse in the vernacular. Much was coy and guileless, but notable exceptions were written in spoken Scots' natural idioms. John Buchan (1875–1940) vigorously criticised the Kailyard school and, on becoming editor of the *Scottish Review* in 1907, told Lord Rosebery its aim was 'to deal with all interests, literary, political and social, with something Scottish in the point of view. We want to make it the centre of a Scottish school of letters such as Edinburgh had a hundred years ago.'[3] Buchan, later a bestselling novelist, had also written (without publishing) some passable poems in Scots although he admitted, introducing *Poems, Scots and English* (1917), that

> Scots has never been to me a book-tongue; I could always speak it more easily than I could write it; and I dare to hope that the faults of my verses, great as they are, are not those of an antiquarian exercise.[4]

Better known to most readers was the poetry of Charles Murray (1864–1941), a poet from the north-east of Scotland who continued to write in the vernacular despite emigration to South Africa. In his frequently anthologised poem 'The Whistle' he shows lively feeling for the language and cadences of the Aberdeenshire farming countryside; his wartime poems, notably 'Dockens afore his Peers' and 'Fae France' continued in that vein. Other north-east poets following Murray, both during and after World War One, include Marion Angus (1866–1946), Violet Jacob (1863–1946), David Rorie (1867–1946) and Mary Symon (1863–1938).[5]

The first reaction to the declaration of war in Scotland, as elsewhere in Britain, was of excitement and relief. Contemporary evidence shows that thousands of Scottish people were prepared to voice their support for war, finding themselves participating in demonstrations of national pride and patriotism often bordering on hysteria. Even realists who should have had their feet on the ground were caught up in the excitement. Shortly after war had been declared the novelist and journalist Neil Munro (1863–1930) travelled by train to Glasgow from his home in Inveraray and later shamefacedly admitted:

> [W]hat silly patriotic and romantic elations were stirred in me when I found that already there were armed guards on every railway viaduct, on reservoirs, and the Loch Long torpedo testing station. All along the Callendar-and-Oban and West Highland Railways, the fiendish ubiquity of German spies, and their readiness to start immediately blowing up culverts and railway bridges, or poisoning us at our kitchen-taps, were already taken for granted![6]

By that time Munro was a successful novelist – his novel *The New Road* (1914), an adventure in the tradition of Stevenson, had just been published – but even he was caught up in the excitement and wanted to do something. Many others shared that sense of enthusiastic conviction that gave the war's early days an unreal quality, creating a feeling that war was a great adventure and man transformed and liberated from the doldrums of a humdrum existence. Chivalry, self-sacrifice and heroism were the catchwords of those early days and very few did not respond to their call.

Artless verses flooded by the thousand into local papers speaking of the noble necessity of doing one's duty; everywhere tub-thumping patriotism was rife and the elation found its way into mainstream literature. Two years later, long after the initial enthusiasm had waned, Neil Munro produced a series of poems under the collective title of 'Bagpipe Ballads', published in *Blackwood's Magazine*. By then his son Hugh had been killed in action at the Battle of Loos, serving with 1/8th Argyll and Sutherland Highlanders and he himself had visited the Western Front as a correspondent. Yet, as he told his publisher George Blackwood, the poems were a compensation of sorts, having been

suggested by the names of bagpipe airs, so that some of them take on that spirit
of braggadocio which comes so natural to youth: and to races like the Gaels who
loiter so much in their past that they are always the youngest and most ardent
when it comes to sentiment – the first and last excuse for poetry.[7]

One of them, 'Hey, Jock, Are Ye Glad Ye 'listed', caught the exhilaration of
those first days of the war:

> Come awa, Jock, and cock your bonnet,
> Swing your kilt as best ye can;
> Auld Dumbarton's Drums are dirlin'
> Come awa, Jock, and kill your man![8]

The mood was echoed in the English poems of James Pittendrigh
MacGillivray (1856–1938) which he published under the telling title, *Pro
Patria*. A native of Aberdeenshire, MacGillivray was a sculptor – after the
war he was appointed the King's Sculptor in Ordinary for Scotland – but
he also wrote poetry in the north-east vernacular. Even when volunteers
started to move across to France and the early battles brought the first heavy
casualties the mood in the country remained strangely optimistic. Following
the Regular Army's deployment in the third week of August 1914, the first
Territorial Force battalions arrived in late summer and early autumn. The
first was the London Scottish, in action at Messines on 30 October – and
these were followed by the volunteer battalions of the New Army. John
Hay Beith (1876–1952), an officer serving in 10th Argyll and Sutherland
Highlanders, celebrated the move in a poem 'K (1)' which he believed
summed up his men's feelings as they set off for France and war:

> And now today has come along,
> With rifle, haversack and pack,
> We're off a Hundred Thousand strong,
> And – some of us will not come back.
>
> But all we ask, if that befall,
> Is this. Within our hearts be writ,
> This single-line memorial:
> He did his duty and his bit.[9]

Beith, a schoolmaster and author turned soldier, usually wrote under the
pseudonym 'Ian Hay' and had attracted an enthusiastic following for a succession of whimsical light novels in the pre-war period. At the outbreak of
hostilities, he volunteered and was commissioned in a New Army battalion
of the Argyll and Sutherland Highlanders. This experience led him to write

monthly sketches for *Blackwood's Magazine* under the pseudonym 'Junior Sub' in order to mask his identity as a serving officer. The first appeared in November 1914 with an account of the tribulations of learning close-order drill. Throughout autumn and winter 'Junior Sub's' musings took the reader through the training of the fictional battalion, the 'Bruce and Wallace Highlanders', until it was ready to cross to France. Brilliantly conceived and narrated in first person and present tense, it was akin to a homely correspondence; the sketches became an immediate bestseller when they were published in December 1915 under the title *The First Hundred Thousand*.

Hay's book is an intensely Scottish account from the perspective of a man who, though born in England, was deeply proud of his heritage, telling his readers early '[W]e are Scotsmen, with all the Scotsman's curious reserve and contempt for social airs and graces.'[10] The novel also provided a keen insight into the military mind, so much so that many brigade and divisional commanders recommended it as reading matter for newly joined officers. For readers at home it was an accurate portrayal of the enthusiasm and optimism of those early days before the New Armies went into action at Loos. *The Spectator* reviewer praised Hay's ability to capture the New Armies' mood while the *Saturday Review* claimed that finally the British soldier had found a voice by making their experience appear 'irrepressibly brave, comical, devoted, prosaic, glorious or dull'.[11]

It was, however, not all patriotism and braggadocio. Two Scottish poets spoke against the glory of war and condemned the Gadarene rush to 'hate the Hun' They are arguably the finest English-speaking Scots World War One poets: Charles Hamilton Sorley (1895–1915) and Ewart Alan Mackintosh (1893–1917). Both were similar in that they were born into Scottish families but brought up and educated in England. They stand, therefore, somewhat outside the contemporary Scottish literary tradition with its emphasis on verse in the vernacular. Both, though, were intensely aware of their heritage: Mackintosh was a Gaelic speaker and Sorley admitted that he felt no sense of patriotism towards England. Both, too, were destined to die during the fighting: Sorley during the Battle of Loos in October 1915 and Mackintosh at Cambrai in November 1917. The poetry of both was published posthumously.

Charles Hamilton Sorley was born in Aberdeen where his father was Professor of Mental Philosophy. When he was five the family moved to Cambridge. He was educated at Marlborough. In December 1913, after gaining a place at University College, Oxford, he spent time in Germany and was attending the University of Jena when war broke out. With a friend he managed to get back to Britain travelling by train and a specially commandeered ferry from Antwerp. Having spent seven enjoyable months in Germany he was disposed to be understanding about the country he had just visited, telling an old school master Wynne Willson in a letter: 'They are a

splendid lot, and I wish the silly papers would realise that they are fighting for
a principle just as much as we are.'[12] What took him aback was the hysteria
and unthinking patriotism. A letter to another friend, Alan Hutchinson,
reflected his exasperation with the mood on his return:

> But isn't all this bloody? I am full of mute and burning rage and annoyance and
> sulkiness about it. I could wager that out of twelve million eventual combatants
> there aren't twelve who really want it. And 'serving one's country' is so unpic-
> turesque and unheroic when it comes to the point. Spending a year in a beastly
> Territorial camp guarding telegraph wires has nothing poetical about it: nor
> very useful as far as I can see.[13]

Even so, despite his cynicism about patriotic impulses, like thousands of
others of his class, Sorley soon joined up as a volunteer and was gazetted
second lieutenant in the 7th Suffolk Regiment, a New Army volunteer battalion. Clearly he realised that he had to serve his country, that joining up was
expected of him, but he refused to take the jingoist's sentimental approach.
There is a delicate irony in the final refrain of one of his earliest war poems
'All the Hills and Dales Along' which he wrote shortly after enlisting. At
first, it appears a traditional soldier's poem, the rhythms reflecting the sound
of marching men but the final lines reveal subtle understanding of military
life's brutalisation and the fate ahead for many fighting soldiers.

> On marching men, on
> To the gates of death with song.
> Sow your gladness, for earth's reaping,
> So you may be glad, though sleeping,
> Strew your gladness on earth's bed,
> So be merry, so be dead.[14]

Sorley first saw frontline service in the spring of 1915 when his battalion
was posted to the Western Front on the Ypres sector, scene of some of the
most intensive fighting of the war. Then he had his first experience of violent
death when one of his bombers accidentally blew himself up with a grenade
while raiding a German trench. Unlike some contemporary English war poets
who exulted in the glory of laying down one's life for one's country – Rupert
Brooke's 'Peace' and Julian Grenfell's 'The Volunteer' come to mind – Sorley
recognised only death's absolute otherness. In the second of 'Two Sonnets',
he reflected on death's nature, likening it to a strange signpost bidding the
traveller towards a 'homeless land and friendless', a place to avoid, but a fate
the soldier could not avoid. In common with every World War One infantry-
man, Sorley had an intimate relationship with sudden and violent death; it is
not surprising that the theme finds its way into those early war poems:

Such, such is Death: no triumph: no defeat:
Only an empty pail, a slate rubbed clean,
A merciful putting away of what has been.

And this we know: Death is not Life effete,
Life crushed, the broken pail. We who have seen
So marvellous things know well the end not yet.[15]

There is much moral indignation in the focus of Sorley's poetry, much written while he was in the trenches. His poem 'When You See Millions of the Mouthless Dead' was found in his kitbag after he was killed by a German sniper during the Battle of Loos in October 1915; by then he regarded war as a nightmarish activity, quite separate from everyday life experience. In one of his last letters to his friend Arthur Watts, he admitted that the constant casualties and the sight of mutilated men had gnawed at his humanity, leaving an empty shell: 'One is hardened by now: purged of all false pity: perhaps more selfish than before. The spiritual and the animal get so much more sharply divided in hours of encounter, taking possession of the body by swift turns.'[16] In that sense Sorley's work embodies a strong feeling of the poet as witness. Like many other war poets he believed he had to come to terms with the experience of battle and then record it so that others could understand there was no glory in violent death and no victory in the individual's demise.

Mackintosh came from a similar social background to Sorley – middle class and privately educated. Although his family came from Alness in Easter Ross, he was born in Brighton and educated at St Paul's School, London and Christ Church, Oxford, where he studied Classics. At the outbreak of war he enlisted immediately and was commissioned into 1/5th Seaforth Highlanders, a Territorial battalion whose men came mainly from Caithness and Sutherland. Quite early in his military career he refused to be taken in by the feeling that war was anything other than a violent and inglorious activity. Although an earlier poem, 'Cha till McCruimen: Departure of the 4th Camerons', written in February 1915, exulted in the excitement of impending battle with its insistence that the volunteers were marching off to war 'with merry hearts and voices singing', his exposure to battle soon changed his tune. There is a world of difference between the initial exuberance of 'Cha till McCruimen' ('honour and noble pride were calling / to the tune of the pipes and the drum') and a poem like 'Recruiting' which voices Mackintosh's sarcastic opinion of 'fat civilians' and 'girls with [white] feathers' who push young men into uniform while taking no risks themselves. Prompted by seeing a recruiting poster in a railway carriage Mackintosh found the patriotic sentiments vulgar and realised that the gulf between 'washy songs on England's need' and the reality of war was almost unbridgeable:

'Lads, you're wanted! Over there,'
Shiver in the morning dew,
More poor devils like yourselves
Waiting to be killed by you.[17]

Mackintosh also wrote several deservedly popular songs and parodies such
as 'High Wood to Waterlot Farm' and 'The Charge of the Light Brigade
Brought Up To Date' satirising the idea of war as glorious adventure.
However, his reputation rests on the much anthologised poem 'In Memoriam,
Private D. Sutherland' which is a bitter reflection on the anguish felt by the
officers of his battalion following the deaths of men under their command.
The incident prompting the poem was a raid by 1/5th Seaforths on a German
trench on 16 May 1916 which resulted in four deaths including Private David
Sutherland's who, to Mackintosh's great grief, had to be left behind during
the attack. In the eulogy Mackintosh addresses Sutherland's father in words
that could never have been written in the official letter of condolence which
every officer composed to the families of casualties:

So, you were David's father,
And he was your only son,
And the new-cut peats are rotting
And the work is left undone.
Because of an old man weeping,
Just an old man in pain,
For David, his son David,
That will not come again.[18]

In the poem, which takes the form of a Gaelic coronach, or lament,
Mackintosh makes much of the conceit that the officers in his battalion were
standing *in loco parentis* over their men. ('You were only David's father, /
But I had fifty sons.') It sounds paternalistic; on one level it is, but that sense
of duty lies at the heart of the regimental system as it would have been
understood by an officer in a line infantry regiment such as the Seaforth
Highlanders. For most soldiers, the first loyalty was to the regiment and the
battalion in which they served. This was their home and one whose honour
and history they would go to great lengths to protect. It helped that all the
Scottish infantry regiments had their own recruiting areas with the depot
central to the local community and a focus for recruitment. The majority of
the men in the Seaforths were Highlanders or had Highland connections; for
them the regiment became home.

Although Mackintosh was a Territorial officer who had joined for war
service, his letters show his intense awareness of that tribal aspect of the
regimental system and the way in which it could give men solace in time of

danger. He was killed in action during the Battle of Cambrai on 21 November 1917. Mackintosh had no need to take part in the battle. Badly wounded on the Somme at High Wood in the previous year and having been awarded a Military Cross, he was employed in Cambridge training officer cadets and could have stayed there. Yet despite the hardships and terrors of life in the front line, which he deplored, he had come to believe that the experience was a privilege, a rite of passage denied others. The final lines of his last poem, 'War, The Liberator' were a fitting epitaph, not just to him but all Scots who served as regulars and volunteers between 1915 and 1917 and knew what it was like to face the hellish shock of battle:

> Now in all the time to come, memory will cover us,
> Trenches that we did not lose, charges that we made,
> Since a voice, when first we heard shells go shrilling over us,
> Said within us, 'This is Death – and I am not afraid!'[19]

By the time of Mackintosh's death, stalemate had long dominated the Western Front and the war leaders – British, French and German – were at a loss how to break it. War weariness had begun to infiltrate civilian life; the women waiting at home recorded this. It also informed the poetry of Violet Jacob ('Halloween') and Mary Symon ('The Soldier's Cairn'), revealing the despair felt by wives and mothers at the slaughter of so many men on the battle-fronts. In the former's case, the sensation was heightened when she received the news of the death of her only son Harry Jacob, killed on the Somme in the summer of 1916. The response was 'Glory', written in the language of her native Angus countryside: she was born in Montrose in 1863, the daughter of the 18th Laird of Dun. The opening verse expresses the anguish every mother would feel about the death of a child.

> I canna see ye, lad, I canna see ye
> For a' thon glory that's about yer heid,
> Yon licht that haps ye and the hosts that's wi ye –
> Ayes, but ye live, and it's mysel' that's deid.[20]

In her long poem 'The Glen's Muster-Roll' Mary Symon extended that sense of personal loss to other rural communities, touched by war's carnage. Born the daughter of a landowner in Dufftown, Banffshire she took a great deal of interest in the language, customs and lore of her native countryside. Her poetry demonstrates genuine concern for the pain and misery caused by war. In that sense, though it is rooted in a local community Symon knew well, 'The Glen's Muster-Roll' attains a universality of feeling through the dominie's articulation of his personal anguish at the deaths in action of so many of his former pupils, boys he had known and fostered.

My Loons, my Loons! Yon winnock gets the settin' sun the same,
Here's sklates and skailies, ilka dask a' fettled wi' a name.
An' as I sit a vision comes: Ye're troopin' in aince mair,
Ye're back frae Aisne, an' Marne an' Meuse, Ypres an' Festubert;
Ye're back on weary bleeding feet – you, you that danced an' ran –
For every lauchin' loon I kent I see a hell-scarred man.
Not mine but yours to question now! You lift unhappy eyes –
'Ah, Maister; tell fat's a' this means.' And I, ye thocht sae wise,
Maun answer wi' the bairn words ye said tae me langsyne:
'I dinna ken, I dinna ken. Fa does, oh, Loons o' Mine?[21]

Four other poets deserve mention – W. D. Cocker (1882–1970), Roderick
Watson Kerr (1893–1960), Joseph Lee (1875–1949) and J. B. Salmond
(1891–1958) – because they were all frontline soldiers and in their poetry
they refused to be taken in by what was supposed to be war's excitement and
glamour. It is noteworthy that all were journalists and their poetry never
really developed beyond the work they produced during the war. Salmond
wrote most of his verse in the vernacular – like Jacob he was a native of
Angus – and is easily identified as a Scottish writer, but there is another
aspect of his work which distinguishes it from the English experience. This
is the so-called 'reductive idiom', which runs through so much of Scotland's
literature, the 'cocking a snook' at authority. He became an establishment
figure, editor of the *Scots Magazine* and later an official of the University of St
Andrews, but his poem 'Any Private tae Any Private' reveals the antipathy
towards the war felt by most ordinary soldiers. The poem is prefaced by a
newspaper report which suggests that 'owing to the number of young married
men who were being killed, the widows were becoming a great burden to the
State'. The speaker is a soldier who has brought in the body of a dead comrade
called Wullie:

I canna mak' it oot. It fair beats a',
That Wullie has tae dee for God kens what.
An Wullie's wife'll get a bob or twa,
Aifter they interfere wi' what she's got.
They'll pester her, and crack a dagoned lot;
An' Heaven kens, they lave her awfu' ticht.
'A burden to the State'. Her Wullie's shot.
I kenna hoo, I canna lauch the nicht.[22]

There are echoes of the conversational style Siegfried Sassoon used in his
poem 'Base Details' ('If I were fierce, and bald, and short of breath'), but here
Salmond takes the point of view – and voice – of a private soldier sickened by
the death of a friend known all his life and angered by unthinking newspaper

comments. Roderick Watson Kerr creates a similar effect in his poem 'The Corpse'. The speaker introduces the concept of the body lying still on the battlefield after the shooting has stopped – a common World War One image – and then brings the reader up short with the chilling concluding words: 'Thank God! it had a sack / Upon its face!'[23] Joseph Lee's poem 'The Bullet' is equally abrupt and to the point. It is also a poem whose message could be understood by soldier and civilian alike:

> Every bullet has its billet;
> Many bullets more than one:
> God! Perhaps I killed a mother
> When I killed a mother's son.[24]

Three poets writing in Gaelic stand out: Donald MacDonald (Dòmhnall Ruadh Chorùna, 1887–1967), John Munro (Iain Rothach, 1898–1918) and Murdo Murray (Murchadh Moireach, 1890–1964). Both Munro and Murray were born in Lewis and educated at the University of Aberdeen. Both were commissioned in 1/4th Seaforths and both saw extensive action on the Western Front. Murray survived the war, but Munro was killed during the Germans' spring offensive in April 1918. Both felt compelled to write about their experiences and the resulting poetry was first published in An Dìleab, (1934, edited by James Thomson). Munro's poem 'Ar Tìr, 's Ar Gaisgeach A Thuit 'sa Bhlàir' ('Our Land and our Heroes who fell in Battle') originally appeared as two separate poems, but A. I. MacAsgaill's edition of Luach na Saorsa (1970) gives a unified version which has been translated by the poet and critic Derick Thomson (Ruaraidh MacThomais, 1921–). According to Thomson this poem is 'the finest early burgeoning of the "new" poetry of the century. Its novelty lies in metre and rhythm and construction, and it is clear that it was in some ways influenced by the work of his contemporaries in English poetry'.[25] Also published in Luach na Saorsa are the wartime diaries of Murdo Murray containing vivid descriptions of life on the front line in Gaelic and English.

Like Murray, MacDonald survived and returned to his native Lewis where he wrote poetry and songs including 'An Eala Bhan' ('The White Swan') which achieved wide popularity. Born at Choruna near Claddach Baleshare – his great-grandfather had served in the Peninsula, hence the name of the house – he was educated at the village school in Carinish and enlisted in the Queen's Own Cameron Highlanders. Wounded during the Battle of the Somme in the summer of 1916, he returned to active service in the 49th (West Riding) Division as a gunner in a divisional field regiment. Although now in the Royal Artillery, he continued to wear his Cameron cap badge, a sign of his regimental attachment. In common with most poets of the period, MacDonald was repelled by war's monstrous attrition; yet he was also moved by the sense of togetherness and comradeship generated amongst the fighting men. Thomson has detected 'a muzziness of emotional response' in MacDonald's war poems but in 'Oran Arras' ('Arras Song') he displays considerable technical virtuosity and throughout there is a wry acceptance of the soldier's lot.

> Tillidh cuid dhinn slàn,
> Cuid for chàdh lann fala
> 'S mar a tha e 'n dàn,
> Roinn le bàs a dh'fhanas.
> Ghillean, march at ease!

> (Some of us shall return unscathed,
> Some in pain from bloody wounds,
> And, as fate decrees,
> A number will remain behind in death.
> March at ease, men!)[26]

Tellingly, the last line's refrain, a military order, 'march at ease', is given in English throughout, dissociating the soldier's world and that of the Gaelic-speaking Lewis men marching up to the front lines at Arras.

Sixteen years after the war ended Hugh MacDiarmid (Christopher Murray Grieve, 1892–1978) addressed the nation in 'Towards a New Scotland', and asked:

> Was it for little Belgium's sake
> Sae mony thoosand Scotsman dee'd?
> And never ane for Scotland fegs
> Wi' twenty thoosand times mair need![27]

In a sense, MacDiarmid had already answered the question himself. He served on the Salonika front as a Royal Army Medical Corps sergeant and on demobilisation been transfigured, literally and metaphysically. During the war he had written little of value for immediate publication, but in the 1920s began writing poetry in Scots. From this, he evolved the idea of a renaissance movement whose aim was to dissociate Scottish writing from the sentimentality of pre-war vernacular poetry and bring it into line with contemporary European thinking. His first serious publication was *Northern Numbers* (1920) an anthology based on Edward Marsh's *Georgian Poetry*. Two further editions followed in 1921 and 1922. The contributors included many who had written poetry during the recent war: John Buchan, Violet Jacob, Roderick Watson Kerr, Joseph Lee, Neil Munro, Charles Murray and Mary Symon. He founded a magazine, the *Scottish Chapbook*, and began to challenge established literary assumptions in articles for *The Scottish Educational Journal* under the title 'Contemporary Scottish Studies'. His campaign had a political aspect: he was one of the founders of the Scottish committee of International PEN and in 1928 was a founding member of the National Party of Scotland. As described by Catherine Kerrigan, Grieve had used his time in the military to good effect to develop his literary and political ideas:

> With an almost military precision he began putting his plan to transform the Scottish cultural scene into action and within a few years Quartermaster-Sergeant Grieve had metamorphosed into Hugh MacDiarmid, the modern Scottish vernacular poet and leader of what he was optimistically to call the 'Scottish Renaissance'.[28]

Like other poets of the immediate post-war period – Yeats, Eliot and Pound – MacDiarmid was aware of English culture's exhaustion in the 1920s and the need to explore new means of national self-expression. He was also aware that the war had changed the cohesion of European civilisation in general. In those circumstances it would be the duty of countries like Scotland to redeem those cultural values; like many of his contemporaries he realised that in no small measure the global conflict had been fought to protect the rights of small nations. In that respect World War One hastened Scottish literature's development. The war poets are harbingers of that change.

CHAPTER FOUR

Arcades – The 1920s and 1930s
Alan Riach

In the twenty-one years between the First and Second World Wars people in Europe endured either conditions of recovery from war or those leading to a new one, including the Great Depression. These decades saw major developments within that crisis-ridden period that influenced Scottish literature for the rest of the century. Writers, artists, intellectuals returning from the 'Great War' to a small nation whose contribution to the British imperial effort had been evidently disproportionate to its population's size, questioned the cost. Memorials in countless villages and towns throughout the country, to soldiers who fell in that war, are perhaps not memorials to the sacrifice made in the fighting, but rather to those men's loss from the villages and towns to which they belonged. They assert Scottish identity as much as equivalent memorials in Ireland to men who fell in the struggle against British imperialism. The prevalence of kilts, Celtic crosses and cairns are icons of Scottishness complemented by Sir Robert Lorimer's extraordinary Scottish National War Memorial (1927) in Edinburgh Castle, itself one of Scottish history's *loci classici*. At the end of *Sunset Song*, Lewis Grassic Gibbon (1901–35) has Robert Colquhoun say these words: 'They died for a world that is past, these men, but they did not die for this that we seem to inherit.' The lives and values of the men we come to know so well and deeply in that novel remain a hard-edged question for future generations. Hugh MacDiarmid's (1892–1978) first appearance as a by-name was not as poet but as author of a dialogue, 'Nisbet: An Interlude in Post-War Glasgow', where the character of Nisbet commemorates one of Grieve's best friends, killed in the war.

Andrew Crozier's great painting, *Edinburgh from Salisbury Crags* (1927), presents a capital city of tenements, prehistoric geology, soaring cliffs and the ancient castle. There are few figures but a populated cityscape: people live here. As the eye runs up and around the canvas to where the castle seems almost to be turning to look back at you, the question it asks is central to the modern movement and reminiscent of Picasso's *Demoiselles D'Avignon* (1907): like Picasso's prostitutes in their African masks, the castle looks straight back at the viewer. It is not there to delight the observer; it asks you, 'Who's looking? What do you think you're looking at? If this city and the nation whose capital it is go back through generations, political statehood, prehistory, what might not happen in an unforeseeable future?'

The emphasis on the personal, local and national counterpoints the prioritisation of aesthetics in art in the great Modernists' neoclassicism. The primal scream was heard in Stravinsky's *Rite of Spring* (1913) but formal precisions subsequently dominated, as Schoenberg's unironically lush romanticism in *Transfigured Night* (1899) gave way to the rigours of twelve-tone serialism. In 1922, Modernism's high-point year, T. S. Eliot's restrained, compassionate, fragmented narratives in *The Waste Land* (given formal immediacy with Ezra Pound's assistance) and James Joyce's structurally meticulous celebration of the whole human mess in *Ulysses* were contemporary with MacDiarmid's first appearance in print. But where Eliot and Joyce had made their protest by leaving their native countries, MacDiarmid – like Yeats – returned to his, and stayed. While major writers and artists bee-lined for Europe's artistic capital, Paris, MacDiarmid – or rather recently demobbed ex-Sergeant Grieve – married, started a family, and settled in East-Coast small-town Montrose, a local paper reporter, socialist town councillor and Justice of the Peace (giving public lectures on Lenin).

MacDiarmid's explicit political endorsement of Scottish independence and international communism is more understandable in the context of the radical, revolutionary politics of this era. After all, 1922 saw Mussolini march into Rome and form a fascist government in Italy. What immediate good was thought to be achieved in Italy (draining marshes, running trains on time) was not tarnished then by the knowledge we now have of what came in the following decades. National self-regeneration was an emblematic strategy. In Scotland, Modernism was to be enmeshed with political self-determination of a practical kind. If Joyce made his protest by leaving and Yeats his by staying, MacDiarmid, especially after his visit to Ireland in 1928, wanted not only Joycean aesthetic ideals and socialist sympathies, but also the Yeatsian sense of aristocratic, bardic authority and residential commitment to social improvement through state intervention.

As the Labour movement and the Scottish National movement took form in political parties (MacDiarmid was an early member of the Independent Labour Party and a founder-member of the National Party of Scotland), he began a lifetime's occupation of a public, political role. The first British Labour government was voted into power in 1924. In 1923, the Scottish Home Rule Association helped organise a march of 30,000 people through Glasgow and in the same year the USSR was established. Behind these events, the Easter Rising in Ireland in 1916 and the Russian Revolution of 1917 set examples for Scotland in the 1920s.

The decade saw MacDiarmid at the centre of the cultural and political ferment in Scotland. He was writing poems in the language we call Scots that, in David Daiches's words, had all the shock of a childbirth in a church. He was also editing the series of three anthologies *Northern Numbers*, including work by familiar establishment figures like John Buchan (1875–1940) for whom he had real respect, poems which, well-crafted as they were, nevertheless espoused conventional piety and clichéd nostalgia, and younger poets just returned from the war, writing about the unemployed, the exploitation of prostitutes, music-hall vulgarities, so bringing together different Scotlands in a bold attempt to shake up what might be made of the nation.

MacDiarmid's – or rather, Grieve's – account of his war-time experiences, *Annals of the Five Senses* (1923) is important not only for its feverishly vivid depictions of Salonika but for its Modernist prose technique, dense, oblique, sharp-edged, and its lucid, shocking poetry, presenting aspects of the soldier's life which were bound to offend Scottish verse traditionalists. Most extensively, he was writing journalism, syndicated in newspapers throughout Scotland, advocating cultural revitalisation in all the arts and condemning the conservative (and usually unionist) establishment for its death-grip on new expression. Some of this journalism was collected in *Contemporary Scottish Studies*, published in the year of the General Strike, 1926.

In the 1920s, MacDiarmid was an evangelist, a passionate advocate of radical new politics and cultural renaissance. But in the 1930s, he was as far from the centre of such activities as possible, while still remaining in Scotland. He was in the Shetland island of Whalsay, isolated, poor, mentally and physically broken down and, in 1935, close to death. The trajectory from dynamic catalyst to obscure and unpopular eccentric is shocking. His recovery, through the central poem of his career, 'On a Raised Beach' (from *Stony Limits*, 1934) into the later 1930s and through the next four decades, remains astonishing. This is the opening of 'From "The War with England"':

> I was better with the sounds of the sea
>   Than with the voices of men
> And in desolate and desert places
>   I found myself again
> For the whole of the world came from these
> And he who returns to the source
> May gauge the worth of the outcome
> And approve, and perhaps reinforce
> Or disapprove, and perhaps change its course.[1]

MacDiarmid possessed the single driving vision that imagined a complex, multi-faceted interconnectedness in the total cultural product of Scotland's national identity as nobody else had done, probably, since Walter Scott. But many of his contemporaries – artists, novelists, composers and playwrights – worked out their own vision. If MacDiarmid's legacy is a sense of comprehensiveness (if not always coherence), that does not devalue others' singular achievements. An important development has been the scholarly reclamation, the archaeology and revaluation of many of these writers and artists, some of whom MacDiarmid himself thought of little value at the time. There were radical new initiatives in all genres during the interwar period, with still under-explored biographical links and explicit alliances.

MacDiarmid grew up in the era of the Glasgow Boys and the Scottish Colourists, the first truly great artists to bring the innovations of modernity in painting into Scotland. Their magnificent precedents are William McTaggart (1835–1910), a Gaelic speaker who painted the landscapes and people he knew, among whom he had family; Patrick Geddes (1854–1932), the social visionary, town planner and biologist, whose word 'Renascence' for what should happen in Scottish culture was first printed in the 1890s; and the now-familiar artist-architect Charles Rennie Mackintosh (1868–1928), whose sense of what a building could be for the well-being of the people who live in and walk around it was only part of a comprehensive vision Scotland has conspicuously failed to endorse. Both the intellectual challenge of social vision these proposed and the shockingly fresh sensualities of the Post-Impressionist Colourists, bringing French appetite for everyday realities and the eloquent mannerliness of bourgeois city life to counter the blackness and silence of northern Europe, were required in the 1920s to re-imagine Scotland.

Les Peintres de L'Écosse Moderne, the exhibition of F. C. B. Cadell (1883–1937), Samuel Peploe (1871–1935), George Leslie Hunter (1877–1931) and J. D. Fergusson (1874–1961), was held in Paris in 1924 and was followed, also in Paris, in 1931, by the exhibition *Les Peintres Ecossais*. It was as if, by moving between Scotland and France, these artists were bypassing London altogether. Perhaps this is one reason they have been so radically undervalued by the British/English art establishment. Through the 1920s and 1930s, while MacDiarmid remained in contact with the major figure of Fergusson, he grew closer to the determined Modernist work of two other artists: first, William MacCance (1894–1970), whose *Structures in a Landscape Setting* (the title is indicative) of 1922 relates closely to his other works of the time, some literally illustrating MacDiarmid's poems; and second, William Johnstone (1897–1981), cousin of the composer F. G. Scott (1880–1958). One of Johnstone's major paintings, *A Point in Time*, was worked on throughout this period and ostensibly completed in 1932, although in its swirling, quasi-organic, semi-mechanical forms, it embodies an abstract vision of lyrical unfolding, and brooding, portentous threat. Many of Johnstone's paintings have their roots in a lyrical vision of Scottish Borders landscapes, but he moves from there to a profoundly impressive abstract, painterly vision, revealing moments of tension, dynamic action, authoritative power and momentary occasions like no other artist of his time. As McTaggart prefigures Impressionism, some of Johnstone's works prefigure the action painting of Jackson Pollock and the New York school, though he is a greater artist than Pollock. Scotland has no Jack Yeats, a single, dominating figure whose paintings present Ireland and the people of Ireland in the full spectrum from tragic to comic. But perhaps the artist MacDiarmid was closest to in terms of a lyric identification with the Borders was William Gillies (1898–1973). There is more work to be done in these interdisciplinary studies.

Since the 1980s especially, more work has been done on the revaluation of writing by women in these decades, particularly Catherine Carswell's (1879–1946) *Open the Door!* (1920) and her *Life of Burns* (1930). Carswell's rich portrayal in the former of both the heroine Joanna and Glasgow (and the Glasgow Art School) remain vivid, and her revitalisation of Burns gave offence to the pious. Less magisterial work of fine quality was also produced by the sisters Mary (1865–1963) and Jane Findlater (1866–1946): Jane's *A Green Grass Widow and Other Stories* (1921) and *Beneath the Visiting Moon* (1923), which the sisters co-authored, were published towards the end of their career, which began in the 1890s. Daughters of the manse, their precise, gentle comedies of observation and manners belying darker depths of unspoken emotion foreshadow the work both of women novelists and those men who made women their central characters, most importantly Lewis Grassic Gibbon. Gibbon is well-known, but equally evocative depictions of northeast Scotland are Nan Shepherd's (1893–1981) *The Quarry Wood* (1928) and Willa (Anderson) Muir's (1890–1970) *Imagined Corners* (1931), while Naomi Mitchison (1897–1999), in *The Corn King and the Spring Queen* (1931), produced an immense mythological reconfiguration of the relation between men and women in society; her *oeuvre* follows this through from ancient times to the present in later books and in memoirs like the semi-autobiographical *Lobsters on the Agenda* (1952).

Renowned and loved as Grassic Gibbon's *Scots Quair* trilogy remains, it is worth emphasising how significant the experience of women was for him in other novels and in his short stories. His first novel, which he acknowledged with his own name, James Leslie Mitchell, was *Stained Radiance* (1930), largely set in London but with principal characters from Aberdeenshire; its heroine undergoes an abortion at the centre of the novel. Mitchell's writing is fascinatingly close to, but utterly different from that of D. H. Lawrence. For both men, the experience of women is central and the political emphasis upon this is an important departure from patriarchal assumptions. For Lawrence, the women are very much his subjects: authorial patriarchalism inhabits all his evocations of their experience. There is always a cloying sense that Lawrence knows what is best for them. For Gibbon, however, the sense of sympathy and human, or creatural, understanding is a very different thing. The women central in his novels and stories, including the eponymous *Gay Hunter, Three Go Back* and *The Lost Trumpet*, are not ciphers in a masculine vision but the acknowledgements of possibility for future visions. There is a flavour of this also in the poignancy of J. M. Barrie's (1860–1937) late work, *Farewell, Miss Julie Logan* (1932), where an ageing minister and a young woman represent their lost and potential selves in a more than merely naturalistic or straightforwardly allegorical way.

The almost supernatural poise of Barrie's novella also characterises the strange writing of David Lindsay (1876–1945) in his masterpiece, *A Voyage to Arcturus* (1920) and its successor, *The Haunted Woman* (1922). Lindsay's later novels are fascinating, but difficult and more laboured. *Arcturus* is an underground classic, on the list of Harold Bloom's 'Western Canon' classics of world literature, and should be read by everyone.[2] Beginning with a science fiction proposition, in which an interstellar spaceship takes a small group from Scotland to a far-distant planet, the novel exfoliates a fantastically intricate, vividly colourful exploration of human motivation, emotional urges and desires, almost as a direct contradiction of the Calvinist doctrine of predestination. It is as if the novel slowly and compellingly demonstrates that nothing is predetermined, everything that happens emerges from motives and desires that are too deep to be analysed and controlled. Yet it is not a thesis but a haunting story, full of tension, characters in opposition and struggle, and profound resolution. *The Haunted Woman* seems like a conventional ghost story, but again repays close attention as it reveals itself to be about the repressions of sexuality and, especially, feminine sexual expression. It is as suspenseful, frightening and gripping as Henry James's *The Turn of the Screw*. It is worth noting that Lindsay's space-and-time travellers and their predecessor in H. G. Wells's *The Time Machine* (1895) may have informed the thinking behind the extraordinarily popular book by J. W. Dunne, *An Experiment with Time* (1928), and Dunne's book may have influenced Gibbon.

A far more extrovert and bodily engagement with reality was Eric Linklater's (1899–1974). After prohibition in the United States in the 1920s, Linklater's picaresque, satirical novel *Juan in America* (1931) opened up an exuberant inhabitation of city life, albeit on the other side of the Atlantic. Fionn Mac Colla (1906–75), in *The Albannach* (1932), created one of the most memorable novels of a young Highlander growing up, but the city he comes to in the central section of the novel is as disastrous and foul, corrupting and foetid, as the corresponding version of Dublin in Joyce's *A Portrait of the Artist as a Young Man* (with which *The Albannach* stands comparison). Similarly, Edwin Muir's (1887–1959) *Poor Tom* (1932) is a quasi-autobiographical account of a squalid Glasgow and its murderous effects on his family, while Gibbon, in *Grey Granite* (1934), creates a vivid cityscape partly conflating Aberdeen

and Dundee but also including scenes of political protest and police brutality that may have been modelled on events the author saw and reported as a
journalist in Glasgow. Rarely acknowledged as such, these works all prefigure
the more recent city fiction of Gray, Kelman and even Welsh. With them,
however, we should note the most famous, widely-read and sensationalist
novel of urban violence, Alexander MacArthur (1901–47) and H. Kingsley
Long's *No Mean City* (1935). Written with journalistic realism, but containing intermittent editorial comments of some sanctimoniousness presumably
written by Long, the narrative of this novel has its power and tensions, its
value as a record of social practice, such as 'the shirricking' (the vocal public
criticism) of the main gang-leader by his offended girlfriend; but its realism
and explicit editorialising are also its limitations as a novel. What might
be done with characters and circumstances such as these remained for later
writers to develop.

Edwin Muir, in *Scottish Journey* (1935) gave a Grierson-like documentary
view of Scotland, memorably retraced by James Campbell, in *Invisible Country*
(1985). Parts of Muir's travel book are beautifully written, fluent, poised and
delightful; parts, however – such as the description of the Highlands and their
mountains – are classically 'purple prose' showing all the excesses of journalism and none of the shrewd measurements and allegorical force Muir's poems
were to develop. It was Linklater again, in *Magnus Merriman* (1934), who
depicted urbane living (in London and Edinburgh especially) in a comically
autobiographical novel which takes a healthily derisive view of the Scottish
Nationalist movement before moving the main character into a mode of
committed support for the idea of independence. Ultimately, however,
disillusioned with politics, Magnus settles with a strong-willed, independently-minded Orkney woman in whose matriarchal authority he finds some
welcome shelter. Dated in some respects, *Magnus Merriman* remains a subtle
and challenging novel about the value of commitment, the temptations of
being human, conservative endorsements of power that the farming world
inhabits and happily lucid, city-based qualities of urbane wit and humour.
There is also a hilarious portrait of MacDiarmid (which MacDiarmid himself
enjoyed hugely).

Through these decades, a number of composers should be noted in relation
to the work of the writers. This could be a chapter in itself, but mention of
John Blackwood McEwan's (1868–1948) *A Solway Symphony* (1922) suggests both the long career of this wonderful composer whose string quartets
are amongst the finest in the literature of small ensemble writing and also
the dedication to a local habitation he emphasised in his symphonic work
and orchestral tone-poems based on Border Ballads. The song-settings of the
magisterial F. G. Scott, such as 'The Eemis Stane' (1924) or the masterpiece,
'Milk-Wort and Bog Cotton' (1932) are clear indications of a sophistication

and mastery the equal of anything in Europe or America. Scott, besides having been MacDiarmid's schoolteacher, was an austere and deeply insight-ful friend to many writers associated with the Scottish Renaissance move-ment. He interacted too with Gaelic poetry, setting George Campbell Hay's (1915–84) poems to music, for example. His role remains under-researched as his music remains undervalued (though the CD of his songs, *Moonstruck*, has been widely praised).[3]

In fiction, John Buchan continued to write an increasingly moving epitaph to nineteenth-century priorities, in *The Path of the King* (1921) and foresaw twentieth-century political revolutions in *The Courts of the Morning* (1929), while his Scottish novel *Witch Wood* (1927) applied the same moral dilem-mas, with which he was as familiar as Joseph Conrad, to Scotland's histori-cal conflict between devotees of pagan and orthodox worship. Buchan saw deeply into what was at stake in conflicts that were superficially no more than sensational. In *The Three Hostages* (1924), the popular genre of 'thriller' or 'shocker' (Buchan's term) belies the political thrust of the questions involved. Like Conrad, Buchan displays rather than endorses unlikeable or even despicable characteristics, and usually leaves them open for question. He knows what is at stake and what it costs to maintain what he values. This is perhaps why MacDiarmid, politically at the other extreme, had such high praise for him, especially his anthology, *The Northern Muse*.

Buchan's literary ambiguity is shared by R. B. Cunninghame Graham (1852–1936), another writer connected closely with Conrad (as was Neil Munro). Graham's *Doughty Deeds* appeared in 1925, the same year as Hitler's *Mein Kampf*. The following year, Neil Gunn (1891–1973) published *The Grey Coast*. In 1927, there was Cunninghame Graham's *Redeemed* and in 1930, Gunn's *Morning Tide* and Cunninghame Graham's *Thirty Stories and Sketches*, edited by Edward Garnett. It seems fortuitous that these works were appearing at the same time as Gandhi was beginning his campaign of civil disobedience in India and St Kilda was being evacuated. Cunninghame Graham's international provenance in an increasingly post-imperial world and Gunn's intensely-observed and politically-committed evocations of the people of Caithness and Sutherland are wonderfully complementary ways to bridge the end of the nineteenth century to the 1930s and the rise of the idea of a new Scotland. Gunn was to be active in the nationalist movement of whose party Cunninghame Graham was a founding member. Meanwhile the popular A. J. Cronin (1896–1981), in *Hatter's Castle* (1931) delivered a posthumous pastiche of the anti-Kailyard classic, George Douglas Brown's *The House with the Green Shutters* (1901) while his 'Dr Finlay' stories con-tinued the Kailyard tradition Douglas Brown seemed to have revolted against. Cronin was immensely popular, perhaps the richest author Scotland produced between Scott and J. K. Rowling.

Meanwhile, as MacDiarmid's left-wing political assertions became increasingly explicit (with *First Hymn to Lenin* in 1931, *Scots Unbound* in 1932 and *Second Hymn to Lenin* in 1935), Edwin Muir was developing a different poetic, in *Chorus of the Newly Dead* (1926), *Variations on a Time Theme* (1934) and later work. Muir's despairing, nightmarish visions of a Europe in which fascism was to grow terribly (brilliantly represented in 'The Good Town', published in *The Labyrinth*, 1949) were a different kind of poetry from that rooted in nationality though no less international in outlook, exemplified and endorsed by MacDiarmid. MacDiarmid's friend, the fine poet William Soutar (1898–1943), published his *Poems in Scots* in 1935, endorsing MacDiarmid's judgement of the intrinsic value of writing in Scots. Soutar was to develop a different strategy from MacDiarmid's, writing attractive Scots poems for children, seeing a new generation as the rising tide which would bring the full 'Renaissance' he and his contemporaries had hoped and written for.

Disillusioned with idealist social aspirations, Muir was having none of this. Things came to a head in 1936 when he published *Scott and Scotland*, saying that the only way forward for Scottish literature was that it should be written in English. MacDiarmid, infuriated, responded by editing *The Golden Treasury of Scottish Poetry* (1940), including poems in Scots, English, translated from Gaelic and Latin – but nothing by Muir. The Gaelic poetry had been translated with the help of Sorley MacLean (1911–96) and it is important to note that through the 1930s MacLean and George Campbell Hay were both writing poetry in Gaelic that was to revolutionise the identity of poetry in that language in the later twentieth century. The greatness of Campbell Hay's achievement was not fully realised until his complete poems were edited and published in 2000, but MacLean's breakthrough volume, *Dàin do Eimhir*, was first published in 1943 and emphatically endorsed MacDiarmid's vision of a multi-vocal, multi-lingual literary Scotland. At the time, MacLean was caught up in the war, and his poems were helped into publication by Douglas Young (1913–73). Young himself, as a translator as well as original, polymathic poet, did crucial work to riddle the Scottish poetry scene with poems from, and in, different languages, but most significantly his translations from Gaelic made sure that that language was central in the literary world's understanding of modern Scottish poetry. Yet Muir had a point: Irish authors writing in English have an international readership in the twenty-first century still denied to MacDiarmid and Soutar. MacDiarmid, however, won the argument: a nation is a place of many voices. To quote Cairns Craig, 'The national imagination [. . .] is a space in which a dialogue is in process [. . .] in a territory [. . .] whose borders define the limits within which certain voices [. . .] are listened for, and others resisted [. . .]'.[4]

This is nowhere more evident than in the plays produced through the 1920s and 1930s alongside a vibrant popular variety theatre. One might summarise by suggesting that working-class drama like that of the coal-miner Joe Corrie (1894–1968) – *In Time o' Strife* (1928) or *Hewers of Coal* (1937) – occupied one theatrical space where the language was largely vernacular Scots; the intellectually challenging, highly articulate plays of James Bridie (1888–1951) like *The Anatomist* or *Tobias and the Angel* (both 1930) or *A Sleeping Clergyman* (1933) occupied another, written largely in heightened, rhetorical, Scots-inflected English; and Robert McLellan's (1907–84) plays, like *Jamie the Saxt* (1937) were historical dramas concerned with matters of political power and national identity of immediate twentieth-century relevance, but written in a Scots synthesising his native Lanarkshire idiom with other dialects into a rich, often ornate, often very funny rhetorical Scots. In the twenty-first century, it is possible to hear all these voices in a complementary polyphony. In the 1920s and 1930s, they were more often in opposition. And the rise of Unity Theatre and working-class drama, alongside the development of the Citizens Theatre that was to come, demonstrate not only conflicts of interest and audience but also an astonishing diversity of theatrical expertise and wilful experimentalism. It was an exciting time and the legacies of these theatres – variety traditions, working-class drama, plays of political protest, plays of moral ideas and intellectual argument – are with us today, and in some respects portend more in the twenty-first century than some of the vital matters that concerned writers of fiction and poetry, which may seem more deeply located in their own times.

In 1936, the Spanish Civil War began, the BBC started its television service, and the Saltire Society was founded to begin committed work on reclaiming the cultural production of Scotland's past. In 1937, Neil Gunn's *Highland River* looked back through the epoch of World War One and the Scottish National Party, looking forward, pledged to oppose conscription from Westminster. Did they know what was coming? Certainly, decades are never neat divisions but by 1939 there were definite signals that something was ending, something different about to emerge. John McNeillie's (1916–2002) notorious *Wigtown Ploughman* (1939) is an overwhelming presentation of the most awful excesses of a farming society, with, at its core, viciousness, brutality and passionate indignation at human limitation. Its anatomisation of character and motive is pure surgery. Its apotheosis of violence is Greek. It should be noted that McNeillie, or Ian Niall, was also the author of one of the most affectionate autobiographies, *A Galloway Childhood* (1967), so the earlier novel is not the whole story. Indeed, Niall or McNeillie is a neglected novelist well worth rediscovering. Better-known, James Barke's (1905–58) epic novel, *The Land of the Leal* (1939), accumulates a tragic and climactic panoramic vision of rural, farming Scotland, as if *Sunset Song* were re-imagined from the point of view of the ending of *Grey Granite*. The horrifically realistic scene where a dead calf has to be extracted from its mother's womb stands as brutal, but convincing, emblem of an aspect of the era. Realism has a Russian power in this book, but realism seems not to be enough. We will come to learn this again more deeply later in the century, first in the 1940s when Edward Gaitens presents Glasgow working-class people limited; but not defined, by external realities, who have working imaginations and dreams; and then in the 1980s, when Alasdair Gray shows us how realism and perspective need to be challenged and vision renewed, to deal with new realities, new contexts for language and humanity. Joyce's *Finnegans Wake*, also 1939, is sometimes described as a marvellous vision of eternal recurrence, the river running back to its source and the journey endlessly returning through the pluralism and puns of all the resources of language, but its ending is also the story of all the particularities of character, relationship, pattern and form running into an encompassing sea – absolute closure: 'Whish! A gull. Gulls. Far calls. Coming, far! End here. Us then. Finn, again! Take. Bussoftlhee, mememormee! Till thousendsthee. Lps. The keys to. Given! A way a lone a last a loved a long the'

And World War Two was beginning.

CHAPTER FIVE

Twentieth-Century Scottish Drama

Donald Smith and Ksenija Horvat

However the position might have changed by the end of the century, in 1900 prospects for a distinctively Scottish theatre were mixed. The national drama inspired by the fiction of Sir Walter Scott had waned, persisting in amateur productions or on the professional margins. In terms of popular entertainment, music hall or 'variety' was supreme and variety played to a British and imperial market place, dwarfing in scale the audience for plays. Since the mid-nineteenth-century expansion of the railways, drama touring was also based on a British market and London was the dominant hub. In London there was a nascent art theatre appealing to a niche audience of *literati* and intellectual reformers. Scots, including William Sharp, the proponent of Celticism, and William Archer, critic and translator of Ibsen, played an active part in this late nineteenth-century movement, but their efforts were largely disconnected from Scotland's cultural scene.

This overall situation was altered by the formation in 1909 of Alfred Wareing's Glasgow Repertory Company, which began to build an audience for 'art' theatre including Shaw, Ibsen and Granville Barker, alongside other European playwrights like Gorky and Chekhov. Scottish writers also involved included Neil Munro and J. A. Ferguson, whose *Campbell of Kilmohr* was the first of a long tradition of modern Scottish plays about the Highlands. Nonetheless, Scottish drama in itself was not the priority. Unfortunately Wareing's company succumbed to the onset of war in 1914 and had to wait for its genuine successor until the emergence of subsidised repertory theatre after World War Two. Meantime, however, the enterprising Scottish National Players reactivated the movement for a national drama, directly inspired by Dublin's Abbey Theatre. The Players drew strength from the burgeoning amateur movement and stimulated an audience for new Scottish drama through both city-based seasons and touring.

From the late 1920s, commercial repertory companies began to emerge in Edinburgh, Glasgow and Perth (1935–). Some, such as the Brandon Thomas and Wilson Barrett Companies in Edinburgh, were oriented towards British theatre or, as critics like R. F. Pollock and Hugh MacDiarmid argued, English theatre.[1] Others, like Rutherglen Repertory Theatre (1939–44 in its first manifestation), were closer to the national drama movement and – following the 1929 foundation of Edinburgh College of Speech and Drama, Scotland's first drama conservatoire – interested in training professional actors. This prefigures the mixed cultural economy of professional theatre that became dominant in Scotland in the 1940s and 1950s.

It is too easy, however, to read this narrative retrospectively as one of inevitable progress. The reality for aspirant theatre artists, particularly playwrights, must have been intensely frustrating. Apart from the overall poverty of opportunity, writers had either to move beyond a distinctively Scottish audience to pursue a professional career or confine themselves to a very limited market. The result could be to deprive an emergent artist of those vital linguistic and social factors that give the playwright context, or to allow the stay-at-home writer so few production opportunities as to prevent their natural development. Both factors undoubtedly caused real damage, yet talented playwrights did emerge and, against the odds, laid the foundations of a modern Scottish repertoire. Some of these key writers will be discussed here in their own right and the contrasts and similarities between them considered.

The sense of living between different worlds is central to the work of J. M. Barrie (1860–1937). Barrie begins in fiction as a social satirist with an uncanny eye for detail and the capacity to display and manipulate his characters for humorous or emotional effect. But his art developed primarily through theatre, and his delineation of character deepened, as did the way in which the plays expressed his own conflicts. The social satirist is seen to good effect in *The Admirable Crichton* (1902) and in *What Every Woman Knows* (1908) where Barrie plays off the small town world of Thrums (his native Kirriemuir) against the big city, Scotland against England, and men against women. But the playwright's wistful evocations of experience beyond reductive social norms become, in other plays, the main theme, though one subtly critiqued and at times emotionally exposed. Such works include *Peter Pan* (1904), *Dear Brutus* (1917) and *Mary Rose* (1920).

Apart from the *Peter Pan* phenomenon, *Mary Rose* may be Barrie's stage masterpiece, because of its combination of superbly economical depiction of character and social situation with intimations of an extraordinary other world. Perhaps the aftermath of World War One gave a special resonance, but the play also reflects Barrie's underlying, profound metaphysical melancholy. He skilfully uses his thematic structure in every scene's construction. Throughout, characters operate on different levels of knowledge and awareness, continually challenging the audience to realign its understanding. In the final scene, Barrie pushes this technique almost to breaking point, but not beyond, as the ghost of Mary Rose sits on the knee of her long lost son, without realising who he is:

MARY ROSE	Nice buckles.
HARRY	I like your hair.
MARY ROSE	Pretty hair.
HARRY	Do you mind the tuft that used to stand up at the back of – of Simon's head?
MARY ROSE	Naughty tuft.
HARRY	I have one like that.
MARY ROSE	Oh dear, oh dear, what a naughty tuft.
HARRY	My name is Harry.
MARY ROSE	Harry, Harry, Harry, Harry.
HARRY	But you don't know what Harry I am.
MARY ROSE	No.[2]

Played with the superb technical control that Barrie demands, this can be unbearably tender and poignant and, to the end, unresolved. Unexamined prejudices have often led to Barrie's being neglected. He connects with a broad public, while remaining a consummate theatre artist.

Barrie's family became middle class through education: implicit in his life and art are the conflicts of 'the lad o' pairts' whose achievements at once elevate him socially and divide him from his roots. Joe Corrie (1894–1968), by contrast, was a Fife miner and, although later in life he made a precarious living as a writer, his art continued to be shaped by the experiences of his own social class. His early theatre experiences come from the popular melodramas of the penny geggie, the inherent drama of local story and folksong, and the influence of the music hall. His ambition was to achieve greater realism without abandoning the need for a 'People's Theatre', and to entertain. First one-act plays, such as *The Shillin'-a-Week Man* (1927) were performed by the local Bowhill Players at 'free-and-easy' concerts arranged to raise money for soup kitchens and cheer mining communities following the impact of the General Strike and subsequent National Lockout of 1926. These plays were later taken up by the Scottish National Players and extensively produced by amateur groups. But the Players' reading committee, which included two fellow playwrights John Brandane and James Bridie, turned down Joe Corrie's first full-length work *In Time o' Strife* (1928). Corrie publicly accused the panel of rejecting his play on political grounds and, though the accusation was rejected with snide comments on Corrie's talents, he was right. The play was too uncomfortably and powerfully direct for the National Players' middle-class preferences.[3] The Bowhill Players later toured it nationally with huge success.

In Time o' Strife's strength is its focus on family household dramas as metaphor for, and embodiment of, wider social struggle. Characters are defined, but not restricted, by their situation and language: Corrie invests passion and linguistic energy to demonstrate that human beings can rise above unjust oppression:

LIZZIE   My mammie was greetin' when I came hame frae the schule the day . . .
            Gimmie a piece, daddy.
            (*Enter JEAN, wearily, an empty basket in her hand.*)
JOCK   Hoo did you get on, wife?
JEAN   I'm beat, Jock, there's no' a grocer or a baker in the toon'll gi'e me a
            crust.
JOCK   (*rising*) Get oot my pit claes.
JEAN   (*rising*) No you're no dain' that.
JOCK   What else can be done?
JEAN   You came oot wi' your neebours, and you'll go back wi' them.
JOCK   And have we to dee o' hunger?
JEAN   Something'll turn up yet.
JOCK   Oh! For God's sake ha'e some sense. What can turn up?[4]

The rejection of *In Time o' Strife* did not prevent its production, but it did damage Corrie's long-term playwriting development, depriving the young playwright of professional productions until his art was fully formed. It is to his great credit that he stretched his own boundaries in plays such as *Hewers of Coal* (1937) and the ghost play *Martha* (1935), but his isolation as a theatre artist thwarted the emergence of a major dramatist.

The same can be said of Ena Lamont Stewart (1912–2006) for related, yet different, reasons. Raised in Glasgow, a minister's daughter in a poor area of the city, Stewart had access to a highly developed amateur scene and in due course to Glasgow Unity Theatre, a professional company devoted to plays of working-class experience. Her husband Jack Stewart became an actor with Unity and encouraged his wife's writing ambitions.[5] Her first full-length play, *Starched Aprons*, produced by Unity in 1945, was a commercial success. The workplace setting, in a hospital, foregrounds a group of working women, each individual, independent and unmarried. The speech of each is subtly differentiated to reflect their class background and attitudes. *Starched Aprons* went on to be produced in Liverpool, Cardiff, Edinburgh and London. The success of Unity's production was partly due to the company's progressive rehearsal methods and a positive relationship between Stewart and the director, Robert Mitchell. This led to Mitchell's asking the young playwright to write about the thirties from the woman's perspective. The result was *Men Should Weep*.

Stewart's second full-length play, produced in 1947, is a family household drama with wider social and political resonance. It embodies a forceful, almost fatalistic, depiction of the price paid by women and children for the poverty of a whole community. Oppressive social conditions are mirrored within the household by the sexual and economic subjection of woman to man. Stewart was to rewrite *Men Should Weep* substantially in the 1970s, giving the women characters greater power to effect change. It was further reworked for its immensely successful 1982 revival by 7:84 (Scotland) Theatre Company. The male/female power nexus remains, however, the animating core:

JOHN   Naw, I didna think ye'd be for bidin.
         (*He picks up her coat, has a good look at it, flings it aside.*)
JENNY   And neither is ma Mammy bidin! Or the kids! You can dae whit ye like. I'm takin a hoose for them in a decent pairt of the toon.
JOHN   You're . . . daein . . . *whit?*
MAGGIE   It's true John, Jenny says . . .
JOHN   I'd an idea I wis the heid o this hoose.
MAGGIE   John, listen! Jenny's got the key money, an she kens . . .
JENNY   I've a friend factors property; I can get ye a four room an kitchen, rare an open, near a park. An . . . I'll can help ye wi the rent.
JOHN   Oh, you'll can help wi the rent? Oh, very fine! Very fine! I'll fair enjoy havin ma rent paid by one o your fancy men.[6]

Glasgow Unity Theatre went out of business in 1951 when it failed to obtain funding from the Scottish Committee of the Arts Council, formed in 1948. With Unity's demise, Stewart's playwriting career went into cold storage until the 1980s revival, with the sole exception of two one-act plays, *Walkies Time for a Black Poodle* and *Towards Evening*, presented in the 1975 Scottish Society of Playwrights' Netherbow season. This was not just a case of changing theatrical fashion, since companies such as the Gateway continued to produce Scottish plays; it was the loss of the only professional company keen to develop Stewart's style of socially-committed theatre that undermined her career. Other companies were preferred for political and social, as much as artistic, reasons, so depriving Scotland's first twentieth-century woman playwright of the creative development which her considerable talent clearly deserved.

In contrast to Stewart's urban world, Robert McLellan (1907–84) had a rural background and drew throughout his life on the spoken Scots of his country childhood. He was interested in the dynamics of Scottish society, class and language, but he chose to examine them through historical otherworlds. In this way, McLellan draws attention to the Anglicisation of Scottish culture and to a loss of identity and autonomy that has personal and social, as well as national, value. He established a productive relationship with the emergent repertory theatres in the 1930s, 1940s and 1950s, but his style of social comedy was seen as dated by the increasingly peer-conscious directors of the 1960s. Revivals, however, began again in the 1980s.

The ambitious historical drama *Jamie the Saxt* (1937) is generally regarded as McLellan's major play because of the complexity and interest of its central character. However, McLellan's comic control of Scots conversation is also deployed to brilliant effect in *The Flouers o' Edinburgh* (1948). There is comic sparkle and verve in this dialogue but also a delving into Scottish psychology and acute social satire:

LORD S   Leave us, Jock.

JOCK   Aa richt, for a whilie, but I'll sune hae to come in and mask the tea, and there'll be mair folk comin to the door. (*Muttering as he goes to the kitchen*) Losh, what a sicht. Mair lace nor a lassie.

CHARLES   The insolent dog! Did you hear him?

LORD S   Can ye blame the man?

CHARLES   Father! What do you mean?

LORD S   I said 'can ye blame the man?' When did ye stert to talk and dress like an Englishman?

CHARLES   (*with a faint sneer*) Do you want me to talk and dress like the men here?

LORD S   Ye belang up here, dae ye no? Ye were born Scots.

CHARLES   I am British, father. The terms 'Scotch' and 'English' became obsolete with the Union.

LORD S   Did they? I'll wager ye winna fin mony Englishmen caain themselves British and stertin to talk and dress like Scotsmen.

CHARLES   Can you blame them? Their language is much more refined than ours, and their clothes infinitely more tasteful.

LORD S   Their language is faur ower refined, as they caa it, for oor vocal organs. Ye may think ye mak no a bad shape at it, but compared wi a real Englishman ye're like a bubbly-jock wi a chuckie in its thrapple. As for yer claes, they wad sit weill on a lassie, but they're haurdly fit weir for a man. Hae they been peyed for?[7]

Despite the wheel of fashion McLellan stubbornly stuck to his task and produced a corpus of work devoted to Scottish theatre and continuously enjoyed by Scottish audiences in both professional and amateur settings.

The last major playwright of this pre-war era is James Bridie (Osborne Henry Mavor) (1888–1951). He was the most prolific and the most influential as regards the emergent institutions of professional theatre in Scotland. Yet Bridie's career straddled the amateur and professional theatre, Scotland and England, and the commercial and subsidised sectors. He is a comic satirist and sceptic, who revels not just in character, but in religious and moral ideas. His drama contrasts sharply with the naturalism of Corrie, Lamont Stewart or McLellan, because he employs non-naturalist techniques including time-shifts, symbolism, dream sequences, older theatrical forms such as masques and types, and abstract moral debates. Sometimes Bridie stirs his heady brew to superb storytelling effect, but in some plays the plot and its resolution seem to part company, as if he had lost patience or creative focus or just run out of time.

Although a less precise and obsessive authorial presence than Barrie, Bridie also creates otherworlds. Some of his heterocosms are unified creations in which the representational logic embraces realism and the archetypes of romance. This is seamlessly achieved in *Tobias and the Angel* (1930), one of Bridie's most performed works, but it is also deployed with great cunning in plays such as *The Anatomist* (1930), *Mr Bolfry* (1943) and *Dr Angelus* (1947). In these, extraordinary or morally offensive behaviour creeps up on the spectator cumulatively before one's defences are established. Humour is employed throughout as a medicine that assists in swallowing uncomfortable truths. In other works such as *Sleeping Clergyman* (1933), *The Queen's Comedy* (1950) and *The Baikie Charivari* (1952), Bridie sets up two worlds and moves the action between them. In yet another group of plays, Bridie fuses realism and surrealism into one strange yet convincing whole. Examples of this type include *Gog and Magog* (1948) and *Daphne Laureola* (1949)

Bridie's theatrical success rate is remarkably high, and he continued to innovate and experiment to the close. What Bridie sometimes lacked was a strong directional counterweight to rein him in and play devil's advocate. It is certainly noticeable that Bridie's best work comes from collaborations with strong producers such as H. K. Aylife, Barry Jackson and Alastair Sim in directorial mode. It is unfortunate that he did not have more opportunities to work with Tyrone Guthrie who was one of the Scottish National Players' first professional producers, and a sympathetic critic of his talent. Bridie's dramas deserve revival, but there is a clear role for contemporary adaptation, editing and direction to present the pungent essence of the playwright in new cultural and theatrical conditions.

Bridie's wider influence on the development of professional theatre has been blamed for thwarting Glasgow Unity and the careers of playwrights such as Corrie and Lamont Stewart. There is justice in this charge, yet Bridie also deserves credit for the emergence of Glasgow Citizens Theatre (1943), the Arts Council's Scottish Committee (1948), and the College of Drama at the Royal Scottish Academy of Music (1950). It seems fitting, then, that it was Bridie who, in 1948, orchestrated the Edinburgh International Festival production of Sir David Lindsay's *Ane Satyre of the Thrie Estaitis*. This heralded a new professionalism and internationalism yet, in typical Bridie fashion, it was founded on a late-medieval play saturated in moral argument. The team that Bridie brought together included adapter Robert Kemp, director Tyrone Guthrie, the cream of Scotland's acting talent and, on the advice of Sadie Aitken, the Church of Scotland's General Assembly Hall. Establishment man, alchemist, animateur and comedian – all sides of Bridie were evident in this triumph.

Robert Kemp (1908–67) was to give further impetus to playwriting in Scotland in the 1950s with comedies like *The Other Dear Charmer* (1951) and *The Penny Wedding* (1957). He was associated with the Edinburgh Gateway Company (1953–65), situated in the Elm Row theatre space, catering predominantly for Edinburgh's middle class with a mixed repertory of new writing, popular plays and adaptations of known classics. Perhaps even more influentially, he was also the first playwright to translate Molière into Scots, his *Let Wives Tak Tent* (1948) nurturing a link between French acting styles and Scottish physical comedy. This vein of linguistic energy and social satire remained pivotal for Scottish audiences through the century. The strand of translation and adaptation regained prominence from the 1970s on with translation-adaptations such as Liz Lochhead's of *Tartuffe* (1986) and *Patter Merchants* (1987); Stephen Mulrine's of Alexander Gelman's *A Man with Connections* (1988); Bill Findlay and Martin Bowman's of many of Michel Tremblay's plays including *The Guid Sisters* (1989), *The Real Wurld?* (1991) and *Hosanna* (1991); Bill Dunlop's of Aeschylus's *The Oresteia*, entitled *Klytemnestra's Bairns* (1991); Ella Wildridge and Tom McGrath's adaptations of Tankred Dorst's *Merlin* (1992) and *Merlin – the Search for the Grail* (1993); Edwin Morgan's *Cyrano de Bergerac* (1992); R. L. C. Lorimer's and David Purves's separate translations of Shakespeare's *Macbeth* into Scots (both published in 1992); and David Greig's of Euripides' *Oedipus the King* (2005), to mention only a representative few.

Since the 1950s Scottish playwrights have developed a style of realistic drama with a strong political slant. Roddy McMillan (1923–79), a former Unity member, was among those who successfully incorporated social criticism and theatrical innovations: *All in Good Faith* (1954) and *The Bevellers* (1973) dealt with stark realities of working-class life in the manner that drew from, but did not imitate, earlier workplace drama. Another playwright featuring strongly from the 1940s was George Munro (1901–68): *Gold in His Boots* (1947), *Vineyard Street* (1949) and *Gay Landscape* (1958) were imbued with naked realism. Multiplicity of approaches has, however, always been common in Scottish drama. Though differing in their styles, playwrights like Corrie, Lamont Stewart, Munro and McMillan heralded Scottish drama that provided political debate in Scots, with strong elements of tradition and popular culture, as John McGrath (1935–2002) would infuse into his plays for 7:84 (Scotland).

In the early 1960s, an already existing gap between artistic provision and the tastes of, particularly, younger audiences widened and theatre companies rapidly lost audiences. Amongst those affected was the Gateway Company. In the 1950s, it had promoted the work of such significant playwrights as Kemp, McLellan, Bridie, Alexander Reid, T. M. Watson, Graham Moffat and James Scotland. In 1961 it premièred Ada F. Kay's (1929–) *The Man from Thermopylae* following the broadcast of an earlier version in 1956 on BBC Radio's Home Service. In 1965, the Gateway effectively became the Civic Theatre Company at the Royal Lyceum, while the Citizens tried its hand at experimental theatre by staging increasingly foreign output, with an exception of Stewart Conn's (1936–) *Break-Down* (1961). Meanwhile, a new writing theatre was born in the bosom of Edinburgh's Lawnmarket, seeking to revitalise Scottish playwriting. The Traverse Theatre (1963) became a platform for alternative creative voices that were political, philosophical and experimental. Amongst the writers who wrote for it were C. P. Taylor, Stanley Eveling, Stewart Conn, Eddie Boyd and Joan Ure.

Like Ena Lamont Stewart in the 1940s and 1950s and Ada F. Kay in the 1960s, Joan Ure (Betty Clark) (1918–78) remains a lonely female in Scottish playwriting circles until the late 1970s. In an example of art imitating life, the focus of her plays is always firmly upon the lack of opportunities for writers, and in particular for women writers, in Scottish theatre of the 1960s and 1970s. In *Take Your Old Rib Back, Then* (1974) and *Make a Space for Me* (1977) she mocks the obsession with producing only tried successes, and shying away from new work as being commercially precarious. Her preoccupation is always with women's position in society, and the choices that they face, and her representation of mothers as resentful nurturers, jealous of their daughters' achievements as in *Me Jane, You Elfie! Who Needs Paisley Adams?* (1978), somewhat resembles Sharman Macdonald's (1951–) later exploration of mother/daughter relationships. Still, though similarities in themes and considerations may urge one to think that not much has changed in twenty years, there is also a sense in Macdonald's work – for example, *The Winter Guest* (1997) – of acceptance and reliance upon one another. Ure often neglects this strong element of solidarity through suffering and a bond of love in her plays. Jan McDonald suggests that one of the reasons Ure's plays were not readily produced during her lifetime was that her writing was before its time, both in form and content.[8] McDonald's assertion is surely true. Ure's experimentation with lyricism, movement and symbolism made her plays as hermetic as it made them immediate. It is this contradiction that continues to baffle audiences and critics alike. Her sardonic stance, the intransigent feminist critique with which she explores the fallacy of sisterhood and separate-spheres models, was often shunned by the overwhelmingly masculine post-Calvinist oligarchy of Scottish theatre.

Within this, however, there was in the 1970s a renewed interest in Scottish themes and Scottish playwrights. The Royal Lyceum's artistic director Clive Perry encouraged this, appointing Bill Bryden (1942–) his associate in 1970 and producing Stewart Conn's *The Burning* in 1971. This play can be read as a response to McLellan's *Jamie the Saxt*, offering a fresh outlook on the Scottish past that differed from earlier plays in both form and content. Such revisionist questioning of Scottish historical material and, by extension, the nature of Scottish society was also nurtured by Stephen Macdonald, artistic director at Dundee Rep (1973–6) and, following Perry, the Lyceum (1976–9). Lyceum plays – like Bryden's *Willie Rough* (1972), revisiting World

War One union activity on the Clyde or Ian Brown's (1945–) *Carnegie* (1973) and *Mary* (1977), interrogating mythic icons through innovative and challenging dramaturgy and vivid theatricality – paralleled Dundee plays like Hector MacMillan's (1929–) *The Rising* (1973) and *The Royal Visit* (1974) with their fresh radical views of nineteenth-century events. MacMillan's *The Sash* (1974) satirised sectarianism, provoking strong audience reaction in Glasgow. Meantime, plays like John McGrath's *The Cheviot, the Stag and the Black, Black Oil* (1973) and Tom Gallacher's (1934–2001) *The Sea Change* (1976) reflected the economic reality of the fast growing oil industry in the North Sea. Both raised questions regarding national and personal identity in the face of exploitation of the Highlands and environmental resources. The former was presented by 7:84 (Scotland), founded by McGrath and Elizabeth MacLennan on their return to Scotland in 1973 with well-established theatre, television and film careers south of the border. They fulfilled their intention of touring to remote areas of Scotland to reach new audiences who might not have experienced theatre before. Other McGrath plays like *The Game's a Bogey* (1974) and *Little Red Hen* (1975) explored Scottish history and social reality, drawing inspiration from grassroots, popular and folk influences. In 1974, McGrath expressed his belief that theatre is a tool for change, 'the way people find their voice, their solidarity and their collective determination'.[9] While McGrath's writing and radical social ideology clearly inspired the work of later theatre companies such as Borderline, Benchtours or Clyde Unity, his edgy vision proved later too in-your-face for a New Labour society leaning towards the middle. By the time *Hyperlynx* was produced in 2002, McGrath's work was already seen as old-fashioned, perhaps one of the reasons it has not yet at the time of writing become part of the newly-established National Theatre of Scotland's repertoire.

A criticism often made of the Scottish playwriting of the 1970s is that it had a masculinist and, often, macho focus. Certainly all the plays referred to in this context so far have been by men, while the dominant aesthetic outside of the revisionist historical drama referred to was urban, West-Coast and often workplace- or street-based as in Roddy McMillan's *The Bevellers* (1973), Bryden's *Benny Lynch* (1974) or Tom McGrath's (1940–2009) *The Hardman* (1977). Such a stance can, however, be overstated. Conn's *Play Donkey* (1977) explores the life of a mercenary from Leith caught fatally in the travails of African civil war; and Giles Havergal's Citizens Theatre from 1969 explored a visual European theatre aesthetic which produced new playwriting, translations and adaptations by the house dramatist Robert David Macdonald (1929–2004). Within the context of Havergal's alternative aesthetic, Macdonald's' *Chinchilla* (1977) ostensibly concerning the Diaghilev company was seen as exploring the Citizens' company's own politics while his *Summit Conference* (1978) engaged with political issues through the relationship of Hitler's and Mussolini's mistresses. C. P. Taylor (1921–81) investigated alternative dramaturgic visions in his *Columba* (1973), in which dance was a integral part of the play, and *Good* (1981), in which music became an extra dimension, as he explored the disintegration of a German intellectual sucked into Nazism. In short, while there was a new concentration on contemporary Scottish themes in the 1970s and the writing of the period was male-dominated, it would falsify the picture not to recognise the wide range of dramaturgical experiment undertaken and the wide range of internationally-engaged subject matter.

This experiment and broad outlook continued to develop through the rest of the century. The Caithness-born playwright, director, theatre historian and poet, Donald Campbell (1940–), for example, was important for the whole strand of drama that dealt with issues of national identity expressed through poetic structure and realistic Scots. *The Jesuit* (1976) and *The Widows of Clyth* (1979) presented two different modes of Scottish realities, respectively political loyalty against the backdrop of religious fanaticism and a working-class sense of female camaraderie in times of social crisis. *Till All the Seas Run Dry* (1981), *The Fisher Boy and the Honest Lass* (1990), *The Ould Fella* (1993) and *Nancy Sleekit* (1994) have since focused on observing and critiquing modernity through the prism of historic and quasi-historic settings. His adaptations of Sir Walter Scott's novels, *The Heart of Midlothian* (1988) and *St Ronan's Well* (1989), and first translation into English of Malin Lagerlof's *The Lighthouse Prisoner* (1996) continued to explore these issues.

The vitality that the 1970s Scottish theatre revival offered to its audiences faced setback in 1979. Then, after a majority of Scots voted for a Scottish Assembly in a referendum, its establishment was obstructed by what was widely seen as constitutional trickery, requiring more than a simple majority. In the same year, the Conservatives under Margaret Thatcher came into power, where they were to remain for eighteen years. For Scotland, this raised fundamental questions of democratic accountability in a context where Thatcherite politics of privatisation and the breakdown of 'society' challenged playwrights and other artists. Yet Scottish theatre thrived artistically on a fountain of possibilities. John Byrne's (1940–) *The Slab Boys Trilogy* (1978–82), for example, straddles the key year 1979. It not only established him as a populist dramatist with his fresh urban outlook on the life of young working-class adolescents, but marked a transition from retrogressive working-class drama to a vibrant use of Scots to undermine conservative working-class stances and explore edgy aspirations for new life. His 1987 television drama, *Tutti Frutti*, became a hit, firmly establishing his popularity with television audiences and leading to a stage musical adaptation (2006) by the National Theatre of Scotland. Work that had grown out of drama in search of varieties of national expression of working-class experience in language that would ring true to its audience now reached fruition in plays that spoke about multivalent Scottish experience – rural and urban, individual and communal, past and present, male and female.

The 1980s saw a rise in the number of women playwrights, helped by the new writing workshops organised by the Traverse Theatre and its artistic director Peter Lichtenfels, who produced, for example, Liz Lochhead's (1947–) *Blood and Ice* in 1982. These women playwrights now established themselves in Scottish theatre circles writing drama that is poetic, lyrical, dynamic, exploratory, angry, melancholic and evocative, always focused on women's experiences, and challenging accepted social roles. They include Marcella Evaristi (1953–), Ann Marie di Mambro (1950–), Lochhead, Sue Glover (1943–) and Rona Munro (1959–). Evaristi and di Mambro are particularly interesting as they write about women's experience from a uniquely Italian-Scottish perspective that had not previously been seen on the Scottish stage. Some of these authors, such as Sue Glover, came from radio, while others like Liz Lochhead were established writers in other genres. Lochhead, a renowned poet, collaborated with others on the Glaswegian comedy circuit co-writing comic revues like *A Bunch of Five* (1982) with Tom Leonard, Dave Anderson, Dave McLennan and Sean Hardie and *A Pie of Damocles* (1983) with Leonard, Alasdair Gray and James Kelman. The need to explore national identities now corresponded to the need to define personal identity in Lochhead's *Mary Queen of Scots Got Her Head Chopped Off* (1987). There, Scottish history is revisited from a female perspective. Lochhead also plays with the notion of linguistic identification, something Evaristi had explored already in her review *Mouthpieces* (1980). In that, she turned on its head an earlier notion that political betrayal is always equalled with linguistic betrayal. Lochhead's subsequent Mary is heavily French-accented, while the purest Scots is spoken by John Knox in an indictment of religious, or any other kind of, extremism. Evaristi's female characters in *Mouthpieces* offer a sharp-witted critique of the inequality that underlies language as a tool of social, political and gender oppression.

In 1981–2, Glasgow's Tron was established as a writers' theatre, its repertoire including works by established names and newer playwrights like Evaristi, Lochhead, Peter Arnott (1962–) and Rona Munro. Arnott's *White Rose* (1985) dealt with issues of women's roles in war against the background of the Russian struggle against the Nazis. His *Thomas Muir's Voyage to Australia* (1986) panoramically, if rather clumsily, presents the Scots radical Muir's attempts to bring liberty against the machinations of a corrupt establishment and his transportation. Jenny Killick's arrival in 1984 as the Traverse's director introduced such figures as John Clifford (1950–) and Chris Hannan (1958–). Clifford's *Losing Venice* (1985), exploring imperialism and political power, became an international touring success, followed by *Ines de Castro* (1989) and his formal experiment in *The Light in the Village* (1991) about village life in India. Clifford is highly prolific and his work, unique in its lyricism and unflinching humanity, was then for some time largely ignored in Scottish theatre, despite his international reputation. His version of *The Queen of Spades* (2002), translation-adaptation of de Rojas's *Celestina* (directed by Calixto Bieito for the 2003 Edinburgh International Festival), *God's New Frock* (2005) and *Faust I* and *II* (2007) have drawn attention again, despite all causing a degree of critical bafflement.

One of the main features of Scottish drama as it moved into the 1990s was its emphasis on contemporary themes: change, loss of old beliefs and value systems, traditions and myths, and search for new standards and values. Although AIDS in Scotland emerged primarily in the intravenous drug-taking community, the myth of AIDS as a predominantly gay illness dominated the 1980s and 1990s. In reaction to this, such plays as John Binnie's (1965–) *Mum, Dad, There is Something I've Got to Tell You* (1986) and *Accustomed to Her Face* (1993) and Ian Brown's *Wasting Reality* (1991) addressed issues of acceptance of homosexuality and the price paid by HIV/AIDS sufferers and their loved ones. Other contemporary Scottish playwrights redefined Scottish identities in the context of global changes in plays like David Greig's (1969–) *Stalingrad* (1992), *Europe* (1995) and *One Way Street* (1995). Chris Hannan's *Elizabeth Gordon Quinn* (1985) had dealt fairly orthodoxly with working-class Glasgow aspiration and delusion. His *The Baby* (1990) was, however, a modern tragedy, using the ancient Roman setting of the last days of Sulla's dictatorship to draw parallels with Thatcher's rule. His *Shining Souls* (1996) returns to Glasgow, this time addressing contemporary working-class aspiration. Rona Munro's *Bold Girls* (1990) explored Northern Ireland violence, while Sue Glover's *Bondagers* (1991), set on a Borders farm in the nineteenth century, explored male–female power relations, although both plays can be seen as a metaphor for political and social change in contemporary Scotland. Contemporary Scottish plays now speak of redefinition and reversal of gender roles within family structures, as in Sharman Macdonald's *When We Were Women* (1988) and *The Winter Guest* (1993), unemployment as in Lara Jane Bunting's (1969–) *My Piece of Foreign Sky* (1996), public and domestic violence as in Rona Munro's *The Maiden Stone* (1994), the revolution in sexual ethics and AIDS as in Iain Heggie's (1953–) *Politics in the Park* (1993) and Ann Marie di Mambro's *Brothers of Thunder* (1994), and social change brought by the oil industry as in Duncan McLean's (1964–) *Julie Allardyce* (1993).

In the late twentieth and early twenty-first centuries, dramatists offer new perspectives. The work of women playwrights continues to gain in prominence. Nicola McCartney (1972–) explores pluralities of voices and redefinition of history in *Heritage* (1998), Zinnie Harris (1973–) looks at the breakdown of old values and reinventing identities in *Further Than the Furthest Things* (2000) and survival in the post-war world in *Midwinter* (2004). Catherine Lucy Czerkawska (1950–) writes about themes of loss and alienation in *Wormwood* (1997) and *Quartz* (2000) while Anne Downie (1939–) recounts chauvinist attitudes towards women in *Parking Lot in Pittsburgh* (2002). Grace Barnes (1965–) follows up her interest in Shetlandic language and culture in the plays such as *Wir Midder da Sea* (1999) and *Circles in Tides* (2002), while in *Babylon Burning* (2006) she approaches the theme of the Iraqi war. Other playwrights offer an engaged view of international politics, including Gregory Burke (1968–) in *The Straits* (2003) and *Black Watch* (2006) and David Greig in *Damascus* (2008). Attention is also on devolutionary politics as in Stephen Greenhorn's (1964–) *Dissent* (1998) and on economic politics as in David Greig's *The Speculator* (1999). Authors increasingly try their hand at writing plays with regional interest and in Scots regional dialects as in Burke's *Gagarin Way* (2001) and Iain F. MacLeod's (1973–) *Homers* (2002). They also explore more intimate, complex tales of individual struggle to match social acceptance and personal desire as in a trio of plays built round questions of child abuse: Mike Cullen's (1959–) *Anne Weiss* (1997), Douglas Maxwell's (1974–) *Decky Does a Bronco* (2000) and David Harrower's (1966–) *Blackbird* (2005). Harrower particularly has explored more fraught areas of human life, from his debut *Knives in Hens* (1995)–exploring the passions of love, marital strain and infidelity–and his bleakly comic intergenerational *Kill the Old, Torture their Young* (1998) on. His *365* (2008) explored, in an innovative production by Scottish National Theatre director Vicky Featherstone, the lives of children in need of care as they seek a way of adult living in a social work practice flat.

The rich variety of perspectives, from regional to global, historical to popular, political to intimate is a sign of Scottish drama's confidence and maturity. From the 1960s on this variety was enhanced, developed and supported by the work of such BBC Scotland radio producers as Stewart Conn, Gordon Emslie, Patrick Rayner, Marilyn Imrie and Tom Kinninmont. Still, for every success story, there are ten tales of the struggle that faces those authors whose work remains eclipsed by popular trends and semi-forgotten on the fringes imposed by the theatre mainstream. If the upward trend in quality and exuberance of indigenous writing is to continue, Scottish theatre must find a way of rediscovering and re-introducing the works of such remarkable individuals to wider audiences.

CHAPTER SIX

The Modern Scottish Literary Renaissance

Roderick Watson

This chapter analyses selected aspects of the modern Scottish literary renaissance in the foundational 'first generation' years between 1920 and 1945, looking most especially at key texts that deal with the nature of identity from Hugh MacDiarmid (1892–1978), Nan Shepherd (1893–1981), Lewis Grassic Gibbon (1901–35) and Neil Gunn (1891–1973). The renaissance agenda made much of looking outwards, but arguably the versions of identity offered in these works go so far 'outwards' as to leave 'Scottishness' behind, and to problematise the conception of identity itself.

This is not to say these authors initiated the outward perspective nor even the Scottish revival of cultural confidence. Its stirrings can be traced back at least as far as Patrick Geddes's (1854–1932) 'Celtic renascence, now incipient alike in Literature and Art' which he announced in 1895 as the best way towards 'the revival and development of the old Continental sympathies of Scotland'[1] – a line MacDiarmid was later quick to adopt. Nor should we forget the paintings and designs of Charles Rennie Macintosh and Margaret and Frances Macdonald in Glasgow, which had wider links to the Arts and Crafts movement, Art Nouveau, the Jugendstil of Belgian Victor Horta and the Catalan Modernisme of Antoni Gaudi. In short, a certain 'renaissance' was in the air by 1900, its 'modern', outward looking and theorised elements already established by visual artists. In these circles, the organicism of 'Celtic' art in Scotland was losing its twilight associations, mixing genres and incorporating elements from numerous centres of culture to be re-appraised in what amounted to internationally proto-Modernist terms. The same impulse had the Scottish Colourists looking to French Post-Impressionism. J. D. Fergusson (1874–1961) in particular theorised a link between the Fauves' vividness, Bergsonian movement and his understanding of 'rhythm' in art (which he later associated with a Celtic sensibility). This led to his becoming art editor for the avant-garde journal *Rhythm* in London in 1911. Fergusson associated what he took to be the characteristically dynamic graphic line of Celtic art with the most modern in the *Rhythm* group's agenda:

Our intention is to provide art, be it drawing, literature or criticism, which shall be vigorous, determined, which shall have its roots below the surface, and be the rhythmical echo of the life with which it is in touch. Both in its pity and its brutality it shall be real.[2]

Fergusson's vision was resolutely international. He commissioned illustrations (with Fauvist, Rayonnist, Vorticist and Cubist elements) from Samuel Peploe, Natalia Gontcharova, Gaudier-Brzeska and Picasso. On eventually returning to Scotland in 1939 he took up the same cause as art editor of *Scottish Arts and Letters*, for five issues between 1944 and 1950, going on to illustrate the Maclellan edition of *In Memoriam James Joyce* in 1955. The pioneering and cross-disciplinary 'renaissance' of visual artists in the first decade of the century should be better recognised than it is in literary circles, though Tom Normand's study *The Modern Scot* is an indispensable guide.[3] MacDiarmid, then, was by no means first to propose 'to get rid of our provinciality of outlook and to avail ourselves of the Continental experience.'[4]

It is, nevertheless, difficult to imagine the then-modern 'renaissance' and rise of Scottish cultural and socio-political self-confidence, without the indefatigable if vividly various and uneven theoretical and critical inputs from C. M. Grieve and his newly discovered alter ego 'Hugh M'Diarmid' as they came to be published in *The Scottish Chapbook* in 1922 and in 1923 in *The Scottish Nation*. Following Gregory Smith's 1919 study *Scottish Literature: Character and Influence*, MacDiarmid's 'Theory of Scots Letters' made much of 'the Scottish instinct' represented by a psychology and a vernacular language seen as 'the perfect expression of the Scottish race'. The overtly essentialist aspects of his case have generated understandable reservations among critics ever since. Yet the actual *products* of that agenda have often actually challenged the notion of any single stable national, cultural, psychological or personal identity, despite (or perhaps because of) its new definition of 'Scottishness'. MacDiarmid's espousal of the notorious 'Caledonian Antisyzygy' spoke for instability and contradiction at the heart of identity; this is the creative core paradox of Scottish cultural nationalism, at least in its earlier years and its best productions. From this position a case can also be made, as we shall see, for the renaissance's contribution to literary Modernism's emergence.

Douglas Gifford has written of darker paradoxes within the so-called renaissance, pointing out how soon the prevailing spirit of cultural renewal and rebirth changed to one of acute pessimism, from Edwin Muir's (1887–1959) vision of Scotland as a place of 'smoke and dearth and money everywhere' presided over by Burns and Scott as 'sham bards of a sham nation' ('Scotland 1941'), to the deeply pessimistic 'rejection of Renaissance values' that characterised post-war Scottish novels, even (or especially) George Friel's and Robin Jenkins's brilliant work.[5] Gifford's is a persuasive critique of canonical reputations, refreshingly recognising tensions implicit in a movement of reinvention whose later output served only to revisit *The House with Green Shutters* (1901) and George Douglas Brown's old cry of pain. Similarly, Gordon Williams's *From Scenes Like These*, as late as 1968, might seem the final blow to any possibility of rebirth in a ferociously forensic Balzacian dissection of Scotland as a place of agricultural brutalism, damaged masculinity and ugly, provincial urban hopelessness.

Having said that, early renaissance writing presents a more complex, nuanced, theoretically alert account of identity, meaning and being than either the movement's strategic, but often limiting and potentially essentialist, emphasis on unique 'Scottishness', or the realism and despair of later 1930s literature might suggest. In fact, there is a Modernist energy and optimism in MacDiarmid's espousal of the concept of antisyzygy, and simplistic notions of origin, truth and identity (Scottish or otherwise) are actually deconstructed in Shepherd's *The Weatherhouse* (1930), Gibbon's *Scots Quair* (1932–4) and Gunn's *Highland River* (1936).

If we leap ahead a little, we gain a sense of the day's prevailing critical and cultural values (and what the renaissance set out to overthrow) by touching on MacDiarmid's and Muir's quarrel over the publication of *Scott and Scotland* (1936). Apart from Muir's analysis of the history of Scots, and his odd notion that one might think in one language and feel in another, as if language did not of itself dictate either mode (assuming 'feeling' is a linguistic act in the first place), there is, throughout the text of *Scott and Scotland*, a repeated and revealing assumption about homogeneity and autonomy as cultural imperatives:

> The prerequisite for an autonomous literature is a homogeneous language [. . .] For this homogeneous language is the only means yet discovered for expressing the response of a whole people, emotional and intellectual, to a specific body of experience peculiar to it alone.[6]

The quasi-imperial assumptions behind such a monological definition of culture and experience,[7] blind as it is to internal differences of region, class and gender (not to mention the manifestations of Bakhtinian polyphony that are implicit in the novel form itself), soon become all too clear in Muir's statement of blunt intent:

> A Scottish writer who wishes to achieve some approximation to completeness has no choice except to absorb the English tradition [. . .] if he thoroughly does so his work belongs not merely to Scottish literature but to English literature as well.[8]

Muir meant well in his hopes of modernising Scotland, of course, although his recommendations are disturbingly similar to Lord Macaulay's in his 'Minute on Education' (1836):

No Hindu who has received an English education ever remains sincerely
attached to his religion. It is my firm belief that if our plans of education are
followed up, there will not be a single idolater among the respectable classes in
Bengal thirty years hence.[9]

Muir's stance may also be influenced by Matthew Arnold, whose *On the Study
of Celtic Literature* (1867), while praising Celtic languages for their past literature, pronounces them unfit for the modern world, urging their extinction:

I must say I quite share the opinion of my brother Saxons as to the practical
inconvenience of perpetuating the speaking of Welsh [. . .] The sooner the
Welsh language disappears [. . .] the better for England, the better for Wales
itself [. . .] For all modern purposes [. . .] let us all as soon as possible be one
people; let the Welshman speak English, and, if he is an author, let him
write English.[10]

Also talking about literature's crucial role as intermediary between education and culture, MacDiarmid's 1931 essay, 'English Ascendancy in British
Literature', anticipated elements of postcolonial theory by pointing out that
Britain itself was culturally and linguistically plural, and the stronger for
being so:

The reading publics of Great Britain have been blinded to four literatures full of
very distinctive values, of absorbing technical interests, and of very diverse
potentialities, and the further development of these four literatures have been
practically inhibited. Surely all this represents an enormous loss.[11]

Few critics today would deny MacDiarmid's opening point that 'there are
many varieties of English' nor that 'a racy native turn of speech is better than
any stilted phraseology, especially for literary purposes'.[12] Cairns Craig has
explored the implications of this and argued extensively that the Scots tradition's cultural and creative strength, then and now, lies in this heterogeneity:

In Leonard, Kelman, Dunn and Lochhead – and many others – writing in
Scotland becomes the exploration of the intersections between, and the spaces
between, a multiplicity of different dialects and grammars. It is the very lack of
unity in Scotland's linguistic situation which makes their writing possible.[13]

More recently this insight further developed into an argument that the condition so deplored by Muir, and regularly seen as sadly divided and unstable,
was the forerunner of what we would now call a much broader postmodern
condition.[14] Those texts of dysfunctional division – going back at least to
Hogg's *Confessions of a Justified Sinner* and Stevenson's *Jekyll and Hyde* – have

been reinterpreted as subtle critiques of the Enlightenment project and harbingers of modernity, or indeed postmodernity. Thus what was once seen as a peculiarly Scottish pathological condition has broadened its critical and theoretical scope to reflect on the contemporary human condition. In a post-structuralist and postcolonial critical context, it is Muir's unhealthy fascination with a 'whole people' and their notionally homogeneous, autonomous and singular culture that now seems deeply suspect.

MacDiarmid began as wholly engaged with internal heterogeneity, instability and flux. The six prose 'psychological studies' of *Annals of the Five Senses* were completed by 1919 (largely composed by 1917 while he was serving in Salonika), but not published until 1923. The dates are significant: they show Grieve had a powerful vision of creative psychological complexity, simultaneity and dissonance before ever encountering Gregory Smith's case for 'Caledonian Antisyzygy'.[15] Every story in *Annals*[16] describes a common sensibility, on fire with different impressions and thoughts in a swirl of ceaseless activity, multiple, various, eclectic and finally, paradoxically, coherent. The following examples, all from 'Four Years' Harvest' (which has an autobiographical element), will illustrate the work's spirit:

He was like an ant-heap stirred: thoughts and memories ran about in all directions at the same moment [. . .] (p. 41)

And now his mind was like a hayrick aflame [. . .] (p. 56.)

So his moods came and went [. . .] like grasses in the winds [. . .] and he heard the voice of his overself, deep within him, with the 'unwinded clearness and unnatural sequence' that informed the controlled and muffled notes of Farmer Oak's flute 'boding an incommunicable thing' (p. 60.)

I have written at length elsewhere that the 'incommunicable thing' these stories try so brilliantly (if unevenly) to communicate is ultimately the internal experience of Bergsonian flux, *durée* and *élan vital*.[17] Indeed, the protagonist of 'The Never-Yet-Explored' recognises that '"the essence of life lies in the movement by which it is transmitted"', a direct quotation from *Creative Evolution* (1907), translated in 1911. The reference to that 'incommunicable thing' at the end of the story and the mention of Gabriel Oak, with a paraphrase of Hardy's lines from Chapter 2 of *Far From the Madding Crowd*, introduce another aspect of this extraordinary collection of stories, which Grieve admitted he had 'designed' rather than written. Unreferenced quotations, both marked as quotations and unmarked, proliferate, amounting to a densely intertextual exercise and prophetically poststructuralist insight into how literary texts, and indeed our own consciousnesses, are generated:

> The old lady described Shakespeare as being 'full of quotations.' So are
> my studies [. . .]

> As fish are seen through an aquarium so these perhaps strange fish of mine are
> discernible almost entirely through a 'strong solution of books' – and not only
> of books but of magazines and newspaper articles and even of speeches.[18]

MacDiarmid was to return to his 'strong solution of books'[19] in the writing of
Lucky Poet and as the guiding structural principle in his later 'poetry of fact'
with its epic catalogues and extensively unacknowledged prose borrowings.
Critical debate about whether this is plagiarism or a new kind of writing
continues,[20] but MacDiarmid's shift from the essentially late-Romantic – if
defamiliarised – utterance of his early lyrics towards his epic later work's intertextual and impersonal collaborative texts does have a claim to critical cred-
ibility in terms of poststructuralist theory like Barthes's claim that 'the text is
a tissue of quotations drawn from the innumerable centres of culture'.[21]

It is little wonder that MacDiarmid was so taken by Gregory Smith's proposal that Scottish literary tradition tends towards 'the piling up of details'
the 'completed effect' of which 'is one of movement', while any apparent
literary or cultural unity is revealed on closer scrutiny to be 'under the stress
of foreign influence and native division and reaction, almost a zigzag of contradictions'.[22] Such a cultural theory placed his own fascination with such
states at the centre of a national literary tradition. Writing in the same year
as 'English Ascendancy in British Literature' and making the same point
about the need for 'the decentralisation of literature', he 'renewed [the]
Scottish plea for diversity as against uniformity in keeping with our essential
national genius'.[23]

The contradictions of MacDiarmid's rhetoric are all too obvious here,
when his case for decentralisation, variety and contradiction simultaneously
invokes the notion of an 'essential national genius'. But in a later passage
he cites the ideological importance of 'dynamic myth' (he is referring to
Dostoevsky and 'the Russian Idea'). This was to be the most fertile dynamic
myth of his own literary production, not least because it links his own and
early Modernism's fascination with change, flux and Bergsonian flow:

> The essential point is that all fixed opinions – all ideas that are not entertained
> just provisionally and experimentally [. . .] every identification of Scottish
> genius with any particular religion or political doctrine [. . .] and above all the
> stupid (since self-stultifying) idea that ideas are not of prime consequence [. . .]
> and that it is possible to be over-intellectual – are anti-Scottish – opposed to
> our national genius which is capable of countless manifestations at absolute
> variance with each other, yet confined within the 'limited infinity' of the
> adjective 'Scottish'.[24]

The *creative* power of MacDiarmid's interpretation of 'antisyzygy' needs no emphasis, since it is the driving inspiration and dynamic force behind his best work from this period, most notably *A Drunk Man Looks at the Thistle* (1926). But the foundations of this restless energy were first laid in the 'psychological studies, essays, mosaics (call them what you will)' that were the *Annals of the Five Senses*. Gregory Smith gave MacDiarmid a theory that could marry the poet's Bergsonian drives to a programme of literary and cultural renewal with a claim to historical continuity. Here is a national idea whose founding principle is to challenge the monological stability of just such definitions, along with a wider socio-political argument (with what we would now call postcolonial overtones) in favour of literary diversity and plurality and the 'decentralisation' of all cultural hegemonies. In this, the Scottish literary renaissance's agenda can be seen as an early manifestation of the wider and later postcolonial process by which other cultures developed counter-discursive strategies against dominant European or anglocentric claims to universality, wary of essentialism, and alert to the dangers of simply replacing the 'centre' with the 'margin'. There are Modernist – even postmodernist – aspects to MacDiarmid's case for the provisional, experimental, relative and transient, as expressing the spirit of 'antisyzygy', even as he identifies that spirit with a specifically Scottish identity that his own case's logic would seem to undermine. His argument remains a powerful, necessary, and theoretically telling counter-discourse to the cultural imperialism of Muir's monological vision of culture.

There are still further counter-discourses to be discerned in early Scottish renaissance literary productions, also to do with the destabilisation of autonomous identity, homogeneity and certainty. It is no coincidence that several key prose fiction texts from this period should deal with specifically female identity – as a realm of doubly-marginalised experience perhaps – within the Scottish context's long-standing patriarchy.

In the 'development novels' of Catherine Carswell (1879–1946), Willa Muir (1890–1970) and Nan Shepherd (1893–1981), for example, issues of class, autonomy and freedom of choice loom large – from the imbalance between creative escape and the Edwardian constraints of polite metropolitan society that are such a feature of *Open the Door!* (1920); to the darker machinations of small town bourgeois masculinist society in *Imagined Corners* (1931), with its closing hints of a more radical sexual liberation; to the trajectory of education, escape and a self-discovery deeper than books, while also affirming an almost equally radical return to the resolutely local that is *The Quarry Wood* (1928). In each case and differently, these show characters subverting dominant modes of social – and generic – expectation. But these authors also ask questions about identity that go beyond female emancipation politics. Carol Anderson and Aileen Christianson chose a phrase from

Nan Shepherd to characterise this trajectory – 'journeys into being' – citing
Patricia Waugh's observation that women writers of this period

> have sought alternative conceptions of subjectivity, expressing a definition of
> relationship which does not make identity dependent axiomatically upon
> the maintenance of boundaries and distance, nor upon the subjugation of
> the other.[25]

Arguably some of these female perspectives on alternative subjectivity begin
to challenge the apparent stabilities of identity itself, whether we consider
ourselves part of the 'imagined communities' of 'men', 'women', or indeed
'Scotland'. This is especially the case in the work of Nan Shepherd, most
notably in The Weatherhouse, and in Lewis Grassic Gibbon's brilliant imagining
of Chris Guthrie. Here again, two early Scottish renaissance foundational texts
challenge the very conceptions of identity upon which one might imagine the
case for 'Scottishness' would depend – a 'counter-discursive' strategy indeed.

Alison Lumsden has written specifically on this,[26] although arguably The
Weatherhouse raises questions of signification, truth and meaning that relate
to all being and all knowing, rather than a specifically female struggle between
the Kristevan semiotic of 'feminine identity' and the patriarchal symbolic
order of language – the law of the father. (The semiotic is not gendered in
any case.) Nevertheless, Nan Shepherd was all too aware of the gulf between
the world of felt experience and the world of words, as she noted in a letter to
Neil Gunn in May 1940, admiring his capacity to bring the two together:

> To apprehend things – walking on a hill, seeing the light change, the mist, the
> dark, being aware, using the whole of one's body to instruct the spirit – yes that
> is the secret life one has and knows that others have. But to be able to share it,
> in and through words – that is what frightens me [. . .] It dissolves one's being.[27]

The Weatherhouse is full of such moments of dissolution,[28] characters coming
into contact with a world – or rather realm of being – beyond language,
beyond easy distinctions of 'right or wrong' or 'true or false' or the comforts of
science or religion, and certainly beyond self.

This is what, in The Weatherhouse, the war-wounded Garry Forbes encounters when he sets out to refute what he sees as the lies of fantasist Louisa
Morgan and her claims to have been engaged to his now dead friend David
Grey. Before the war Garry was an engineer used to seeing the world as a
material and wholly calculable thing, a place of binary simplicity and black
and white distinctions:

> The complexity of human motive and desire had not come home to him, and
> he supposed, without thinking much about it, that right and wrong were as

separate as the bridges he helped to build and the waters over which he built them. But [. . .] limits had shifted, boundaries been dissolved. Nothing ended in itself, but flowed over into something else [. . .] (p. 118.)

Characters realise that the world we live in – even our sense of who we are – is inextricably bound up with the figments of desire. This was the root of Louie's lie, as she constructed herself around an imagined romance, and yet even her feeble fantasy will speak a wider truth:

'I am made like that. I live all the time – oh I am going to scourge myself – in what I want other people to be thinking about me, until often I don't know – indeed, indeed, I don't – what I really am and what I have thought they are thinking I am.' [. . .]
Garry was looking in amazement.
'I should have thought the difference between truth and a lie was clear enough,' he said as she paused.
'Oh no, no, it's not – not clear at all. Things are true and right in one relationship, and quite false in another. (p. 105.)

Cairns Craig has noted how this novel subverts the nature of writing itself (which is one of the ways in which we try to make an account of reality) by the indeterminacy of such insights and by 'enacting the falsity of the imagination at the level of its own plot':

Imagination infects and distorts; the narrative of *The Weatherhouse* is a tissue of imaginations, from which the truth has to be redeemed precisely by negating the kind of fictionalising which the characters, in imitation of their author, but in denial of her fundamental values, are only too prone to commit themselves to.[29]

Indeed, the book ends with a profound *jeu d'esprit* about its own operating principle, in which Garry's fiancée remembers her childhood days with Louie and Louie's dog 'Demon' (the name is not insignificant):

'Nonsense!' rapped Miss Theresa. 'Louie had never a dog.'
'But I remember. I can see him. A whippet hound he was.'
'Nonsense! She hadn't a dog. She wanted one [. . .] And after a while she used to pretend she had it – made on to be stroking it, spoke to it and all.'
Lindsay [. . .] pondered. The dog, bounding among the pines, had in her memory the compelling insistence of imaginative art. He was a symbol of swiftness, the divine joy of motion. But Lindsay preferred reality to symbol.
'Queer, isn't it? she said, coming out of her reverie. 'I remembered Demon was a real dog.' (p. 199.)

In the most subtle and profound ways, *The Weatherhouse* challenges our understanding of truth and fiction, the real and the imagined as well as our capacity to know them and the very grounds for our own sense of who we are and what the world is. In face of such insights, the question of a specifically 'Scottish' identity seems less than pressing.

On the same issue of 'identity' Lewis Grassic Gibbon's *Scots Quair* trilogy provides an all too familiar *locus classicus* in the *Sunset Song* passage about the two Chrisses – the 'Scots' Chris and the 'English' Chris – but in fact the trilogy's engagement with identity is much more subtle and puzzling than this would suggest. In symbolic terms the trilogy makes much of its sense of historical continuity in the way that Chris has a special relationship with the standing stones, the Kaimes, and finally with Windmill brae and the Barmekin, as each novel unfolds. She has a vision of ancient Pictish life on a wild night on the Slug road, and weeps for the Covenanting folk – her folk – persecuted at Dunnottar Castle in the seventeenth century. Yet her own trajectory in the novel is acutely discontinuous – haunted by the past – but seemingly ever more remote from her own sense of who she is, and in her capacity for relationships. After the sad failure of her third marriage – over before it was begun – and facing Ewan's increasingly alienating and alienated dedication to revolutionary politics, she returns to her place of origin to find no comfort: 'her little shelter in Cairndhu a dream of no-life that could not endure', thus travelling full circle to arrive at a deeply ambiguous closing scene in which she either falls asleep or dies on a rainy hillside.

In fact there are several Chrisses in the course of the trilogy – a 'third Chris' and then 'many Chrisses' each one seemingly increasingly remote for her own sense of who or what she is herself. In *Cloud Howe* – pregnant for the second time – she stands by the gravestones in Segget (echoing the standing stones of happier times) in a passage marked, in symbolic terms, by a continuity only of separation and extinction:

> She seemed to stand here by the kirkyard's edge looking back in the stones that marked the years where so many Chrisses had died and lay buried – back and back, as the graveyard grew dim, far over those smothered hopes and delights, to that other Chris that had been with child, a child herself or so little more, and had known such terror and delight in that [. . .][30]

She will lose the child, of course, as the spinners will lose their cause, as her husband will lose his life, as she will even lose young Ewan, her first-born, to the ruthless cause he has adopted. The progress of the trilogy is the slow stripping away of all that has made her what she is. Chris Guthrie, the strongest character in the trilogy, an icon of linguistic and regional identity, ends as enigma. In summarising how Chris has been interpreted over the years, Isobel Murray rightly declines to see her simply as 'Chris Caledonia', a symbol of the nation, or as 'woman personified'.[31] But if we do entertain this possibility, even for a moment, the implications of such a reading are deeply disturbing. National symbol or not, she is given over to defeat and death in the end, and Chris Guthrie's special affinity to the land (which is an affinity to geological time and change) has led only to her complete erasure. What is 'identity' or 'nationality', after all, *sub specie aeternitatis*? Grassic Gibbon was no Scottish nationalist, of course, but his vision of Chris and the final unknowability of being is more searching than any quarrel with the then-contemporary politics of national reconstruction and identity. It is a counter-discourse that problematises the nature of identity itself, and hence of continuity, tradition and renewal, even as it provides the 'renaissance' movement with a foundational text.

In the many books of origins, escape and return that characterise the renaissance literature of this period, Neil Gunn's *Highland River* stands out, and indeed its mixed narrative tone makes it equally singular in Gunn's own *oeuvre*. Its highly complex modernist narrative structure comprises a series of flashbacks and flash-forwards – a nest of Chinese boxes – often triggered by an image or an associative memory as the text gradually reconstructs a single narrative from a succession of looping strands. Douglas Gifford has referred to this as an 'innovative use of prolepsis and analepsis',[32] while Francis R. Hart calls it 'an intricate "systolic-diastolic" rhythm that plays against the linear river'.[33] This last point is relevant: the controlling trope of the whole novel is that of tracing the river of identity back to its roots in a journey upstream to the 'source'. Yet the time- and perspective-looping narrative structure of the actual book subverts all such conceptions of recoverable coherence and even of continuity itself. It is we the readers who reconstruct Kenn's life (with difficulty), even as he himself struggles to understand his own past life.

The narrative voice of the novel is equally divided between an immediate, powerful and extensive use of free indirect discourse and a more detached and ironically realised quasi-Godlike authorial voice that seems to observe its own observations in a slightly puzzled manner, as if for the first time. Throughout the book Kenn's memories are triggered by poetic and associative symbols and echoes – we might imagine we are looking back, with him, to spots of time in a golden Wordsworthian youth. Yet the text has a contrary movement and a contrary voice, associated with Kenn the scientist, whose searchingly forensic analysis regards his past self with a degree of detached incomprehension:

But the small figure does not hear the singing ecstasy in the wings; has no knowledge of the eyes that presently peer at him, noting with scientific care every breath of expression, each detail of the face [. . .]

For Kenn had forgotten the fear, the wonder, the sudden heart-beat, the strangeness, the sense of adventure, the ominous quality in known things when encountered in lonely places. He had forgotten what it really was to be young [. . .]

Kenn waits in the trees watching him with profound attention, for the little
figure out there is himself.[34]

As their correspondence shows, Neil Gunn shares Nan Shepherd's sense
of the sheer strangeness of being and unknowableness of the relationship
between mind and physical world – not to mention the difficulties of catch-
ing this in language. As with Grassic Gibbon (and indeed MacDiarmid's early
poems) there is a sense in which the 'bonnie lowe o' Eternity' erases all the
petty distinctions of who and what we are in any mundane, socio-political or
nationally-determined sense:

Into the timelessness in which the great ball of the earth revolves and circles and
drives onward into space, lit by sunlight and moonlight and starlight, towards an
end or an endlessness of which not the slightest glimmer reaches us.
      And so in some way past comprehending, the small boy sticking his toe in
the mire of the drowned earth becomes one with the grown-up scientist watching that same earth from an astronomical point above it and wondering, as he
stares in front of him, Whither? And, occasionally, Why? (p. 108.)

Gunn's final joke about identity in this, his greatest and most challengingly
Modernist novel, comes with its conclusion and the Zen-like moment when
he traces the river to its actual root, only for that, too, to disappear into the
boggy hole of his own subjectivity. The figments of his desire had imagined a
beautiful shore, but the reality seems plainer and truer:

Suddenly, before his very eyes, the stream vanished into the earth. His dismay
was vague and ludicrous. From his map-gazing he knew that his river should rise
in a loch. He could not have been mistaken. This loch was to have been the end
of his journey. Like the Yogi in his pilgrimage to Lake Mànas!
      And here it was coming out of the earth itself. The realism mocked him. He
had actually thought of a loch with shores of sand and water grey in the
evening light [. . .]
      He climbed over broken ground. Remembering how they listened-in to the
earth when boys, he lay down and put his ear to the ground. Faintly he heard
the surge of the stream away underground. So it was not lost! But listening more
acutely, he realised that what he heard was the surge of the river of his own
blood. (p. 238.)

Nature plays its final joke when the stream reappears further on and Kenn
discovers the loch after all. By then Gunn's point has been made about the

elusiveness and the meaninglessness of origins, as Kenn's eye takes him to the mountain beyond the loch. From this mountain one might see the Caithness plain, with the Orkneys beyond; and beyond them, 'the immense chasm of space'; and beyond that 'what lay in his heart and his mind' (p. 241). These passages, with their symbolism of deception, humour and endless recursion, lead only to our own subjectivity, and the figments of our desire, even as we search for those longed-for and impossible roots and origins. The final symbol of *Highland River* is the humble bog-asphodel, guardian of that boggy hole of life and death in ooze. Kenn does not even put it in his buttonhole, but walks off with it, forgotten, in his hand.

It seems appropriate to close with Gunn's Zen joke and doubtless the sound of one hand clapping. The point is that the best creative writers of the socio-political counter-discourse in favour of Scottish cultural identity (at a time when that was under considerable threat) ended by problematising the concept of identity itself. Paradoxically, this may have been the early Scottish Renaissance's most significant achievement as a contribution to Modernism and literary theory.

CHAPTER SEVEN

Literature and
World War Two

Douglas Gifford

There is an immense – and continuing – body of writing that records, laments and occasionally celebrates World War Two's impact on individuals and communities. This chapter can consider only some of Scottish writers' most vivid and poignant commentaries in poetry, fiction and drama, bearing witness to those effects. It explores major Scottish writers who foresaw, fought and remembered the war. Its texts express the damaged, disrespectful, myth-making, yet impressively enduring nature of Scottish writing within and about the 1939–45 British conflict. It also considers home responses for those bombed, evacuated, objecting conscientiously, or seeing their families permanently blighted. War literature arguably falls into two groupings: that directly affected, produced in the post-war quarter-century; and later secondary re-imagining. War's long shadow lingers in contemporary works like Andrew Greig's (1951–) *That Summer* (2000) and Alison Kennedy's (1965–) *Day* (2007).

Fiction

War is never far from Eric Linklater's (1899–1974) fiction, whether as background and reminiscence for the picaresque hero of *Magnus Merriman* (1934) or later centring on it. *Private Angelo* (1946), dedicated to the Eighth Army is surely, however, pre-eminent in Scotland's war fiction, its savage satire on war and profound empathy with humble predicaments and suffering setting it alongside the great war novels of Hašek, Vonnegut and Heller. Americans and British are liberating Italy, although, as the peasant Angelo wryly comments, liberation by bombing villages is somewhat confusing. A cast of fanatics, collaborators, devious aristocrats, bullying Nazis and profiteers rampage through Italy. Like Voltaire's *Candide*, the narrator's voice is of a kindly simple storyteller, understating events' actual horror. Angelo, like Schweik or Billy Pilgrim, archetypally symbolises enduring ordinariness; professing to lack the *dono de corragio*, he emerges, beaten, cuckolded, as ultimate hero of the ordinary, his fundamental decency carrying him, shivering yet unconquered, through nightmare. *The Dark of Summer* (1956), powerful, complex and haunting, is Linklater's other great war novel. Told by a self-deprecating soldier seeming close to Linklater himself, it ranges through the Faroes, the Norwegian debacle, the Western Front and the later Korean war, a tale of ancient betrayals and war's legacy in dreams (anticipating redemptive dream's significant role in Linklater's later work). *Roll of Honour* (1961), part novel, part long poem, recalls through a retired schoolteacher's memories his contemporaries, those he taught, and how their grotesquely varied lives ended. More clearly than most, it reveals Linklater's sense of human life's absurdity, life as existentialist adventure.

Some novels deal with far-flung war. At their head stand Stuart Hood's (1915–) stark 1950 novellas. *The Circle of the Minotaur* has a communist partisan returning after the war, to find old fascist-communist feuds die hard. *The Fisherman's Daughter* has an escaped prisoner (nationality unidentified, but Allied) in a dream-like web of difficulties, facing the choice of settling safely with peasants or striking northwards across the river. Hood's terse, minimalist writing has affinities with Hemingway, expecting readers to flesh out bleak situations. James Allan Ford's (1920–2009) *The Brave White Flag* (1961), drawing on experience of Japanese internment after Hong Kong's fall, tells the epic story of imminent invasion and Japanese occupation's terrible pressures. Conventional British militarism breaks down, but becomes something inspiring, bringing out essential human decency across the British-Chinese spectrum, surviving nightmare through mutual support.

Two novelists deal with France's agony in very different ways. Bruce Marshall's (1899–1987) *Yellow Tapers for Paris; A Dirge* (1943) is a savage, Waugh-like anatomisation of Paris life before and during war, and a profound lament for France's collapse. His alternation between poor Parisians' conversations and the corruption, stupidity and betrayal of politicians, bosses and their wives, all in denial about Hitler and clinging to the hope of the Maginot Line, is by far the most trenchant criticism of pre-war attitudes by any Scottish writer. Criticised at the time as gross, Marshall's brilliant juxtaposing, with coruscating wit, of low and high Paris is convincing. Catherine Gavin's (1907–2000) novels are more sympathetic to the French. Two of her four Scottish novels deal with the war, anticipating her French Resistance trilogy. *The Black Milestone* (1941) involves war-separated Scottish and French lovers and a German submarine landing. *The Mountain of Light* (1944) moves through war in Norway, Holland, Brittany and London's Blitz. Later she produced the French Resistance trilogy, *Traitor's Gate* (1975), *None Dare Call it Treason* (1978), and *How Sleep the Brave* (1980). From France's fall in 1940 to the 1944 Normandy landings, central to all is division of loyalties between de Gaulle, distrusted by Britain and America, and those like Jacques Brunel, who steer between Free French de Gaulle and Vichy.

At first sight Neil Gunn's fiction has little to do with 1939–45 war action (although *Highland River* (1937) is a classic Proustian account of recovery from World War One trench nightmare). Appearances deceive. *Young Art and Old Hector* (1942) (the names symbolically echo legend) presents the deceptively simple Highland adventures of young Art, yearning to be allowed to reach the forbidden river. Exploration of individualism and freedom's significance beside community and tradition leads to the crowning adventure of *The Green Isle of the Great Deep* (1944), one of the greatest Scottish novels, primarily concerned with issues raised by war. Like Edwin Muir's poetry, Gunn's approach transmutes actual events into a timeless world. His small wartime Highland community is shocked by atrocities, but especially by totalitarian mind-control, seen as destroying the soul. Hector and Art, exploring the river, fall in and drown – or dream. They come to in the Green Isle, the Celtic paradise, Tir-nan-Og, now a nightmare parody of paradise, a totalitarian state where eating the country's fruit is, like art and any questioning of the state, forbidden. As in Muir's 'The Combat', the humble pair should be destroyed easily, but, as Art goes on the run and becomes symbol of freedom, old Hector's ancient wisdom recalls God: human wisdom and endurance, together with Art, will triumph. Three novels followed, continuing Gunn's preoccupation with war's shadow. In *The Shadow* (1948), the shadow is of both a murder in a small community and the London Blitz. *The Silver Bough* (1948) explores a war-damaged landowner's regeneration. *The Lost Chart* (1949) is simultaneously about a real chart of crucial West Coast defence positions and how humanity has symbolically lost its way, living in fear of a Third World War.

Gunn, from the Highlands, and Robin Jenkins (1912–2005), from the industrial Lowlands, are two of Scotland's greatest novelists. Several Jenkins novels concern war's impact on the home front. *The Cone-Gatherers* (1955) may seem far from war, but closer reading reveals Jenkins's underscoring of the Argyllshire woods' local war between the psychopathic gamekeeper Duror and the innocent cone-gathering brothers (again, shades of 'The Combat'), against the world war's threatening background, from the opening page's destroyer moving down the Clyde to the last page's warship. More explicit, *Guests of War* (1956) is one of Jenkins's finest novels. Its unique presentation of urban and rural upheaval caused by evacuation of thousands of children, and many mothers, from Gowburgh (Glasgow) to Langrigg, a sleepy Border town, documents a major, too-readily forgotten aspect of the war, and how conventional town and country values collided, raising huge questions about what peacetime Scotland should become.

Jenkins was abroad for almost ten years; the later Scottish novels are more complex and ambiguous. Two return to the war period. *A Would-Be Saint* (1978) presents Gavin Hamilton, a figure of impossible Christian decency, a conscientious objector presenting a challenge to all with muddled and hypocritical moralities. Gavin works in the Argyllshire forests, gaining army officers' grudging respect: the crucial war-relevant question this unresolved novel leaves is whether his conscientious objections stem from genuine idealism or a kind of masochistic egotism. Similar questions arise regarding the eponymous *Fergus Lamont* (1979), whose bizarre life, moving from Gantock (Greenock) slums to national celebrity as the seeming-ideal war hero to disgrace and redemption on a remote Scottish island and final obscurity in old age represents Jenkins at his most elusive. Is Fergus self-deceiving hypocrite or misunderstood genius? Sometimes he plays the role of aristocratic soldier, sometimes angry people's poet. While he gains a Military Cross, he disarmingly questions his own courage, arrogantly believing himself a kind of secular elect, unable to be killed ('I had a greatness in me, too valuable to be lost'). Thus war plays its part in the novel's meaning; but only a part, one ambiguous element in the rag-bag of Scottish identities Fergus struggles to hold together. Ultimately, we see him as a deeply flawed version of Scotland itself, its clash of classes and cultures, couthy and critical, and its all-too-suspect mythologies, from 'Scottish soldier' to 'lad o' pairts', Kailyard to island cottage.

Fred Urquhart's (1912–95) writing is much neglected. His first novel *Time Will Knit* (1938) tells of working-class Edinburgh life. On war's outbreak, he was a conscientious objector and in 1940 his first collection of short stories, *I Fell for a Sailor*, was published. His writing sensitively captures wartime atmosphere and attitudes, as in *The Clouds are Big with Mercy* (1946), *The Ferret was Abraham's Daughter* (1949), where Bessie Hopkiss attempts escape from urban squalor as a GI bride, and the short story collection *The Last GI Bride Wore Tartan* (1947). These, arguably the best of their time, deal with the war relatively soon after it finished. While Urquhart continued to write short stories and novels, younger novelists re-encountered the war and its related issues several decades later, re-imagining them from new perspectives.

At their head stands Allan Massie's (1938–) *A Question of Loyalties* (1989), revisiting France's travails under Nazi occupation. It relates the quest of a middle-aged, sceptical Frenchman, Etienne de Balafre to find out the truth about his Vichy collaborator father, who, like many collaborators, hated communists even more than Nazis. Petain, Laval, de Gaulle move convincingly amongst fictional lesser players, dividing their loyalties and leaving haunting relics of guilt, easy condemnation and rootlessness. *The Sins of the Fathers* (1991) is its thematic sequel. In 1980s Buenos Aires, English Rebecca and German Franz, in love, introduce their respective parents. Rebecca's Jewish father recognises Franz's father as his wartime captor, a top-level German war criminal. His exposure and extradition by Mossad leads to Kestner's Israeli show-trial. The tragedy reveals subtle nuances of pain and guilt, blurring clear-cut edges, exploring fundamental questions of duty clashing with morality in ways as profound as any fiction of the kind. *Shadows of Empire* (1997) concludes Massie's trilogy exploring the West's decline in its post-war traumas. Alec Allan, a wealthy cabinet minister's journalist son, recounts his involvement with Spain and Germany. Surveying family members' differing ways in responding to the period's crises, one embracing communism, another leaving permanently for Malaysia, another becoming a German fascist, Alec, like Etienne, becomes trapped in *anomie* resulting from the clash and ambiguities of causes. These novels are among the most deeply reflective and insightful fictional treatments in English of events around World War Two.

A long gap separates Stuart Hood's early and later fiction. The latter lies in the distinguished (and neglected) group, *The Upper Hand* (1987), *The Brutal Heart* (1989), *A Den of Foxes* (1991) and *The Book of Judith* (1995). The first uses war as backcloth for its story of betrayal, as dour hypocrite James Melville seeks to destroy the partisan war hero, his polar opposite, Colin Elphinstone. The second is set amidst German post-war terrorism. The third is a complex postmodernist novel moving from actual war to war games in San Vito thirty years later, all undercut by the possibility that everything is the fantasy of a mind trapped in a mental den of foxes, a lair of 1939–45 memories and traumas. *The Book of Judith* narrates the last days of Franco and a hard-line British communist's betrayal to his death by his wife.

Jessie Kesson's (1916–94) *Another Time, Another Place* (1983) (filmed by Michael Radford for Channel 4 in the same year) must be the finest account of prisoners of war in Britain. The novel's perspective is of a sensitive and lonely crofter's wife projecting her dreams of romance and escape onto three Italian prisoners living in the bothy next door, and working alongside her in the dreary fields. The Italians are sensitively portrayed – sympathy can be found for even the Neapolitan rascal and seducer Luigi – while Kesson gently satirises entrenched Scottish and British narrow-mindedness. She captures how exotic foreigners, Americans, Poles, even prisoner Italians, revealed dangerously different worlds to Scots trapped in insularity.

Civilians could be prisoners differently. Tom Gallacher's (1934–2001) *The Wind on the Heath* (1987) presents actress Annie Jeynor moving through bewildering historical movements, from involvement with the Black-and-Tans and the General Strike to the Suez crisis. The novel's centre sees her caught in Nazism's rise in Germany, from which she escapes to America. Meanwhile Meg Henderson's (1948–) *The Holy City* (1994) relives the 1941 Clydebank Blitz. This novel is the most detailed and committed account of one of Britain's worst blitzes; it also pictures traumatised Jimmy Ryan, the invalided commando, presenting a real insight into the extremities of mental as well as physical war damage.

Arguably, however, the most impressive re-creations through research and imagination of the war are recent, Andrew Greig's *That Summer* (2000) and

Alison Kennedy's *Day* (2007). Greig revisits his joint long poem *A Flame in your Heart* (with Kathleen Jamie, discussed later) as fiction. Again the contrast is between the tranquil beauty of England's landscape and the Battle of Britain's sudden violence in its skies. Len is the Hurricane pilot; Stella, his radar-operator. Their war-time affair, their colleagues, Polish exile pilots, upper-class characters contradicting their stereotypes by their courage, all bring a war back to life that is filtered for us through book and film images. Even more effective is Kennedy's award-winning *Day*. Her achievement is the greater because her central figure is a kind of English Everyman of the People's War. Alfred Day is a working-class Staffordshire boy with an abusive father, finding a replacement for family in his Lancaster bomber crew. The novel's subtlety lies in its dual time scheme: in 1949 Alfred is in a made-up POW camp, the set of a war film; moving back in memory to the horrors of boyhood and war, the experience becomes therapeutic, allowing him to cleanse his poisons. Kennedy's feat is to convey a sense of the ordinary person's life and suffering in wartime Britain.

Echoes of war are heard beyond these specifically war novels. Apart from the many popular novels like Alistair MacLean's (1922–87) and Douglas Scott's (1926–), much subsequent fiction carries too many indirect impressions to record here. For brief example: central passages of Alasdair Gray's (1934–) *Lanark* (1981) emphasise wartime blackout and Duncan Thaw's young life's austerity and bleakness; William Boyd's (1952–) epic *The New Confessions* (1987) takes his embarrassingly candid, neurotically selfish international filmmaker protagonist through two wars; Janice Galloway's (1956–) *Foreign Parts* (1994) presents two social workers' cathartic French holiday whose ostensible purpose is to let Rona find her grandfather's Normandy grave, the graveyards symbolising women's problem with men, macho war's waste of lives; Iain Banks's (1954–) *A Song of Stone* (1997) turns war into surreal, unlocated and unidentified nightmare. Less seriously, George Macdonald Fraser (1925–2008) created several comic short story collections around his disreputable Private McAuslan, including *The General Danced at Dawn* (1970) and *McAuslan in the Rough* (1974).

Poetry

Poetry provides some of the most moving records of war and personal involvement therein. As with fiction, war's prospect looms through the 1930s: until his death, in some twenty-odd poems explicitly about war, William Soutar (1898–1943) expresses the decade's feelings as Franco, Hitler and Mussolini's ruthless fascism reveals itself, war becoming reality. His forebodings are mainly in English, rather than Scots, in poetry sharing something of Edwin Muir's (1887–1959) search for fabulous expression.

'Armistice Day 1936' satirises 'our sacrilegious silence which now screens /
the mounting of the murderous machines'; 'Spring Offensive' tells how 'the
young men prepare to die'; 'Bravery' has the 'treacherous trumpet-shout /
summon to deeds of death'. Many poems hint at the background of war, but
extend their anger to even wider issues, as in 'The Guns', where wavering
cries of birds predestined to death 'like the words of an international peace'
stand for humanity's cry. Muir's poetry of struggle of Fable and Story within
and without himself anticipates war; late 1930s and early 1940s poems like
'The Wayside Station' and 'The Refugees' embody timeless personal and
general human agony. As always, Muir's responses express themselves as
allegories, distilling aspects of violence and corruption into sinister, dream-
like tableaux, as in 'Then' or 'The Combat', the first seeing all wars symbolised by a blood-stained wall, the second having a killing beast powerless to
destroy its apparently defenceless victim – the endless struggle simultaneously evoking totalitarianism's atrocities in Europe and the eternal struggle
in individual and history between Evil and Good. In Gaelic, Dòmhnall
Ruadh Mac an t-Saoir (Donald MacIntyre) (1889–1964) won the 1938
bardic crown at the Mod in Glasgow with a dense rich allegory of a boat
travelling through a threatening storm, Aeòlus agus am balg (Æolus and the
bellows), a poem shot through with the forebodings of war.[1]

It may be surprising to realise that poets, not novelists, saw most action;
particularly three whose immersion in war produced the most deeply felt and
profound poems of battle and death. First, Hamish Henderson's (1919–2002)
Elegies for the Dead in Cyrenaica (1948) gained the Somerset Maugham Award
in 1949. The ten elegies, followed by 'Song for the Heroic Runners', are,
however, only a fraction of Henderson's war poetry, the most extensive of any
Scottish poet's. In his Collected Poems and Songs (2000)[2] (edited by Raymond
Ross with invaluable notes from Henderson regarding his poems' inspiration
and situations), nearly two-thirds of the volume is war-related. It follows
young Henderson from his mother's death to school in Dulwich and, in '4
September 1939', the loss of innocence: 'an incendiary dawn is prelude to this
soft morning / First morning of the new war'. This early poetry feels its way
into new worlds – 'En Marche' 'unsiccar o the foe I seek' – but soon lampoons
fellow soldiers, with affection and respect, but trenchancy towards backslid-
ers, as in rollicking send-ups like 'Pioneer Ballad of Section Three', or 'Ballad
of the Creeping Jesus'. (Henderson's love of and facility with the irreverent
and satiric traditional ballad form hallmarked his post-war poetry.) Here, in
deceptively jovial doggerel, is Rommel and his 'stubby guns on bulgy tanks'
with 'The Fall of Tobruk' unflinchingly facing facts. But just before the great
elegies the poems change, as in 'Death as a Dancer' and 'Lines to a Fool': their
mood darkens, as Henderson finds 'a curse of sandy hell's on me'. The Elegies
are the most unified series of war poems we have (given that Campbell Hay's

ambitious *Mochtàr is Dùghall/Mokhtâr and Dougall* remained unfinished). Sorley MacLean introduces the 1977 edition of the *Elegies*, finding the poems arose from the desert's weird doppelganger effect, where mind gave way to mirage and looking-glass effect. Henderson himself said the desert became for him 'the symbol of our human civil war', where 'the roles seemed constantly to change', so that 'There were no Gods and precious few heroes'. What Henderson clings to amidst shifting sands and moralities is simple, basic humanity: 'we should not disfigure ourselves / with villainy of hatred'.

Henderson continued writing powerful war poetry: 'So Long', his laconic farewell to Africa, 'Song for an Irish Red Killed in Sicily' and 'Lament for The Son', where he imagines an Italian father's grief. Besides these are stirring ballads for singing, written for fellow-soldiers, like the famous 'Fifty-First Highland Division's Farewell to Sicily', and Henderson's contemptuous response to Lady Astor's implied criticism of the Eighth Army, 'The Ballad of the D-Day Dodgers'. The first group have metaphysical depth and a constant insistence on civilised humanity's crucial importance, while the second are poems of camaraderie and encouragement. With this distinction a question arises which cannot be answered here, why Henderson's later creativity worked in the second rather than first vein. There are later fine songs – 'The John Maclean March', 'The Flyting of Life and Death', 'The Freedom Come-All-Ye' – but arguably Henderson never again attained the earlier war poems' power and completeness. Nevertheless, he remains the greatest Scottish World War Two poet.

Hardly far behind, however, are the two Gaelic poets Somhairle MacGill-Eain (Sorley MacLean) (1911–96) and Deòrsa Mac Iain Dheòrsa (George Campbell Hay) (1915–84). Iain Crichton Smith places MacLean's *Dàin do Eimhir/Poems to Eimhir* alongside MacDiarmid's *A Drunk Man Looks at the Thistle* (1926) as twentieth-century Scotland's greatest poetry. One of that sequence's two major themes is the poet's guilt at failing to fight fascism in Spain, and his agony at suffering Europe's cry. The other moves through MacLean's feelings for inspirational women, and his guilt and anger at his own weakness and their fates. On hearing of his first love's marrying another, MacLean reveals how his European agony intermingles with his loss:

Cha d' ghabh mise bàs croinn-ceusaidh
an èiginn chruaidh na Spàinn
is ciamar sin bhiodh dùil agam
ri aon duais ùir an dàin?

(I did not take a cross's death
in the hard extremity of Spain
and how then should I expect
the one new prize of fate?)[3]

Thus the two themes are not separate; the horror of Europe and the power of ideal love juxtapose in a great cry for freedom and beauty.

The Cry of Europe recurs in the long poem *An Cuilithionn* (*The Cuillin*, 1939). Here it merges with the poet's reflection on the Highlands' and Scotland's suffering. Both poems are, however, preludes to some of the finest poetry of the war, found mainly in the grouping *Blàr* (*Battlefield*) (1942–3) in *O Choille gu Bearradh* (*From Wood to Ridge*) (*Collected Poems*, 1989). 'Dol an Iar'('Going Westwards'), 'Alasdair MacLeòid', 'Gluasibh gu Deas'('Move South'), 'Curaidhean'('Heroes'), 'Glac á Bhàis' ('Death Valley') and ' Latha Foghair'('An Autumn Day') form a group of explicit commentaries on the desert war leading up to El Alamein (where MacLean was seriously wounded). 'Going Westwards' takes up the guilty theme, MacLean feeling he goes to war in shame, far from love of country or woman. But a newly-aware note for the ubiquitous suffering of humanity enters; Belsen, the Clyde Blitz, Guernica are paradoxically distant, but present. The poet finds no heartfelt rancour against his hardy desert enemies, imprisoned like himself. Detached compassion pities the body of the German boy killed in 'Death Valley'; a puny Englishman of immense courage is wept for in 'Heroes' as a great warrior of England. These are great poems of lament for the brave dead, whoever they are.

George Campbell Hay's war poetry has little of MacLean's valuing of enduring heroism, instead seeing war as dictators' meaningless madness. Onlooker rather than participant in war, Hay originally intended to avoid any involvement, his cause being that of Nationalist friends like Douglas Young, who saw their quarrel as with England before Germany. He gave in, and went with Ordnance to Tunisia, where his language skills brought him respect for the Arabs –'Atman' expressing preference for the ordinary Arab victim rather than his judge. The actual war poems are few – barely a dozen – yet 'Bisearta' ('Bizerta') has astonishing intensity in its vision of how the blaze's fury above the doomed city becomes animate Evil with pulse and heart. A dead man wishes a great wind to blind the masters of war for the horrors they have brought about in Italy and Africa in 'An t-Òigear a' Bhruidhinn o'n Ùir' ('The Young Man Speaking from the Grave'); 'Esta Selva Selvaggia'('The Savage Wood') is a ten-part cacophony, mingling Clyde Blitz with the crashed bomber that missed docks, destroying a home, an Italian girl's posthumous, poisonous revenge on soldiers who shot her, a French torturer, and other scenes of horror across the world, ferociously culminating in a ten-language litany, bitter and questioning, yet arguing 'they started it' – while the poem says simply 'Listen to yourselves. Beware.' Events like these permanently scarred Hay: in an earlier poem, 'An Lagan' ('The Hollow'), he wondered if, on returning to his sacred places in Argyll, he would find his soul.

Michel Byrne has speculated that perhaps this damage prevented Hay from completing his most ambitious poem, which was to have linked the lives and deaths of an Arab and a Scot. *Mochtàr is Dùghall* is the magnificent incomplete

account of the shared destiny of Arab Mokhtâr and Gaelic Dougall. A thousand lines tell of Mokhtâr's forefathers, their courage in defying oppressors
and search for spiritual truth. A draft poem of Dougall's story survives, as he
sails in grey ships in the U-boat-haunted Atlantic to Africa, where his predestined death awaits. Was dealing with the fate of Dougall too hard for Hay?
What we have concludes:

Mort nam marbh is mort nan naoidhean
nach do ghineadh – crìoch dhà shaogal.

(Murder of the dead, murder of the children
never begotten – the end of two worlds.)[4]

Other Gaelic poets writing strongly about the war are well represented in the
magnificent *An Tuil: Duanaire Gàidhlig an 20mh Ceud* (1999), the anthology
of twentieth-century Scottish Gaelic verse edited by Raghnall MacIlleDuibh/
Ronald Black.[5] One might single out, perhaps, the magnificent, itchy,
satirical war-prisoner poem, 'Deargadan Phòland' ('The Fleas of Poland') by
Aonghas Caimbeul, 'Am Puilean' (1903–82), whose prose account of the war
(and the rest of his life besides), *Suathadh ri Iomadh Rubha* (*Touching on Many
Points*) has become a classic of Gaelic autobiography.[6]

David Robb[7] has recently rediscovered the war poetry and extensive
unpublished prose of Alexander Scott (1920–89), whose fighting (and
wounding) with the Gordons in France gained him the Military Cross. Robb
argues that Scott did not publish the eighteen poems written during the war
because he did not consider them good enough – yet it would be fascinating
to have available one of our important poet's poetry coming from battle's
immediate experience. They range from descriptions of soldiers asleep, or
awaiting rescue, or as sentries, to his own acknowledged terror before going
into action. Surprisingly, only one poem, 'How Strange It Is' describes actual
battle ('machine guns chattering shrill hysterical laughter'). There is a group
of six post-war poems, including the magnificent 'Coronach', with the dead
crying to him ('You hae the words we spak / You hae the sang we canna sing').
Yet paradoxically he would not respond to their call, that he should 'tell hou
the sudden nicht / cam doun and made us nocht'.

It is a truism that those in the thick of war preferred thereafter not to speak
of it. This may explain why so many poets' intense war experience reveals itself
in few poems, often, like MacLean's or Scott's, grouped together, a class apart.
Another version of this separation is found in Robert Garioch's (1909–81)
three extended poems 'The Bog', 'The Muir' and 'The Wire', grouped in
Section II of his *Collected Poems* (1977). These move direct experience of captivity and war into strange realms somewhere between Edwin Muir's timeless

worlds and Kafka's surrealism. Humanity's struggles, bogged down, trapped in a limbo-like moor, penned in by barbed wire, are simultaneously life's struggles (as in his allegory 'Sisyphus') merged with battle and imprisonment's imagery and conditions. With Muir's similar poems, they are perhaps the finest expressions of their kind, universalising war as metaphor for the human condition.

Many other poets similarly present such occasional, yet intense, glimpses of their war experience. William Montgomerie (1904–94), with a handful of poignant poems, remembers, for example, his torpedoed brother, 'skull and skeleton now', or another Montgomerie, nothing now, 'under the cold bone of the moon' in the Sahara. J. K. Annand's (1908–93) experiences in Atlantic convoys produced poems like 'Atlantic 1941', 'Action Stations' and 'Sailor's Grave', vigorous poems in Scots and English full of the sea and naval action. Annand could also produce poems where war action gave place to fine appreciation of incidental beauty, like 'Sun Worship', where dawn amidst icebergs awes hardened sailors, or 'On the Fo'c'sleheid', where pellocks (porpoises) racing before the vessel become symbols of hope. In Egypt, G. S. Fraser (1915–80) produced *Home Town Elegy* (1944) and *The Traveller Has Regrets* (1947), sensitive poems for people and places indirectly haunted by 1930s and 1940s wars. Edwin Morgan's (1920–) experiences in the North African desert as a private in the Royal Army Medical Corps are described in some of the poems in the sequence 'The New Divan' from the book of that title (1977), and his journey around Africa on a troop ship is the location for his fine poem 'The Unspoken' from *The Second Life* (1968).

There are also those at home, or sidelined from active service. Men dominated war poetry; yet some of the most striking accounts of war at home are in two women's poems. Naomi Mitchison's wartime experience may lie most fully in her autobiographical volumes, *You May Well Ask* (1979) concerning 1920 to 1940 and *Among You Taking Notes* (1985), her magnificent wartime diary for Mass Observation, but a long poem like *London Burning* is one of the most detailed and vivid poetic accounts we have of blitz. She also devotes a section of her 1978 collection, *The Cleansing of the Knife*, to 'The War Experience'. Here Kintyre's ongoing life, hearing the distant war through unreal radio voices, is set against the section's central poem, her translation of Diament-Berger's passionate lament, 'The Burial of Elie Gras', Franc-Tireur who died for France. '1943' concludes the section, contrasting nature's spring renewal with war's continuing threat.

Olive Fraser (1909–77) served in the cipher department of the Royal Navy, WRNS and Naval Intelligence till the Merseyside Blitz in March and May 1941, which may have caused nervous breakdown. Her pain can be read in 'War and After War: 1940–1949'. Her innate humour shows in her 'The Home Fleet', juxtaposing Nazi linking of guns and butter with her view of the war in her garden as guns and cabbages.[8] Her longing for peace shows through

'VE Day 1945' and 'Victory Ode', while her agonised appeal to God to restore her faith in 'After War' poems I and II anticipates her later breakdown: 'Here dost the violence of the mad world come / Nightly to threaten by my sleepless bed.' It is pleasing to know she later fully recovered.

Many of Scotland's major poets preferred to leave the subject of war alone. Ruaraidh MacThòmais/Derick Thomson (1921–) speaks of it rarely, as in the fine 'Marbhrann do Shomairle MacNeacail' ('Elegy for Sam Nicholson'), where he recalls his friend, one of a bomber crew lost over Germany, or much later, in 'Anns an Ospadal' ('In the Hospital'), where for both Thomson and his dying friend their wartime experience is a wound, 'seeping through the joyous flesh'. Maurice Lindsay, whose Byronic poem-autobiography *A Net to Catch the Winds* (1981) candidly acknowledges his physical inability for war, although 'I was, of course, no cowardly escaper / having resigned myself to killing's chance', nevertheless occasionally captures well, as in his early poems, 'London 1941' and 'Home on Leave', the effects of war at home. Clearly a fuller survey would fruitfully explore much further, evaluating these domestic experiences. Writers like J. F. Hendry (1912–86) (*The Bombed Happiness*, 1941), Joseph Macleod ('Adam Drinan') (1903–84) (*Women of the Happy Island*, 1944), and Anglo-Scots such as Norman Cameron (1905–53) and Gavin Ewart (1916–95) deserve fuller discussion than possible here.

But what of MacDiarmid, with experience of both wars, yet, by the second, making poems of such shocking unconventionality that Muriel Spark thought he might well have been tried for treason? In *The Revolutionary Art of the Future* (2003), a collection of rediscovered poems by John Manson, Dorian Grieve and Alan Riach, his feelings about World War Two are clear. They describe the range of MacDiarmid's war poems as 'satires on Goering and Hitler, an attack on the Munich agreement, protest against conscription, and the treatment of "heroes" of World War One'. The most striking poem must be 'On the Imminent Destruction of London, June 1940', where MacDiarmid realises, 'horror atrophying in me / that I hardly care', since, to him, London is 'the Earth's greatest horror' in its opposition 'to progress and prosperity in human existence'. Yet, before reacting, one should remember he was not alone in his immense dislike. George Campbell Hay – and even John Betjeman, in his famous invocation, 'Come friendly bombs' – express similar feelings. The unpublished poem simply reveals the depth of MacDiarmid's dislike of what he saw as total English dominance of culture and economics in Britain. Likewise, 'The German Bombers' attacks 'The leprous swine in London town' for failing to pass on air-raid warnings to Scotland, intent only on their own protection.

Finally, yet impressively, as with fiction, as time passes, the war and its issues re-emerge, recreated through reading, imagination and empathy. Tom Scott (1918–95) heads this group, writing in Scots and English with great passion about war's folly and evil. The difference between earlier war poetry and his is that Scott's is not so much about individual places and horrors like 'Death Valley' or 'Bisearta', but a more general and politicised anger, rolling all wars into one. An early poem, 'Ceol Mor', exemplifies this: it laments unspecified Scottish dead, and its grief, pity and love can refer to any century. *At the Shrine of the Unkent Sodger* (1968) uses the Edinburgh Castle memorial to reflect in the same general way on the pity of war, insisting capitalism is at its root. An even longer poem, *This Dirty Business* (1986), covers all fronts from Russia to Japan, Far East to African desert. Despite passages of real power, the poem's sheer scale, and its remorseless moralising, is less effective than the more focused and directly involved poems of Henderson, MacLean and Hay.

Scottish, but London-based and unplaceable, George Macbeth (1932–92), editor of *Poetry Now*, was prolific in his war poetry. Outstanding is his *A War Quartet* (1969) where in four extended sequences ('The Desert War', 'Autumn Victory', 'Under the Sea', 'At Stalingrad') he presents an overview of war from the perspectives of a British tank commander, a Spitfire pilot, a U-boat captain and a German infantry officer. He aims at a newsreel documentary effect, admitting that 'too young to fight, too old to forget' his poem can only be 'dream-like trauma' from obsessive memory. His imagining (and use of sources, from Keith Douglas to a U-boat logbook) is convincing. El Alamein and the Battle of Britain come across as strange dreams remembered by survivors. Forgiveness and regret dominate in these records of decent men: the crew are 'prepared for death / in ungauged heroism', but ' the betrayed were mine / surrendered into life'. The commander decides for life, while amidst Stalingrad's carnage, 'the only man / of all that death-sped army left alive' fires his last shell into the snow.

Over sixteen years later, memory haunted another generation. Collaboration between Kathleen Jamie (1962–) and Andrew Greig (1951–) produced an astonishing projection of imaginations reliving the Battle of Britain in *A Flame in your Heart* (1986). Set in that mythic 1940 summer, and broadcast on radio, this is the love-and-death affair of Len and Kate, fighter pilot and radar operator, in their early twenties, snatching what moments they can in pubs and countryside, as war dictates. The voices change; letters intrude; the song of the title hangs in the air as though from a distant radio. The result is intensely nostalgic, a poetic drama-cum-documentary evoking collective memory. With Greig's *That Summer* and Kennedy's *Day* it marks the high point of contemporary treatments of the never-ending story.

Drama

Linklater's popular radio drama-conversations, *The Cornerstones*, *The Raft* and *Socrates Asks Why* (1942), and *The Great Ship* and *Rabelais Replies* (1943) succeeded as official propaganda (how war would be won) and intelligent discussion of both war issues and future Britain (what, exactly, were we fighting for?). His coda, *Crisis in Heaven* (1944), a stage play where an array of the dead, including Florence Nightingale, Abraham Lincoln, Voltaire and Helen of Troy philosophise lengthily about the ethics of war and peace, was less successful. His friend James Bridie (1888–1951), Scotland's leading dramatist of the war and post-war period, makes surprisingly little of war; it impinges rather than figures. *Mr Bolfry* (1943) comes closest; with two bored soldiers (and the Reverend McCrimmon's formidable niece Jean) billeted in a wartime Highland manse summoning the devil (Mr Bolfry) war appears to matter. Jean explains to Bolfry that the West is fighting Hitler. Bolfry appears not to know Hitler, claiming instead he started war. The ensuing discussions typify Linklater's and Bridie's universalising, quasi-philosophical treatment of the period's conflicts; unspecific, tending to archetype, like Bridie's ambitious debate about war's timeless nature in *The Queen's Comedy* (1950)

Scottish theatre had other post-war preoccupations: McLellan and Kemp concern themselves with social and language problems, and Ena Lamont Stewart women's marginalisation. Later Scottish theatre continued war's relegation to the background: John McGrath (1935–2002) explores 1950s National Service in *Events while Guarding the Bofors Gun* (1966); Bill Bryden's (1942–) *Benny Lynch* (1975) focuses mainly on pre-war years, but culminates in the 1943 Clyde bombing, Benny's defiant drunken disintegration set against war's cacophony. Exceptional is W. Gordon Smith's (1928–96) monodrama *Jock* (1972), powerfully telling the Scottish soldier's, and Scotland's, (hi)story, linking periods through Russell Hunter's performance persona as a military museum keeper. Again World War Two is secondary to age-long war and debates like the moral validity of mindless regimental or national loyalty. Substantial representation of that war – more precisely, its underlying politics – is perhaps found only in two plays, one ranking as one of modern Britain's greatest theatre pieces, C. P. Taylor's (1929–81) *Good* (1981). This anatomisation of seeming-decent German Professor John Halder's slow entanglement in the Final Solution astonishingly fuses flawless drama and profound psychological analysis. The title is key: Halder, his wife, mistress and Jewish friends believe him a good man. He tries to be, but through inexorable pressures, self-deceit and vanity (Hitler praises his book on euthanasia's validity) he betrays everything and everybody he professed to believe in. At the appalling conclusion, Halder arrives at Auschwitz's gates to become moral adviser. The other play dealing directly with war's politics and moralities, Peter Arnott's (1962–) *White Rose* (1985), also avoids a British location, focusing on the Battle of Stalingrad in 1942, as experienced (and fought) by legendary woman pilot, Lily Litvak, the Russian White Rose, her lover Captain Alexei and her engineer friend Ina. Atrocity and suffering are vividly presented through documentary, conversation and poetic monologue.

Yet two major themes arguably pull apart the play: sexual politics, as Lily struggles with her hatred of Germans and her fellow-Russians' women-demeaning attitudes, and Arnott's strident denunciation of human savagery. Liz Lochhead's (1947–) later *Britannia Rules* (1998) achieves greater sympathy, portraying working-class urban children evacuated to the countryside, while acutely exploring class and gender differences in Scotland then and, by implication, now.

Thus, while Scottish dramatists – and writers generally – continue exploring World War Two and war generally, this never-ending story is now usually employed as context rather than foregrounded. Yet Gregory Burke's (1968–) magnificent *Black Watch* (2006), ostensibly focused on Iraq, tells the bigger story of Scottish soldiers and their loyalties, desert war's immediacies giving way to the same question as Smith's in *Jock*, and so many other Scottish writers': why do ordinary human beings go to war?

CHAPTER EIGHT

Arcades – The 1940s and 1950s

Moira Burgess

If a strictly non-professional historian looks back from the colourful, complex, multimedia-supplied early years of the twenty-first century, the two decades of British history stretching over the 1940s and 1950s tend to be obscured by a kind of smog. In this slightly *1066 and All That* view, there are the hectic 1920s and 1930s – depression, bright young things, the threat of war – and then the 1960s, the heady days of *les évènements*, the Age of Aquarius, the Beatles. In between lies a repressed grey world. News of the great events in World War Two and the Cold War is doled out in cut-glass accents on the radio, and later, grudgingly, on black and white television, to a population queueing for rations, utility goods and snoek or other such fish (or processed meat) substitutes for the food they were used to pre-war.

If such a view of history is inaccurate, the parallel view of Scottish literature during the 1940s and 1950s may be almost equally ill-judged. These two decades are often given fairly short shrift in literary histories, as if, after the great days of the Scottish Literary Renaissance in the 1920s and 1930s, Scottish literature is waiting for the outburst of new writing which began in the 1960s and swept onwards from there. A second wave of the Renaissance is acknowledged during the 1940s and 1950s, but there is a difference:

> Renaissance values seemed to many to come dangerously close to many aspects of German National Socialism of the '30s and '40s [. . .] Suspicion [. . .] persisted long after 1945, and this, together with disillusion and scepticism stemming from the prevailing drab urban greyness of the '50s, led to a rejection by writers of the values and beliefs of 'Renaissance' writers.[1]

Great works like Neil Gunn's *The Silver Darlings* (1941), Sydney Goodsir Smith's *Under the Eildon Tree* (1948) and MacDiarmid's *In Memoriam James Joyce* (1955) are thus seen as singular landmarks in a rather depressed and uneventful literary scene, in the 'drab urban greyness' of a world recovering from war.

But in fact there has seldom been a livelier or more varied period in Scottish literature, and that is true in all the genres – poetry, fiction and drama.

Supporting all kinds of literary activity, too, there was a network of Scottish-based book and periodical publishing, hardly credible today, which will be looked at more closely later in this chapter. If we pick out, almost at random, the year 1947, we find MacDiarmid's A Kist of Whistles and George Campbell Hay's Fuaran Sleibh (not to mention Hamish Henderson's Ballads of World War II, privately published to elude the censor); Naomi Mitchison's The Bull Calves and J. F. Hendry's (1912–86) Fernie Brae, both novels long delayed by the fortunes of war, as well as Sydney Goodsir Smith's Carotid Cornucopius and Eric Linklater's short story collection Sealskin Trousers; and Ena Lamont Stewart's stunning play Men Should Weep, given its first staging by Glasgow Unity Theatre. In hindsight, bliss was it in that dawn to be alive.

It is right too to mention, from the same year, Guy McCrone's (1898–1977) Wax Fruit and Compton Mackenzie's (1883–1972) Whisky Galore, together with their near contemporaries, George Blake's (1893–1961) Garvel novels[2] and James Barke's (1905–58) Immortal Memory series which energetically fictionalised the life of Burns.[3] Barke and Blake are probably better regarded in literary circles – when they are regarded at all – for their pre-war proletarian fiction,[4] but in the 1940s and 1950s, when Barke turned to Burns and Blake to the shipbuilding dynasties of Greenock which he knew from childhood, they became household names. Their later works, like McCrone's Victorian Glasgow sagas[5] and Mackenzie's Highland comedies,[6] were popular novels in more than one sense: people were reading them, recommending them to each other, looking out for more.

A concern for Scottish culture in the broadest sense, too, begins to be visible in these decades. Following the foundation in 1951 of the School of Scottish Studies at Edinburgh University, Hamish Henderson and others began their historic expeditions to collect songs and stories from the Highlands and the traveller community. Henderson was also involved in the Edinburgh People's Festival of folksong and music, inaugurated in the same year, and indeed in the whole folksong revival of the time.[7] In another country-wide movement perhaps less often remarked on, drama clubs were being set up in cities, towns and villages, providing first-hand experience of acting, directing and stage-craft, through the activities of the Scottish Community Drama Association, founded in 1926; local venues from cinemas to church halls were packed out for the competitive drama festivals held each year.[8] It all made a good background for the beginnings of the Edinburgh International Festival, whose establishment is another highlight in that notable year of 1947.

A chronological survey of Scottish literature in the 1940s and 1950s throws up surprises as well as the expected names. The first five years have their own particular quality, since they are largely taken up by World War Two. The previous chapter in this book has surveyed the responses of Scottish writers to the war and its legacy to later generations, but there were difficulties too

on the home front: publishers had to contend with paper shortages and production quotas, and theatres with blackout and air-raids. Nevertheless Neil
Gunn published a novel in every year between 1940 and 1945, including
The Silver Darlings,[9] and new plays by James Bridie were produced almost as
regularly: these included *Mr Bolfry* (1943), a 'depiction of the drab and petty
reality of World War II as opposed to the notion of an epic struggle between
good and evil'.[10] Sorley MacLean's *Dàin do Eimhir* (1943) and George Bruce's
(1909–2002) *Sea Talk* (1944) appeared from the Glasgow publisher William
Maclellan, whose role as a facilitator of Scottish literature will, again, be considered later in this chapter. Compton Mackenzie completed his six-volume
magnum opus *The Four Winds of Love* (1937–45):

> one of the most ambitious Scottish novels of the twentieth century [. . .] The
> novel's concluding vision of a Catholic Christian confederation of small Celtic
> nations captures the author's eccentric political romanticism perfectly.[11]

The underrated Bruce Marshall produced *All Glorious Within* (1944), a
novel impossible to pigeonhole about a Catholic priest in a very Protestant
Scotland. Fred Urquhart, who had come to notice in 1938 with his novel
Time Will Knit, published the first of his superb (and superbly titled) short
story collections, *I Fell for a Sailor* (1940),[12] and Fionn Mac Colla (1906–75)
his dark novel on the Highland clearances, *And the Cock Crew* (1945).

But perhaps most startling, even though they can be seen as a development of an earlier movement, were two books from unknown writers whose
backgrounds were far from literary or academic. The 1930s had seen a fashion
for 'proletarian' fiction with an urban, industrial setting, such as the pre-war
novels of Barke and Blake. Much better known than their work was – and is
– the famous, or notorious, *No Mean City* (1935). It was written by Alexander
McArthur (1901–47), an unemployed Gorbals man, in order (according to
himself) to show up the poverty and intolerable living conditions in his area
of Glasgow, but tidied up for publication, probably heavily revised, and possibly sensationalised by a London-based journalist, H. Kingsley Long. Perhaps
predictably with such a pedigree, the novel polarised opinion: it was banned
from Glasgow city libraries, but never out of print for sixty years.[13] Rightly
or wrongly, it was seen as being written to shock; whatever McArthur's
intention, it has never been seriously taken as a realistic picture of the urban
working class.

The short stories of Edward Gaitens (1897–1966) in *Growing Up* (1942)
are immediately recognisable as something quite different. Gaitens too was
brought up in the Gorbals, and there is probably an autobiographical element
in the picture of the young protagonist observing and responding to his
Glasgow tenement background of family, shipyard work and unemployment.

Gaitens is probably now better known for his 1948 novel *Dance of the Apprentices*, which, while drawing heavily on the short stories – six of the ten stories from *Growing Up* appear as chapters in the novel – expands on the experience of the character Eddy (or the author Gaitens) as a conscientious objector in World War One and in the 'world fit for heroes' after the war.

Tom Hanlin (1907–53) too emerged from an uncompromisingly proletarian background. His short novel *Once in Every Lifetime* (1945) is set in a mining community similar to Armadale, West Lothian, where he grew up and worked as a miner for twenty years. On its favourable reception by reviewers Hanlin left the mines, publishing short stories and two more novels, *Yesterday Will Return* (1946) and *The Miracle at Cardenrigg* (1949), before his early death.

The second half of the 1940s began with what might be regarded as another descendant of *No Mean City*, which similarly gained considerable popularity. Robert McLeish's (1912–80?) play *The Gorbals Story*, produced by Unity Theatre in 1946, was a fiercely comic, passionately sincere account of the postwar housing crisis in Glasgow which played to packed houses in its home city, on tour and in London; it was filmed in 1950.[14] Also in 1946 Eric Linklater, who kept up a steady production of novels, short stories and memoirs throughout the period, published his war novel *Private Angelo* (considered elsewhere in this volume), probably to be counted among his masterpieces.

Some of the highlights of 1947 have already been listed; others, for it was indeed an *annus mirabilis*, included the dark small-town novel by Dorothy K. Haynes (1918–87), *Winter's Traces*. Haynes published one other novel, *Robin Ritchie* (1949), but is most notable for her short stories, many of which introduce a highly unsettling element of fantasy and even horror into an apparently realistic situation; her first collection, *Thou Shalt Not Suffer a Witch*, appeared in 1949. In 1947 too came a significant anthology of short stories, *No Scottish Twilight*. 'The younger generation [of Scottish writers], which has started to write during the past few years – especially since the beginning of the war – has devoted a great deal of attention to this medium,' wrote the editors, Maurice Lindsay (1918–2009) and Fred Urquhart.[15] Urquhart has already been cited as a novelist and short story writer, and Lindsay is ubiquitous in this period (and long after) as both editor and poet. His groundbreaking anthology *Modern Scottish Poetry* appeared in 1946, and his own first collection in Lallans, *Hurlygush*, in 1948. The closing years of the 1940s also saw such landmarks in Scottish poetry as Sydney Goodsir Smith's *Under the Eildon Tree* (1948), Hamish Henderson's *Elegies for the Dead in Cyrenaica* (1948), and Edwin Muir's *The Labyrinth* (1949).

Arguably, Muir's greatest poems were written in the 1940s and 1950s. In the previous two decades he had held a central position alongside MacDiarmid, F. G. Scott and others as creative artists working together in what came to be known as the Scottish Cultural Renaissance. Famously, however, he disengaged from this group after the publication of *Scott and Scotland* in 1936, to which MacDiarmid and F. G. Scott both took exception. As a poet, Muir's language was English, not Scots, and his disposition was profoundly different from that of his more Scotocentric contemporaries. In *The Narrow Place* (1943), with poems like 'The Wayside Station' and 'The Good Man in Hell' he was developing his own vision quite uniquely and this came to inimitable stylistic mastery in the allegorically-entitled *The Voyage* (1946) and most especially *The Labyrinth* and *One Foot in Eden* (1956). The title poems of these volumes might show Muir yearning for the idyllic securities of his childhood, but the symbolic power of his writing escalates beyond mere nostalgic autobiography or sentimental special pleading. There is major achievement in poems like 'The Combat' (which is almost impossible to describe except in abstract terms of an ancient battle between good and evil) or 'The Good Town' (one of the century's most essential poems about the pervasive European ethos of the increasingly Cold War), both from *The Labyrinth*. This achievement is developed in 'Scotland's Winter' and 'To Franz Kafka' from *One Foot in Eden*. If MacDiarmid could achieve poetic effects in Scots impossible in English, Muir for his part could create atmospheres and demonstrate profoundly serious moral truths in his English-language poetry that might be impossible in Scots.

Not far into the 1950s a notable series of events brought about considerable changes in Scottish society and literature. These were the death of George VI in 1952, the coronation of his daughter Elizabeth in 1953, and – much more influential than either – the coming of television to Scotland. It would have come anyway, but flickering images of the king's funeral were displayed in the shop windows of a few forward-thinking Scottish retailers in February 1952, and the televising of the coronation ceremony in June 1953 was what put TV sets into Scottish living-rooms (though, as yet, only into a few). The emergence of Scottish literature on television will be discussed later in Ian Brown's and Colin Nicholson's chapter; here it should be noted that radio was, and had been for many years, another of the support services which facilitated the publication of Scottish work. A substantial series of radio plays, *Annals of Scotland*, broadcast over the winter of 1956–7, dramatised fifteen Scottish novels ranging – chronologically and thematically – from the Kailyarders to Tom Hanlin, interspersed with talks on the past, present and future of Scottish literature.[16]

If the official proclamation of a new Elizabethan age was not entirely to the taste of Scots – who, historically, had no part in the first one, since it happened before the Union of the Crowns – still it is possible to see some fresh names and directions as the new decade takes shape, alongside established writers like Bridie (who died in 1951);[17] Naomi Mitchison, dividing her time between Scottish fiction and innovative fantasy;[18] and MacDiarmid, who published his major work *In Memoriam James Joyce* (discussed elsewhere in this volume) in 1955. W. S. Graham (1918–86) and Norman MacCaig (1910–96) had both published poetry in the early 1940s as part of the New Apocalypse movement, but Graham's *The Nightfishing* and MacCaig's *Riding Lights*, both in 1955, showed them to be major poets in their own right. In drama, the actor Roddy McMillan made a notable debut as a playwright – not to be followed up for some twenty years[19] – with *All in Good Faith* in 1954, a work in the tradition of Glasgow Unity Theatre where he had begun his career. Two of the most significant new names of the decade were those of Derick Thomson/Ruaraidh MacThòmais (1921–), whose first collection *An Dealbh Briste* (*The Broken Picture*) appeared in 1951, and Edwin Morgan (1920–), whose first collection *The Vision of Cathkin Braes* and translation of *Beowulf* both appeared in 1952, though his full voice was not heard until the 1960s. The year 1952 also saw the appearance in the newly-launched journal *Gairm* of Sorley Maclean's masterpiece 'Hallaig', inspired by and reacting to the Clearances on Raasay. Another was the novelist Robin Jenkins, who, after a debut novel set in the Highlands, *So Gaily Sings the Lark* (1950), turned, in *Happy for the Child* (1953), to a depressed industrial landscape which he made very much his own.[20] He returned to the Highlands also in *The Cone-Gatherers* (1955) and other work of this decade,[21] building up in both modes a series of complex, ambiguous novels which continued until his death in 2005.

By the second half of the 1950s great names were still at work – Edwin Muir with *One Foot in Eden* in 1956, MacDiarmid with *Three Hymns to Lenin* in 1957 – and, valuably, there was a move towards assessing Scottish writers and their work through memoirs and criticism (exemplified on a small scale in *Annals of Scotland*). Muir's revision of *The Story and the Fable* (1940), simply titled *An Autobiography*, appeared in 1954, and Neil Gunn's memoir *The Atom of Delight* in 1956, while Alexander Scott published *Still Life*, a biography of William Soutar, in 1958. But there were also surprises in store. Compton Mackenzie, whose Highland comedies had kept people amused throughout the 1940s, completed his fiction oeuvre with *Thin Ice* (1956), a thoughtful novel about a homosexual politician. Equally striking was Jessie Kesson's powerful, semi-autobiographical *The White Bird Passes* in 1958; Kesson had been virtually unknown till now, though she had been publishing and broadcasting short stories and drama for some years.

As mentioned earlier, Scottish literature of this period was well served by a support system hardly to be found today. The publishing scene of the 1940s and 1950s is worth a brief mention. While the major Scottish publishers by then had London offices – a sensible commercial move, only in hindsight casting a shadow of the wholesale emigration to come – Edinburgh was still home, for most of the period under review, to Constable, William Blackwood, Oliver and Boyd, Chambers, Nelson and Blackie; and Glasgow housed both editorial and production sides of the massive firm of Collins. Scottish writers looking for a publisher found as much expertise and enthusiasm in Scotland as anywhere else. In any age there is work perceived as non-commercial or non-mainstream which needs a small publisher ready to take a risk, and that was catered for too in the period under review. Serif Books in Edinburgh published, among other good things, Maurice Lindsay's *Hurlygush* and Sydney Goodsir Smith's *Under the Eildon Tree* in 1948, Naomi Mitchison's *Men and Herring* in 1949, and a *Selected Poems* of Marion Angus, edited by Lindsay, in 1950.[22] Macdonald Printers, also in Edinburgh, published work by Robert Garioch and Alexander Scott, and in Glasgow Caledonia Books and Scoop Books brought out editions of Glasgow poets like John Kincaid.

But by far the most significant of the small publishers, ubiquitous in the 1940s and 1950s and active into much more recent times, was William Maclellan, based in Glasgow. His groundbreaking *Poetry Scotland* series, slim attractive books with eye-catching cover designs, included work by MacDiarmid, W. S. Graham, Sydney Goodsir Smith, Douglas Young – the list goes on. He published the novels already mentioned – important first novels, which might otherwise never have seen the light of day – *And the Cock Crew*, *Dance of the Apprentices*, *Fernie Brae* and *So Gaily Sings the Lark*. In the wider field of Scottish culture he published F. Marian McNeill's four volumes on folklore, *The Silver Bough*, and George Bain's unmatched *Celtic Art*. And he was the publisher of MacDiarmid's great and difficult poem *In Memoriam James Joyce* (1955). It is simply impossible to overstate Maclellan's importance in this period, particularly in the genres of poetry and fiction; a much-needed biography is on the way.[23]

Drama is a special case, in that the publication of plays does not necessarily accompany performance, but it too was well supported during the 1940s and 1950s, with the appearance of a clutch of repertory theatres,[24] some of which have survived into the twenty-first century. The Byre Theatre, St Andrews, founded as an amateur theatre in 1933 to become professional in the 1940s, and Perth Theatre, becoming Scotland's first building-based professional repertory theatre in 1935, both housed professional companies throughout World War Two. In the face of approaching war, Dundee Repertory Theatre was established in 1939 and performed weekly repertory during the 1940s and 1950s. Rutherglen Repertory Theatre also began life in 1939, at first as the MSU Repertory Theatre, named for its founder the actor Molly S. Urquhart; renamed in 1945, it continued until 1959.[25] Park Theatre in Glasgow opened in 1940 as a theatre club, intended by its founder John Stewart to develop into a fully-fledged new theatre. Post-war building restrictions made this impossible, and the Park closed in 1949. John Stewart moved on to establish in 1951 what became his legacy, Pitlochry Festival Theatre. Again because of building restrictions, Pitlochry opened in a tent and after it blew away in 1953 operated for many years in a steel framework with an interior designed – in tribute to its pioneering opening – to look like a tent. Stewart died in 1957, but his company has continued, moving to a custom-built modern theatre in 1981, something of a landmark of cultural tourism with its attractive setting and congenial repertoire, changing plays each night in a manner unique in Scotland and rare in the UK.

It should be noted that these companies, and the slightly later Edinburgh Gateway Theatre (1953–65), by no means confined themselves to producing Scottish plays, though they did offer some. The perception, reasonable enough if unfortunate for Scottish literature, was that a wider-ranging repertoire made commercial sense. More significant for Scottish drama was Glasgow Unity Theatre, founded in 1940 by bringing together several of the city's amateur dramatic groups. Its viewpoint was socialist and its aim to bring theatre to the people, specifically to a working-class audience. While the repertoire was international, Unity soon began to include new Scottish work such as The Gorbals Story of 1946, and Ena Lamont Stewart's plays Starched Aprons (1945) and Men Should Weep (1947). The company closed down in 1951, but its influence through the later work of its actors and playwrights has been considerable, arguably stretching as far as, and even beyond, the radical and thoroughly Scottish theatre of the 1970s, exemplified by the popular 7:84.[26] Contemporary with Unity's high period was the 1943 establishment of Glasgow Citizens Theatre, the pet project of James Bridie, whose Holy Isle was revived as its first production. Very different from Unity in ethos and purpose, the Citizens too has always presented an international repertoire, but in its early years this included a good proportion of new Scottish writing; the names of Robert McLellan, Robert Kemp and Alexander Reid, for instance, regularly appeared.

A final link in what may be regarded as support services remains to be noted. The researcher looking through Scottish newspapers and magazines of the period will be surprised, not so much at the writers to be found there, but at where they turn up. Popular weekend pages in The Glasgow Herald and in evening papers published short stories not only by the comparatively well-known Naomi Mitchison and Tom Hanlin (both with several stories in the Glasgow Evening Citizen in 1949) but by a newcomer like Archie Hind (in The Glasgow Herald during the 1950s), ten years before his epic novel The Dear Green Place (1966). Neil Gunn, under the pseudonym Dane McNeil, was a regular contributor to the Scots Magazine in the 1940s. Scotland's (SMT) Magazine in the 1950s ran a long series of articles by Alexander Reid on contemporary Scottish writers, as perceptive and valuable now as they were then.

'Little magazines', as always, rose and fell: *Scots Writing, New Scot, Chapbook, Scottish Journal, Scots Review* (in several incarnations), as well as the longer-lasting titles *Poetry Scotland, Saltire Review, Scottish Arts and Letters, Lines Review*. By contrast with more short-lived titles, the immensely important Gaelic literary journal, *Gairm*, was founded by Derick Thomson and Finlay J. Macleod in 1952, to run for 200 volumes, brought to an end in 2002 only by the editor/publisher's own decision not to pass it into other hands. It constitutes perhaps the longest running such journal in Scottish literary circles, never mind Gaelic ones. Less predictably, the socialist weekly *Forward* and the economics journal *Scotland* found room for book reviews and literary pieces. The picture is of a country at home with its culture, where literature fitted in happily alongside business and politics and the previously noted movements in folk music and community drama.

The dynamics of change, however, continued. The last year of our period, 1959, saw George Friel's first novel *The Bank of Time*; George Mackay Brown's poetry collection *Loaves and Fishes*; and – not her first novel, but the one that fully confirmed the promise of *The Comforters* in 1957 – Muriel Spark's *Memento Mori*. Springing from the seed-bed of the 1940s and 1950s, another great age of Scottish literature began to flower.

CHAPTER NINE

Language, Hugh MacDiarmid and W. S. Graham

John Corbett

In March 1955, the year of the publication of Hugh MacDiarmid's *In Memoriam James Joyce* and W. S. Graham's *The Nightfishing*, a literary dinner was held to present an award to John Betjeman. In a book on poetic language, published three years later, the critic John Press recalls a *Daily Telegraph* report on the dinner, which was made newsworthy by Lord Samuel robustly denouncing much recent poetry as being afflicted by 'this fashion of deliberate and perverse obscurity', citing lines by Dylan Thomas to illustrate his point.[1] MacDiarmid and Graham's poetry can generally be accused of 'deliberate and perverse obscurity', and indeed the two major poems published in 1955 directly address the vexed issue of poetic language, if in quite different ways. With particular reference to these two poems, this chapter explores each poet's linguistic concerns in the context of contemporary and later attitudes to language and literature.

Christopher Murray Grieve, or 'Hugh MacDiarmid' (1892–1978) and William Sydney Graham (1918–86) might be seen as poets whose literary careers and poetic concerns are diametrically opposed. MacDiarmid's early lyrics brought him literary fame, and his combative personality, controversial political interventions and poetic ambition sustained his public profile and won him a circle of followers and a loyal audience, even when his style and opinions chopped and changed over the decades. During his life, he combined his poetry with careers as a journalist, editor, controversialist, political activist and academic, without ever yielding to the temptation of the kind of stable employment that might bring financial security and temper his opinions. His poetry in Scots and English is public, attention-seeking and encyclopaedic in reference. In twentieth-century Scottish letters, he is an inescapable monument, and he is still a household name, even amongst those who read little or no poetry.

By contrast, W. S. Graham is still a less celebrated figure, even in literary circles. Born and raised in industrial Greenock, he served his apprenticeship as an engineer before enrolling in Newbattle Abbey, an Adult Education College, in the late 1930s. He published his first collection of poems in the early 1940s; around this time, through David Archer, his publisher, he came into contact with poets (including MacDiarmid) and artists who converged on Archer's flat and the Arts Centre that Archer had opened on Scott Street in Glasgow. Through these personal contacts, Graham moved with his partner and their daughter to Cornwall in 1944; there, amongst the colony of artists in St Ives, he spent much of the rest of his life, with occasional sojourns in North America, London and Paris. His poetry, in English peppered with the stray Scottish word, is inwardly directed, philosophical, elusive. It suffered from general neglect: after the appearance of *The Nightfishing* in 1955 he published no collection until *Malcolm Mooney's Land* in 1970, followed seven years later by *Implements in their Places*. During this long period he contributed to the sustenance of his family by selling manuscripts of his work to friends and patrons. With the publication of his *Collected Poems* in 1979, and the public admiration of such cultural icons as Harold Pinter, Graham's standing gradually grew. Since his death, his poetry has been relaunched by the prestigious publisher Faber, his letters have been edited, and his work as a whole has received dedicated attention from an expanding coterie of enthusiasts. Monographs have been published by Lopez (1989)[2] and Francis (2004)[3] alongside a critical anthology edited by Pite and Jones (2004),[4] while *Malcolm Mooney's Land* is one of three key texts chosen by Christopher Whyte to evoke the 1970s in his survey of *Modern Scottish Poetry* (2004). It is interesting to note that MacDiarmid's *In Memoriam James Joyce* is one of Whyte's three key poems of the 1950s.

Despite the apparent gulf between the life and literature of MacDiarmid and Graham, a comparison of their work yields considerable insights into Scottish poetry in the mid-twentieth century and its relationship to broader cultural concerns. This chapter takes as its starting point Alan Riach's suggestion, in his extensive discussion of MacDiarmid's later poetry: 'It seems to me that Graham and MacDiarmid might be considered as poets whose enquiry into the nature and function of language is equally essential, but which led them to develop completely different poetics.'[5]

An explicit engagement with language is clearly crucial to the poetry of both Graham and MacDiarmid. Douglas Dunn, in his foreword to Graham's *New Collected Poems* contrasts the erudite 'synthetic English' of MacDiarmid's *In Memoriam James Joyce: A Vision of World Language* (1955) with Graham's obsession with 'communication itself, with the imperatives of listening and reading, and the improbability of being entirely heard or understood'.[6] A concern with language is by no means confined to Graham and MacDiarmid. Shari Benstock characterises Modernist poets' assumptions in terms that apply equally to MacDiarmid and Graham:

> The one sacred belief common to them all seemed to be the indestructibility of the bond between the word and its meanings, between symbol and substance, between signifier and signified. Multiple linguistic experiments – juxtaposition

of like words, typographical experimentation, translations of language into the dreamworld of the night or the idiolect of the mad – only reinforced the linguistic claims on meaning. The word was the one thing in this modern world that remained sacred: it survived wars, resisted the claims of materialist culture, masked despair and exposed cultural hypocrisy. The word held within it the possibilities of restructuring and rewriting the world. The writer would succeed where God had failed.[7]

For Benstock, the writer who showed Modernists the way was James Joyce, who with *Finnegans Wake* had mastered and re-imagined the potential of language, releasing its energy anew. MacDiarmid's *In Memoriam James Joyce* pays explicit homage to the Irish novelist, and, according to Matthew Francis, Joyce was cited by Graham as one of the major influences on his work, and 'was arguably the greatest and most durable of them all'.[8] Of course, the poetry of MacDiarmid and Graham shares at least one distinctive quality with the later fiction of Joyce: all of these writers are very difficult to read. This fact is so obvious as to be a commonplace, and yet the challenging quality of their work is worth revisiting, because, although MacDiarmid and Graham's poetry might be difficult to read for similar intellectual motivations, it is not, as Riach observes in the quotation above, difficult in the same way.

The 'difficulty' of modern poetry has troubled many readers and critics; a live issue in the 1950s, it resurfaces even today. In 1958, John Press published *The Chequer'd Shade: Reflections on Obscurity in Poetry*, which begins with an account of the literary dinner alluded to at the very beginning of this chapter. Fifty years later, a feature article on current poetry, written by John Mullan in *The Guardian*, attests to the fact that difficult poetry and adventuring in dictionaries remain fixtures in the poetic firmament. Rather than Dylan Thomas, however, the avant-garde poet in question is J. H. Prynne (to whom Lopez's monograph on Graham is dedicated):

> Prynne's poems are likely to defeat the common reader; even an admirer calls them 'dense and alarming'. Though most have a poetic shape on the page, there is no recognisable human voice speaking to you in them. They are places where vocabularies from different places (economics or science, for instance) unexpectedly intersect. They do not tell stories or describe experiences. They are usually about language itself. They will probably not make you look at nature afresh, but they might send you for an interesting trip through the Oxford English Dictionary.[9]

The construction of the 'common reader' is itself a critical response to a set of challenging poetic strategies. The 'common reader' is someone who might well query the value of engaging with a poetry that, from poets such as MacDiarmid and Graham through to Prynne, flaunts its dense, alarming near-incomprehensibility. From the perspective of the late 1950s, Press's defence of obscure poetry appeals to spiritual qualities that only a departure from the expected norms of everyday language can evoke:

> Poetry is less a means of communication than a way of communion, more intense, more profound and more personal than the casual intercourse of our social life. Those who desire to share in this communion must learn to accept the strangeness and even the obscurity of a world in which the syntax and the vocabulary of analytical reason have been transformed into the grammar of assent and the language of the heart.[10]

Press's vocabulary of 'communion' and his assertion that linguistically difficult poetry can conjure an intense, profound and personal response in those who accept its challenges echo MacDiarmid's Introduction to *In Memoriam James Joyce*. MacDiarmid's Introduction and the poem that follows it both envisage an intellectual elect. Quoting an unnamed contemporary who asks 'Why should the fences be lowered till even the donkeys can jump them?',[11] the poet forms an allegiance with John Milton and T. S. Eliot, both of whom demanded for their work 'fit audience, though few'. MacDiarmid's intellectual élitism does, however, allow for self-mockery, as when he describes his poem as 'jujitsu for the educated'.

Graham, too, writes obsessively in his poetry about the difficulty of communicating, a difficulty compounded, for the 'common reader', by the wilful opacity of his writing. His early poems followed the contemporary trend of the 'New Apocalyptics', a grouping of predominantly Scottish, Welsh and Irish poets such as Dylan Thomas, J. F. Hendry, Norman MacCaig and G. S. Fraser, who sought to bring a rapturous intensity and fervour to their poetry. It is the kind of poetry easily represented by a brief sequence of lines such as the following, from 'The Sixth Journey':

> With Judas my head, the thunderclapping hub
> The joywheel ring of tempest-engendered wrack
> Peels round my Crusoe sky a drunken almanac
> Lights on this Galway inish my island's negro
> And swings the wrinkling sea on a servant hinge.[12]

The reader is faced with the challenge of making sense from this string of potent and provocative cultural images ('Judas ... Crusoe ... negro'), Anglo-Saxonish compound modifiers ('thunderclapping ... joywheel') and half-obscured syntax ('the ring ... peels round ... lights ... and swings'). The relationship between the phrases is ambiguous: does the joywheel ring light my island negro on this Galway inish, or does the joywheel ring light on this Galway inish, which *is* my island negro? The 'common reader' might complain that whichever reading is preferred, the outcome is nonsensical. We shall return to the issue of interpretation later; for now, it is sufficient to note that while Norman MacCaig relinquished and disowned his poetry of the New Apocalyptic period, Graham continued to uphold the value of his earlier work. Indeed, much of his more celebrated and ambitious later work develops the themes and techniques found in his early verse.

Both *In Memoriam James Joyce* and *The Nightfishing* are long poems. The former was the result of a protracted process of composition and reconfiguration lasting two decades, while Graham finished his first draft of the latter in 1949. The two poems represent, as Riach observes, a very different set of poetics, linked by a fundamental interest in language. MacDiarmid's 'vision of world language' is a voracious autodidact's common-place book versified: a long, energetically rambling collage of prose passages reworked and assembled into a piece of found art. The materiality of the poetic enterprise is accentuated in the original publication by 'decorations' by J. D. Fergusson, described in MacDiarmid's Introduction as 'that splendid octogenarian and doyen of Scottish painters, who knew James Joyce in Paris'.[13] Fergusson's 'decorations' announce the poem as an *objet d'art*; while controversial in their day, the many 'plagiarisms' in the poem situate it as an *objet trouvé* in the line of Marcel Duchamp's 'readymades', his bicycle wheel, urinal and bottle-rack, exhibited as sculptures, to public consternation, from 1915 on. The appropriation of found texts into 'original' poems was always central to MacDiarmid's versifying and can be seen in his ransacking of Jamieson's dictionary for his early lyrics. *In Memoriam James Joyce* extends and intensifies the process. Robert Crawford notes that

> The technique of building fragments of older work into a new text was a common modernist practice, used by Pound, Joyce, Eliot and others, but, as in the case of Eliot, so with MacDiarmid this collage technique could bring charges of plagiarism. Later he would take long passages of other people's prose and, often with a very fine feel for line-breaks and verse movement, realign them as verse.[14]

The 'long passages of other people's prose' in *In Memoriam James Joyce* were largely unacknowledged by the poet himself, and it has been left to sleuthing if sympathetic commentators such as Kenneth Buthlay and Alan Riach to track them down.[15] The sources include novels such as T. H. White's well-known *The Sword in the Stone* (1938) and less familiar sources such as J. S. Martin's *Orchardford* (1924) and John Buchan's *A Prince of the Captivity* (1933). If there is a continuing unease about MacDiarmid's silently reworking passages from these sources into his own work, it is mitigated by the acknowledgement that transgressive, even unethical, practices can be seen in the light of Modernist appropriation of 'ready-made' texts. That Joyce offered a direct model for the method MacDiarmid adopted is evident in Eloise Knowlton's observations on the 'difficulty' of *Finnegans Wake*:

> So, what is difficult about *Finnegans Wake*? Simply put, it has no quotation marks, no means of bordering one semantic unit from another or one period of history from another. It has no ultimate singular source by which to name and refer it, reliably. It has no narrator, no 'author.' [. . .] It is from our necessarily fixed positions as modern (not yet as 'postmodern') that we find the textuality of *Finnegans Wake* transgressive, unsettling, *out of control* [original emphasis].[16]

This passage could easily be adapted to describe *In Memoriam James Joyce*. It too has no quotation marks, acknowledging the diversity of voices that contribute to its textuality. Author and interlocutor waver, unreliably. It celebrates unity by insisting on diversity, takes us on a roller-coaster trip beyond the settled solidities of individual perspective, and denies us the comfort of expected poetic conventions. Christopher Whyte is one of a range of critics to affirm that MacDiarmid's technique of uncontrolled collage is a meaningful attempt to redefine what it means to be a poet in a post-Romantic age; he notes that:

> Concepts such as originality, subjectivity and intellectual property collapse in the maelstrom of MacDiarmid's compilation which, though it can sound both overwhelming and forbidding when described like this, is at the same time an entertaining and enormously playful text.[17]

Whyte is pleasingly sensitive to the playfulness that offsets the seeming intellectual arrogance of *In Memoriam James Joyce*; after all, in his Introduction to the poem, MacDiarmid appeals not only to an intellectual élite but to 'Miss Mae West', whom he quotes approvingly as having observed, 'Well, Shakespeare had his technique, and I have mine.'[18] MacDiarmid's poetic technique in this poem is 'to illustrate the concept [. . .] of the unity of all mankind' by explicitly and repeatedly placing the reader in the uncommon position of having fully absorbed the 'literature of all times and languages, the merely good as well as the great'.[19] Time and again the reader is exhorted to recall that he enjoys a dizzying command of knowledge. By accepting the exhortation, the reader might aspire to the spiritual condition that Press alludes to in *The Chequer'd Shade*, namely, a profound communion with other minds that results in an altered perception of the world. The poem addresses the reader directly, sometimes positioning that person as James Joyce, sometimes as W. B. Yeats, sometimes as the poet's wife, Valda Trevlyn, but always as someone who has read and understood a wealth of literature, science and myth in a dazzling range of often untransliterated languages. J. D. Fergusson's illustrations sit alongside a rash of glyphs whose meaning is both concrete and (to the 'common reader') elusive. To be the ideal reader of *In Memoriam James Joyce* is to join the interlocutor in a privileged community of hyper-intellectuals, whose sagacity encompasses all human endeavour. It is not an easy reader-position to adopt; the narrator continually urges you to recall texts and writers with whom you are likely only to have the merest, if any, acquaintance; for example:

> This rag-bag, this Loch Ness monster, this impact
> Of the whole range of *welt literatur* on one man's brain,
> In short this 'friar's job' as they say in Spain
> Going back in kind
> To the Eddic, 'Converse of Thor and the All-Wise Dwarf'
> (Al-viss Mal, 'Edda die lieden des Codex Regius' 120, I f)
> Existing in its present MS form
> Over five centuries before Shakespeare.
> You remember it?[20]

While Shakespeare remains a cultural benchmark, both in the Introduction and the body of the poem, MacDiarmid is notoriously, unapologetically, anglophobic in his sentiments throughout the text, most explicitly in the section 'England is our Enemy'. Further examination shows that it is a cast of mind that MacDiarmid associates with 'Anglo-Saxondom', a genteel philistinism sanctioned by 'English official literary criticism' that might be summed up best as a lack of national ambition, a complacent tendency to belittle rather than enlarge. MacDiarmid identifies this belittling mindset with the advocacy of 'Basic English', a reduced form of English devised in the 1930s by C. K. Ogden for use in the teaching of English to speakers of other languages[21] and championed by I. A. Richards.[22] However, MacDiarmid rebuts what he refers to as 'linguistic imperialism', anticipating by over three decades Robert Phillipson's 1992 volume which takes this phrase as its title.[23] In *In Memoriam James Joyce*, MacDiarmid engages explicitly with the Basic English movement (which in an altered guise has returned in the form of current debates on English as a lingua franca today; see, for example, Jennifer Jenkins, *World Englishes*).[24] MacDiarmid acknowledges that the adoption of Basic English as a world language would carry with it the implication that 'We are richer, more numerous / More civilised, more virtuous than the rest!' and suggests instead that a world language might be composed of a core vocabulary assembled from 'the vast international vocabulary which already exists'.[25] This suggestion triggers a typical digression on potential sources of an international vocabulary and grammar, sources that include Sanskrit *sūtras*, the grammar of Wasiri Pashto (an Afghan language), various Chinese languages, Greek and Latin, three dialects of Albanian, Japanese, Hebrew, Yiddish, Tupi (an Amazonian Indian language), Continental and Brazilian Portuguese, Castilian and Argentinian Spanish, Bantu, Amerindian languages, amongst others. MacDiarmid, of course, in this poem and elsewhere, advocated a 'poetry of fact'; it is useful to lay the stress on the first rather than the second of those two nouns: fact is here the substance from which a poetic perspective is distilled.

MacDiarmid's technique for evoking this poetic perspective, then, is to place his readers in a position where they experience a totalising epiphany, a position where they are imaginatively conversant with all the languages and literatures of the world and so apprehend imaginatively the unity of all humankind. This technique is one source of the 'difficulty' of this poem – the reader might think they need to know all the allusions, references, citations and quotations, overt and covert, in all the languages and scripts referred to and represented. They do not. They just need to accept MacDiarmid's generous invitation to *imagine* that they know them, and, like him, to snarl at anyone who might wish to belittle their vision or offer a pallid 'Basic' alternative. Despite its notorious 'difficulty', if the reader accepts the near-omniscient role offered, *In Memoriam James Joyce* can be, as Christopher Whyte acknowledges, 'an extremely easy poem to read'.[26] The arcane knowledge, languages and scripts on ostentatious display can be relished simply as displays of humankind's endless diversity and ingenuity; quarrying for deeper meaning can be reserved for later contemplation.

In contrast, as we have already seen, W. S. Graham's poetry places more immediate obstacles in the way of the reader's comprehension. The obscurity of his poetry is more in line with that identified by John Press in *The Chequer'd Shade*, namely, a departure from the expected norms of syntax and lexical usage. Matthew Francis argues that Graham, particularly in his early poems, uses the figure of 'catachresis', that is, the deliberately unusual collocations of words, or even incongruous images, such as the following:

My need reads in light more specially gendered and
Ambitioned by all eyes that wide have been
Me once.[27]

Here the collocations are incongruous and perplexing: why should 'need' 'read'? Why should 'light' be 'more specially gendered'? How has 'light' been 'ambitioned by all eyes'? The grammar does not help, the syntax playing against the line division to suggest first that 'all eyes' have been 'wide' before suggesting that 'all wide eyes' have been 'me once'. Francis follows Michael Riffaterre in arguing that catachresis is a signal that the reader should strive beyond the literal meaning of the language towards a metaphorical significance.[28] The 'common reader', picking up *The Nightfishing*, then, faces a different set of challenges from those afforded by *In Memoriam James Joyce*. Instead of being swiftly borne along in a role that implies superhuman erudition, Graham's reader must slowly puzzle out the sense of evocative, but semantically opaque, wordings. The rewards, no less than the effort demanded, are different.

Gnomic poetry is as old as any recorded literature in the English language. Anglo-Saxon poets compressed images and deferred meanings in their riddles, elegies and religious visions. Chris Jones has argued strongly for a rediscovery of Old English poetics by Modernist writers, and he notes that Graham acknowledged that Ezra Pound's translation of 'The Seafarer' was beside him when he was composing The Nightfishing.[29] Jones also remarks on the occasional influence of Old English versification on Graham's other poetry, most obviously 'The Voyages of Alfred Wallis', which is marked by unusual compounds and heavy alliteration. Another more immediate and pervasive influence is T. S. Eliot's Four Quartets, whose phraseology The Nightfishing persistently echoes, as Ian Sansom observes: '"N. F." is in fact stuck together from little bits from "Tommy E.", beginning with an echo from "The Dry Salvages" [. . .] and continuing with many reminders of the rest of Four Quartets.'[30] There are other poems that could be referred to, not least Robert Lowell's The Quaker Graveyard in Nantucket (1946), which, like 'The Seafarer' and 'The Dry Salvages' is one of a sub-genre of Modernist poems that treat of sea-voyages and drowning in an elegiac mode. Matthew Francis confirms this point: 'A glance at any anthology of poetry of the period [1930s and 1940s] reveals a number of laments for the drowned.'[31] The Nightfishing, in common with many other poems by Graham, therefore invites its readers to make sense of its linguistic conundrums against a narrative frame of seafaring that extends back to the earliest verse in English and which enjoyed a recrudescence in the Modernist period. The ubiquity of the sea in Graham's poetry is perhaps at the root of Robert Crawford's characterisation of the 'surging obscurity' of his earlier work.[32] Its presence might be explained by Graham's upbringing in the Clydeside port of Greenock; it might equally be explained by the attraction of the archetypal trope of sea-voyaging to many Modernist poets.

The Nightfishing, then, offers the reasonably erudite 'common reader' a set of familiar images – the haunting bell from 'The Dry Salvages', the cry of gulls and the lonely voyager from 'The Seafarer', the sea's harvest from The Quaker Graveyard in Nantucket – and so the poem can at least be quickly apprehended as a variation on a theme. However, as in Graham's earlier, more apocalyptic work, the elusiveness of the literal sense of many of the lines ensures that the reader cannot regard their meaning as unproblematic.

In his exploration of Graham's poetic language, Mathew Francis[33] invests a substantial part of his argument in suggesting that Graham's 'difficulty' represents a critique of the metaphor of language as a conduit, that is, Graham's poetry problematises the view of language as a simple container for transferring ideas from one individual to another. This metaphor is unquestioned in MacDiarmid's 'vision of world language'. The notion that language is a conduit, and that it therefore automatically evokes a particular cognitive response lies (however ironically) behind some of the litanies in *In Memoriam James Joyce*; as in, for example, the following extract:

And [we] are learned in all manners of hypnagogic images
Verbal reflexes, visual onomatopoeia
Word-physiognomy, colour associations, tactile values,
The psychological experiences differentiating
Noun-consciousness from verb-consciousness,
And the adjective state of mind from the adverb.
The psychomotor effects of different sound combinations,
The fact that poetry is largely tonal and that the sounds of poems,
Especially those of lyric poetry, yield of themselves
A mood comparable to that of the original poem [. . .][34]

The suggestion here, particularly in the last lines quoted, is that the substance of language is a guarantee of its meaning, or at least of its mood. W. S. Graham struggles with the contrary notions that there is in fact no guarantee that he will find the right words to convey his ideas or mood, and that, even if he is satisfied by his own wordings, he cannot be sure that they will have communicated his thoughts and emotions effectively. *Malcolm Mooney's Land* contains two of the most familiar of many, many lines that address the inadequacy of communication. Graham asks: 'Have I not been trying to use the obstacle / Of language well? It freezes round us all.'[35] Frozen wastes, inhospitable seas, chasms whose silence is punctuated by the surreal ringing of neglected telephones – these images do not hold sufficient meaning in themselves but invoke metaphorical interpretations from readers who are primed by their knowledge of poetry, intensified by the shock of Graham's obscure rhetoric, to read texts non-literally.

The linguistic theory best suited to guiding the 'common reader' through Graham's work is not the structuralism celebrated by MacDiarmid, but later pragmatic approaches to textual interpretation formulated by linguistic philosophers such as Paul Grice and John Searle.[36] Grice famously sought to account for the human capacity to understand non-literal utterances by devising a 'cooperative principle' underpinned by four 'maxims', namely quality (that is, tell the truth), quantity (give a sufficient amount of information), manner (avoid obscurity) and relevance (remain on the topic of conversation). As Grice recognised, much communication is characterised by the breaking or 'flouting' of these maxims, and indeed most literature flouts the maxim of quality (by being fictional), quantity (by leaving the reader to infer information), manner (by being 'perversely and deliberately obscure'), and relevance (by being about strange or elusive topics). Grice's point is not that the flouting of the maxims disables communication; rather it enriches it by signalling that the co-operative reader must resort to *implicatures* to make sense of the utterances. And so, say, the co-operative reader makes sense of Ezra Pound's 'In a Station of the Metro' by establishing an unstated connection of relevance between the apparition of the faces in the crowd, and petals on a wet, black, bough. A co-operative reader will recognise that the simple assertion of these two images in conjunction with each other is sufficient to reveal a hitherto unrecognised truth, and the reader may conclude that the manner in which the comparison is made is therefore orderly and transparent.

Of course, if the reader considers that the writer is *not* co-operating, and simply producing meaningless babble, then communication breaks down. The distinction between the co-operative and unco-operative reader, the reader who will work with the poet in the mutual construction of meaning versus the reader who simply throws a book of 'difficult' poetry across the room, perhaps correlates to the Modernist notion of the 'fit audience' versus the 'common reader', though some poems, like Graham's earlier oeuvre, seem to defeat even his more ardent admirers. Even a fit audience must still be teased with exotic reading positions, sensuous imagery, ghostly allusions to a rich tradition, or the promise of a metaphorical understanding. We see Matthew Francis adopting several of these strategies in his analysis of *The Nightfishing*:

> [T]he narrator's equivalent of home is language. The ghost crew to which he belongs is the community of all those who have used the language before him. For this reason, like the Ancient Mariner, surrounded by his ghostly shipmates, he is a lonely and alienated figure, but at the same time not alone. Language is both the ghost crew and the sea itself, 'the all common ocean' whose 'lonely behaviour' causes him to cry 'headlong from my dead'.[37]

The Nightfishing is read, here, metaphorically, as a voyage to fix and capture language, seen variously as the ghost crew (with its allusion to Coleridge), the sea, and the shoals of herring that are being fished. The critic's engagement with the poet to co-construct meaning through the medium of the poem is itself a necessary negotiation of individual perspective and scholarly authority; it is part of an echoing, overlapping, ongoing dialogue between a 'fit audience' of sympathetic critics, more sceptical 'common readers' and the poets themselves. MacDiarmid, in his typically provocative manner, does the sums and calculates 'the fraction of readers / for the best work today' as five per one hundred thousand.[38] His work and that of Graham in the mid-1950s represent different ways of using the 'obstacle of language' to challenge that minority of readers without losing their co-operative and sympathetic engagement.

CHAPTER TEN

Post-War Scottish Fiction – Mac Colla, Linklater, Jenkins, Spark and Kennaway

Bernard Sellin

It is always convenient to categorise literary history into periods, movements or groups. Scottish literature has been no exception if, for example, we bear in mind the amount of attention paid to the first twentieth-century Literary Renaissance. The claim has also been made that we have a second Literary Renaissance gathering talents who appeared in the 1980s and after, now the modern voices of Scotland. In between lies the uncertain ground of the mid-twentieth century, a period which may have been neglected and which is even perhaps in the awkward situation of having to lay a claim for better recognition. This seems true of the fiction of the period, sometimes over-shadowed by achievements in other fields, such as poetry or drama. With the exception of Muriel Spark, the authors included in this chapter have received little sustained critical attention. One of them at least has often been presented as a neglected writer, Robin Jenkins.

This chapter is concerned with writers whose production either started in the 1950s and 1960s, or began in the 1930s before extending into the post-war period. This period witnessed many challenges to accepted social and literary norms all over Europe, for example in the form of the *nouveau roman* in France or the 'Angry Young Men' in England. However, when attention is paid to individual works, it is not easy to find unity in literary periods which extend over several decades. Two of the authors treated in this chapter, Fionn Mac Colla (1906–75) and Eric Linklater (1899–1974) might be described as survivors from the first Literary Renaissance, whereas the other three can be associated more clearly with the literature of the second half of the twentieth century: Robin Jenkins (1912–2005), Muriel Spark (1918–2006) and James Kennaway (1928–68). Some of them had exceptionally long careers. All together they offer a wide range of experience and approach that bears witness to the variety and vitality of Scottish fiction over a period covering a large part of the century. Considering their output and their careers' length, it is impossible to do justice to them in any single chapter. This chapter's ambition will be limited to underlining some of the main directions which the Scottish novel took over that period.

> A competition in cruelty, a contest of horrors – that is no unfair description of
> much that has characterised and befouled our century, but humanity – dextrous
> and slippery humanity – survived the degradations and avoided the deepest
> morasses of a dark epoch, and left a comment on our times in its open prefer-
> ence for stories of escape.

This comment from Eric Linklater's autobiography, *Fanfare for a Tin Hat*
(1970), seems to set the tone for much post-war Scottish fiction, while
opening a possibility of escape and redemption which, to some extent, con-
tradicts the bleakness of the verdict.

What Linklater had in mind, of course, was the catastrophe of total war
which afflicted Europe and the world on two occasions, leaving the survivors
stunned, if not bitter. Linklater took part in World War One, this 'outrage
against common sense, as well as against humanity', he wrote.[1] His autobiography is as much a personal account of the horrors of war as a celebration of
survival, a fanfare for the tin hat which indeed saved his life. Hence mixed
feelings which found their way into one of his most famous books, *Private
Angelo* (1946). Drawing from his memories of the first war, Linklater depicts
episodes of the allies' landing in Italy in 1943, at a time of confusion that also
lends its uncertainty to moral positions. Whereas the reader expects a tale
of courage upholding strong moral values and celebrating victory, the book
turns out to be an ambiguous, if funny, account of self-help whose picaresque
anti-hero, lacking the *dono di coraggio* praises survival more than anything
else. Hence the final lesson: '[W]e have learnt the most useful of all accom-
plishments, which is to survive!' By choosing an Italian as his main character,
Linklater was prepared to meet objections from British war veterans, but it
would have been interesting if, instead of an Italian, the character had been
a soldier from one of the allied armies fighting Nazism. Why not a Scottish
soldier? No doubt the book is to be read as a pleasant comedy, but it remains
characteristic of Linklater's fiction of escape – also found in the Juan series
– in which negative elements tend to be obliterated by a definitely comic
approach, with the danger that the irony may confuse the message.

There is no such ambiguity in Robin Jenkins's work, particularly where war
is concerned. Nothing could be more different from Linklater's enthusiasm
in joining up . . . and being rejected because he was too young. A staunch
opponent to war in all its forms, Jenkins was a conscientious objector in 1939
and it was not before 1946 that he returned to normal civilian life. This was
his response to war and his own method of survival, but it had little to do
with escapism or lack of courage. Jenkins claims that moral weakness and
a refusal to face reality are chiefly responsible for the present degradation.
Although there is not a single passage depicting war action, it is a theme that
runs though his work, but which he chooses to treat indirectly. *A Would-be*

Saint (1978) deals with the experience of limits, when a young conscientious objector is – almost – ready to die, not for his country, but for his ideas. *Guests of War* (1956) recalls the experience of ordinary people having to leave the Glasgow conurbation for the safety of nearby villages. In all of them, including *The Cone-Gatherers* (1955), war is more than a permanent threat to serenity and normal life. It becomes the supreme form of evil and a genuine test for the individual's commitment. There is never any suggestion that you can join the war and try to save your life. Joining is already a form of compromising acceptance. Only in *Fergus Lamont* (1981) do we find an oblique, ironic presentation in which war becomes an instrument of promotion and success, at least until the final chapter, which serves to take the reader back to the realities of the blitz. For such a demanding moralist as Jenkins, the only acceptable answer implies a rejection of war and of everything that is associated with it. It is not enough to say 'I'm not responsible. I did not see the bomb fall.' Jenkins's response is 'What did you do to prevent the bomb?'

In a similar way, Jenkins would have objected to Linklater's nonchalance. For the former there is hardly any escape and, in truly Presbyterian fashion, the only option is paying the price. Against expectations perhaps for writers who all experienced it, World War Two is not a recurrent theme in their fiction as if they had made theirs the Labour Party's motto 'Never again'. Readers are more likely to find an oblique presentation in which the war stands as a background or a symbolic message (Jenkins' *Cone-Gatherers*). The war is hardly evoked in Kennaway's novel of army life, *Tunes of Glory* (1956). And in the case of Linklater the contrast is striking between his autobiography, *Fanfare for a Tin Hat*, steeped in military action, and his novels of escape. Though their lives overlapped, Jenkins and Linklater expressed views that are almost antithetical. In Linklater's work, disaster is kept at a distance, neutralised by comedy and a definitely optimistic spirit which chooses to enhance what is positive in human experience. Jenkins, on the contrary, constantly swerves between hope and despair, but, as one character of *The Cone-Gatherers* puts it, 'The human mind [. . .] ranges from heaven to hell; and usually stays a long time in the latter place.'

In spite of the diversity of their works, the writers discussed in this chapter also provide evidence that, over the period considered, Scottish fiction was never as rooted in the national territory as might have been expected. Jenkins spent some ten years outside Scotland and wrote about Malaysia, Afghanistan and Catalonia. Linklater himself, with an English grandmother and a Swedish grandfather, was born in Wales, then lived in England and elsewhere. His most famous novels are set abroad – Italy, America or China. Kennaway settled in England early in his career. And for Edinburgh-born Muriel Spark, it was chiefly Italy that provided both the escape and the sense of exile. In their own way, each expressed dissatisfaction with the Scottish experience, ranging from outright rejection to painful compromise, hence the numerous tensions we find in their works.

Although, at the beginning of his career,[2] Jenkins praised attachment to the country, he became more and more conscious of the limitations imposed on the Scottish writer and found himself in an uncomfortable position, torn between loyalty to the nation and the appeal of novelty and new themes. Although he later came to express doubts about his departure from Scotland, he found that his books on Afghanistan and Malaysia (*Dust on the Paw, The Holy Tree, A Figure of Fun*, for example) offered a welcome opening towards new cultures, provided opportunities to parallel East and West and helped to reduce the feeling of parochialism that has haunted discussion of Scottish literature. James Kennaway started writing about Scottish society in *Tunes of Glory* (1956) and *Household Ghosts* (1961), but, inevitably, his imagination was attracted to the circles that surrounded him in London. 'It never crossed Kennaway's mind that he should ever live in Scotland,' wrote Trevor Royle, his biographer,[3] adding that 'he had no interest in the everyday concerns of contemporary Scotland and its society, which he disliked for its "touchy patriotism and conservatism of an unbelievable fast hue"'. And yet the rejection is never final, which adds interest and complexity to Kennaway's situation and makes him a good example of the divided loyalties we find in the writers of the post-war period. Even in the most 'English' of his books, there is always a double perspective. Not only is the Scottish connection usually preserved via a character embodying some positive values of the old country (truth, loyalty, courage, political commitment, working-class attachment), but the way his novels develop often shows that it is not easy to eradicate this origin. Although the circles he depicted were close to a tradition which looked more English than Scottish, the English middle class provided no model of excellence for this 'exile who cannot conceal his affection for home',[4] in a manner reminiscent of Robert Louis Stevenson. As for Muriel Spark, her departure from Scotland took place early, at the age of nineteen, but it would have been inevitable so imperious was her quest for experience outside the narrow circle of Edinburgh life. Eventually, the quest for experience turned into a sense of deprivation, a 'constitutional exile', as she felt she was 'moving from exile to exile'.[5] Consequently, her themes reach beyond Scotland to encompass an international experience that includes London in *The Ballad of Peckham Rye* (1960) and *The Girls of Slender Means* (1963), New York in *The Hothouse by the East River* (1973) and Geneva in *Not to Disturb* (1971), to mention only some examples.

The most internationally successful Scottish novelist of her generation, Spark also raises the question of national identity and the freedom of imaginative art to go beyond national boundaries. In the same way, we could ask: where are the Scottish elements in Linklater's two most famous novels, *Juan in America* and *Private Angelo?* The defence would argue that these are only two examples in a production which does include books about Scotland, some of them going back to early Scottish history as in the pre-war novel *The Men of Ness* (1932). Or that a widening of imaginative territory does not imply a betrayal of one's roots. It may even be welcome.

One writer who expressed an almost excessive attachment to his roots is Fionn Mac Colla (Tom MacDonald), certainly an exception among the writers considered in this chapter. The internationalism displayed by Linklater, Spark or Kennaway finds little echo in his output which is limited both in size and range. Although his first book was published as early as 1932, the rest of his novels appeared after 1945, and even some of those posthumously. Most of *And the Cock Crew* was written in 1935, but the book was published only ten years later, in 1945. What they have in common is an attachment to the Highlands which is nowhere better expressed than in *The Albannach* (1932), the story of an adolescent in conflict with his family and community who decides to leave for Glasgow. The book, like other titles by Mac Colla, is a passionate hymn to Highland culture, its language and traditions, a lament for the past and a powerful indictment of the modern city. If the modern novel put an end to the tendency to look backward with nostalgia, as it has been claimed, then Mac Colla is an exception, belonging more to the spirit of the interwar period than to the second half of the twentieth century, though he shares many elements with Iain Crichton Smith.

Mac Colla is also an exception in the way he writes about religion, a theme which had always permeated Scottish literature, but which, by 1945, was beginning to lose its prominence just as the Church was releasing its grip on society. Running against the current, Mac Colla turns repeatedly towards this theme, with the risk of endowing his oeuvre with a definite old-fashioned aura, though it is not devoid of coherence. The blight affecting the Highlands has a name: the Presbyterian Church. It is this desolation that Mac Colla's books lament endlessly:

> [T]hen the dark days came, with a new kind of religion that changed old ways, stopped the song on the lip, and let the wind out of the pipes with a squealing of drones. Then the folks began going abroad till none were left, but the old people and bairns.[6]

The Ministers (1979) is a rather stilted narrative that bears evidence of Mac Colla's interest in intellectual debates. Another minister is at the centre of *And the Cock Crew* (1945), once more a story of divided loyalties. As in *The Albannach*, the contrast between two of the main characters, Maighstir Zachary, the minister, and Fearchar the poet, embodies a fundamental opposition between two visions, although here the minister is genuinely in doubt about the impact of the Clearances. Mac Colla's investigation into the causes of present disorder was carried further in *At the Sign of the Clenched Fist* (1967), an ambitious intellectual analysis which again confirmed his interest in metaphysical debate.

Dissatisfaction with religious orthodoxy extended into the second half of the twentieth century. Mac Colla, like Spark, opted for Roman Catholicism. There was no need for such conversion in the case of Robin Jenkins. A non-believer, he was brought up in a family in which religion hardly counted and he never contemplated joining a particular Church.[7] Yet, a quick glance at some of his titles is enough to suggest an obsession almost as deep-rooted as Mac Colla's, though more subtle. *Some Kind of Grace* (1960), *A Toast to the Lord* (1972) and *A Would-Be Saint* (1978) develop the paradox of a writer who claims no particular attachment to religion, but whose imagination is permeated with religious motifs, either to produce satirical portraits of religious fanaticism and narrow-minded behaviour or express a need for spiritual values dramatically absent from our secular world. At a time when morality was becoming slightly old-fashioned in fiction, Jenkins – like Mac Colla perhaps – may have been running against the tide, but he insisted that his were the only issues worth considering. Though it is possible to place his work in a Scottish tradition which has often been obsessed with evil and the distinctions between right and wrong, Jenkins is never more fascinating than when he goes beyond clear-cut oppositions to indulge in the ambiguities of moral positions: the 'holy fool' caught in his own trap (*The Changeling*, 1958; *A Figure of Fun*, 1974) or the arrogant egotist who feigns pangs of conscience (*A Very Scotch Affair*, 1968; *Fergus Lamont*, 1979).

Muriel Spark shares with Jenkins the problem of 'how to write about religion in a world that has lost faith'[8] and an ability to distance herself from her work. Both are interested in moral issues, have a keen eye for the absurdities of human behaviour and favour oblique presentations that give scope to irony. They also meet in a similar taste for distortions which, eventually, verge on the grotesque. When Spark confesses '[W]hat I write is not true – it is a pack of lies,' Jenkins echoes by saying, 'I love writing things that are not true.'[9] Though Spark is not a writer that Jenkins usually mentions among his favourites, there is no doubt that a novel like *The Ballad of Peckham Rye* (1960) which centres on a fraudulent, though charismatic, intruder who disrupts the small world of a London suburb bears similarities with some of Jenkins's works.

Although Muriel Spark's background was part Jewish, part Church of England, and although she left Scotland early, she could not avoid the moral influence of her native city. 'I think the puritanical strain of the Edinburgh ethos is inescapable,' she wrote.[10] Like Jenkins and Mac Colla, she is haunted by the permanence of evil. Occasionally, it even becomes a form of pure evil, 'at first too incredibly evil to seem real' as Fleur Talbot realises in *Loitering with Intent* (1981). Like Jenkins, she writes about the moral consequences of individual action, a responsibility which is all the more formidable as it concerns a person having power over others, as in the case of Jean Brodie. A teacher, she has the responsibility of shaping girls into adults, but where she is wrong is in the fact that she considers her pupils as extensions of her own self. 'She has elected herself to grace,' says Sandy in the book, just like the heroine of Robin Jenkins' novel, *A Toast to the Lord* (1972). In that book, Agnes Tolmie, like the hero of Hogg's *Confessions of a Justified Sinner*, is persuaded that she can do no wrong since she has God on her side. Jean Brodie, like Agnes Tolmie, is also responsible for disaster without even realising it.

This religious emphasis in at least three of the writers represented here may appear unexpected in mid-twentieth-century writers, when religion was already sharply on the decline. On the one hand, it stresses how difficult it was to get rid of the negative impact which, in Scotland, the Church exerted on society and on the collective imagination up to the second half of the century. On the other, it enhances the paradox of writers who, though not necessarily religious believers, expressed their dissatisfaction with a dominant materialistic society and their need for spirituality.

All the novelists considered were close observers of their society, but differences in their own backgrounds and their main interests explain why they do not show the unity that might be expected in a period celebrated for the attention paid to social realism, political commitment and recognition of the working class as major components of society. The Scottish novel, over that period, continued to develop separately, with little similarity with the contemporary English novel. We do not find, for example, in the books under examination a counterpart to what has been called 'the condition of England novel', an attempt to scrutinise the social and historical situations of postwar Britain carried out in a predominant vein of social realism reminiscent of nineteenth-century fiction. It would be difficult to talk of 'the condition of Scotland novel' as writers under discussion not only tended to locate their works within a personal context, but also expressed doubts about a purely national perspective. It is, indeed, debatable whether these writers' ambition was to represent Scotland and Scottishness. In this respect, the contrast with Lewis Grassic Gibbon and Neil Gunn is clear. As we have seen, for many of them the priority was to distance themselves from Scotland, either geographically or spiritually. This was true for Linklater, Spark, Kennaway and, to some extent, Jenkins. Only in Mac Colla's work do we find a definite attempt to present what looks like the state of the nation, however negative the verdict may be. Yet, we also note that his world, the rural world of the Highlands, was already estranged from the experience of the majority of people living in Scotland at the time. The amount of attention paid to the past is another dissociation from the realities of the present. Mac Colla is also the only writer who insisted on the importance of national identity and whose political views expressed this commitment. He was one of the first members of the National Party of Scotland, as early as 1928, and when asked to give a brief summary of his life and career he started with the words 'I was from as far back as I can remember a – horrid, inadequate word – nationalist.'[11] Jenkins's position is more difficult to assess in so far as he always refused any party affiliation, but the intensity of his national commitment can hardly be questioned, though he was often torn between feelings of pride and disgust. Like many others, he was ready to put the blame on the English 'for Scotland being the wee dump that it is', a statement which says as much about the author's longing as his despair.[12]

It is also true that this selection of five writers leaves out a number of others, whose first work appeared somewhat later, who may have paid more attention to social conditions, among them George Friel, William McIlvanney, Gordon Williams and Archie Hind. Although the working class, which had appeared significantly in the production of inter-war fiction,[13] provides a background for many of the early novels of Robin Jenkins, plots tend to focus on individual issues more than on collective interests or perspectives. The industrial worker seldom appears in his work, and neither does he in the novels of his contemporaries. The plot of his first book is exemplary of this withdrawal from work-related issues: *So Gaily Sings the Lark* (1951) tells the story of a disenchanted young man who leaves the mining district where he grew up for the promises of a quieter rural village. Kennaway's Scottish novels are set in a similar environment (rural Perthshire here) though they have little trace of romantic idealism. Mac Colla's favourite background is the Highlands. The Scottish city seldom offers an essential component of narratives and when it appears, in *The Albannach* (1932), the picture evokes hell on earth.[14] Spark's *Prime of Miss Jean Brodie* (1961) presents interesting glimpses of Edinburgh in the 1930s, a multi-faceted city whose 'puritanical strain' was 'inescapable'. For Robin Jenkins the city is Glasgow, but once more it is its moral nature that attracts the writer. 'The unrelenting morality of his native Glasgow could not be shaken off' reflects the hero of *A Very Scotch Affair* (1968), but for Jenkins the issue is a reconciliation between spiritual progress and the handicaps attached to the modern city (violence, destitution, ugliness). Often it seems that survival is to be found away from the city, in some bucolic, utopian rural village – *Guests of War* (1956), *The Changeling* (1958) – but the country is never exempt from evil. Jenkins' message is probably closer to the lesson in *Fergus Lamont* (1981): a return to the city of one's origins is necessary, however painful it may be. To find a convincing representation of modern city life, one must turn towards Kennaway's London novels such as *The Bells of Shoreditch* (1963) with its representation of business circles, glittering champagne parties and a less appealing view of the infancy of Metroland.

Of all the writers examined here, Kennaway is the one whose work projects a definite image of post-war Britain. His plots may revolve around family affairs, stories of lies and betrayals, and his narratives may resort more and more to dialogue, yet the social and political context is never allowed to go unnoticed. References to the main issues of the period (devaluation, currency crises, Suez, the Algerian war, student protest, prime ministers) root the stories in a context whose uncertainties seem to echo the human crises when they do not simply provoke them as in *The Bells of Shoreditch* or *The Cost of Living Like This*. 'Long ago in 1945 all the nice people of England were poor': the opening words of Spark's *The Girls of Slender Means* (1963) projects an ironic image of fairy land which should be taken cautiously. The bomb buried in the garden actually explodes near the end of the plot, shattering to pieces the utopian world of the May of Teck Club. And the hero of Linklater's *Position at Noon* (1958) is the bankrupt descendant from an old family whose only prospect of survival lies in running away from wife, children, mistress and debts. None, however, depicts such a bleak world as Jenkins, the disenchanted world of post-war Britain seen through the lens of a Scottish novelist who does not seem to be living in the same society as that of Harold Macmillan's 1957 remark, '[M]ost of our people have never had it so good.' *Happy for the Child* (1953), *The Thistle and The Grail* (1954) and *Just Duffy* (1988) tell the same story of deprivation and spiritual blight which colour much of the Scottish fiction of the period, a darkness which, occasionally, is relieved by humour and compassion, but which leaves little doubt about Jenkins's pessimism.

Many post-war novels, including Scottish ones, can be considered in terms of a reaction against 'the asocial experimentation of modernist fiction'.[15] The writers mentioned here do not foreshadow the evolution, indeed the revolution, which was to be so noticeable when Gray's *Lanark* (1981) appeared. All are writing within conventional norms inherited from the nineteenth-century realist novel, with occasional breaks in the regularity of the narrative: Robin Jenkins's *Fergus Lamont* with its double voice or Kennaway's *Household Ghosts* with its switches from one narrator to another. Only in Muriel Spark do we find a constant fascination with the favourite modes of modern fiction (time shifts, multiple perspectives, irony) and an insistence on the artificiality of novels, in works such as *The Prime of Miss Jean Brodie* or *Symposium* (1990).

These novelists do not represent the whole production of the mid-twentieth century, but they indicate the most significant directions which fiction took over a period which covers years of great political and social change, and showed interest in renewing the modes of modern fiction.

Analysis confirms a verdict which has been made before: generalisations are dangerous, the concept of a distinctive Scottish novel is perhaps more problematic than may appear. None of the novelists mentioned here is writing within a clearly identified tradition. On the contrary, they are all trying to express very personal views which are, inevitably, coloured by their different backgrounds, experiences, philosophies. They do not even share the same Scottishness. At least three of them clearly set their works within an international perspective, which may indicate that the idea of oft-lamented parochialism in Scottish fiction should be revisited. Muriel Spark, Eric Linklater, James Kennaway, even Robin Jenkins, never give the impression that they were prisoners of the Scottish scene. They appear so liberated that, sometimes, it is even difficult to find the connections. Nor is allegiance to the working class a constant element of their works: in their association with the middle class, they follow the evolution of literature in general and of Scottish society in particular, though they maintain a high degree of critical independence. The one feature that they tend to share is a recurrent preoccupation with moral issues and the consequences of one's actions. Only in Fionn Mac Colla is this near-obsession closely associated with the Church, but it gives Scottish post-war fiction a distinct spiritual and moral tone which is absent from much of the period's English fiction.

Linklater's fiction of survival may have been echoed by the title of William McIlvanney's book of essays, *Surviving the Shipwreck* (1991), but the two do not share the same views of what was at stake. In contrast with the writers belonging to the previous and the following generations, political issues seldom appear, even when writers were known for their personal political views. Their concern dealt with more private issues (faith, commitment, preserving spiritual values or one's integrity). The imperatives of survival condition, if not a grim outlook, then at least views devoid of idealism or nostalgia for the past. In that sense, such writers are coming to terms with the realities and complexities of the modern world within their period. Following them, a new generation was to carry that quest further into the realms of language, narrative technique, politics and social dissatisfaction. Yet, judging from the tone of their books, the need for survival is still there.

CHAPTER ELEVEN

Arcades – The 1960s and 1970s

Ian Brown and Colin Nicholson

At the 1963 Edinburgh Festival drama conference in the McEwan Hall, a naked woman was wheeled across the gallery. Following Lord Curzon's injunction, the lady did not move; the event lasted less than a minute; the ensuing tabloid stramash was lively. Jim Haynes, Kenneth Tynan and John Calder put together this 'sixties happening'. Calder and Haynes had organised a 1962 Festival International Writers Conference, a highlight being the mutual contempt of Hugh MacDiarmid's (1892–1978) calling Alexander Trocchi (1925–84) 'cosmopolitan scum' and Trocchi's riposte: 'stale porridge'. Elements of this hint at four constituent transformative strands in 1960s and 1970s Scottish literature: affront to established *genii loci*, new performative modes, more cosmopolitanism and domestic revitalisation.

Transformation was not, of course, just positive. Edinburgh had been a great, even a world, publishing centre. This faltered when, in 1962, the Thomson Organisation bought Nelson's, leading to that great firm's break-up: Edinburgh operations closed and in 1968 printing facilities were sold. This began a slow, steady attrition of old, important publishing firms that continued and worsened into the 1980s and 1990s. Oliver and Boyd, bought by the *Financial Times* in 1962, closed in 1990. In 1980, once-titanic William Blackwood and Sons merged with Edinburgh printers Pillans and Wilson. Large Scottish publishers were losing identity. Even William Collins was taken over by Rupert Murdoch's News Corporation in 1987, and merged with Harpers of the US. Yet small independent publishers emerged. In 1973, Canongate was founded, while in 1969 Edinburgh University Student Publications was established, later becoming Polygon.[1]

Both literary and publishing transformation happened during globalisation's and mass television's first major impact. Commercial television launched in Scotland on 31 August 1957 and BBC2 started on 19 May 1964. The Edinburgh Festival's development as a producer of influential international work was well-established. Its first, 1947, manifestation featured Louis Jouvet's production of Molière's *L'École des Femmes*, inspiring Robert Kemp's 1948 *Let Wives Tak Tent*. By the early 1960s, the Festival and Fringe delivered international innovative exploration. A 1962 Fringe production in the basement of Jim Haynes's Paperback Bookshop, by George Square, led to the Traverse Theatre's 1963 foundation in a former doss-house and brothel in James Court, David Hume's Old Town address, off the Lawnmarket. Initially, this theatre presented somewhat traditional fare, including, for example, Shaw's *Candida*; quickly it found a new-writing identity, its first original play being Stanley Eveling's (1925–2008) *The Balachites*, opened on 30 July 1963.

Poetic change was also afoot, notwithstanding continuing and sometimes acrimonious argument about fit speech and preferred form that Edwin Morgan (1920–) in 1962 called 'the language problem, the problem of Scottishness'. His perception of its then-current evolution into 'something of an incubus', rooted in its feelings and effects – 'shake it off and you leave scars and puncture marks [. . .] making it all the more difficult for the Scottish writer to develop integrally'[2] – shows an impatience to move on. MacDiarmid's *Collected Poems* (1962) confirmed his pre-eminence as Scotland's major poet and laureate of Scots precisely when pressure for change was building soon-to-be irresistible heads of steam. After the false starts of the 1940s, it was clear that with *Riding Lights* (1955), MacDiarmid's close friend Norman MacCaig (1910–96) had, at forty-five, effected a remarkable make-over, finding a viable voice. *A Common Grace* (1960), *A Round of Applause* (1962), *Measures* (1965), *Surroundings* (1966) and *A Man in My Position* (1969) mark MacCaig's emergence as the major Scottish craftsman in English. Between the guardian of Scots, impatient with transgression, and the practitioner of English lucidities whose Scottishness is undoubted, we read polarities that animated verse production. Iain Crichton Smith (1928–98) developed autobiographical myth as grounding framework for his explorations of Gaelic culture's crisis and his own alienations from and accommodations with his upbringing's repressive ideology, bringing a taut, incremental, psychologically-driven prose that has left deep marks on Gaelic writing. He moved into fiction to fund his poetry. His first and finest novel *Consider the Lilies* (1968) existentialised the Clearances' impact through its ageing protagonist Mrs Scott. He also produced a stream of vibrant and challenging stories and novels, many fictionalising, to profound effect, autobiographical memory and personal recollection.

Clearly such developments offered new ways of expressing and delivering literary works, whether through new spatial relationships (the transverse Traverse so-named by happy misnomer) or Beat Poetry's new forms. London's landmark 1965 Albert Hall *International Poetry Incarnation* saw Trocchi scheduled alongside Allan Ginsberg, Adrian Mitchell, Gregory Corso, Lawrence Ferlinghetti – and Hugh MacDiarmid. Meanwhile, Scottish poetry's cosmopolitan scum – Morgan, Trocchi, Ian Hamilton Finlay (1925–2006) and Tom McGrath (1940–2009) inter alia – vigorously explored new expressive avenues. As Eleanor Bell observes:

Morgan, alongside other poets of his generation including Gael Turnbull, Maurice Lindsay, D. M. Black and Alan Jackson, has often cited the 1960s as a major source of inspiration – with the beginnings of space exploration, new forms of musical experimentation, the growth of counter-cultural forms and the importance of the Beat writers representing some of the most influential cultural developments.[3]

These were feisty, combative times for Scottish writers.

This was partly because political statehood's continued absence provoked continuing elaboration of cultural difference, a struggle as much internal to Scotland's regional variations as one of directly finding and developing international relationships by importation, translation or adaptation. The MacDiarmid–Trocchi spat followed a more serious confrontation in the same year, after the January *Scottish Field* carried an attack by Tom Wright and Hugh Rae on the 'attitudes and dogmas of the older poets'. Because a perception had developed that the 'Lallans boys' held most critical and editorial positions of influence, younger poets found 'a massive road block in their way'.[4] On 12 March 1962, *The Scotsman* provided national coverage to Edwin Morgan, who pulled no punches. He alleged established writers had 'not been notably sympathetic to the changes now taking place in Scottish poetry', leaving no doubt about whom he held responsible for cultural deafness:

> Mr MacDiarmid will have to find other grounds for his opposition: in particular he will have to come to terms with the criticism that his own kind of aggressive, dogmatic, proprietorial Scottishness may not be the best for Scotland, and may in fact be the very thing that is holding Scotland back at the present time.[5]

Despite perceptions of establishment refusal to engage (notwithstanding MacDiarmid's own 1959 welcome to the Beat generation),[6] radical change was well under way. Magellan for much pioneering navigation was Morgan, who in 1962 'published his "Beatnik in the Kailyard" essay, recommended the San Francisco poets in "The Beat Vigilantes" and wrote such poems as "The Death of Marilyn Monroe"'.[7] His *Poems of Thirty Years* (1982) show how much he trail-blazed during the previous two decades. Yet leaving him out of account demonstrates how widespread the movement for change was. An early sign of innovative energies was Ian Hamilton Finlay's first collection *The Dancers Inherit the Party* (1960), minimalism playing colloquial voice into patterned utterance to show up-to-the-minute awareness of West-Coast American practice. A year later Finlay's Wild Hawthorn Press, established in Edinburgh with Jessie McGuffie, published experimental collections by Louis Zukofsky, Lorine Niedecker and Jonathan Williams. Contemporaneously, Finlay established a poetry magazine called *Poor. Old. Tired. Horse* after a line in a Creeley poem. Morgan contributed; MacDiarmid thought the magazine 'utterly vicious and deplorable'.[8] *The Dancers* was followed by the combined Glasgow demotic, pictorial dimension and folk-tale idiom of *Glasgow Beasts, an a Burd, Haw, an Inseks, an, aw, a Fush* (1963), which Finlay described as 'a wee buik / for big weans', further provoking MacDiarmid's ire. But this bestiary was also based on the Japanese 'tanka', a form much older than the haiku, sometimes incised in stone. Finlay was already working towards the concrete forms that would contribute importantly to international avant-garde, not least through his poetic garden at Little Sparta, started in 1968. Meanwhile, Ivor Cutler (1923–2006) was exploring the surreal logic of the everyday though poetry, prose and children's books, but above all by performance. From 1959 on he was widely broadcast, worked with rock musicians (featuring in the 1967 Beatles film *Magical Mystery Tour*) and was taken up from 1969 by John Peel's and Neil Innes's progressive radio and television programmes. He became in time, in Peel's words, probably the only performer to be featured on Radios One, Two, Three and Four. He also performed on records, like the gently satirical 1978 LP *Life in a Scotch Sitting Room*, often accompanying himself on a harmonium.

Kenneth White (1936–) claimed of his first beginnings that 'as a Scot', he 'felt closer to America than to England'.[9] Yet, his sense of Scottish origin and upbringing feed a life-time's development of subjectivity impatient with ethnic or territorial definition and more rewardingly engaged with Gaia than with Gallup. Despite the 'intellectual nomadism' (the title of his Sorbonne doctoral thesis) of his life's work, the attention to natural phenomena he uses to secure his science-based cosmology was honed on Scottish landscapes. Though virtually unknown in Scotland then, White's work during the 1960s and 1970s marks a significant contribution to technique and possibility, repeatedly laying out a Scottish autobiography in other locations and perspectives, often exotic and always effectively rendered. The future University of Paris Professor of Twentieth-Century Poetics habitually specifies a Scottish speaker for adventures in cross-border relationships that refuse confinement by nationalist narrative. Another poet of similarly purposeful nomadism is Alastair Reid (1926–), also a prose writer and translator of South American writers. His poetry has a marked lightness of touch and a precision shared with his pellucid prose style. Like White, he has made his writing elsewhere, living, after war service, in Spain, France, Switzerland, Morocco, Greece, the United States and also in South and Central America and working since the 1950s for *The New Yorker*, while always remaining imaginatively grounded in Scotland.

Eschewing avant-gardeism for personal observation on native soil, and insisting on Scots as the language of feeling, Duncan Glen's (1933–2008) extraordinarily prolific output did much to sustain a conversational vernacular. He founded Akros Publications in 1965, editing the journal *Akros* until its demise in 1983. While a stream of Scots anthologies and other Scottish writing poured from Akros, inventive energies ran along several circuits. Robin Fulton's (1937–) quiet, reflective manner of self-definition, signalled by *Instances* (1967) and refined over the years, modulated different keys from much Scottish writing around him. From 1967 to 1976, he edited *Lines Review* and the associated books that Callum Macdonald's publishing house brought out, enriching the field by maintaining high standards.

Efforts to codify appropriate modes for writing in Scots continued, as did resistance to them. Finlay's use of local urban speech in *Glasgow Beasts* preceded the 1969 appearance of Tom Leonard's (1944–) first phonetic foray into working-class demotic in 'Six Glasgow Poems'. Radically politicised, and by turns hilarious and unsettling, Leonard's inventive sound world extends the field open to writing in Scots. It responds differently to Edwin Morgan's suggestion that while the 1920s 'MacDiarmid "renascence" of a general synthetic Scots [. . .] can still be felt, and learned from [. . .] the move should now be towards the honesty of actual speech'.[10] Partly for this reason Morgan welcomed Liz Lochhead's first collection *Memo for Spring* (1972), containing the seeds of her grittily ironised, working-class feminism. Morgan's promotion of actual speech also appealed to Robert Garioch (1909–81), who had started publishing in the 1940s. In the 1960s and 1970s his redactions into Edinburgh working-class speech idiom of Giuseppe Belli's racy, vulgar and blasphemous nineteenth-century sonnets in the Roman dialect become entertaining and insightful poems in their own right. What has been said of Belli (1791–1863) holds as true for his Edinburgh interlocutor: he has 'erected a lasting poetical monument' to the people of his city.[11] Change locations and something similar might be said of Douglas Dunn (1942–). After testing his mettle in Philip Larkin's city of words with his first collection *Terry Street* (1969), Dunn's return to Scotland marked a significant turn to history and politics lyrically conceived, best represented in his 1979 collection *Barbarians*. In manifold ways, Scottish selfhood – spatialised, ironised or provocatively reconstructed – is topic, theme and project in a variety of writing concerned to establish multiple possibilities through specific voice and context.

The resurgence of Gaelic poetry is often pinned to the cloak of Somhairle MacGill-Eain's pivotal *Dàin do Eimhir* (1943), but in many ways the 1960s and 1970s definitively broke the mould and saw the emergence of new poetic forms and the dominance, for the first time, of free verse and academic poets. Key voices were Iain Mac a' Ghobhainn (Ian Crichton Smith), mentioned above, and Ruaraidh MacThòmais (also writing as Derick S. Thomson, 1921–), whose three-part national and cultural allegories, and explorations of the internal tensions in his feelings for his home island of Lewis, heralded new intelligence and psychological honesty. In the 1970s both were to break further with traditional practices and images, MacThòmais in his punchily political collection *Saorsa agus an Iolaire* (1977), and Mac a' Ghobhainn in his iconic *Biobaill is Sanasan-Reice* (1965) and the 1974 collection *Eadar Fealla-dha is Glaschu*, introducing urban and urbane, sub-Beat rhythms, best witnessed in the Ferlinghetti-influenced 'An t-Òban' ('Oban') from *Biobaill is Sanasan-Reice* and from the 1974 collection, 'Innsidh mi dhut mar a thachair' ('I'll tell you how it happened'): 'Co-dhiù thug e gu m'chuimhne / cruachan-mònach, muir is teine, / etcetera' ('Anyway it brought to my memory / peat-stacks, sea and fire, / etcetera').[12] That vague but dismissive 'etcetera' signalled a defiance towards Gaelic poetic and cultural convention, evoked also in Derick Thomson's criticism, and the lively debates within his reliable and foundational journal *Gairm* (1952–2002). It was a period of cultural convulsion superbly captured by Ronnie Black in the Introduction to his *An Tuil*.[13] Another academic poet, Dòmhnall MacAmhlaigh, further pushed at the limits of verse form and of cultural, especially religious, questioning. He was also responsible for bringing Gaelic poetry much further into the Scottish literary mainstream with his *Nua-Bhàrdachd Ghàidhlig* (1976). This canonised, and in its Introduction put forth something of a retrospective manifesto for, the 'new' poetry in Gaelic in the work of five individuals (MacGill-Eain, George Campbell Hay, MacThòmais, Mac a' Ghobhainn and MacAmhlaigh) and, by appealing to the non-Gaelic reading public in this way, may be said to have further widened the gap between conventional Gaelic poetry and this new breed of poets.

It was not, however, the first publication in these decades to attempt to bridge the language gap in poetry. Iain Crichton Smith's translation of portions of *Dàin do Eimhir* appeared as *Poems to Eimhir* (1971), and through it Somhairle MacGill-Eain's work became known to a wider British and, importantly, also an Irish audience, having a signal impact on poets such as Seamus Heaney. This coincided too with MacGill-Eain's own re-emergence as a poetic voice, one that had not lost its political bite and resonance. His poems of the 1960s and 1970s are critically neglected, but can sometimes bring forward to the politically-charged atmosphere of the late 1960s the craggy, searching honesty and willingness to interrogate violence that characterised his earlier work. In 'Palach' (first published in *Scottish International* in 1970) he reflects on how once (like MacDiarmid) he would have welcomed the advance of the Red Army into the West, imagining a bonfire of money, and not the 1968 self-immolation in Prague of the student protester, Jan Palach, *an ceòthran* 'this little smoke'. This is added to the accusatory accumulation of smoke from the gas-chambers, from Hiroshima, from China with a cryptic nod towards the other 1968 students in his closing lines 'Chan eil cheann-teagaisg 'nam chainnt: / tha dusan Palach anns an Fhraing' ('There is no text in my words: / there are a dozen Palachs in France').[14] He returns to the jarring antitheses of *Dàin do Eimhir* and *An Cuilithionn* (*The Cuillin*) in 'A'

Bheinn air Chall' ('The Lost Mountain') which appeared in a special *Lines Review* issue in 1970:

A chionn 's gu bheil Vietnam 's Uladh
'nan torran air Auschwitz nan cnàmh
agus na craobhan saoilbhir ùrar
'nam prìneachan air beanntan cràidh.

Dé'n t-sìorruidheachd inntinn 's an cuirear
Ameireaga mu Dheas no Belsen,
Agus a' ghrian air Sgurr Urain
's a bhearraidhean geàrrte 'san sneachda?

(Because Vietnam and Ulster
are heaps on Auschwitz of the bones,
and the fresh rich trees
pins on mountains of pain.

In what eternity of the mind
will South America or Belsen be put
with the sun on Sgurr Urain
and its ridges cut in snow?)[15]

Engagement with the new moment was not purely the younger generation's preserve.

Such radical reshaping of poetic space was complemented by radical reshaping of theatre space. As early as 1948, on Sadie Aitken's suggestion, Robert Kemp and Tyrone Guthrie converted the Kirk's Edinburgh Assembly Hall to produce Kemp's version of Sir David Lindsay's *Ane Satyre of the Thrie Estaitis* on a conventional thrust stage in an unconventional space, something widely explored later in non-theatre Fringe venues. In the 1960s, experiment in the very conventions of theatrical spatial orientation took off. The Traverse audience-stage relationship was developed further in the versatile second (Grassmarket, 1969) Traverse, while both the Festival's international companies and, increasingly, theatre events outside the Festival sought new production loci. In 1968, the just-vacated Festival box office in Cambridge Street on the current Traverse site was remodelled internally to present, in an irregular round, Jerzy Grotowski's Laboratory Theatre's *Acropolis*, a terrifying, mind-expanding exploration of (in)humanity setting a severely-edited Polish classic text in a concentration camp. Luca Ronconi's Haymarket Ice Rink promenade *Orlando Furioso* (1970) demonstrated imaginative theatrical potential in new 'found-space' audience–performer relationships. Many explored this further, including Tom Buchan with *The Great Northern Welly*

Boot Show (1972), and, later, Bill Bryden with *The Ship* (1990) and *The Big Picnic* (1994) and John Tiffany with *Black Watch* (2006). André Gregory's Manhattan Theatre Project *Alice in Wonderland* (1971 Festival), reconfiguring Grotowski's vacant box office "'[mirrored] the Vietnam War, or the Age of Aquarius", in the sense that it spoke to the widespread helplessness and loss of control experienced during that time'.[16] Richard Demarco (1930–), a Traverse founder, produced creatively, sustaining Scottish and international artists. He introduced Joseph Beuys's performance art and Tadeusz Kantor, whose *Dead Class* (1975), where Kantor himself acted teacher, presiding over seemingly-dead characters confronted by mannequins representing their younger selves, had particular impact. Demarco cross-fertilised thinking across literary, performance and visual arts. Yet he was far from alone: Hamilton Finlay and Tom McGrath were similarly pioneering. Such artists encouraged what the present authors have called border-crossing and 'Reconfiguration of the Possible',[17] which continues to mark Scottish literary culture.

It should not be thought, however, that innovation took place only outside established theatres. In the 1960s the Citizens' was an enterprising company within the framework of then-orthodox repertory theatre. Four particular productions mark its enterprise: Iain Cuthbertson directed Albert Finney in an innovative 1963 production of Pirandello's *Henry IV* and premièred John Arden's *Armstrong's Last Goodnight* (1964), while Michael Blakemore and Michael Meacham premièred Peter Nichols's *A Day in the Death of Joe Egg* (1967) and in 1968 presented the acclaimed production of Brecht's *Arturo Ui* starring Leonard Rossiter. The Close Theatre, the Citizens' experimental response to the Traverse, opened in 1965 and presented lively programmes until a disastrous 1973 fire closed it. Meantime, Edinburgh's Gateway Theatre had a strong policy of new writing until, when Edinburgh Corporation established the Civic Theatre at the Royal Lyceum in 1965, it voluntarily wound itself up to clear the way for the new company. Indeed, the Royal Lyceum Company, Gateway stalwart Tom Fleming being first artistic director, was the Gateway in another guise. Clive Perry, succeeding Fleming in 1966, took time to find his stride, but with a young Richard Eyre as associate, and from 1970 Bill Bryden, he initiated a new phase of Scottish playwriting. Many major playwrights of the next three decades emerged under him and his successor (1976–9), Stephen MacDonald, who, having spent three successful years at Dundee, came to Edinburgh with an enterprising new-writing policy, most of it in Scots. The many writers developed by Perry and Macdonald include Stewart Conn, Hector MacMillan, Bill Bryden, Ian Brown, Roddy McMillan and Tom Gallacher. The 1970s Lyceum was echoed and reinforced by the new-writing Traverse under Chris Parr's directorship (1975–81), which nurtured playwrights like C. P. Taylor, Tom McGrath, Billy Connolly, Michael Wilcox and John Byrne, as well as Dundee/Lyceum playwrights like

MacMillan and Brown. This new writing was complemented by the work of BBC Scotland's Radio Drama Department, led by Gordon Emslie and Stewart Conn: Hector MacMillan's *The Rising* and *The Royal Visit*, for example, were both broadcast before being produced in 1973 and 1974 respectively at Dundee. The Citizens' headed in another direction after Giles Havergal's 1969 arrival. His first season employed the traditional star-led repertory fare of his previous theatre, Watford Palace, including *Heartbreak House* with the then-young James Fox as a ludicrously unbelievable Captain Shotover. This policy failed and, in 1970, he and his co-directors, Philip Prowse and Robert David MacDonald, launched a *Hamlet pour épater les bourgeois* and, thereafter, decades of innovative, cosmopolitan productions. Visual imagery and stunning theatricality reinterpreted classics and engaged new writing, especially by MacDonald, that matched the Citizens' group aesthetic. While theatres like the Byre at St Andrews and Pitlochry seemed to present tamer fare, Joan Knight arrived at Perth in 1968 and within the limits of her contexts steadily subverted expectations. She presented, for example, the only Scottish professional production so far of David Hare's and Howard Brenton's controversial *Pravda* and supported new writing outside the big cities. Following the 1973 example of 7:84 (Scotland), various new touring companies sprang up, including Borderline (1974–) and Fir Chlis ('Northern Lights'), the first professional Gaelic-language company (1978–81)

For fiction, it seems retrospectively fortuitous that R. D. Laing's *The Divided Self* should have appeared in 1960, speaking directly as it does to the linguistic divisions constituting Scotland's psychological terrain. While his title could lead appropriately into any reading of Iain Crichton Smith (later to refer to himself as a 'linguistic double man'),[18] it covers a range of issues explored by novelists. Muriel Spark's *The Ballad of Peckham Rye*, also published in 1960, is readable as both extending Laing and foreshadowing a seemingly inevitable complicity between finished text and the Calvinist predestination that Scottish writers have customarily anathematised. The warping power of belief, and belief in power, forms the substance of Spark's next, *The Prime of Miss Jean Brodie* (1961): Brodie's connections with and disconnections from conflicted history and sexuality unravel a fate as inevitable as anything Calvin imagined. By 1970 Spark was negotiating, in *The Driver's Seat*, an impossible quest for self-definition in conditions of personal isolation, while the narrative explores a postmodern and apparently contradictory predicament of existential responsibility enmeshed in textual predefinition. Between *Dust on the Paw* in 1961 and *Fergus Lamont* in 1979, Robin Jenkins (1912–2005) produced a string of novels, further securing his 1950s reputation, where the quest for value by characters variously dislocated from community and context is both deepened and extended. Jenkins's fiction investigates contested relationships to Scotland's past and its unfolding present, including child characters uncertain of their origin that Cairns Craig considers 'one of the fundamental narrative tropes of the modern Scottish novel'.[19]

Three younger novelists led a new-writing surge: Alan Sharp (1934–), Archie Hind (1928–2008) and Gordon M. Williams (1934–). Sharp's *A Green Tree in Gedde* (1965) and its sequel *The Wind Shifts* (1967) delivered newly-direct writing about west of Scotland life and young disenchanted Scots' drift to London and the Continent. The proposed trilogy's third novel never appeared and, after producing a radio play and two more novels, Sharp moved to Los Angeles, becoming a highly successful screenwriter, often of Westerns, a genre he drew on for his *Rob Roy* screenplay (1995). Hind's *A Dear Green Place* was a sensation on its 1966 publication, winning the *Guardian* fiction award and becoming the object of media attention as representing a new approach to writing about Glasgow, breaking with its sometimes-mawkish gang-literature tradition. The novel is properly a landmark, opening an urban landscape in ways productively developed by Alasdair Gray, James Kelman and William McIlvanney. Famously, however, though Hind produced some Citizens' and Close Theatre reviews and novel fragments, *Fur Sadie*, he suffered writer's block, never fulfilling his rich promise. Williams's fourth novel *From Scenes Like These* (1968), again dissecting modern west of Scotland life, was highly regarded and shortlisted for the 1969 Booker Prize. Like Sharp, however, popular forms drew him, writing the 1969 *The Siege of Trencher's Farm* which was filmed as *Straw Dogs* (1971), ghost-writing autobiographies for footballers like Bobby Moore, Terry Venables and Tommy Docherty, writing for television and, with Venables, inventing the popular detective Hazell. For different reasons, all three were diverted from the initial impulse that made them such promising figures in the 1960s: clearly, for two of them the attraction of other media represented an irresistible draw.

George Friel (1910–75) at first sight parallels the work of these three, all of whom work within a realist tradition. Yet Friel achieves a very particular synthesis of realism and expressionism making his Glasgow a city both closely observed and simultaneously nightmarish, even chimerical. His first novel, *The Bank of Time* (1959), and last, *An Empty House* (1974), have been undeservedly out of print for a long time. When he is remembered, it is for his intervening Glasgow trilogy: *The Boy Who Wanted Peace* (1964), *Grace and Miss Partridge* (1969) and *Mr Alfred MA* (1972) with main characters dislocated and off-balance within their worlds. Against gap sites, middens, smoky pubs, back-closes and stairheads, they seek other values. The Boy, Percy Phinn, fantasises himself a philosopher, creating a bizarre religion of money. He sees himself leading his followers to higher values; they see him, for a time, as a soft touch. In his final flight to find himself – in London – he is lost, not even sure how to tip in a restaurant car. Miss Partridge seeks her vision of grace for her young neighbour Grace, her worldview in conflict with the back-close fumblings of her younger neighbours and down-to-earth priorities of her older ones. Mr Alfred seeks the solaces of literature while drowning in drink, disillusion and eventually delusion, seeing his city taken over by juvenile delinquency, violence and vandalism until in final phantasmagoric chapters he is confined by mental illness. Friel achieves distinctive clarity and intertextual definition. Standing in the challenging and stimulating space between James Hogg, Samuel Beckett and Alasdair Gray, he has not always received the recognition he deserves.

The 1970s also saw a resurgence of the twentieth-century development of the novel in Gaelic, following the stuttering start represented by the three novels of the 1910s and 1920s referred to in Cairns Craig's chapter. The outstanding contribution to the resurgence is surely Tormod Caimbeul's (Norman Campbell's) *Deireadh an Fhoghair* (*The End of Autumn*, 1979). Meg Bateman praises the 'organic form of this masterpiece and its sinuous streams of consciousness',[20] while Michelle Macleod and Moray Watson talk of its uncomplicated setting in which 'really only three characters [. . .] play an active part'.[21] Later in the same paragraph, they see the novel using 'three old friends to explore notions like memory, friendship, belief and fear [through] language [at times] slow and rambling, echoing the movements and thought processes of the ageing characters'. Some passages, they say, suggest traditional Gaelic poetry and the whole represents 'village fiction', yet offers 'a strong hint of modernism throughout and an important development in the Gaelic novel'.

In the screen genres, work by popular Scottish novelists was adapted. Ian Fleming's James Bond novels began the sequence of film adaptations with *Dr No* (1962) and Alistair MacLean's popular action novels were consistently transferred to film during the 1960s and 1970s, though these authors were often not recognised as Scottish. The dominant representation of Scottish life on television was often sentimentally, regressively and typically embedded in *The White Heather Club*, presented on BBC between 1958 and 1968. Certainly the programme never commended itself to the intelligentsia then nor has it since. Yet, at its peak it was watched by ten million viewers and made Andy Stewart an international star. Television was, nevertheless, the most fruitful screen medium in terms of recognisably Scottish prose adaptations. Neil Munro's (1863–1930) work was first presented as a series of six episodes, *Para Handy – Master Mariner*, in 1959–60 starring Duncan Macrae. Three subsequent series, *The Vital Spark*, written by Bill Craig, starred Roddy McMillan between 1965 and 1974, and, later, two series in 1994–5, *The Tales of Para Handy*, starred Gregor Fisher. A. J. Cronin (1896–1981) inspired *Dr Finlay's Casebook*, which ran to 191 BBC episodes over eight series (1962–71) and was later revived by ITV in new series (1993–6). Both of these series sentimentalised Scottish life, although the latter could address important themes. Original television writing complemented adaptations, though tending to comprise Scottish versions of established genres. The school soap *This Man Craig* (1966–7) employed Jack Ronder, Tom Wright, George Byatt and others; the historical romance, *The Borderers* (1968–70), employed Ronder and Bill Craig; and Eddie Boyd (1916–89) created the hard-boiled detective series, *The View from Daniel Pike* (1971–3). While none achieved *Dr Finlay's Casebook*'s impact, they did provide opportunities for Scottish dramatic talent, occasionally addressing less stereotypical topics.

This activity allowed significant talents to cut their teeth and the 1970s set new standards. Pharic Maclaren, producer of *Para Handy – Master Mariner* (whose director was the legendary James MacTaggart), produced the landmark 1971 BBC adaptation of *Sunset Song*, directed by Moira Armstrong, who had earlier directed episodes of *The Borderers*. In 1971, adaptations of George Mackay Brown stories, 'A Time to Keep', 'The Whaler's Return' and 'Celia', by John McGrath, directed by MacTaggart, replicated *Sunset Song*'s excellence. McGrath's *The Cheviot, the Stag, and the Black, Black Oil* (1973), first staged by 7:84 (Scotland), was broadcast in 1974. In the same year Armstrong directed for *Play for Today*, Maclaren producing, Roddy McMillan's *The Bevellers*, a Royal Lyceum 1973 première. In 1976 the same team provided *Clay, Smeddum and Greenden*, Bill Craig's adaptations of Grassic Gibbon short stories. As with the rest of Britain, *Play for Today* was a significant outlet for Scottish writing. These important adaptations created an atmosphere where Peter McDougall's (1947–) original Scottish trilogy could be broadcast. *Just Another Saturday* (1975), *The Elephant's Graveyard* (1976) and *Just a Boy's Game* (1979) explore 'crises in Scottish masculinity against a backdrop of sectarian violence, gangland mythology and post-industrial decline'.[22] All this represented some change from *The White Heather Club*'s – much-derided, yet much-loved – 'stale porridge'. By 1980, established *genii loci* had been affronted, new performative modes developed, cosmopolitanism embraced and the domestic revitalised. However disappointing the 1979 referendum outcome might be, transformation was afoot.

CHAPTER TWELVE

The (B)order in Modern Scottish Literature

Carla Sassi

The dynamic nexus constituted by interrelated processes of bordering, order-ing and collective identity has been amply investigated in the past twenty years from a number of different disciplinary and theoretical standpoints. 'Border theory' today is largely grounded on the work of American/Chicano cultural critics, who have investigated the power of boundaries as both literal and figurative barriers, fostering an essentialist view of culture and thus as commanding and violent tools of inclusion and exclusion; but who have also highlighted how borders can be valuably reread as sites of encounter, of 'politically exciting hybridity, intellectual creativity and moral possibility'.[1] If the power of borders is essentially divisive, in fact, the power of liminality is dialogic and affiliative. Seen in this perspective, borderlands potentially foster 'the opening [of] new forms of understanding,'[2] and indeed may become '*the* privileged locus of hope for a better world'.[3]

Even though Europe has a similarly dramatic and turbulent history of con-testation of geo-political boundaries, often generating conflicts and genocide, but also fostering hybridisations and precarious liminalities which continually undermine the orders created by mainstream cultures and by official state his-tories, European thought has seemed largely unable to offer a theorisation of liminal aesthetics as radical and wide-ranging in its implications as that articu-lated along and about the US/Mexican border. And yet, the border paradigm has discreetly inhabited European literature and literary studies in the past decades, to surface with growing intensity after the fall of the Iron Curtain – as witnessed, for example, by Triestine scholar Claudio Magris's writings on east central Europe, which, while focusing on the 'local', shifting boundaries of a specific transcultural macro-region, also provide an admirably wide-ranging corpus of reflections on the border as a complex, contradictory but extraordi-narily enriching experience. In his words, '[T]he border can be a stimulant or an obsession, an opportunity or a curse, a place where it is easier to know and love the other or easier to hate and reject him; a place to make contact or to exercise intolerance.'[4] In locating history and power in the liminality of the border, and in identifying in this a part of an important European paradigm,

Magris, along with a host of other writers and scholars, has valuably contributed to the ongoing construction of new, more flexible ways of rereading and retheorising the entrenched national/regional identities of Europe. And yet, so far, for understandable reasons, the greatest part of such a growing corpus of investigations has been mainly focused on what is regarded as the most divisive of borders – the ideal line separating western from eastern macro-regions, juxtaposing conflicting modernities and conflicting political values.[5] But how would such theories evolve if they delved further into the intricate network of Europe's marginal/ised and shifting national/(micro-)regional identities – in the continuous friction between the rhetoric of the border articulated by historical nation-states and numberless acts of resistance staged by intersecting, overlapping or bordering identities? The reply to such interrogation is obviously beyond the scope of the present chapter, which rather examines how the question of (b)orders – internal and external, real and symbolic – has been represented and theorised by Scottish critics and writers in the period between World War Two and the restoration of the Scottish Parliament in 1999. Yet even the articulation of a specific case study may contribute fruitfully to a more lucid articulation of European theorisations in this field.

By highlighting the centrality and exploring the specificity of the border paradigm in modern Scottish literature we do not intend to suggest that such a paradigm is the only interpretative key to Scottish literature. The subject is too vast and diversified for that. Nor do we intend to provide, due to obvious limitations of space, an exhaustive panorama of writers and writings involved with such a complex and cogent question. What follows is an attempt rather to map out some of the recurring or most significant attitudes and visions, and to identify in them distinguishing traits and lines of cohesiveness.

In order to provide a wider contextualisation, it is useful to point out that border-crossing as a thematic device is a recurring feature in post-Union Scottish literature. Walter Scott, Susan Ferrier and R. L. Stevenson, for example, not only staged it frequently in their novels, but also creatively reflected upon the value and power of linguistic, cultural, geographical and psychological borders. Nineteenth-century Scottish literary border-crossers like Scott or Ferrier – if a generalisation can be made – should be described as 'translators': they represented difference not with a view to promoting separation, but rather to bridging cultures. They envisaged a 'British' future when England and Scotland would be forced into increasingly combining relationships with one another, and yet would also be allowed to save their individual features. Their twentieth-century colleagues found themselves in a deeply changed political context when Scotland, with the demise of the British Empire, gradually shifted from the status of equal partner in the imperial enterprise to that of a marginal, culturally threatened 'region'.[6] In the course of the twentieth century the border between the two nations became more and more the site of encounter between a dominant culture and a resistant one – the dialogue turning more tense and problematic. The lack of a 'hard' border, along with the increasingly homogenising pressure from London and an internal difficulty in delineating a monolithic idea of nationhood, fostered in Scotland the development of multiple 'soft' borders and boundaries, along and across regions, social classes, dialects and languages. The gradual decline of the ideal of Britishness, defined in the eighteenth century as a 'genetic *concordia discors*' where different ethnic strains, individually clearly defined, contributed towards the building of a greater polity,[7] was not replaced by an ideal, univocal demarcation line separating Englishness from Scottishness, but by a turbulent proliferation of cultural boundaries, tearing not only self from other but also – as we shall see – self from self.

It is mainly at a creative level that, in the early twentieth century, this complex and extremely fertile context finds its most remarkable expression. Scottish Modernist writers like Hugh MacDiarmid, Lewis Grassic Gibbon and Catherine Carswell stage border-crossings – both as individuals and in their literary work – that in many ways differ from those of their nineteenth-century colleagues. Their urge to 'make sense' of a downtrodden and marginalised Scottishness is combined with a restless quest for new words and new concepts to reshape the idea of 'home', often against the grain of early twentieth-century dominant nationalist ideologies. MacDiarmid redefines Scottishness by valorising hybridisation and liminality; Gibbon, like Carswell, dislocates himself permanently in England, where he projects onto Chris Guthrie – the celebrated heroine of his *Sunset Song* (1932) – his own complex and painful borderland experience. Chris *embodies* the border – a border that indeed divides self from other but also tears self from self, as in one of the best-known passages of the novel:

> [T]wo Chrisses there were that fought for her heart and tormented her [. . .] you wanted the words they'd known and used, forgotten in the far-off youngness of their lives, Scots words to tell to your heart, how they wrung it and held it [. . .] And the next minute that passed from you, you were English, back to the English words so sharp and clean and true.[8]

Carswell's similarly painful negotiation with her selves, which led her to theorise that 'what we term identity' is a 'curious, frail thing',[9] also led her to explore over and over again her own liminal stance in terms of the intangible parameters of her being. Carswell challenged ontological fixed categories by juxtaposing her own individual experience:

> Most people, I have noticed, pride themselves, perhaps rightly, on their exclusiveness [. . .] I am inclusively constituted. I like aristocratic people and common people, British people and foreigners [. . .] I enjoy every sort of food and drink that human beings eat, and thrive on it.[10]

After World War Two, up till the 1990s, the (b)order remains firmly at the centre of Scotland's cultural concerns. The legacy of writers like MacDiarmid and Gibbon has a great impact on at least two generations of Scottish writers, who take on the task of (re)defining Scottishness, of setting new cultural boundaries and thus of reclaiming it from cultural humiliation or downright denial from the centre. Indeed, as Angus Calder has observed, '[T]he key to Scotland's story in the last third of the twentieth century was a swelling sense of difference from England' – a veritable 'addiction to difference'.[11] Twentieth-century Scotland then is a 'borderland' in more than one of the canonical senses: more and more contested *and* entrenched as a nation, it has become 'remote' from the metropolitan centres of Europe, which ignore, throughout the greater part of our period, its extraordinary cultural output. But Scotland is also a borderland in so far as its imagination gravitates obsessively around its own complex and shifting cultural boundaries – on the one side resisting assimilation to England and thus closing up against its southern border, on the other side opening up to the Continent and Ireland[12] through its writers, scholars and translators' impressive engagement to retrieve and valorise the lost networks of reciprocal making with other European countries.[13]

Scotland's 'swelling sense of difference', however, is not accompanied by a smooth or easy critical/theoretical debate on the nature and the potential of such 'difference': under the pressure of England's national(ist) rhetoric, unable to follow in Ireland's footsteps in claiming a postcolonial status, Scotland lacks ready-made models to make sense of its own predicament. Emerging from the indeterminacy which fostered MacDiarmid, Gibbon and Carswell's experimentalism, a gradual bifurcation of critical approaches to Scottishness becomes evident in the course of our period – for the sake of simplification we will describe them as 'nationalist' and 'post-nationalist'. As for the first approach, it comes as no surprise that in the post-war period the lure of traditional nationalism is powerful in Scotland, and that many scholars – perhaps inevitably, as such ideological framework is deeply ingrained in European culture – refer, implicitly or explicitly, to it. Within such framework, however, Scotland's complex predicament (of a multi-lingual, multi-ethnic stateless nation) can only be defined as inadequate at best, a 'failure' at worst. The well-known vein of self-reproach, or self-hatred,[14] marking both critical studies and literary texts in this historical period, may indeed be, at least in part, ascribed to Scotland's resistance at being assimilated to a narrow nationalist paradigm, as well as to the lack of adequate political/cultural models to make sense of its status. There are scholars in our period, however, who do appropriate nationalist discourse with a certain degree of confidence and manage to articulate an essentialist celebration of Scotland's literary tradition, defined as an organic and consistent construction, as is the

case with the writings of influential critics and literary historians like Kurt
Wittig[15] or Francis Russell Hart,[16] whose impact left its mark on generations
of critics and students. The gradual shift to a post-nationalist approach can
be largely ascribed to the growing authority of postmodern and postcolonial
theories, even though Scottish Studies scholars have been somewhat slow
in acknowledging such influence.[17] The questioning of the nationalist paradigm – which has undoubtedly undergone an acceleration in post-devolution
criticism[18] – and the search for an integrative or substitutive paradigm have
gone hand in hand with implicit or explicit questioning of the very concept
of national (b)order – an important sub-theme of the debate on Scottishness,
which discreetly surfaces in most critical writings throughout our period.
What follows is an attempt to gather and sift some among the most meaningful contributions in this field.

Cairns Craig in the essays collected in *Out of History* – all published in
the early 1980s – describes Scotland's as a peripheral culture by-passed by
history – 'invisible' in so far as not entirely assimilable to the 'organic core' of
'English' culture. Craig also questions the idea that the nation need 'be the
defining boundary of significant tradition, even if we continue to use "tradition" as a central concept in our critical vocabulary'[19] pre-figuring 'very different configurations in our "cultural maps"'.[20] 'If we look at the literary map of
Europe,' Craig continues, interpreting John Orr, 'what we see is not so much
a tradition as a series of peripheral writers producing, sometimes in complete
isolation, very similar world views.'[21] By calling for 'a mode of writing history
that can make sense of the formative role of peripheral cultures rather than a
mode of writing history which always subsumes the artist from the periphery
into the historical formations of the centre,'[22] and by revaluating Scotland's
'being between', Craig goes a long way to shift the critical focus on 'marginality' to that on 'liminality'. By debunking T. S. Eliot's myth of tradition and
claiming that 'culture is not an organism, nor a totality, nor a unity: it is the
site of a dialogue, it is dialectic, a dialect – it is being between'[23] he indeed
identifies in relational dialectics a new paradigm, apt to tell Scotland's predicament, but also to transcend it by linking it to transnational realities.
Roderick Watson takes Craig's theorisation a step further when he explores
the complexity of the cultural boundaries shaping Scottishness across and
along regions, languages/dialects, social classes.[24] Cultural resistance, according to Watson, is associated with the establishment and the celebration
of a distinctively polyphonic articulation of 'national' identity in literary
texts. He also formulates a post-nationalist agenda when, after remember-
ing how for Fanon the concept of the nation is 'the material keystone which
makes the building of a culture possible,'[25] he asks himself: 'Once that bridge
has been built – might we not throw away the keystone?' The bridge may
indeed collapse, but 'between the rabble and the bridge', 'beyond the ruins

of unifying discourses, grand narratives, unmediated narrative authority and singular national cultures'[26] there might be – Watson implies – the possibility of a new, different 'order'.

Alan Riach, in his investigation of Wilson Harris's 'fractal poetics', prefigures the same possibility, in more concrete terms. Riach explores the opacities of a complex writer whose work resists being pigeon-holed in traditional or even postcolonial categories and identifies consonances with Scottish writers. Harris's work, in his words,

> is a literature of fractal energies, and also a way of reading literature which keeps the fractal dynamics that shaped its creation constantly in mind. It follows that the securities Harris offers, like the securities offered by his contemporaries in Scotland, will be contingent, constantly deferring any achieved resolution.[27]

Riach borrows and adapts Benoit Mandelbrot's theory of the fractal (a model of many 'rough' or 'chaotic' phenomena in the natural world, such as the shapes of mountains, coastlines and clouds, revealing a hidden non-Euclidean, infinitely complex geometry) to highlight how the shapes and boundaries that one order of thought presents as meaningless chaos may indeed acquire a beautifully symmetrical meaning under the lens of another order. Rethinking the (b)order always requires a transgressive act of border-crossing, as implicitly suggested by Riach's making sense of Scottish literature through the rereading of a West Indian writer, but also through his interpreting a literary text by engaging a dialogue with scientific reasoning. Border-crossing, or border-defying, as a personal life-strategy as well as a strategy radically to unsettle and question nationalist constructions of Scottishness is enacted by Christopher Whyte, both in his poly-linguistic literary work (in English and Gaelic and as a translator from several European languages) and in the comparative approach of his criticism. His poetics are unmistakably a borderland poetics – his own (in)voluntary liminal status (as gay, as ex-Catholic in a predominantly Protestant country, as a non-native writer in Gaelic, as a self-uprooted scholar who lived in Italy for twelve years and has now settled in Hungary) is the privileged standpoint from which he can perceive both the value and the elusiveness of borders, as when he travels 'from central Europe down [. . .] to the coast of the Black Sea, beginning in one of these places that has names in three languages – Ljubljana, Laibach, Lubiana –' discovering 'a linguistic continuum that gradually transforms Slovenian into Bulgarian, embracing Croatian, Serbian and Macedonian', a continuum 'with transitions so multifarious and imperceptible' that it is impossible to 'say this is where one language stops and another begins.'[28] The idea of Scottishness, as can be inferred from Whyte's critical writings, can be preserved, if at all, only at the cost of its systematic displacement. R. D. S.

Jack, partly in line with Whyte's vision of trans-border cultural continuities, promotes a valuable model of 'transcultural nationalism'. His emphasis on the 'polymathic origins' (in cultural and linguistic terms) of Scottish literature, underpinning autochthonous ideas of Scottishness prior to 1707, as opposed to modern definitions of Scottishness, reliant on the myth of 'a homogeneous language called "Scots"',[29] also goes a long way to problematise Scotland's cultural boundaries.

Beyond 1999 Scottish criticism is marked by a growing interest in issues of liminality, of (b)order questioning/crossing. At least two essays are worth mentioning as they explicitly address this specific set of issues as central to the expanding field of Scottish Studies. Aileen Christianson's 'Gender and Nation: Debatable Lands and Passable Boundaries'[30] explores the work of twentieth-century Scottish and Irish women's writing and the question of 'how conjunctions and disjunctions between the marginality of our female-ness and of our nation are to be figured'.[31] Drawing on feminist and postcolonial theory, Christianson points out how conventional cultural boundaries have been largely constructed on male values, excluding women from a full sense of identification with the Scottish nation. In 'The Border Crossers and Reconfiguration of the Possible: Poet-Playwright-Novelists from the Mid-Twentieth Century on', Ian Brown and Colin Nicholson observe how an increasingly relevant number of writers have staged 'border crossing and boundary transgression in Scottish literature', 'working in different genres, even in different art forms and languages', thus identifying in liminality, both as a predicament and a strategy, a distinctive marker of contemporary Scottish literature and culture.[32]

As suggested by Brown and Nicholson, it is possibly at a creative level that the most interesting and consistent theorisations of the border can be gleaned. While writers are often subject to the same theoretical and ideological constraints as (academic) scholars are, they no doubt have a greater degree of freedom in dealing with or eschewing them as well as suppler tools and strategies to represent the complexity of a 'debatable land'. The following is an attempt to offer a survey of their contribution, structured on the three basic and interconnected properties of (b)orders: that of a site of resistance/containment (border-making); that of a site of passage or point of escape (border-crossing); and that of a site of encounter and hybridisation (border as liminal space).

Border-making in our period is largely an experimental activity, rife with tensions: the idea of a 'proliferation of borders' introduced at the beginning of this chapter is a figurative attempt to convey the complexity and the difficulty with which writers try not so much to define Scottishness (a normative goal that does not pertain to literary texts, which has nonetheless polarised the attention of generations of critics), but to make sense of their 'being

Scottish' as well as of being in the world. It is possibly appropriate to start this survey with Tom Scott (1918–95) – a scholar of medieval literature, a translator and a poet in Scots and in English. In his work the discerning eye of the medievalist, trained to recognise a European common, intercommunicative literary space across linguistic, religious and ethnic borders, colluded with the vocation of the poet/translator, searching and testing his native language (so he described Scots) against the literary languages of other countries/regions and ages, in an endeavour to re-inscribe Scotland's silenced literary voice in the 'English' as well as in the European canon. Scott's idea of being Scottish is largely grounded on linguistic (porous) boundaries, but also on social class and gender ones, as one of his most famous heroes testifies. Brand the Builder – giving a title to a long poem[33] – belongs to a well-established line of Scottish working-class male heroes, from Lewis Grassic Gibbon's Ewan in *Sunset Song* to William McIlvanney's and James Kelman's protagonists. For the celebrated folklorist, Gramsci scholar and ballad writer Hamish Henderson (1919–2002), who revisioned Scotland tracing the songlines and the oral culture of the 'people', boundaries are more explicitly social and ideological (centred on the socialist/communist ideal). Henderson identified the expressions of the 'subalterns' in the working classes, rural communities, gypsies and travellers, the counter-cultures on which Scottish national identity should/could be regrounded.

   If Scott's and Henderson's border-making entails intensive border-crossing, as both writers engage in an active dialogue with other European cultures, for other writers the same act seems to involve cultural as well as geographical closure, as with George Mackay Brown (1921–96), whose microcosmic Orkney islands – the privileged background of his fiction, as in his mesmerisingly poetical novel *Greenvoe*[34] – are a remote borderland, located at the geographical and cultural margins of Europe. Brown's regionalism, however, should not be seen simply as a seductive manifesto for cultural monogamy, but also as a response to Scotland's difficulty at imagining the national community along traditional tenets. Regionalism – as a reterritorialisation of national identity – plays a central and complex role in twentieth-century Scottish literature. The region does not necessarily have a metonymic function in this context, but works rather as a corrective paradigm, either restoring a civic ideal of continuity between place and *polis* (as in Brown or McIlvanney) or valorising individual agency/resistance as opposed to the homogenising effect of a conventionally constructed nationhood (as in Iain Crichton Smith).[35] Regional boundaries, as much as social boundaries, overlap and intersect, problematising but also closing the horizon of the Scottish (post)nation, as the continuity and transparency of the region is achieved at the cost of excluding those who do not belong to it – socially and ideologically, in most cases, rather than ethnically as is the case with most European nationalisms. In so far as regionalism valorises locality as a site of resistance to homogenisation or cultural imperialism, and in so far as the 'regional' community may suggest an 'affective community', regulated by friendship and *humanitas* as opposed to the coercive and impersonal structure of the (nation-)state,[36] this alternative model undoubtedly represents a valuable corrective paradigm. Yet the risk of regionalism sanctioning the rooted evils of exclusive nationalism are real and evident in the powerful literary strain that rigidly connotes Scottish nationhood as male, working-class and, ideologically, as socialist or republican.

Within this context, a gendered revision of 'being Scottish', gaining momentum in the last third of the twentieth century, has indeed opened up Scottish literature to new interpretative paths. Liz Lochhead's (1947–) *Mary Queen of Scots Got Her Head Chopped Off* is a kaleidoscopic re-appropriation of the myth of the most famous and most vilified Scottish female monarch, which goes a long way to debunk the spell of the (male) Scottish protago-nist.[37] The two queens – Mary and Elizabeth – reproduce the centuries-long history of enmity between Scotland and England and stand for the difference between the two countries. But while Lochhead's text deploys all the binary oppositions which traditionally represent the queens' antagonism (Catholic/ Protestant, virgin/whore, oppressor/oppressed and so on), the ironic anach-ronisms of the play and the fragmentation into the multiple female identi-ties adopted by each of the monarchs stage a deconstruction of traditional notions of (male/military) heroism and of patriarchal values on which such oppositions are largely grounded. Lochhead's queens, displaced in time and space, locked in bitter antagonism and yet very similar to each other, comic and tragic, realistically human and stereotypically iconic, regal and plebe-ian, playfully and seriously destabilise centuries of male-centred, monolithic representations of nationhood.

Not all questionings of the (b)order are playful. Glasgow-born and Lewis-raised, Iain Crichton Smith's (1928–98) liminal characters may be comic, but they are also marked by a deep tragic vein as bilingual, bicultural misfits who are hopelessly caught up between two enemy cultures. A great part of Smith's fiction in English was devoted to voicing the downtrodden Gaelic-speaking minority, historically locked up in a ruthless subordinate relation with the English-speaking majority. He was, however, one of the Gaelic writers, alongside Derick Thomson/Ruaraidh MacThòmais and Aonghas MacNeacail, who dared question the defensively essentialist values that still dominated both the English-speaking and the Gaelic-speaking communities, even though with different political agendas (aggressive for the former, defen-sive for the latter). Murdo, the native Gael who is the protagonist of his three semi-autobiographical novellas – 'Murdo' (1981), *Thoughts of Murdo* (1993) and 'Life of Murdo' (2001)[38] – is affected by a lucid 'madness', expressed in his inability to come to terms with the rigid polarisation of the two languages which structures the social life of the remote Hebridean island where he was born and lives (and – metonymically – of Scottish society at large). Murdo is both unable and unwilling to keep the two linguistic/cultural codes separate and to use them in their 'appropriate' context. His bilingualism then develops into a radical space that subverts hierarchies, and where separate systems of signification and different symbolic worlds are brought together in a relation of perpetual interference:

> He would find himself speaking as follows: 'I have much homework to do *an nochd*'. (The explanation for this is that he would start the sentence in English, then remember that his mother preferred Gaelic, and switch to that language. If he had spoken English to his mother she would have called him a snob and not a son of hers.) All this caused Murdo to appear very strange. Thus the reverse might happen at school and he might say, '*Chan eil mo* homework again'.[39]

Murdo is possibly one of the most radical of all Scottish liminal characters. To a greater extent than Gibbon's Chris, he *embodies* the border, which painfully cuts through his self, tears him apart. His de/constructive madness represents both a unique attempt to speak of the power and the value of liminality and to shape – albeit tentatively – a new order out of the old one.[40] Alasdair Gray's (1934–) *1982, Janine* (1984) takes us through a twenty-four-hour journey into the consciousness of a middle-aged, alcoholic failure – spiritually mutilated by the invisible boundaries (ethical, cultural, social, sexual) at work within Scotland's and Britain's culture and society. If for Murdo the piecing together of his sundered self is possible only within the restricted space of the literary text and the trilogy ends with a note of defeat,[41] for Jock, the narrator-protagonist of the novel, the same possibility seems slightly more concrete when, at the end of the novel, a new horizon opens up for him, as well as for the country he stands for:

> I will stand on the platform an hour from now, briefcase in hand, a neater figure than most but not remarkable. I will have the poise of an acrobat to step on to a high wire, of an actor about to take the stage in a wholly new play. Nobody will guess what I am going to do. I do not know it myself. But I will not do nothing. No, I will not do nothing.[42]

It would be difficult to find a more effective figuration of a proactive declaration of liminality in Scottish literature. There is both determination and uncertainty in Jock's fresh departure – a tight-rope walk towards a new, unknown and yet enticing order.

It is possibly appropriate to conclude this chapter with a brief reference to a novel that, written at the end of our period, shows remarkable self-consciousness about identity theories, and thus both links up with the works discussed so far and distances itself from them, heralding a partly different approach to similar issues. *Trumpet*[43] by Jackie Kay (1961–), awarded the 1998 Guardian Fiction Prize, is loosely inspired by the life of Billy Tipton, the American jazz pianist who was discovered to be biologically a woman after his death in 1989. The novel memorably stages the multi-liminality of Joss Moody, a black jazz trumpeter, African by father, Scottish by mother, woman by birth and man by choice – a character who questions (b)orders and boundaries by enacting freely his life choices and who nonetheless honours each of the categories/identities whose conventional boundaries he trespasses. Like other characters, he is the emanation of an author with whom he shares similar life experiences/ideologies: Kay is a black Scot of Nigerian descent, brought up in Glasgow by (white) adoptive parents, a lesbian and a committed poet and writer who has voiced the unease of those minorities who have been excluded from traditional mappings of Scottishness. Like Kay herself and unlike the characters of the novels discussed in the present chapter, however, Joss is empowered by his liminality to transform himself and to transform the society in which he lives.

In the changing/changed climate of the post-devolution age, 'discontinuity and adaptability have become Scotland's cultural trademarks',[44] as Schoene has pointed out. The post-nation, 'no longer regarded, or led to regard itself, as exclusively Scottish and thus found or finding itself lacking, becomes free to reconceive itself in broader terms [. . .] as situated within a vibrant network of interdependent cultural contexts'.[45] Here, the challenge which crushes Murdo and daunts Jock is at last turning into a concrete and joyous opportunity. And, from a theoretical standpoint, twentieth-century Scotland's hazardous and problematic quest for a new (b)order undoubtedly stands out as an immensely fertile and enticing field of inquiry.

CHAPTER THIRTEEN

The Seven Poets Generation

Robyn Marsack

Shortly after the 1979 referendum when Scotland seemed to have lost its chance for devolution, Alexander Moffat painted a generation of Scottish poets who, he thought, shared 'a passionate concern about Scottish history and culture [and] played the leading role, both in their verse and prose, in shaping the artistic conscience of this country'. He produced a series of individual portraits, based on sketches of the poets whom he travelled widely to see in their own homes. The group portrait, *Poets' Pub*, was an attempt to 'evoke the romance of Edinburgh's bohemian life of the late 1950s and early 1960s', when Moffat himself had encountered it. The space was a compound familiar setting, and the central figure is the poet who is now the most obscured of the group – Sydney Goodsir Smith – who died before Moffat began his series. 'I think all the others would have wanted Sydney to be the central figure: he was the great character of all the poets and wrote many fine verses about Edinburgh pub life.'[1]

This chapter explores the painting as an icon of Scottish literary culture, placing the poets in the context of their own male-dominated, literary milieu and, at the time the painting was made in 1980, not long after Margaret Thatcher had become prime minister of a Conservative UK government. This was a generation for whom Hugh MacDiarmid was exemplary, but his presence – at once stony and combustible – was succeeded by the shape-changer Edwin Morgan as the century tipped towards its conclusion. Morgan empowered the younger generation – not least the women, who generally found MacDiarmid's influence rebarbative and the pub door hard to open, unless as muse rather than makar. It glances at what lies outside the frame, too, at the poetic world that lay beyond the confines of the Abbotsford and Milne's bar, where the 'heroic laughter of Sydney Goodsir Smith could be heard [. . .] every day'.[2]

A detail of *Poets' Pub* forms the cover image for Murdo Macdonald's historical survey, *Scottish Art*,[3] in the series published by Thames and Hudson aimed at the general reader. It is perhaps a surprising choice: a McTaggart landscape, a Scottish Colourist's flowers or seascape, something by Charles

Rennie Mackintosh or one of the more recent Glasgow Boys might have been expected. But here is Scotland advertised as a masculine nation of smokers, drinkers and writers, perhaps convivial, perhaps argumentative – the facial expressions are neutral – certainly in an urban setting. It suggests that Scottish writers are as great an asset to the nation as its landscape, but raises the question of whether the Scottish poet is, necessarily, MacDiarmid's 'drunk man'.

Another group literary portrait comes to mind, William Roberts's portrait of the Vorticists at the Eiffel Tower restaurant with Wyndham Lewis, Ezra Pound and a new issue of *Blast* at its centre – figures similar to MacDiarmid in their energy and ability to stir things up in all directions. In Roberts's painting, set in 1915, but painted in the 1960s, there is a greater sense of a cohesive group, not bound by nationality but by the *Blast* manifesto. Even if all were not signatories, the ripple of controversy, subversion and determination to make things new (at a point when indeed the old world was being blasted to smithereens) spread out to all of them.

It is doubtful that the Scottish painting's poets were ever in the same room – even the same pub – at the same time. They did not sign up to any manifestos and, unlike the Vorticists, they in fact had strong rural connections: MacDiarmid by the 1950s was living in Brownsbank Cottage near Biggar; Mackay Brown returned to Stromness in 1962; MacLean was in Plockton; MacCaig spent much time in Assynt; Crichton Smith was teaching in Oban for over twenty years from 1955. As a collective, they did not exist; as drinking companions, as admirers of each other's work, as the public face of Scottish poetry in those years, they shared an identity fixed in the painting. Here, the central trio is of Hugh MacDiarmid (born Langholm, 1892), George Mackay Brown (born Stromness, 1921) and Sydney Goodsir Smith (born New Zealand, 1915), who seem to be in conversation; then three poets who look over the viewer's shoulder, in one direction: Norman MacCaig (born Edinburgh, 1910), standing casually, cigarette between his fingers; Iain Crichton Smith (born Glasgow, 1928, but brought up on Lewis), slightly anxious behind MacDiarmid, and over on the right-hand side, Robert Garioch (born Edinburgh, 1909), somewhat apart. Standing behind Crichton Smith, looking in the opposite direction with a faint frown, is Sorley MacLean (born Raasay, 1911), while Edwin Morgan (born Glasgow, 1920) sits next to Garioch but seems to gaze directly past MacCaig's shoulder, as though abstracted from the group altogether – and being a Glasgow poet not much given to drinking in the Rose Street pubs, this is perhaps emblematic. In the lower foreground, bearded and hatted and looking like a figure from a Wyndham Lewis painting, is the poet and MacDiarmid's biographer, Alan Bold (born Edinburgh, 1943).

The background suggests both the 'romance' and the politics of bohemian life, but also the realities of Edinburgh's streets: a naked Muse figure curled in a chair; the unsteady progress of a man negotiating steps with his stick (this depicts the art critic John Tonge, author of the pioneering 1935 *The Arts of Scotland*); an anonymous figure evoking despair; a figure recalling Robert Capa's famous photograph of a soldier shot in the Spanish Civil War; the Edinburgh skyline; and a figure with unfurled flag – revolution, perhaps with a hammer and sickle. The black-stockinged woman on the far right may be a streetwalker, or even one of the students who came to the Rose Street bars in the hope of seeing Scotland's best-known writers gathered there, like the narrator of Alasdair Gray's novel *1982, Janine* :

> The bar was crowded except where three men stood in a small open space created by the attention of the other customers. One had a sombre, pouchy face and upstanding hair which seemed too like thistledown to be natural, one looked like a tall sarcastic lizard, one like a small shy bear. 'Our three best since Burns,' a bystander informed me, 'barring Sorley, of course.'[4]

Unlike Roberts's tight (and exuberant) composition, Moffat's gives a sense of the international context from which these poets' work emerged and with which they engaged, as well as the specific location of Scotland's capital, home to only three of them, although both MacLean and Mackay Brown had studied there.

Despite Moffat's claim for Goodsir Smith's centrality to the imagined gathering, MacDiarmid draws the viewer's attention first, and remains the towering figure of Scottish poetry in that period. In 1952 he wrote an essay, 'The Dour Drinkers of Glasgow', for an American magazine, taking pleasure in defining the characteristics of Scottish pubs, which were for 'connoisseurs of the morose', none of those tarted-up places with music and arty effects – or women, really. True Scots, he writes, in a typical tone of unassailable authority:

> do not like the confiding, the intimate, the ingratiating, the hail-fellow-well-met, but prefer the unapproachable, the hard-bitten, the recalcitrant, the sinister, the malignant, the saturnine, the cross-grained and the cankered, and the howling wilderness to the amenities of civilisation, the irascible to the affable, the prickly to the smooth [. . .] In short, we are all poets (all true Scots – that is, all Scots not encased in a carapace of conventionality a mile thick) of *l'humeur noir* [. . .]

This will not quite do as a characterisation of the seven poets pictured with him, even if MacDiarmid himself – especially in his public role – answered to the extremity of the description. In this same essay he speaks of the Scot as having

> sloughed off his literature, history, native languages and much else over the past two and a half centuries. Another and equal mystery is the way in which he is

today resuming them [. . .] There is a widespread agreement that a great Scottish National Reawakening is in progress.[5]

MacDiarmid was willing to wait before pronouncing on that. (A dozen years later, he contested the seat of the then-prime minister, Alec Douglas-Home, in the 1964 general election, as a communist candidate, having broken with the Scottish National Party.) In the 1950s, MacDiarmid was publishing almost as prolifically as ever: *In Memoriam James Joyce* (1955), *Poems of Hugh MacDiarmid* selected by Oliver Brown (1956), *The Battle Continues* (1957), *Three Hymns to Lenin* (1957); in 1962 his first *Collected Poems* were published.

One vital figure missing from this group portrait is an Edinburgh publisher, described thus by Angus Calder in his obituary:

> It is also true that Callum Macdonald would often quietly be of the company. It was he who persuaded MacCaig to cease to be 'McCaig'. He published Iain Crichton Smith's first slim volume of poems, then, decades later, the collected poems of Garioch, and of his fellow Gael Derick Thomson. When he set up *Lines Review* in 1952, MacDiarmid, Sorley MacLean, MacCaig and Goodsir Smith were on his editorial board [. . .] Macdonald's outlook was never parochial. He was a man of wide vision, not a Milne's Bar groupie. A reserved, dignified Gael, he stood, fag and glass in hand, on the verge of many a literary gathering, where, with his immaculate suit and tie, he might have passed for a modest Highland draper accidentally present, but was actually a subject of awe among those who knew how devoutly he had obeyed his ruling passion for poetry.[6]

Looking at Scottish publications of the 1950s in the Scottish Poetry Library, Macdonald is the recurrent publisher: Alan Riddell's *Beneath the Summer* and Goodsir Smith's *Cokkils* (1953), Garioch's *Masque of Edinburgh* (1954), Smith's *Omens* (1955), Tom Scott's *An Ode til New Jerusalem* (1956), together with Serif, owned by the somewhat mysterious Joseph Mardel, who was also publishing Sydney Goodsir Smith – *Under the Eildon Tree* (1954) – alongside poets outside Moffat's frame like Maurice Lindsay and Derick Thomson. Smith had a third publisher in the venerable firm of Oliver and Boyd, which also published Alexander Scott's *Selected Poems* (1950) and George Campbell Hay's *O Na Ceithir Airdean* (*From the Four Airts*, 1952). Meanwhile, Mackay Brown was taken up by the Hogarth Press as Norman MacCaig had been before him, with *The Storm* (1954) and *Loaves and Fishes* (1959). MacCaig published *Riding Lights* (1955), *The Sinai Sort* (1957) and *A Common Grace* (1960).

Crichton Smith, MacCaig, MacLean and Garioch all made their living for many years as schoolteachers. Sutherland by day, Garioch by night, says, writing to a friend in 1961, that he likes 'being in Edinburgh, and I like meeting the literary boys, who are to be found in a strictly limited set of howffs [. . .] There is a good deal of sojourning to Calum [sic] Macdonald's late at night of a

Friday: he is very robust in his hospitality [. . .] It is a nice walk home over the
Meadows in the morning. N. MacCaig mostly presides everywhere, as is his
due.'[7] MacCaig spoke unreservedly of his love for MacDiarmid, yet managed
to follow his own path unswervingly: 'He must have altered the convolu-
tions in my brain [. . .] but he didn't influence me as a writer, because his wild
desires and powerful intentions weren't the same as mine at all.'[8] MacDiarmid
nevertheless thought highly of him, entitling his review of *Riding Lights*, 'The
Norman Conquest'. Dismissing most of modern Scottish poetry as 'soggily
and indiscriminately affectionate', he sees MacCaig's work as standing 'in the
sunshine of the Gaelic classical tradition', and adds a personal note: 'He is one
of the exceeding few in Scotland with whom one can have a thorough-going
technical discussion on literary matters,' and at ceilidhs in his house: 'A wor-
thier choice of piobaireachd and Gaelic songs can be heard than ever reaches
the microphone or the concert platform.'[9]

    The language issue is surely crucial: how are these men speaking, not so
much to each other – although Mackay Brown speaks of 'night-long word-
splurgings', sometimes carried on after the 10 p.m. closing time at MacCaig's
house – as to their readers? MacLean's reputation was heralded by his co-
publication with Robert Garioch of *17 Poems for 6d.* (1940), but it came
to rest on the *Dàin do Eimhir* (*Poems to Eimhir*) published in 1943, and even
in that truncated form – its full extent was not revealed until Christopher
Whyte's edition in 2003 – recognised as 'the greatest Gaelic book of this
century', as Iain Crichton Smith later described it; and on 'Hallaig', first
published in *Gairm* in 1952, his re-imagining of the Clearances on Raasay.
In 1952 also, Hugh MacDiarmid was claiming that MacLean's 'unpublished
An Cuillin poem is a great Communist poem and by far the greatest Scottish
Gaelic poem since the days of the '45'.[10] What place could Gaelic find in the
resurgent Scottish nation, if that was what it was? The answer is still unclear,
but it was MacLean who took into Gaelic poetry the politics of the twentieth
century and the lessons of poetic Modernism. And, importantly (and partly
through provision of concurrent English translations), he claimed the attention of the key arbiters of Scottish literature in mid-century, thereby staking
an unalterable claim for Gaelic poetry in the otherwise mainly non-Gaelic
speaking howff. While MacLean represents Gaeldom in the *Poets' Pub*, along
with Iain Crichton Smith, their near contemporaries George Campbell
Hay and Derick Thomson are shadow presences. Hay, a Gaelic learner with
a prodigious vocabulary and skill in the language, had entered a mental
institution in 1948 from which he did not emerge until 1960, but published
collections in English and in Gaelic in 1948, and a further Gaelic collection
in 1952. Ruaraidh MacThòmais/Derick Thomson, brought up in a bilingual
household in the same village as Crichton Smith, also brought out his first
collection in 1952, *An Dealbh Briste* (*The Broken Picture*). His influence on

subsequent Gaelic poets has been considerable, not least through his long guardianship of *Gairm*, the magazine he founded and edited from 1952 to 2002. The Gaelic poets have a possible contemporary readership of about 10,000 in their original language, Christopher Whyte has estimated, and he points out that their work is mainly read within the body of Scottish poetry in English translations, generally those made by the authors themselves.[11]

Obviously the dominant position of the English language was hotly contested by the poets of the Scottish Renaissance movement. Writing to J. K. Annand in 1955, Garioch asks:

> Do you realise that you and I belong to about the last age-groups to have spoken Scots as laddies in the ordinary way of life? I'm not sure, but I fear that must be about true, at least in places like Edinburgh [. . .] This resurrected word Lallans surprised me when I came home from the war, but the accompanying activity surprised me even more, and there seemed to be the exciting atmosphere we never used to have [. . .] But I don't care much what it is called, so long as there is interest, which there never was very much of before the war, or so I excuse myself for wasting such years of time and now I try to make up for it. But I find it very hard to get onto a clear line of development, and keep writing in different styles.[12]

Garioch was both in and out of the mainstream. Sydney Goodsir Smith noted in his Introduction to Garioch's *Selected Poems* that his first two books he 'printed himself on a small hand-press and sold personally by hand, too, which is probably the best way to sell poetry'. This volume was the first easily available and substantial selection of his poems but was not published until 1966, although Garioch was 'one of the best-known names in a Scottish literary movement that its enemies have amusingly called an establishment!'[13] His choice of Scots was, he said, for its music; but also as a reaction against a very English upbringing. The difficulty of writing in Scots of whatever kind, and of being published, persisted. Maurice Lindsay persuaded Faber and Faber to publish the pioneering *Modern Scottish Poetry: An Anthology of the Scottish Renaissance 1920–1945* in 1946, but could not prevail with a proposal to publish a collection in Lallans by himself, Goodsir Smith and Douglas Young. T. S. Eliot wrote:

> [I]t might be injudicious from your point of view to have such a book brought out in London. It would imply to many of the public the suggestion that Scotland was unable to publish its own poets and that recognition, like everything else, had to be centred on London.[14]

Or as Garioch put it to Michael Schmidt thirty years later, '[I]t may be that selling Scottish books in Scotland is like selling breeks to Heilanmen'.[15]

Such difficulty was compounded when the language used was Sydney Goodsir Smith's, 'a language he invented and which no one else ever wrote or spoke or could conceivably have done', wrote MacDiarmid, who compared him at various times to Burns and James Joyce, and to Lewis Carroll.[16] He was born in Wellington (New Zealand) and educated in England; moving to Edinburgh in his teens, he found his direction through Scotland and MacDiarmid's example. As MacCaig wrote, 'With the suddenness of a conversion he seceded from English, adopted Scots, and never wrote a poem in English from then on, until he died,' in 1975, aged only fifty-nine.[17] Of the eight poets in Moffat's painting, only Morgan did not contribute to the memorial volume published by Macdonald in the year of his death, but then he had written a spirited essay in the New Saltire (spring 1962) about the 'language problem', singling out Goodsir Smith's controversial play The Wallace. When Morgan saw it at the 1960 Edinburgh Festival, he wrote, 'I found it hard to believe that such a talented and sensitive man could write, theatrically and stylistically, as if the whole of twentieth-century drama had passed him by – Brecht for presentation, Miller or Williams for language.'[18]

In this essay, 'The Beatnik in the Kailyard', Morgan argued that the Scottish Renaissance movement had set up two aims that were 'hard to keep compatible [. . .] it would risk dealing with contemporary subjects and would experiment with new forms, but [MacDiarmid] also wanted it to be unmistakably Scottish, if possible by a revival and extension of the Scots vocabulary'. He proposed that the ideal – given that Scottish speech itself was very fluid in register – would be to 'preserve an unanguished flexibility in this matter of language'. In this 'large freedom from anxiety' over language that he saw in MacDiarmid, Morgan himself also rejoices. Anxiety, however, was palpable at the turn of the decade. Morgan goes on to discuss the publication of the anthology Honour'd Shade (W. and R. Chambers Ltd, 1959) or, rather, its reception in the columns of The Scotsman. This was a collection of new Scottish poetry marking the bicentenary of the birth of Robert Burns, initiated by the Scottish Committee of the Arts Council of Great Britain, and edited by MacCaig. All eight Pub poets were among the twenty-seven included. There was a great deal of argument about the existence of a 'Rose Street Group', centred in Edinburgh and biased towards Lallans. After the 'many weeks of inflammatory toing and froing' in the correspondence columns had died away, a group of seven 'non-Rose-Street non-contributors to the anthology put together a tape recording of readings of their own poems and called it Dishonour'd Shade'. They all wrote in English, although Morgan remarks of Ian Hamilton Finlay that his work had as Scottish a 'flavour [. . .] as a "Scotch-at-all-costs"-er could ask for'. More importantly, Morgan saw that the argument over the anthology, although lively and fascinating in its way, indicated that Scottish literary life was not in a particularly healthy state. He quoted from a letter by Tom Scott, in which Scott stated flatly that 'The sense of community, of abundant, vigorous social life has almost completely gone. There is a wealth of talent [. . .] but something vital has gone, or almost gone. That something is Scotland.' Morgan could not agree with the diagnosis or the cure proposed by Scott, but he felt that the situation was 'rightly indicated', and this leads him to a passionate indictment of the 'prevailing intellectual mood of indifferentism and conservatism': this in a period which Angus Calder characterises as the 'all-time apogee' of Unionism, 'with Tories winning an actual majority of the vote in 1955 and Labour abandoning Home Rule soon after'. Calder maintains that on the surface, there 'was little life (bar the folk-music revival) in Scottish culture in that period'.[19] Morgan goes further:

[The] result in 1960 is a gap between the literary and the public experience which is surprising and indeed shocking in a country as small as Scotland [. . .] the world of television and sputniks, automation and LPs, electronic music and multi-storey flats, rebuilt city centres and new towns, coffee bars and bookable cinemas [. . .] How ridiculous to list distinguishing features of contemporary culture – material ones at that! Yet material differences in society imply spiritual, moral and aesthetic differences, and although writers can struggle along for a time on language, on myth, on nature, on 'eternal emotions', there comes a day of reckoning when they realise that they are not speaking the same terms as their audience.[20]

It was the sea-change of the 1960s that makes *Poets' Pub* a historical moment. Peter Kravitz, the influential editor of the revived *Edinburgh Review* (1984–90), and editorial director of Polygon, declared of the painting in 1997:

[T]his mythic combination marked the end of an era when poetry eclipsed prose, Edinburgh lorded it over Glasgow and women were left outside the pub of Scottish literature. The idea that you could fit Scotland's best writers round one table is inconceivable now.[21]

Justified Sinners – An Archaeology of Scottish Counter-Culture (1960–2000), edited by Ross Birrell and Alec Finlay, provides a kaleidoscopic view of the activities of those years: basement readings; the explosive encounter at the 1962 Edinburgh Writers Conference of Hugh MacDiarmid and Alexander Trocchi; the influence of men as diverse as R. D. Laing and Richard Demarco; the culture wars waged by Ian Hamilton Finlay – this world still looking very male-dominated. Morgan, in his letter written for the book, declared that he would almost date his life as beginning from 1960 instead of 1920:

Yes, I go along with the idea of a Scottish spring. It was genuinely a time of beginnings, a time of openings, and I always felt that those who left Scotland then – e.g. Kenneth White, Douglas Dunn – were too impatient and should have stayed. New international configurations – Scottish-American, Scottish-Russian, Scottish-Brazilian – appeared. New genres like concrete poetry and sound poetry challenged a fair amount of opposition. I remember Hugh MacDiarmid growling in 1970, 'I'd hate an Ian Finlay poem on my gravestone.'[22]

Morgan, along with Garioch, was on the board of the magazine, *Scottish International* (1968–74). Garioch seemed less excited than Morgan by the events of the decade:

Sam [Sorley] Maclean [sic] has been in Edinburgh, an important event, in fact, and he has been going over a tape-recording made at that sit-in in Aberdeen which we [at the *Scottish International*] are going to publish [. . .] He is very seriously concerned with poetry, but little interested in setting it before the public [. . . Maclean and George Davie] work somewhat in a state of despair. Perhaps I am wrong, and am only seeing them through my own visors. But I wonder if we all have a feeling of things falling about our heads.[23]

Kravitz characterises *Scottish International* as curious in several respects, under its editor Bob Tait's guidance treating MacDiarmid as a poet among equals instead of installing him high on a throne. It also tried to cover Glasgow comprehensively for the first time. Here was a different aspect of the language question, as seen in Tom Leonard's 'The Good Thief', published in *Scottish International* in January 1968, the *Glasgow University Magazine*'s printer having refused to print some of his poems because of their language. That tumultuous year[24] resonated for Scottish literature: Leonard, Morgan's *The Second Life*, Iain Crichton Smith's most famous novel, *Consider the Lilies*, and MacCaig's *Rings on a Tree*. As Edward Heath set up the Scottish Constitutional Committee under Sir Alec Douglas-Home, Finlay began to construct his garden at Little Sparta.

Even at this heady time, the women still have not made their appearance. Moffat's painting is true to its period in pushing them to the margin. Violet Jacob and Marion Angus, both praised by MacDiarmid, had died in 1946 and were not identified with the Scottish Renaissance movement. Helen Cruikshank, who was and who lived much of her life in Edinburgh, died in 1975. Their work was unevenly anthologised. Serif published the *Selected Poems of Marion Angus* in 1950, with a memoir by Cruikshank, but women are conspicuously absent from the Scottish Poetry Library's holdings for the 1950s. One perhaps unexpected entry there is Muriel Spark's *The Fanfarlo and Other Verse* (1952), her first poetry collection, but of course Spark had left her native Edinburgh in 1937 and became better known as a novelist than as a poet. Christopher Whyte observes:

When, in the person of Liz Lochhead, a woman at last came to occupy an uncontested space on the poetic scene, she had little awareness of Scottish predecessors, and had to invent herself, and her speaking position, more or less from scratch.[25]

Memo for Spring (1972) was Lochhead's first volume and the enabling presences for her were chiefly Morgan and Tom Leonard.

Amongst those presences that hover beyond the frame, the poet arguably most missed is another Sydney, W. S. Graham, born in 1918 in Greenock. In 1943 he left Scotland for Cornwall, and there he stayed, out of the picture. *The Nightfishing*, which established his reputation, was published by Faber and Faber in 1955 (he owed much to Eliot's encouragement). Graham's tone is often very personal, conversational, belying the emotional depths and technical skills of his poetry, a very distinctive music. MacDiarmid, in an unsigned review in the journal *The Voice of Scotland* of Kurt Wittig's *The Scottish Tradition in Literature*, commended his treatment of the Scots language, but maintained that Wittig was

> not able to deal as effectively with such phenomena as the poetry of W. S. Graham or Norman MacCaig or the later multilinguistic epics of Hugh MacDiarmid. This is a pity since these represent the growing end of Scottish poetry and call for an increasing intellectualism that is in accord with one of the deepest elements in our Scots tradition [. . .][26]

Graham did visit Scotland when he could afford to, was included in *Honour'd Shade*, and corresponded for years with Morgan. In 1969 he wrote to William Montgomerie:

> Have I given up Scotland? Not that I know. I certainly couldn't write the poems I do without being Scots. Of course I have great bouts of homesickness for Scotland, the land and the people. But the selfconsciousness of what the Scottish art scene seems to be today embarrasses me tae hell.[27]

The readings he gave in Edinburgh, Glasgow and Dundee in 1981 turned out to be his last visit. He wrote to Tom Leonard:

> It was a pleasure and a nice excitement to meet you that night in the iris of The Third Eye [. . .] Sauchiehall Street wasn't the same. I wasn't the same. It was a different kind of night-time. The Firth of Clyde is my place. I came back a bit homesick.[28]

Perhaps Graham saw *Poets' Pub*, which was exhibited in Glasgow's Third Eye Centre in 1981, along with individual portraits and photographs. For that

occasion Marshall Walker taped interviews with six of the poets, and Neal
Ascherson wrote the catalogue text for the book *Seven Poets*, which included
reproductions of Moffat's portraits and photographs of the poets by Jessie
Ann Matthew. This, too, became the historical document of a particular,
post-referendum period.

Ascherson, in his Introduction to the catalogue, sees the group portrait as a
powerful reminder that the Scottish Renaissance is 'over and done with [. . .]
part of the past':

> It was hoped, even assumed, that the literary revival would fuse naturally with a
> political revival. This did not really happen. The European pattern of cultural
> nationalism, with the poet on the barricade and the lexicographer of the national
> language elected president of the new republic, was not repeated in Scotland. It
> is instructive that none of these seven, except for Iain Crichton Smith, signed up
> actively with the Scottish resurgence of nationalism in the seventies.[29]

Perhaps, after all, the 'passionate concern for Scottish culture' that Moffat
saw as their common denominator was less important to these poets than
the search for the best language in which to write the best of which they
were capable, to take in as much or as little of the changing world as their
individual temperaments allowed: a landscape, a city, or everything from
Glasgow to Saturn. 'How Scottish are you?' Marshall Walker asked MacCaig,
and he replied vehemently:

> Hundred per cent. Infuriated with distilled water. I don't like the Scots and I
> don't like their history [. . .] I think everybody's awful, except when you meet an
> individual instance, and some of them are so wonderful and marvellous [. . .]
> and don't tell me they came from their filthy history.[30]

Now this image is part of Scotland's literary history, with male poets smoking
in pubs as they are no longer able to do, and the painting itself exists in a
world that Morgan predicted would be 'more fast, more clean, more "cool"
than the one it leaves behind.'[31]

CHAPTER FOURTEEN

Language and Identity in Modern Gaelic Verse

Michelle Macleod

Sociolinguists and (linguistic) anthropologists have long believed that language is one of the key factors in determining a person's identity. One eminent scholar, Joshua Fishman, states in the Introduction to his *Handbook of Language and Ethnic Identity* (1999) that

> although language has rarely been equated with the totality of ethnicity, it has, in certain historical, regional and disciplinary contexts been accorded priority within that totality [. . .] How and when the link between language and ethnicity comes about, its saliency and potency, its waxing and waning, its inevitability and the possibility of its sundering, all need to be examined.[1]

Fishman also believes that when one's 'ethnically associated language is restricted or denigrated, the users who identify with it are more likely to use it among themselves (and to organise in order to have it accepted and recognized by others) than if no grievance existed'.[2] It is perhaps not surprising, therefore, that issues relating to language – language loyalty, language death, language shift and the relationship between language and identity and language and location – are common in modern Gaelic poetry. At a time of increasing linguistic fragility, Gaelic writers and poets have often been fierce defenders of the language and have perhaps contemplated more than most the consequences to one's identity should the language be lost. Perhaps in some way their writing is equivalent to Fishman's 'organisation' to improve status as well as embodying their own examination of the link between language and ethnicity.

This chapter will concentrate on the works of George Campbell Hay (1915–84), a poet in many languages, a nationalist and keen supporter of the Gaelic language, and Derick Thomson (1921–), possibly the twentieth century's most prolific Gaelic scholar and poet and also a Scottish Nationalist. It will also discuss how other poets have referred to the issue of language, and by way of contrast with the 'senior' poets, the issue will be considered in the works of subsequent generations with examples from poets for whom the language was learned in childhood: Aonghas MacNeacail (1942–), Myles Campbell (1944–), Mary Montgomery (1955–) and Anne Frater (1967–), and from those who came to Gaelic later in life: Meg Bateman (1959–) and Christopher Whyte (1952–). Some reference will also be made to the Gaelic poetry of Iain Crichton Smith (1928–98), the issue of whose bilingualism in his poetry the present author has discussed elsewhere.[3]

George Campbell Hay did not learn Gaelic as his first language, neither was he a native bilingual; he did, however, learn Gaelic at a young age and in an informal environment from his aunts and from fishermen in Tarbert, Kintyre.[4] Hay spent much of his youth in Kintyre and returned to Argyll frequently as an adult; he considered himself to be a Gael. Unlike the other poets considered in this essay, Hay's perception of Gaelic is almost uniquely associated with traditional speakers and mostly with the traditional Gaelic-speaking areas. Of course, Hay stopped writing before any of the other poets considered here and he wrote mostly in an era when, although one would have had to acknowledge the weakened state of the Gaelic language, the fatalism that is now associated with its survival was not so strongly felt. In Hay's poetry there is a pervading sense that language and location cannot be separated in any discussion of Gaelic identity.

In the poem 'Aig an Fheurlochan' ('By the Grassy Lochan') Hay describes an incident where he is addressed by the wind, which is a metaphor for Gaelic language. The wind tells the poet that it has travelled much throughout Scotland, naming among others places in Argyll, Rannoch, Lorne, Sutherland, Barra, Uist, Mull, Lewis, Islay, Jura and even Edinburgh. These are, of course, all places where Gaelic language and culture is or has been vibrant. Hay's reference to Gaelic's existence as the language of the royal court is particularly poignant: he highlights the creative side of the Gaels:

> Bha uair 's bu leamsa am fearann
> Eadar Sealtainn is Tuaidh
> An Dùn Èideann nan rìghrean
> bhithinn cinnteach à duais.
> Bhiodh teudan gan riaghladh
> a chur rian dhomh air duain,
> is gum freagradh gach balla
> do dh'aicill is uaim.

> ('There was a time that mine was the land
> between Shetland and Tweed.
> In Edinburgh of the kings my
> reward was assured.
> Harpstrings would be tuned
> to accompany my songs,

and every wall would echo
with vowel-rhyme and alliteration.)[5]

The voice now admits to the poet that it has retreated, having been damaged
in the past, to live with the Gaels in the countryside where it will be safe
and protected.

In 'Fòlachd is Àrach' ('Lineage and Rearing') in the 'Dùghall' ('Dougall')
section of the long (unfinished) poem *Mochtàr is Dùghall* (*Mokhtâr and Dougall*)
Hay attempts a definition of the Gael (and, of course, Dùghall); again, the
Gael is associated with nature, and particularly the rugged landscape of the
Highlands and Argyll. To the question: 'Ciod e th' annainn, a chlann mo
dhùthcha? / Ciod e th' annainn is a bha 'n Dùghall?' ('What are we children of
my country? / What makes us and what made Dougall?')[6], he responds:

Bu Ghàidheal e, 's bu bhlàth a dhùrachd
don chànain àrsaidh a rinn a dhùsgadh
o 'chadal creathlach; san d' rinn e sùgradh
ri leannan anns a' choille chùbhraidh.

(He was a Gael, and warm was his regard
for the ancient tongue which woke him
from his cradle sleep; and in which he courted
his love in the fragrant woods.)[7]

Hay continues by stating that Dùghall was also a Scot; for although Hay clearly
recognised two distinct native cultures in Scotland – that of the Gael and the
Lowlander – he never portrayed any tension between the two cultures. By
contrast, he recognised this as a quality of Scotland and one that should be celebrated. In 'Gum Chur an Aithne' ('By Way of Introduction'), for example, he
makes claims to dual identity 'nam dhalt' aig Gàidheil, 's mi leth-Ghallda' ('fostered by Gaels, and I half Lowlander').[8] Hay's ease with the two cultures is in
distinct opposition to later Gaelic poets (such as Thomson and Iain Crichton
Smith) who very often felt a tension between the cultures to which they
belonged (perhaps because the second culture was a more anglicised one?).[9]

Dùghall and other Gaels are nearly always placed in rural Gàidhealtachd/
Highland settings. In 'Fòlachd is Àrach' Hay uses an extended metaphor of
the felling of a forest to refer to the repeated tyranny suffered by the Gaels
throughout their history. Hay believes adamantly, however, that there is
hope for the Gaels and using the tree imagery he shows that, in spite of heavy
damage, there is resilience:

Ach fhad 's a dh'fhanas freumh a dheoghal
brìgh na h-ùrach, 's a chur snodhaich

suas fon rùisg, le driùchd is soineann,
thig failleanan ùra o na stocaibh
gu 'cur 'na tuiltean uaine molach
air ais far am b' uaine I roimhe.

(But as long as one root survives to suck
the juice of the earth and to send sap
rising under the bark, in dew and sunshine,
fresh saplings will sprout from the stumps
and in time restore floods of green bush
where there was greenness before.)[10]

Hay is equally respectful of Scotland's native cultures, having written in
both Scots and Gaelic, but although the poem 'Air Suidh' Artair Dhomh
Mochthrath' ('On Arthur's Seat One Morning'), displays a fondness and
respect for Edinburgh and its surrounding area, there is a passion about the
Gaels' regular pilgrimage from Edinburgh to Kintyre. Hay goes so far as to
say: ''s gur iad a' Ghàidhealtachd 's a' Ghàidhlig an dà nì 's fheàrr a tha 'n
Albainn.' ('for Gaelic and the Gaeltach / are the two glories of Scotland').[11]

As his representation of the pilgrimage to Kintyre above shows, Hay
is not completely naïve to the fact that many Gaels live outside of the
Highlands; in another rare example of a poem which places the Gael
outside of his traditional homeland, 'Na Gàidheil sna Bailtean' ('The Gaels
in the Towns') Hay is quite clear about his desire to make a connection
with other Gaelic speakers: 'nì mi 'n tàladh 's an tatadh 's an taitinn le rann
no dàn' ('I will lure them and fondle them and please them with a verse or
a poem').[12] There is almost a sense here of Hay seeing himself as different
from other Gaels in the cities, and he is forcing himself to be appealing to
them. Perhaps this is an instance of what Christopher Whyte has called
'becoming an "other"':

By choosing to write in Gaelic, in a language used neither by his parents nor in
his own social ambience, Hay had himself crossed a cultural boundary. The
experience of becoming or impersonating an 'other' may well have encouraged
a leap in the direction of other 'others'.[13]

What comes across clearly in Hay's poetry is a true sense of patriotism, and
at times nationalism, and much of this is firmly rooted in his commitment to
the language and culture. As Christopher Whyte has pointed out, Hay's representation of nationalism has influenced many subsequent Gaelic poets:

Hay is a doctrinaire nationalist, with an intransigent fervour characteristic of
the newly converted, who developed a type of poem that was to be enormously

influential on both Thomson and the younger generation of Gaelic poets [. . .]
The process, with Hay, tends to culminate in an overt moral exhortation to
his audience.[14]

Derick Thomson has published seven collections of poetry, from *An
Dealbh Briste* (*The Broken Picture*) in 1951 up to the most recent *Sùil air Fàire*
(*Surveying the Horizon*, 2007); he also published a collected poems *Creachadh
na Clàrsaich* (*Plundering the Harp*, 1982), which contained hitherto unpub-
lished material. Thomson's attitude towards the language and how it affects
his identity is apparent in much of his work, particularly in the early poetry.
There, views on language are bound to culture and the home, in his case the
Isle of Lewis.

In his first collection, *An Dealbh Briste*, Thomson uses nature imagery to
show how Gaelic culture and tradition are dying; these are all inextricably
linked with the identity and sustainability of the community. For example
in 'Asaid' ('Delivery') the poet describes a harvest scene. Superficially everything seems the same as it has done for many years, but nothing is happening:
''S na raointean torrach a' feitheamh an asaid, / 'S cha ghluais duine' ('and
the ripe fields await their delivery, and no man moves').[15] It is not made
clear why the harvest is left uncut; perhaps the skills to do so have been lost.
However, the significance of the lost harvest, which arguably represents the
loss of Gaelic culture, is very important. Without the harvest and crops the
community faces hardship; similarly, without their tradition the community
is not the complete entity it used to be. Instead of the hum of a living community there is a chilling quiet broken only by the heart-breaking cry of a hungry
baby; the image of a baby crying may represent the youth of the place starved
of their culture. Similarly, in 'Chunnaic mi ròs a' fàs' ('Rose'), the fragility
of the language and culture is symbolised by a rose growing on a craggy rock
face. In an attempt to preserve the rose the poet transplants it to a garden
where he hopes that it will grow, but this is a fruitless task: 'Ach O! chan
eil cùram ann a ni a caomhnadh, / No gath bho ghréin an t-saoghail a nis
bheir blàth oirr'' ('But O! There is no care that will keep it, nor ray from the
world's sun that will make it bloom').[16] Perhaps this is a warning that Gaelic
language and culture cannot be artificially maintained, and that language and
society cannot be separated. We see in later Thomson poems his unease with
Gaelic in the non-traditional environment.

One of Thomson's best-known poems, 'An Tobar' ('The Well'), is in a
similar vein to the above. The well is a metaphor for the source of Gaelic
culture; just as the water that the well provides is essential for a community,
so is the wealth of tradition and education that the culture can supply. As one
would expect of a contemporary setting, the village well is now little-used
and overgrown and it is thus hard to find. The poet learns about it only from

an old woman in the village; he immediately compares her to the well. She too is a repository of something precious and is perhaps, in an unfortunate way, regarded as being useless and anachronistic, like the well. Ultimately the old woman dies and the path to the well is overgrown. The death of the old woman means that her knowledge of tradition cannot be drawn on for the continuation of Gaelic culture. Thus, just as the well that provides life-giving water has disappeared, so has an important source of traditional knowledge. A resonant device in this poem which clearly shows the decline in Gaelic tradition is the use of 'tobar' '(well'), 'cogan' ('cogie/basin') and 'meòirean' ('thimble') as diminishing receptacles for the water which has already been shown to be a symbol of the culture.

A final example of Thomson's early work which mourns the passing of Gaelic culture is 'A Chionn 's gu Bheil' ('Since the Picture is Broken'). The poem's structure is formulaic and each verse starts with the incremental repetition of 'a chionn 's gu bheil' ('since the . . .') and then proceeds to describe a separate aspect of decay and the poet's petulant decision seemingly to abandon his culture. The first verse gives an overall impression of how things have changed; the broken picture is representative of how the poet's home has deteriorated culturally:

A chionn 's gu bheil an dealbh briste
Cuiridh mi bhuam e, chan eil buannachd
Ann a bhith 'ga amharc, [. . .]

(Since the picture is broken I will put it from me; there is no profit in looking at it [. . .])[17]

Perhaps the least hopeful image for the future of Gaelic culture is to be found in the final verse: 'Cha chunnt mi na h-eòin bhreaca / A chionn 's gu bheil an nead creachte' ('I will not count the brindled birds since the nest is raided'). The raided nest is a trope for the Highlands. The poet appears to be suggesting that, like the nest which will see no offspring in the immediate future, the cradle of Gaelic culture will also not be productive because it has been continually violated by external forces. This poem does more than simply mourn the loss of Gaelic culture; it shows the poet rejecting what is, as yet, only partially decayed. Of the tree with the withered branch he says: 'Cha chuir mi todhar ris a' chraoibh so' ('I will not manure this tree').

The subject of language is most prominent again in the recent (2007) collection Sùil air Fàire. There is a real poignancy here and a critical and honest reflection on the current language situation. Although not all of Thomson's earlier poems which dealt with language as their subject were positive about the future of the language, these later poems show it in a much-weakened state, particularly in its traditional setting, although he does note the growth of Gaelic in new domains. There is a tension of sorts in this collection between the fading out of Gaelic in its traditional environment, on the one hand, and its use in the new media and amongst young speakers, on the other.

In the section 'Leòdhas A-rithist' ('Lewis Again'), while the poet is not totally pessimistic about the future of the language, he is very clear that the language is in a weakened state. In 'Àros nan Sean' ('Old Folks' Home') the language is compared to an old person; although this is not a new metaphor for Thomson (see 'An Tobar' ('The Well') and 'Catrìona Mhòr' ('Catherine the Elder'), for example), there is more sensitivity and acceptance at what is happening. While initially Thomson describes other places where Gaelic has withered (Kintyre, Perthshire, Braemar, Sutherland), he returns to Lewis and discusses in detail places in Lewis. It could be that Thomson's clever play on place-names which have literal, often physiologically-related, meanings can only be appreciated by readers not familiar with Lewis topography with the help of the translation:

> ach is beag a bha dhùil a'm
> gun tigeadh a' ghagadaich
> buileach cho dlùth orm,
> tachdadh sa bhràighe
> is ciorram an ceòs,
> liota san teanga [. . .]

> ('But had no idea
> that the stuttering would come quite so close to me,
> choking at the Bright/throat
> and maiming in Keose/the hollow,
> lisping in Tong/the tongue [. . .]')[18]

Although the central image of the poem is an old folks' home in which Gaelic, personified by speakers from different areas, will retire too, this is not a sad poem. There is a touch of humour in his description of life in the home, and the rallying call at the end 'Suas leis a' Ghàidhlig' ('Up with the Gaelic')[19] is uttered in determination and hope, rather than despair.

'Cridhe an t-Sluaigh' ('The Heart of the People'*: * signifies author's translation), on the other hand, is much more despairing about the sustainability of the language. While the language was healthy, the intellect and the people thrived. Now that the language is in serious decline, there is a sense of destruction and muting of the intellect:

> 's tha an smùr 's a' ghainmheach
> a' mùchadh nam briathran

's a' càrnadh
saoghal ùr air an uachdar[20]

(and the dust and the sand
is extinguishing the words,
and piling up
a new world on the surface*)

Thomson uses the catastrophic symbol of an earthquake to portray the damage that has been done to Gaelic. He contrasts the Gaelic language and culture in its most vibrant condition, being at the centre of the world, to the earthquake causing the disaster; the shift in status is emphasised by Thomson's clever wordplay with the Gaelic 'cridhe an t-sluaigh' ('heart of the people') and 'crith-thalmhainn' ('earthquake').

Thomson accepts that Gaelic is not completely lost; however, the Gaelic that exists among the younger generations is not one with which he feels particularly comfortable. His unease is palpable even from the title 'Teagamh' ('Doubt'*). This poem questions immediately the condition of Gaelic in modern society: that Thomson even contemplates whether Scotland would be better off without Gaelic rather than with the poor Gaelic of the common vernacular is an indication of his disappointment at what is currently happening in Gaelic:

Cò 's fheàrr:
Alba gun Ghàidhlig,
no Alba le Gàidhlig phiullach an TV?[21]

(What is better:
Scotland without Gaelic,
or Scotland with the raggedy Gaelic of the TV?*)

He mourns the loss of the genitive case in the language practices of the younger generation; he wonders also at the need constantly to learn new vocabulary, presumably a reference to the Gaelic lexicon which is developing, some see unnaturally, to deal with domains not traditionally found in the Gaelic language. He compares the environment of this Gaelic to the environment from which his own Gaelic emerged: ''s an crotal a' dol o fheum / 's gun a dhath air a' chainnt' ('and the crottle going from use / and without its colour on the language'). (Crottle, a rock moss, was traditionally used to dye sheep's wool.) Although Thomson is obviously at odds with this new Gaelic environment, he does not completely reject the new situation.

He refers to Gaelic television again in 'Dh'fhalbh Siud is Thàinig Seo' ('That Has Gone and This Has Come'*). Again Thomson contrasts the traditional, rural society in which he learned Gaelic with modern society. In the former, Gaelic is closely associated with history and heritage and this led to it prospering naturally. This environment, however, is replaced by the metropolitan and monocultural society, represented in this poem as the 'cornflake' replacing 'porridge'. According to Thomson, Gaelic now exists only on the periphery: for example, on road signs, on paste-over translations on children's books and on television programmes at midnight.

Thomson's quandary over the changing nature of Gaelic, and perhaps what this means to his identity, is seen in the ironic 'Thèid sinn dhan t-Sabhal' ('We will go to the Sabhal/Barn'*); the 'Sabhal' referred to here is Sabhal Mòr Ostaig (SMO), the Gaelic college on the Isle of Skye. Here Thomson acknowledges, at least, the good that the college is doing for the survival of Gaelic. It is unclear who else he is referring to when he proclaims 'we' will go to the 'Sabhal' (perhaps other suspicious, traditional Gaels like him), but Gaelic will have a prominent position there, even if it achieves this prominence by being 'caressed' artificially by a computer. Again Thomson refers to the new vocabulary that SMO, in particular, is often credited with promulgating; he is more scathing of it here: 'is stòras de data / a' tighinn às a mhàs' ('and a proliferation of data coming from its backside'*).[22] Thomson is presumably making a reference to the Stòr-dàta (lexical data-base) project housed in SMO. Although there is undoubted recognition from Thomson, there is still unease. The irony is stressed in the format of the poem: it is in the form of a Gaelic (riddle) song with the lines of verse interspersed by meaningless lines of vocables (as is common in traditional verse).

Thomson is not the only poet of the modern era who struggles with 'new' Gaelic. As the present author has shown elsewhere,[23] Iain Crichton Smith is also aware of the difference between the two types of Gaelic and the two environments in which they grow. In his collection An t-Eilean agus an Cànan (The Island and the Language, 1987) Smith also has a poem set in Sabhal Mòr Ostaig, though at its outset rather than the developed stage of the Thomson poem. Smith, like Thomson, compares the traditional Gaelic environment (for example, places like the home) to the new environment. He is also somewhat bewildered by those who learn Gaelic: he gives examples of a Frenchman and a Japanese whose environments and backgrounds are completely alien to him, and he presumes to Gaelic culture.[24] Mary Montgomery goes further than Thomson and Smith in her discussion of the 'new' Gaelic speaker in 'Na Gàidheil Ùra Eile' ('The – Other – New Gaels'), from her first collection Eadar Mi 's a' Bhreug (Between Myself and the Lie*, 1988). She acknowledges that sometimes traditional (native) speakers do not understand how or why anyone would wish to learn Gaelic; it is as if for them Gaelic is only a marker of heritage and genealogy, rather than a communicative tool or a national treasure available to all. She asks the Gaelic learner to forgive her and her sort for being so slow to accept them.

The concept of Gaelic as a heritage language and marker of identity is given some expression in 'oideachadh ceart' ('a proper schooling') by Aonghas MacNeacail in the collection of the same title (1996). Although not ostensibly a 'language' poem, it raises the issue of a collective, racial memory of which the language is a part. Mostly, however, the poem discusses how knowledge of historical events, such as the Clearances, emigration and local history events, unite the Gaels. He repeats throughout the poem: 'cha b' eachdraidh ach cuimhne' ('it wasn't history but memory'). MacNeacail, who has published three collections and two long poems, is not a poet for whom language is a major subject; he is more concerned with the private rather than political or philosophical issues. When he does discuss language, we see at once how he struggles with bilingualism in 'an tùr caillte' ('the lost tower') in a way that is not dissimilar to some of Smith's and Thomson's work; as MacNeacail notes, 'tùr' can also mean reason or sanity:

snàmh anns an eabar ghleadhrach
eadar freumhaichean
mo dhà chànan
an té tha dearg
a' ruith na dealan brisg tro m'fhéithean
's an téile
    coimheach, coingeis, eòlach
mum sheice mar eideadh ciomaich

(swimming in the clangorous mud
between the roots of my two languages
the one that is red
sprinting swift lightnings through my veins
and the other
    alien, indifferent, familiar
wrapped round my skin like prison clothes)[25]

Although not a poet who dwells on the language situation in his work, Christopher Whyte notes that there are issues to do with language surrounding MacNeacail's work: he calls him a 'truly bilingual poet' and contrasts his portrayal of 'Gaelic "otherness"' with MacLean, Hay and Thomson.[26] Although MacNeacail may differ, as Whyte suggests, in his experience of Gaelic language and culture, this does not stop him celebrating it in 'tha gàidhlig beò' ('gaelic is alive'). Dedicated to Catilín Maude, an Irish language activist, singer, writer and actress, the choice of metaphor in this incitement to rejoice in the survival of the language(s) is reminiscent of Hay's 'Fòlachd ia Àrach':

'tha gàidhlig beò'
a dh'aindeoin gach saighead
's i streap nan sìthean
fiùran darach fo h-achlais

('gaelic is alive'
despite all arrows
she climbs the hillside
sapling of oak in her arms)[27]

It is a celebration of the language's survival in spite of the changing environment and it asks too that the language should be defended.

The issue of Gaelic's changing cultural basis is seen in Meg Bateman's third
and most recent collection *Soirbheas* (*Fair Wind*, 2007). Bateman came to
Gaelic as a young adult and has made a successful career for herself as a Gaelic
academic and poet. She is predominantly a poet of the soul and her poems
are usually personal introspections about private emotions. For the most part
Soirbheas is no exception; there are, however, several poems which touch on
Gaelic language culture and what they mean to her. Like several of Thomson's
poems from *Sùil air Fàire*, 'Cànain' ('Language') contrasts the two sets of
Gaelic speakers: those for whom it is a 'heritage' language and those, like the
poet herself, who have come to the language from a different background and
have therefore learned the language differently. The first verse, of this two-
verse poem, describes the 'traditional' Gaelic speakers; their mouths, that is,
their language, are compared to flowers, but like flowers they must expire:

nuair a bha an samhradh aca seachad
is a shearg iad dhan ùir.[28]

(when their summer was over
and they crumpled into dust.)

But there will be new speakers 'Bidh beòil eile ann' ('Other mouths will
come') and their lips will be just like the lips of the other speakers. The poem
ends with almost a rhetorical self-defensive question:

ach gu bheil maitheas san talamh
carson a bhiodh am boltrach staoin?

(and as there is goodness in the soil,
why doubt their sweetness?)

There is a note of defence here, as if some have doubted the worthiness or
authenticity of the 'new' speakers. But Bateman, using the soil as a metaphor

for Gaelic, points out that the language still exists and it now nourishes a new crop of speakers.

A contemporary of Bateman's, Christopher Whyte, has also learned Gaelic and has chosen to write poetry in Gaelic; however, for him it seems that the language is a vehicle of expression only. In the long poem *Bho Leabhar-Latha Maria Malibran* (*From the Diary of Maria Malibran*), he ends with a long attack on the reader who had expected him to write about 'Gaelic' subject matters:

A luchd-leughaidh chaoimh,
chan iad na cuspairean as fheàrr leibh.
Nam b' e bhith còrdadh ribh a bha 'nam rùn,
bu chòir dhomh sgrìobhadh air cùis eadar-dhealaicht'.

'S dòch' air an acfhainn a chaidh fhàgail anns
an t-sabhal lem sheanair caoin, tha marbh a-nis,
gach ainm a bh' oirr', 's an dòigh cheart air an robh
gach ball ga chleachdadh, 's mis' a' caoidh na meirg'
a lobhas iad, 's an traidisean air chall.[29]

(My dear readers,
these are not the subjects you prefer.
If to be pleasing you were my desire,
I should have written on another topic.

Perhaps about the tools abandoned in
the barn by my dear grandfather, now dead,
each name they had, and of course the proper way
to use each part, while I bemoan the rust
that rots them, and the lost tradition.)[30]

Whyte doubts that his readers will accept his work as 'truly Gaelic' as he is not a Gael; obviously for him Gaelic-speaking does not equate with Gaelic identity. His summary, above, of the content of a typical 'Gaelic' poem is almost a parody of one of Anne Frater's poems, 'Ar Cànan 's Ar Clò' ('Our Tongue and Our Tweed'), which mourns the loss of Gaelic language and culture by using an extended metaphor of an old man's loom and cloth being discarded to be replaced by new, colourful cloth. Frater's 'Ar Cànan 's Ar Clò' and 'Am Bodach' ('The Old Man') are reminiscent of some of Thomson's early work, such as 'An Tobar' and 'Catrìona Mhòr'. Interestingly, however, whereas Thomson always uses old women as symbols of linguistic and cultural maintenance, Frater uses old men. Her poem 'Am Bodach', for example, clearly links language death with the death of the old man: the tradition bearer. The old man is clinging to life with the aid of technology, and though others wait for his death, she recognises that there is still some life left in him and begs him not to die:

> Na dùin do shùilean fhathast
> cuir spàirn ort fhèin an aghaidh sàmhachd a' bhàis
> 's thig d' oghaichean gad dhìon.

> (Don't close your eyes just yet,
> struggle against the peace of death
> and your heirs will come to your aid.)[31]

Frater has a section 'Dùthaich agus Cànan' ('Land and Language') in her collection Fon t-Slige (Under the Shell, 1995); like Thomson and Hay, language, nationalism and Gaelic identity are all key themes in her work. There is a sense that she feels whole and complete when at home with her native language, seen for example in the poem 'Aig an Fhaing' ('At the Fank'). There, she clearly shows that it is the Gaelic language that makes her part of the community: ''s mo chànan fhìn 'nam bheul' ('and my own language on my tongue').[32]

Myles Campbell also likens Gaelic to an old man in 'Bi Mar Bhàta' ('Be Like a Boat'*) from the collection Eileanan (Islands); again this poem is a plea to the language to aspire to vitality in spite of its age and condition. Campbell beseeches the language to be like a boat and 'sail, sail, sail'. Campbell is a prolific Gaelic poet, having written five collections and published a comprehensive Gaelic-Irish selection Breac a' Mhuiltein (Cirro-Cumulus) in 2007. Language and identity is not a dominant theme in Campbell's work, although it does appear in some of his poems. One of his most striking works that deals with this topic is 'Cogadh an Dà Chànan' ('Fight of the Two Languages'*) in which the poet's two languages are compared to nursing breasts. The mother's breast produces rich nourishing milk, whereas the foster-mother produces only thin milk; clearly the former represents Gaelic and the latter English. Campbell extends the metaphor by saying that the milk of the foster-mother is no use for making cheese and it goes sour and leaves a foul taste, yet in spite of its apparent flaws, it fights for supremacy:

> ach tha e sabaid
> airson uachdranachd
> air an stapaig mhilis
> a tha daonnan nam bhràigh

> (but it is fighting
> for supremacy
> over the sweet stapag
> that is always in my throat*)

Presumably Campbell is referring to the conflict between the two languages in his daily life, with English achieving supremacy, much to his dislike. Stapag, to which Campbell compares Gaelic, is a traditional sweet dish of milk, cream and oats. Although Corinna Krause refers to a sense of 'nostalgia' in this poem,[33] there is also very much a sense of anger. Krause continues by quoting Paul Barnaby's statement about some of the poetry in the anthology *An Aghaidh na Sìorraidheachd/In the Face of Eternity*[34] tending towards nostalgia and leading to 'grief, resignation, [and] rage in the face of Anglicisation'; she continues to show, using another postcolonial writer, that 'preoccupation with the pure essence of the past, however, becomes a fruitless endeavour'.[35]

There is a sense of tension throughout most of the language-related poems addressed here, and to a large extent this has arisen from the realisation that the language situation has changed and continues to change. While there is often sadness at this, nostalgia is not one of the most dominant themes. There is certainly a sense of love for the language and all that it stands for, and also a sense of bewilderment at the situation the language now faces. This poetry might equate to Fishman's exploration of the complex issue of language and ethnicity or determined language action. But that it is in Gaelic at all cannot simply be explained using ethno-linguistic rhetoric; the Irish poet Nuala Ní Dhómhnaill's belief that she was in fact compelled to write in Irish rather than English is perhaps also fitting here:

> I had chosen my language, or more rightly, perhaps at some very deep level, the language had chosen me. If there is a level to our being that for want of any better word for it I might call 'soul' (and I believe there is), then for some reason that I can never understand, the language that my soul speaks, and the place it comes from is Irish.[36]

CHAPTER FIFTEEN

Arcades – The 1980s and 1990s

Michael Gardiner

The decade from the early 1980s to the early 1990s was as significant for Scottish literary history as that from the mid-1920s to the mid-1930s. Like the 1920s–1930s Renaissance (the 'First Renaissance'), the period saw a crisis of representation accompanying a rethinking of national aesthetics. It is significant not only because of 'how many' writers and 'how important' they were – but also because the period reframed issues concerning the form of the canon and Scottish literature's scope, purpose and autonomy. It would be misleading to say that a politico-constitutional crisis *caused* national literary rebirth in the early 1980s, but a crisis did trigger long-building tendencies, accelerated by the First Renaissance and then the breakdown of the post-war British consensus in the late 1950s and early 1960s. In particular 1979 can be seen as a watershed date, since the country now faced not only the failure of the devolution referendum but also a government which made a virtue of deafness to national issues. A new 'Britishing' period emerged, but without the cohesive pride of Blitz, the Welfare State, or industrial expansion. The new administration faced a downturn while maintaining a combination of monetarist control over public finances and a popularising of social-Darwinist metaphors in business; unemployment more than doubled between 1979 and 1983, and social inequalities became broadly acceptable for the first time since before the war. Not only Wales and Scotland, but England's industrial north and rural edges felt disenfranchised, and even Londoners protested through the Greater London Council, and more than ever the UK state seemed less a form of representation than an oligarchy of financial management. National contexts became increasingly distinct from, and *opposed to*, those of the UK. As Scottish literature enjoyed a revival, Britain as an idea was collapsing more rapidly than at any time since the eighteenth century.

Culture was behind this process; indeed after 1979 the UK government became notably uncomfortable with the term 'culture' itself. A favoured term was 'heritage', which recognised only established values, and fitted the unwritten UK constitution, for which every value is a repetition of what seems to have come before. Fault-lines then formed between ethnic continuity as heritage on one hand and the desire to rewrite the nation in culture on the other. Duncan Glen's nativist magazine *Akros* ended a distinguished history in 1983, and with it a certain form of MacDiarmid revivalism. *Cencrastus*, established in 1979, also titled after a MacDiarmid poem, and also neo-Renaissance, moved away from ethnic and continuant descriptions of national culture and towards more formal political descriptions, and was joined by Joy Hendry's *Chapman* (1973–) and a new series of *Edinburgh Review* (1969–), in defining the tone at the level of small journals.

Culture and literature were not only politically contested, but were more fundamentally sites of contest for the very possibility of politics. A systemic collapse described by Stuart Hall as 'the great moving-right show'[1] began; politics retreated under economic pragmatism. Scottish culture now connoted the possibility of public action as much as it did homeland or belonging, and Scottish culture's historiography shifted in a way it had not since Walter Scott's *Waverley* (1814). If *Waverley* for Georg Lukács 'portray[ed] how historical necessity asserts itself [. . .] through the passionate actions of individuals',[2] 'necessity' had been the management of the state and 'passion' emotional attachment to the nation; and Scottishness a negotiation between the two. But after 1979, 'historical necessity' seemed stretched way beyond emotional bonds in public value.

This makes it unsurprising that the flag-bearer of Scott's Unionist-Conservative conception of progress, Allan Massie (1938–), has not been treated generously by Scottish literary history. Introducing the 1982 edition of Edwin Muir's *Scott and Scotland*, Massie amplified Muir's reading of Scott to describe Scottish culture as an emotional distraction. Massie's own novels map character events onto grand 'historical necessity' during cycles of epochal civilisation change such as World War Two (1989–97) and the Roman empire (1986–2004). Other versions of national historical fiction thrived, from Nigel Tranter's (1909–2000) continuing popularity (*Bruce Trilogy*, 1969–77), to Shena Mackay's (1944–) *Dunedin* (1991) and *Orchard on Fire* (1996 Booker shortlist). William Boyd's (1952–) ex-pat story *A Good Man in Africa* (1981) was perhaps too close to a movement comedy of manners. His *An Ice-Cream War* (1982), set in what is now Tanzania during World War One and Booker Prize nominated, is a good introduction to Boyd's themes, as is the ingenious rereading of Rousseau in *The New Confessions* (1987).

If the search was for an aesthetic which was neither defeatist-pragmatic (Muir, Massie) nor ethnic-revivalist (MacDiarmid, *Akros*), the most significant early advance was Alasdair Gray's (1934–) *Lanark* (1981). *Lanark* is partly negative critique, portraying Glasgow as 'Unthank', a non-space, a blank standing for a failure of Scottish ontology; and Gray's *1982, Janine* (1984) is an unflinching critique of the period's self-hating Tory Scot. But

Lanark is also an encyclopaedia of possibilities in which normal time and space restrictions are suspended, both historically grounded and fantastic, seeking shared values over individualism and 'heritage' and even listing its own influences in an undermining gesture. Recalling *Frankenstein*, Gray's *Poor Things* (1992) resists heritage, rereading reform history, anti-psychiatry, bookmaking, gender training, eugenics, the nineteenth-century turn to anatomy and – as in *Frankenstein* – scientific reason. Using a medical experiment to run these histories through an artificial memory, Gray critiques the imprinting of experience on blank minds which was central to the Bildungsroman in English literature from Henry Fielding to Julian Barnes, and typically understood in terms of John Locke's description of a blank slate preceding personal experience. If the blank slate is positivist and empirical – individual impressions become literary form – Scottish literature after Gray is more dialectical: characters are troubled by previous experiences that are muffled and difficult to voice. This early 1980s aesthetic can be described as Gothic, set against long shadows and empty warehouses, and presaging how hidden languages and experiences would haunt experience.

Lanark's 'Index of Plagiarisms' also recalls a long de-authorising tradition: Hugh MacDiarmid famously (re)worked other writers' material; Edwin Morgan's poetic experiments of the 1960s 'found' poems in newspapers or had them 'emerge', challenging individual authoritative creation; R. D. Laing defined the self as contingent, unstable and complexly dependent; John Macmurray suggested that the knowing subject was less meaningful than the acting agent. The emphasis on the circulation of ideas rather than personal authority demanded a different canonicity – not only different texts, but different organising principles – from 'EngLit', institutionalised study of a literary tradition defined, often in hegemonic and centralising terms, as 'English'. F. R. Leavis's popularisation of the individualistic Great Tradition had had less impact than in England, and had been held off by diverse thinking including G. E. Davie's insistence on avoiding academic specialism and Alexander Trocchi's questioning of New Critical positivism. Resistance to Leavis as restaged in Gray was effectively nationalisation of literary form, since the Great Tradition's *Great* really was the *Great* of Great Britain: idealist, ahistorical and expansive in terms of its boundaries.

Unemployment and de-industrialisation then catalysed a challenge to 'heritage'. Losing the purpose of labour meant losing shared historical meaning. The work ethic could no longer be easily pressed into state service, as Pat Kane pointed out in 2000 in *The Play Ethic*.[3] Workplace drama often moved to pub or street corner, or nostalgia, as in John Byrne's (1940–) retro-Americana – *Slab Boys Trilogy* (1979–82), *Tutti Frutti* (1987), *Your Cheatin' Heart* (1990) – or, on a rural-historical trajectory, Sue Glover's (1943–) powerful weaving of work, marriage and folklore in St Kilda, *The Straw Chair*

(1988), the Borders, *Bondagers* (1991) and Shetland, *Shetland Saga* (2000). The cohesiveness of the urban workplace drama was now deeply troubled, as in Bill Bryden's (1942–) *Civilians* (1981) and *The Ship* (1990). Drama, though, often showed more continuities with 1970s social-realism than fiction. By 1980, under the example of post-Unity playwrights like Bryden, Roddy McMillan and Hector MacMillan, Scottish dramaturgy had generally extended and formalised social realism. John McGrath (1935–2002) followed his condemnation of nationalism's failure, *Joe's Drum* (1979), with *Blood Red Roses* (1980) starkly criticising Scotland's passage from post-war consensus to satellite nation. His 7:84 (Scotland) Theatre Company continued with the 1982 'Clydebuilt' Unity classics season. McGrath's own *Border Warfare* (1989) returned to the style of *The Cheviot, the Stag and the Black, Black Oil* (1973), moving between eras of conflict from ancient times to the 1980s and dramatising the democratic deficit between nation and state. Tom McGrath (1940–2009), active in the 1960s poetry underground, wrote dramas of political misfit including *Animal* (1981) and *The Nuclear Family* (1982), a tense Trident age parody. Peter Arnott (1962–) made an important connection, reprising Bryden's *Benny Lynch* (1974) in *The Boxer Benny Lynch* (1984), following this with *White Rose* (1985) and *Muir* (1986). A similar ethical position underpins Liz Lochhead's (1947–) *Mary Queen of Scots Got Her Head Chopped Off* (1987), but in Lochhead overtly poetic figures are packed in, recalling Edwin Morgan's (1920–) popular experiments. Now a superstar poet, a status consolidated by his Carcanet *Collected Poems* (1990), Morgan had an extensive range of translations, many into Scots, making him an important broker of the First Renaissance. Like Morgan (*Cyrano de Bergerac*, 1992), Lochhead translated French drama, beginning with *Tartuffe* (1986).

Rejecting tabula rasa Bildungsroman and 'heritage', many turned to European Modernists troubled by the disjunction between official history and lived-experience. Dostoevsky was revisited (honouring MacDiarmid's plea in *A Drunk Man Looks at the Thistle*), as were Joyce, Kafka and Beckett. James Kelman's (1946–) *Not Not While the Giro* (1983), *The Busconductor Hines* (1984) and *A Disaffection* (1991) attempt to grasp experience as it slips into distraction and alienation. The struggle for presence in Kelman is not only at the level of story, but also the textual one, in the push-and-pull tension of dialects, emotions, resistances and capitulations, using figures of repetition, hesitation, stuttering, interruption and sudden inexplicable emotion. This becomes masterly in *How late it was, how late* (1994), where a blind protagonist feels out each new experience in the streets. The book famously precipitated a row over its Booker Prize, which, although ridiculous, brought to popular British attention questions of ownership rights to literary language, and so non-standard dialects' relationship to literary experience, recalling Tom Leonard's (1944–) *Intimate Voices* (1984).

The post-heritageist years also saw various structural signs of increasing literary confidence. The Edinburgh International Book Festival, beginning in 1983, expanded to one of Europe's largest. In 1984, the Scottish Poetry Library was established, gathering important documents together, the magazine *Verse* began, and Morgan's anti-'heritage' *Sonnets from Scotland* appeared, aimed at national narrative from first principles. In 1985, Kelman and Gray were collected with Agnes Owens in *Lean Tales*, establishing a tone of spare Glasgow naturalism which stood (and was often over-imitated) throughout the period. That year the Traverse Theatre's 'Points of Departure' season turned to a provocatively national agenda, and three years later the Tramway opened in Glasgow. In 1987–8 an ambitious four-volume history of Scottish literature was published by Aberdeen University Press, and began to set out widely-agreed parameters. In 1989 the same general editor, Cairns Craig, began to series-edit Polygon's *Determinations*, polemical reconsiderations of Scottish cultural history. One of the first of these, edited by Owen Dudley Edwards, was also one of the most significant: the *Claim of Right for Scotland* involved a broad spectrum from politics, arts and public life, nailed the democratic deficit for a general audience and shifted the ground of the Scotland–UK relationship. Further volumes discuss education, labour history, cultural history and party politics, and the series can be seen as an index of this new Renaissance.

In the 1980s, the literary depiction of 'living space' shifted. Jeff Torrington's (1935–2008) Whitbread Prize-winning *Swing, Hammer, Swing* (1992) encapsulated themes of Glasgow regeneration and degeneration popularised by Laing, Trocchi, Gray and the Morgan of 'Glasgow Sonnets' (1972). In 1989 Dilys Rose's (1954–) 'Snakes and Ladders' sympathetically depicted public housing despair, and Janice Galloway's (1956–) *The Trick is to Keep Breathing* put Joy Stone on a semi-fictional late-Thatcher-era housing estate and subjected her to every crumbling organ of the UK welfare state, from salacious housing officer to patronising GP. Rose's stories and novels often circle post-welfare state themes; the psychologists in *Red Tides* (1993) prioritise efficient processing over communication, like Galloway's Dr Stead, recalling the anti-psychiatry of Laing and, in another sense, Muriel Spark's (1918–2006) *The Hothouse by the East River* (1973).

Spark's work in this period was less swayed by the Scottish domestic situation. An early domesticator of the *nouveau roman*, her work had already prefigured the move from empirical realism. Spark remained one of the period's most prominent voices in small and beautifully crafted novels including *A Far Cry from Kensington* (1988), parodying the London publishing industry, and *Symposium* (1991), a comedy of manners set in London and St Andrews. Meanwhile her earlier critiques of gentility, classism, empire-building and sectarianism continued to influence writers as disparate as Ian Rankin and Margaret Elphinstone. The somewhat comparable novelist-of-ideas Elspeth

Davie (1919–95) also consolidated her reputation with *Traveller's Room* (1985), *Coming to Light* (1989) and a wide oeuvre of short stories. Robin Jenkins (1912–2005) modified the tropes of *Fergus Lamont* (1979), a coming-of-age story of a working-class boy as a cipher for social history, in *Just Duffy* (1988), seen through an odd misanthropic boy's eyes, avoiding nostalgia with a powerful social realism. This prolific period for Jenkins encompassed national history – *The Awakening of George Darroch* (1985), staged around the 1843 Disruption – and cultural comparison – *Willie Hogg* (1991), in which Glasgow pensioners are drawn by a communication from the US and *Leila* (1995), a careful negotiation of orientalism. Stuart Hood (1915–), now an immensely under-rated figure who was also an authority on television and a political historian, wrote several sophisticated short novels, including *A Storm from Paradise* (1985), describing a pan-European socialist woman's wooing of a repressed Scottish schoolteacher, drawing modern changes towards rural Scotland, and recalling Lewis Grassic Gibbon's Renaissance themes and his richness and lightness of touch. George Mackay Brown's (1921–96) Orcadian scenes are by contrast *counter*-modern, from *Greenvoe* (1972) to the Booker-shortlisted *Beside the Ocean of Time* (1994), which uses the schoolboy, again, to run ancient Viking tales alongside modern Orcadian ones. Iain Crichton Smith (1928–98) also continued to negotiate an island-based, Gaelic Scotland, describing religious decline in *A Field Full of Folk* (1982), then the strain caused on a Glasgow marriage by the fantasy of returning to the islands in *The Dream* (1990) – between which appeared his *Collected Poems* (1985). He followed earlier collections of Gaelic short stories with *An Dubh is An Gorm* (*The Black and the Blue*, 1985) and *Na Guthan* (*The Voices*, 1991). Meanwhile, his first Gaelic novel *An t-Aonaran* (*The Loner*, 1976) was followed by *Murchadh* (*Murdo*, originally serialised in *Gairm* (106–9, 1979–80) and *Na Speuclairean Dubha* (*The Dark Glasses*, 1989). Murdo recurs subsequently in English in *Thoughts of Murdo* (1993) and *Murdo: The Life and Works* (2001) as Smith wrestles with interactions of Gaelic- and English-speaking identities. Margaret Elphinstone (1948–) similarly worried over the negotiation of nativeness in her unique and fantastic *The Incomer* (1987), turning to Brown-like Nordic saga in *Islanders* (1994).

If science fiction began during this period to meet popular literary fiction, the pioneering figure was Iain (M.) Banks (1954–), whose faux-controversial, best-selling debut, *The Wasp Factory* (1984), was ahead of its time in rendering the life of a young iconic Highland anti-hero for a British audience. *The Crow Road* (1992) returns to the trope of the weird village boy, and in *Complicity* (1993), the zeitgeist-friendly young male voice is of an itinerant journalist. *The Bridge* (1986), sometimes described, with Irvine Welsh's (1958–) *Marabou Stork Nightmares*, as part of a sub-genre of 'coma fiction', shows a debt to Gray in arranging narratives around a single damaged voice.

'M.' Banks's 'hard science fiction' from *Consider Phlebas* (1987) worries over the cultural bankruptcy of perfectly rational progress, connoting the modern difficulties of Enlightenment-Unionist Scotland's civility, and indexing the possibilities of a Scottish science fiction. Similarly Ken MacLeod's (1954–) future-Gàidhealtachd 'Fall Revolution' novels from *The Star Fraction* (1995) force post-Enlightenment questions about the limits of the rational and the human, and do so in a most conspicuously 'nativist' ground – and are perhaps better contextualised if we see Gray's *Lanark* as a Gothic, a fantastic, or a magic realist moment. Sometimes also associated with the fantastic, the poet, playwright, short-story writer and editor, Ron Butlin (1949–), rose from cult status with his closely observed second-person novel of alcoholic ennui, *The Sound of My Voice* (1987). Emma Tennant (1937–) developed her impressionistic psychological tone in *Woman Beware Woman* (1983) and the *Cycle of the Sun* sequence (1987–), and also published among other things a long series of variations on classic Victorian English literature. Also riding a wave of psycho-gender interest, and comparable to Angela Carter, Alice Thompson's impressionistic short novel *Justine*, a series of interlinked neo-decadent paintings of London, won the 1996 James Tait Black Memorial Prize.

The boy's-level story, so central to Scottish literature and film in the 1960s and 1970s, was resurrected and adapted to sectarianism by Alan Spence (1947–) in his accomplished *The Magic Flute* (1990), published just as Glasgow puzzled over European City of Culture status. Andrew Greig (1951–), already an admired poet (*The Order of the Day*, 1990), moved to fiction in the state-of-the-nation mountaineering epic *Electric Brae* (1992), with a tone comparable to that of Banks, and then to an ingenious reworking of John Buchan, *The Return of John Macnab* (1996). Ronald Frame (1953–) (*A Long Weekend with Marcel Proust*, 1986) returned to explicitly Scottish themes with *The Lantern-Bearers* (1999), an elegantly worked story of a musical composer and his Platonic love. Candia McWilliam (1955–) won the 1994 Guardian Fiction Prize for her story of an antipodean boat voyage in *Debatable Land*, elegantly taking in national and other concerns with Sparkean lightness. Meanwhile Thatcher-era values as they continued under John Major, with their individualism and devaluation of labour and community, were meat and drink to the sarcastic, nihilistic junkies of Irvine Welsh's *Trainspotting* (1993). This novel's dropout culture recalls Trocchi's *Cain's Book* (1960), but also documents public culture's paucity in the UK's second-favourite city. Lambasted by nationalist critics from what now looks uncomfortably like class prejudice, *Trainspotting* locates an underground in global, culturally self-important Edinburgh, as does Robert Louis Stevenson's *Jekyll and Hyde* (1886) or Muriel Spark's *The Prime of Miss Jean Brodie* (1961), and is a powerful inside attack on British egoism and boredom. Welsh's *Marabou Stork Nightmares* (1995) is an even more brutal account of class, gender, empire, football hooliganism and sectarianism winding their way through one jug-eared family on an Edinburgh estate.

Welsh's commercial success encouraged the banding and marketing together of some Scottish writers, a subject of both celebration and hand-wringing. Usefully later historicised by Alan Riach,[4] 'Magnetic North' was a 1995 marketing pamphlet produced by Cape and Vintage showcasing Galloway, Kennedy, Duncan McLean (1964–), Leonard, Alan Warner (1964–), Welsh, Gray, Kelman and Owens. The marketability involved a covert politics: Scotland is the magnetic 'North' as it was North Britain for Smollett. It is not coincidental that the years when New Labour emerged were also those during which 'Scottish literature' was identified as globally viable, homogenised, 'spun' and mass-marketed. And although Scottish writers' relationship with London publishing has generally been good and mutually beneficial, to an extent 'Magnetic North' exemplifies a wider gentrification. Some writers, including Kennedy and Kelman, had emerged via the Edinburgh publisher Polygon, which by now looked more interesting than most London imprints. The Clocktower Press in Orkney produced ten booklets from 1990 to 1996, including McLean, Galloway, James Meek (1962–) and famously, some of the stories which would be incorporated into *Trainspotting*: a retrospective anthology is *Ahead of Its Time* (1997). Some, including Warner and Meek, came through the Edinburgh micro-culture of Rebel Inc, founded by Kevin Williamson in 1992 (*Children of Albion Rovers*, 1996). Meek emerged as an engaging storyteller, with a boisterous voice comparable to Gray, in *Macfarlane Boils the Sea* (1989); *Drivetime* (1995) extended the voice, again via the young male protagonist, on a European road trip. *The People's Act of Love* (2005) would further extend his range. McLean, like Welsh, was interested in football hooliganism (*Bucket of Tongues*, 1992) and public exhibitions of perversion (*Bunker Man*, 1995), and had already had a career in drama (The Merry Mac Fun Company) as well as showing strong First Renaissance-agitprop sympathies, echoing Grassic Gibbon in *Blackden* (1994). Laura Hird (1966–) is perhaps the only writer from these circles successfully to pull off a novel in something comparable to Welsh's abrasive Edinburgh idiom, in her compelling *Born Free* (1999).

Some survived the marketing of northern chic better than others. One of the era's strongest voices since her collection *Night Geometry and the Garscadden Trains* (1990), A. L. Kennedy (1965–) in *Looking for the Possible Dance* (1993) presented disjointed insights in the voice of a hero, Margaret Maxwell, moving from Glasgow to London, a journey reversed in *Now That You're Back* (1994). *Looking for the Possible Dance* sets up the 'dance', the ceilidh, as a site of personal and possibly national salvation, but one plagued by insecurities. *So I Am Glad* (1995) makes a boldly anti-realist statement, fantasising the character of Cyrano de Bergerac into life, so reworking

Morgan's (and Lochhead's) dramatic connections in a more fantastic idiom. *Original Bliss* (1997) returns to stories, often of sexual relationships, packing in insights as confidently and passionately as did the Kelman who returned to stories in *The Good Times* (1998). Alan Warner's marketwise *Morven Callar* (1995), further popularised by Lynne Ramsay's film (2002), features a checkout girl who claims authorship of her boyfriend's first novel and is then sold as a strong woman, a salutary conundrum recalling the translation of Highland experience for London publishing. Still, the Scottish activist George McKay has made more telling statements about the rave revolution, as in *DIY Culture* (1998) (cover-puffed by Welsh), and Warner's *These Demented Lands* (1997) is more compelling in describing the guts and grain of the 1990s Highland experience. Warner is also comparable with another metropolitan broker of designer rawness, Andrew O'Hagan (1968–), whose *Our Fathers* (1998) plumbs some of the older staple themes. Crime fiction also strengthened its exportability during the period, perhaps reflecting a longer history of North British uneven development. Ian Rankin (1960–) (*Knots and Crosses*, 1987 and subsequent novels) mixes the visceral social realism of William McIlvanney (1936–) (*Docherty*, 1975; *The Big Man*, 1985) with the rhetorical sophistication of Spark, and has enjoyed a huge dispersal, adding to Edinburgh's moody northern reputation. The late 1990s saw a wave of 'hard' literary crime, sometimes sold as 'tartan noir'. Denise Mina (1966–) has worked on central support systems' breakdown and latent urban violence, as in *Garnethill* (1998). Christopher Brookmyre's (1968–) investigative journalist Jack Parlabane starred in three of his first five novels (1996–2000), which aimed to mix hard crime with political comedy. Allan Guthrie (1965–) and Louise Welsh (1965–) would follow in comparable vein.

Playwrights also took the opportunity of the global-marketing moment to ask loud questions of the nation's form. David Greig's (1969–) *Caledonia Dreaming* (1997) satirises an ambitious Member of the European Parliament trying to bring the Olympics to Edinburgh, while *The Speculator* (1999) features the proto-Thatcherite career of the Scottish banker John Law. Stephen Greenhorn's (1964–) *Passing Places* (1997) visits the back-to-the-Highlands sub-genre in drama as Warner did in fiction, taking Central Belt kids to Thurso in a pointed rereading of Edwin Muir's despairing trek from Orkney in *Scottish Journey* (1935). At the same time there was a Britishing of film, building on the financial success of Danny Boyle's *Shallow Grave* (1994) whose epochal opening sequence restages (probably unwittingly) the exclusions of Enlightenment, when a pan-British trio of brats in Edinburgh's New Town, employed in medicine, finance and journalism, grill a potential flatmate named Cameron. The Britishing moment marks the move away from the neo-pastoral low-budget aesthetic of Bill Forsyth's *Gregory's Girl* (1981) and *Local Hero* (1983) towards the global-British, lowest-common-denominator youth culture aesthetic which re-adapted recent Scottish literary successes like *Trainspotting* (1997) and *Complicity* (2000). *Shallow Grave*'s budgetary leap did, however, make independent exceptions possible, such as Peter Mullan's *Orphans* (1997), Lynne Ramsay's *Ratcatcher* (1999) and Ken Loach's long-term tapping into Scottish rep in the 'Glasgow Trilogy' (1996–2004).

Meanwhile poetry found a more northern North in St Andrews, whose StAnza festival has grown to be one of Britain's most important since its inauguration in 1998. Robert Crawford (1959–) came to occupy an influential position covering poetry – from his collection *A Scottish Assembly* (1990) onwards – criticism and major editing (*The Penguin Book of Poetry from Britain and Ireland since 1945*, ed. with Simon Armitage, 1998). Critically, Crawford traced Scotland's importance to Modernism in *Devolving English Literature* (1992) and *The Scottish Invention of English Literature* (ed., 1998). Douglas Dunn's (1942–) Whitbread Prize-winning 1985 collection *Elegies* confirmed a move away from the Larkinesque model of *Terry Street* (1969) to the more challenging voice of *St Kilda's Parliament* (1981), then later *Northlight* (1988). Kathleen Jamie (1962–) (*The Way We Live*, 1987; *The Queen of Sheba*, 1994) added to the St. Andrews profile, as did Don Paterson (1963–): *Nil Nil* (1993) and *God's Gift to Women* (1997). In the early 1990s *Verse* was edited from here by Crawford and David Kinloch (1959–), and grew into a major international publication. A related, smaller journal was *Gairfish* (1990–5), edited by W. N. Herbert (1961–) and Richard Price (1966–), both with important and popular oeuvres of their own. Two other, quite independent, critic-poets whose poetic reputations have grown more steadily, but very significantly, are Alan Riach (1957–) and Roderick Watson (1943–).

At the far end of the poetic spectrum, Robin Purves's magazine *Object Permanence* (1994–7) introduced some of the most important experimental writers in the English-speaking world, largely to deaf ears (it went the way of Ian Hamilton Finlay's *Poor.Old.Tired.Horse* (1962–7), only later realised to be vitally important). If Edwin Morgan straddled mainstream and experiment with increasing success, Finlay (1925–2006) and Kenneth White (1936–) also continued to extend European connections that had been built since the early 1960s. Finlay's concrete sculptures and books encouraged an Enlightenment-sceptic aesthetic, showing allegiances as wide as Brazilian concrete poetry and French Situationism; White's psychogeography-influenced work described the experience of travelling, writing and environment, often deliberately pitching between genres. French crossovers have been under-examined, despite the importance of Laing and Trocchi, and despite later attempts like Richard Price and David Kinloch's *La Nouvelle Alliance* (ed., 2000). The line through *Object Permanence* also shows that Scots were involved in the Cambridge-London-California experimental movement, particularly Drew Milne (1964–) (*The Damage: New and Selected Poems*, 2001). And also often missed, though not by prestige UK publishers like Paladin, was Thomas A. Clark (1944–), strikingly engaging with Buddhist aesthetics (*Twenty Poems*, 1983).

The 1980s and 1990s might be seen as a watershed period in the develop‑ ment of Scottish Gaelic literature. In 1987, you could walk into a mainstream bookshop and purchase the best of the older generation: Somhairle MacGill‑ Eain's first selected poems, *Reothairt is Contraigh/Spring‑Tide and Neap‑Tide, Poems 1932–1972*, republished by Canongate in 1985; George Campbell Hay's 'lost' poem sequence *Mochtàr is Dùghall* first published in 1982; Donald MacAulay's anthology *Nua‑Bhàrdachd Ghàidhlig/Modern Scottish Gaelic Poems*, republished by Canongate, 1987; the collected and new poems of Ruaraidh MacThòmais (Derick Thomson), *Creachadh na Clàrsaich* (Lines Review, 1982) and the first collection of Aonghas MacNeacail, *an seachnadh agus dàin eile/the avoiding and other poems* (Lines Review, 1986). To this one might add the first substantial critical study of a modern Gaelic poet, in the col‑ lection edited by Raymond J. Ross and Joy Hendry, *Sorley MacLean: Critical Essays* (Scottish Academic Press, 1986), and the invigorating collection of MacLean's own criticism, *Ris a' Bhruthaich*, edited by William Gillies (Acair, 1985). Critically, as well as creatively, Gaelic seemed to be moving towards the mainstream. This new prominence and acceptance by the Scottish liter‑ ary publishing mainstream marked something of a high‑water mark for Gaelic poetry.

There was tension here, however: all of these volumes were produced with facing translations, by the authors themselves. Moving onto a national stage demanded these authors compromise with their other tongue, a compromise that continues to be controversial. Few major collections of Gaelic poetry have been published since in Gaelic only. The 1980s and 1990s also saw the rise of a new breed of Gaelic poet: those who had learned Gaelic in school or university. These poets found, alongside a number of talented native speaker poets, their own 'canonisation' in Christopher Whyte's *An Aghaidh na Sìorraidheachd/In the Face of Eternity, Eight Gaelic Poets* (Polygon, 1991). It was the newer generation's answer to the 'famous five' of MacAulay's anthol‑ ogy, and has arguably been as influential in defining the scope and sound of contemporary Gaelic poetry. By the end of the 1990s, the eldest of this new generation, Aonghas MacNeacail, was stretching further boundaries, with challenging new collections (*oideacheadh ceart/a proper schooling*, 1997), and with a wide variety of artistic collaborations, particularly musical, such as *An Turus/The Journey*, with William Sweeney, premièred at the Glasgow Celtic Connections festival in 1998. Ominously, however, only a few of the poets of Whyte's anthology – Meg Bateman, Maoilios Caimbeul, Whyte himself – have sustained their poetry in quantity or profile, and this against the backdrop of the deaths of three of the most important members of the older generation: George Campbell Hay (d. 1984), Somhairle MacGill‑Eain

(d. 1996) and Iain Mac a' Ghobhainn/Iain Crichton Smith (d. 1998). If these decades began strongly for Gaelic poetry, it was easy by the turn of the millennium to feel distinctly uncertain of its future. For Gaelic prose it was a very mixed period, and its renaissance was unlooked for; it came in the early years of the twenty-first century, with the rise of the imprint Ùr-sgeul. In drama much was hoped for from the theatre company Tosg, founded in 1996 but closed in 2007 without making a lasting impact, although Theatre Hebrides (2002–) now presents bilingual drama on contemporary topics, such as Kevin MacNeil's *The Callanish Stoned* (2006). Michelle Macleod and Moray Watson's detailed discussion of Gaelic prose and drama of this period is an important resource.[5]

During these two decades, the explosion in range across poetry, drama, fiction and criticism was huge. Many of the most important questions about a national aesthetic had been asked, if not all answered. Progress has been mixed. One dubious legacy of the 1990s boom, partly because of critical academic methods which eschewed theory, was a resurgent tendency to nativise the canon, fixing Scottish literature to Scottish history, preferring to be diagnostic about the origins of writers, or of characters. Literature has sometimes been reduced to a cipher for national identity. So, Kennedy is seen to 'represent Scottish women', and so on – diagnoses strenuously resisted by the writers themselves. Jenkins, Spark and Boyd might have been incorporated better into literary history even on those occasions when they are not describing Scottish scenes (or, like Spark, are doing so complexly). More fundamentally, even during the devolutionary phase Scottishness was still often seen as an ethnic belonging, stretching back unbroken – and New Labour management of devolution, nervously silent over the term 'state', somewhat encouraged this. Iain Crichton Smith's celebration poem at the 1999 opening of Parliament went more or less unquestioned when it described the nation as 'three-tongued', but the welding of language to nation is both a great weakness and an ethical problem, since it privileges some languages and turns the nation from state-political to ethnic-nostalgic. In other words, as national redefinition was spread in the 1990s by a new confidence, the marketing of that new confidence sometimes tended to close down the very liberating possibilities that were so needed. Some of the ethnic blind spots of the First Renaissance were amplified. Yet by 1999, local and global had been connected in sophisticated and successful ways, and Scottish literature had defined its concerns – largely relative to the 1960s, though not always realising this. By 2000, devolution had shaken up the UK constitutional situation. 'Scottish Literature' as a legitimate separate field of study was in a sense born during this period.

CHAPTER SIXTEEN

Scottish Contemporary Popular and Genre Fiction

Marie Odile Pittin-Hédon

Popular literature is a volatile notion, involving marketing, publicity and sales figures, but also the more literary, abstract concepts of genre, sub-genre and the shift of our conception of those in the last thirty years. In the case of Scotland, many of the authors of 'popular fiction' make it to the top of best sellers' lists on a regular basis: Iain M. Banks (1954–), Louise Welsh (1965–), Val McDermid (1955–) and, increasingly in later years, Denise Mina (1966–), not to mention the hugely popular Ian Rankin (1960–) and Alexander McCall Smith (1948–) and the worldwide Edinburgh-based literary marketing phenomenon J. K. Rowling (1965–). All those writers contribute to shaping a contemporary literary landscape described by David Lodge in 1992 as 'the aesthetic supermarket', while retaining characteristics of the backgrounds they have chosen to write from, about, or simply to ignore, but which is part of their common vantage point[1] described by Ben Okri in 1986 as 'another country'.[2] The additional issue of genre versus mainstream fiction, the blurring of whose limits prompts comparison with the Scottish Borders' sub-region, the 'debatable lands', affords a unique perspective. This adds to the social and literary dimension yet another one, the broadly political, as those writers operate, in Kevin McNeil's words, from 'the very *heart* of beyond'.[3] This chapter is situated at the crossroads of mass-market publishing and literary issues and debates. It endeavours to chart the shifting borders of the 'debatable lands' of Scottish popular fiction from the fairly stable definition of the 1960s and 1970s to the 2000s, characterised by crossover and hybridisation, justifying Roger Luckhurst's claims (about science fiction) that it has become 'a central cultural node, less a genre than a mode of apprehension'.[4] By examining the works of authors traditionally categorised under the label of genre fiction the chapter will look at the various 'modes of apprehension' to come out of the popular Scottish novel in recent years.

We see through a glass, darkly

Iain Banks pursues two very successful literary careers, publishing both main-stream and science fiction novels whose themes – transgression, duality and doubles, the fearful,[5] and power structures – transcend generic lines. In them, horror is never far from the surface, whether it takes the form of crude and always inventive forms of torture (a monstrous Buddha-like ruler in *Consider Phlebas* (1987) devouring his subjects or, in *The Algebraist* (2004), a melodrama villain's enemy destroyed by the chemically-enhanced growth of his own teeth slowly piercing his brains), or that of the ontologically disturbing blurring of the safe boundary between fiction and reality in language.[6] Horror is embodied in *Excession* (1996) by a species called 'the Affront', who have genetically manipulated their environment to create 'a kind of self-perpetuating, never-ending holocaust of pain and fear'.[7] Banks's Culture novels, with their typical reliance on cognition and estrangement[8] present 'an anarchy'[9] or a 'future anarchist-socialist utopia',[10] a place where a moral collective prevails, and which paradoxically needs violence and pain to restore the validity of the human pitted against drones and AIs. As suggested by Gavin Miller, the post-scarcity society idealised by the culture has also become post-human, propounding as it does an informatic post-vitalist view of life.[11] The foregrounding of terror is compounded by its hopelessly circular structure, as in the frightfully literal, destructive contest of *The Player of Games* (1988) where the empire's name, Azad – meaning 'machine'– and the reversible chapter title 'machina ex machina' provide a sort of dead end in guise of conclusion. No last-minute intervention will save either the empire or even the Culture because the two apparently opposed worlds are ultimately interchangeable, as the text further indicates by disclaiming the Culture's proverbial benevolence – 'Fuck with the culture and you will see how mean it is'.[12]

The contamination of the real world by terror takes place in crime fiction in a different way from science fiction. No cognitive estrangement for Rankin, Mina, McDermid or the other proponents of 'tartan noir'; rather an orchestration of violence connected by Ian Rankin with the dark area he locates on the borders of human consciousness and society, claiming 'people are interested in crime fiction because they are fascinated by the margins of the world, those places where society's rules break down' and because 'they learn how to deal with fear of the unknown'.[13] Val McDermid's novel situated in Scotland (she lives and works in Manchester), *The Distant Echo* (2003) significantly hinges on the biblical quote 'we see through a glass, darkly',[14] itself a metaphor of her own fictional output which cryptically reflects on the specularity of the genre as a whole. As with Banks's novels, the darkening of the material has to do with the reversibility of the process of violence. In *Beneath the Bleeding* (2007), the narrative follows two parallel courses, DCI Carol Jordan and profiler Tony Hill's enquiry into the death of a celebrity football player and what appears to be Yousef Aziz's carefully planned terrorist attack. While a character rejoices over the shift of the country 'from empire to multi-culti in the space of fifty years',[15] the narration itself focuses on 'the precariousness of the bridge between the two cultures' (p. 103). This resolves itself into an escalation in the psychological impact of violence, as is pithily summarised in Aziz's lesson in terrorism: '[W]e create terror, not outrage' (pp. 113–14). McDermid's novels consistently point to the diffuseness of evil – through means of internal focalisation in *Beneath the Bleeding*. This aspect distinguishes them from their predecessors in the 1960s and 1970s, for example the novels of Hugh C. Rae (1935–) in which evil is isolated by being associated with one protagonist. In Rae's *Skinner* (1965), the eponymous character, an unrepenting murderer, is described like a pounding predator; in *The Shooting Gallery* (1972) internal focalisation is used to enhance the melodramatic connection between the murderer and evil:

> The fence was high. Above it he could see an earth banking. He tried to reason the position of the railway line in relation to river and canal. Yule stared at the sky-line; four posts, like gibbets, planted on the breast of an earthwork.[16]

Skinner and Yule may be Ian Rankin's Cafferty's forefathers, but Rankin's novels, like McDermid's, increasingly narrow the gap between the villain and the sleuth. Indeed, while Rebus in *Exit Music* (2007) still describes Cafferty as '[not] just the grit in the oyster' but the 'pollutant poisoning everything within reach',[17] he ends his career desperately giving Cafferty a heart massage in hospital, the novel's last words '[T]ell me he's going to be all right' (p. 380) blurring for ever the distinction between horror and safety. McDermid makes a similar suggestion in *Killing the Shadows* (2000), where psychological profiler Fiona Cameron and her partner and thriller writer Kit Martin are up against a killer using copycat stories as models for his deeds – a copycat copycat. This *mise en abyme* of a fairly conventional crime thriller motif first suggests the recursive aspect of evil and terror, while also commenting on the fiction-writing process. The criminal, a failed writer, recounts his deeds in a diary, thereby reversing the formula of detective fiction: the list of victims and the manner of killing are already pre-written, as is the generic identity of the killer (the mentally disturbed would-be writer), a transformation which makes the book not so much a whodunnit as a 'whydunnit'. This shifts the focus from the actual enquiry (a process at the core of *A Place of Execution* (1999) or *The Distant Echo*) to another, more metaphysical and contextual form of enquiry on what drives evil, or how horror progresses. The composition of the novel, which yokes together emails, death-threat letters, decoded trial exhibits, extracts from the victims' novels and from website publications, simultaneously insists on the realism of the action depicted and dereferentialises it. Combined with the novel's insistence on how people can be stalked on the internet, this gives shape to a sort of all-pervading, multi-format 'virtual' terror. McDermid's world, therefore, instils into the referential world a type of psychological, virtual terror that cannot leave the reader entirely safe in the assumption that, as Kit puts it, 'what he [is] reading [is] fiction',[18] that the violence will stop once he closes the book. The porosity between actual and fictional is also tackled from the point of view of the murderer, who confidently asserts that 'it couldn't have gone better if I'd scripted it' (p. 111) or even puns: 'I'll be writing them off' (p. 60). *Beneath the Bleeding* is a logical outcome of that. With its focus on the society of prying which has come to be symbolised by the World Wide Web (economically summed up by the repetition of the slogan 'REMEMBER YOU READ IT FIRST ON MURDER BEHIND THE SCENES'), it finally encapsulates our relation with (virtual-real) horror in the truism 'societies get the criminals they deserve' (p. 65). This turns the table on the readers by focusing not on the criminal's perceived 'madness' (as in *Skinner*), but on each individual and their own locus of evil, or even on the detectives themselves. As Rankin also recognises about Rebus: 'I *do* think that we all have this dark side [. . .] And in Rebus there is that darkness in him that he is loath to explore, because he is terrified of where it will take him.[19] J. K. Rowling's Harry Potter series, albeit operating in a genre at odds with Rankin's brand of hard-boiled detective fiction, shares with it this preoccupation with violence, terror and death and with the problematic porosity of the good/evil frontier indicated by the planting of one of Voldemort's Horcruxes inside Harry himself.[20] The exploratory nature of her depiction of death parallels Rebus's introspective visions, as the recurring images of verticality indicate:

> Harry jumped to his feet, caught Quirrell by the arm and hung on as tight as he could [. . .] he could only hear Quirrell's terrible shrieks and Voldemort's yells of 'KILL HIM! KILL HIM! [. . .]
> He felt Quirrell's arm wrenched from his grasp, knew all was lost, and fell into blackness, down . . . down . . . down . . .[21]

Louise Welsh, in her own literary version of the crime thriller, carries out this exploration in her three novels *The Cutting Room* (2002), *Tamburlaine Must Die* (2004) and *The Bullet Trick* (2006). The first in particular basks in darkness, portraying a dive into an underworld of pornography, snuff photographs, homosexual encounters, dark secrets and voyeurism unambiguously treated like a lethal impulse. Welsh's muffled universe, obsessively referring to the young woman in the snuff photograph and her forever-muted agony, is paradoxically revealed to be the means to get at the 'truth'. This last concept deviates from its usual meaning in crime fiction, that of finding the culprit, to focus on the real self hidden at the core of the books. Rilke realises that:

> What I had been avoiding was the truth. Like a child hesitating before a keyhole, I wanted to discover hidden secrets, but was frightened that the knowledge, once gained, wouldn't be to my liking and could never be lost.[22]

The hint at the protagonist's innocence serves to indicate the dialectical nature of the search, itself duplicated in an ambivalent light and darkness symbolism best summed up in the oxymoron 'the gloom of the day' (p. 51). Innocent probing, like perversion, leads to an ultimate darkness that the narrative – in a manner strikingly similar to *Harry Potter*'s symbolic motif of the 'he-that-must-not-be-named' – cannot confront. And indeed, when Rilke delves into old books, photographs and etchings, he realises that 'death reached out from their pages' (p. 228), and when finally confronted with the dead body of old Miss McKindless, he experiences an epiphany that extends to Welsh's conception of the genre:

> The pale body washed, scented and tucked beneath the sheets was no longer Miss McKindless. Whatever it was that had made her herself, the essential spirit, vital spark, soul, call it what you will, had departed. (p. 244)

Louise Welsh's fiction, therefore, strays away from the conventional version of the whodunnit, not in order to write, like McDermid, a sort of 'whydunnit', but to focus on a more generic and metaphysical question. A clue carefully left by the author in the shape of a Wordsworth quotation, 'we murder to dissect' (p. 208), is just as much a statement of purpose for the novelist as her explanation for the roots of crime. As Welsh explains in an interview, the mechanics of crime fiction is not what she is primarily interested in: 'So yeah, I think I do have ethics, that there's things that I dislike in books. I dislike when a murder is somehow just a prop.'[23] Indeed, in the aesthetically staged world of *The Cutting Room*, murder becomes all but a prop; it is paradoxically the only entry into the 'essential spirit, vital spark, soul, call it what you will'.

Crossing Borders or Shifting Them?

In *The Novel Now*, Richard Bradford notes that 'fiction as an industry is dominated by what the high cultural literati treats as subgenres'.[24] The development of mass-market publishing, and the sales figures of novels by Rankin, Rowling or McCall Smith, as well as the number of languages their books have been translated into[25], in effect questions the validity of the classification of literature into mainstream fiction, genre fiction and sub-genre. It also underlines the contradictions of the inclusive cultural politics of 1990s Cool Britannia which, however, did not always stretch to an erasure of the impassable frontier between high and low art. The most vocal opponent to this static categorisation is Ian Rankin, who frequently dismisses the distinction as 'rubbish'.[26] Denise Mina is on the contrary quite happy to work from within a genre, claiming that:

Crime fiction gives currency to ideas on a subliminal, populous level, so that they are absorbed into the culture in immeasurable ways [. . .] The truth is that crime fiction, read on buses and beaches, sniggered at by the bigger boys who went to better schools, is a potent social force.[27]

Rankin, in his Introduction to *The Rough Guide to Crime Fiction*[28] sums up the debate by reducing it to its basic, yet crucial question: 'Has crime fiction finally achieved the literary respectability that has long been its due?' This should be understood in terms of both the formal aspects, the crossing of the border between 'literature' and 'genre', and the agenda that transpires behind the mass market sales. Rankin conveys the transformation of the genre over the years spanning the publication of his novels. *Knots and Crosses* (1987) takes in the evolution of gangsterhood from the 1950s to the 1980s, from the Gorbals-type gangs to the 'dope scene'.[29] *Mortal Causes* (1994) describes the way the underclass in Edinburgh has been moved out of sight to the schemes, a motif which Rankin shares with Irvine Welsh. *Dead Souls* (1999) expands on the theme of the Scots as glorious failures, while taking up that of independence. *Set in Darkness* (2000), opening the new millennium, turns to the inclusive, gentrified image Scotland has been building for itself since devolution, with a few comical reflections of the vacuous politically correct thinking behind, for example, the description of foreigners: 'a settler – one of the New Scots. I think that's what the Nationalists call them'.[30]

Louise Welsh, Val McDermid and Denise Mina all comment on their concern with gender politics. In *The Bullet Trick*, the metaphor of magic informs the crime story, with the cutting-up of women both theatrical illusion and homicidal reality, thereby drawing the reader's attention to sexual politics. In *The Cutting Room*, Welsh formally conveys this concern by setting up a dense network of visual references, organised around the central image of the panopticon, a metaphor for the imprisonment of the woman in the snuff photograph. The eye, and its appendages (mirror sunshades, camera, video camera, photocopying machine) cannot distinguish between fake and reality, in the same way that the photograph of the tortured woman seems to allow blood seepage to contaminate the real world:

The same girl, still naked, lies on the wooden pallet [. . .] Pupils unfocused and far back in her head, a mouth that ended with a scream. Her throat has been cut. Blood flows from her wound, slicks its way around the pallet and drips onto the floor. I wonder if it stains the photographer's boots. (pp. 35–6)

When the narrative nears its conclusion and Rilke realises, in a curiously abstruse formula that 'death was a woman, and women were dead' (p. 228), the woman's ordeal is universalised. In a parody of whodunnits, the final clue to unmask the culprit, in this case a woman's powder compact, shows Rilke a reflection of his own face, providing an illustration to McDermid's epigraph to *The Mermaids Singing* (1995), 'the Soul of torture is male'. Mina's output most obviously and consistently departs from the formulaic masculinity of the protagonist of 'tartan noir', by bringing in maverick female investigators – Maureen O'Donnell and Paddy Meehan – in a manner that coincides with the gradual centring of DI Siobhan Clark in the Rebus narratives, or even the patent reversal of gender politics in the detective fiction of Alexander McCall Smith, with his world-famous Mma Ramotswe of the *No. 1 Ladies' Detective Agency* (1998; television film, 2008) and his atypically intellectual Isabel Dalhousie of the Sunday Philosophy Club series. For Mina, the issue of female detectives, and of focusing on women outside the usual circles of power, is a political one:

> Women are labelled mentally ill through the criminal justice system in different ways from men. When women are deemed 'mad' it takes all their agency away; it means she can never have meant to do anything, whereas a man might still have rationality. This all ties in with the idea of women being passive – which is a stereotype the courts preserve very strongly. I wanted to have a female detective who [. . .] had to be proactive and have agency and make moral decisions, though she has a history of mental illness.[31]

In *Resolution* (2001), Maureen's enquiry leads her to a group of foreign prostitutes, and turns into an uncompromising summation of their predicament, concluded by her refusal to let things be. In *The Dead Hour* (2006), set in 1984, mixed with the gritty descriptions of housing estates and unemployed shipyard workers, epitomised by such chapter titles as 'Homeland of Tramps and Whores' or 'The Sad Fate of the Late and the Lost', Mina's consistent wish to focus on the most deprived, the female, transpires:

> Scott Lithgow shipyard was about to shut and if it did thousands of workers knew there were no jobs waiting for them elsewhere [. . .] Mrs Thatcher publicly insulted the workers, and when a committee of wives travelled to London with a petition she refused to meet them.[32]

The focus is unchanging, the feminist agenda being from Mina's own account actually enhanced by its placement within the pages of a popular – accessible – novel. Symbolically, in *The Dead Hour*, Paddy sets herself the task of writing a biography of criminal Patrick Meehan, and fails even to start: the point is elsewhere.

At the other end of the spectrum from Mina or Rankin, Alexander McCall Smith's fiction depicts another country which, before him, had remained relatively undescribed. McCall Smith admits to being 'a bit of a Utopian novelist', adding 'I am not a social realist novelist, I am not really concerned with describing things always as they are; rather, I look at how they might be'.[33] And indeed, his Botswana-based detective series thought by Robert Crawford to 'offer a near-Kailyard Africa sometimes suspiciously free from fearful facts'[34] allows for 'a fantasy of communal cohesion and simple resolution',[35] a detective world which, like that of his Isabel Dalhousie novels, 'returns us to the world of Miss Marple, where everything under the sun can be understood through reference to the microcosm of village life'.[36] McCall Smith's other 'bit[s] of light-hearted fiction',[37] namely the 44 Scotland Street series, but also the Isabel Dalhousie series and the Von Igelfeld trilogy, present a world in which, for example, a German professor of philology discusses everything from the disadvantages of playing Solitaire to a schedule with the Pope, or where Isabel Dalhousie, editor of the *Journal of Applied Ethics*, reflects on the price of a suitable employee, or the advisability of keeping charity anonymous. *The Right Attitude to Rain* (2006) captures the very nature of McCall Smith's kindly feelings towards the world in general:

> They were sitting in a small pâtisserie round the corner from St Stephen Street [. . .] On the table behind them the day's newspapers were untidily folded, outraged headlines half obscured by creases in the paper: WARNS . . . RESIGNATION . . . ERUPTS IN SOMALIA . . . [38]

Declining to write about what the creases in the paper obscure, McCall Smith, in a profound departure from the culture of disaffection initiated by James Kelman, produces gentle middle-class comedies of manners, in which he sometimes, as in *Friends, Lovers, Chocolate* (2005), extends his optimistic feelings in a generalising gesture to the present and future of Scotland:

> He could see the flags on top of the Balmoral Hotel: the white-on-blue cross of the Saltire, the Scottish flag, the familiar diagonal stripes of the Union Jack [. . .] And that, he thought, was what Scotland was like: a small vessel pointed out to sea, a small vessel buffeted by the wind.[39]

While this metaphor ironically points to 'another country' quite literally, McCall Smith can be credited with putting the overworld on the literary map. His novels further help shifting the boundaries of popular fiction by foregrounding the particularly intimate rapport he enjoys with his readers. This he has done his very best to maintain, by inviting readers to write to him on his website as well as having leaflets handed out at his public appearances, discussing the lives of his fictional character as if they were real people. The likeability of his characters, the effect of interactivity created by the author's relationship to his readers, as well as the innocuousness of the world depicted in his books has successfully created the illusion of the breaking down of barriers between fiction and reality, in a sense much more pervasive than the mere inclusion of recognisable places in his novels. This can be seen when Scottish MSP for the Highlands and Islands Mary Scanlon chooses Mma Ramotswe as her ideal dinner party guest on Holyrood TV, claiming that 'she's just everything that you expect in a strong woman.'[40] This links McCall Smith with J. K. Rowling, as they share the celebrity status of their characters.

A. S. Byatt in 'Harry Potter and the Childish Adult' concedes a sort of anthropological value for Rowling's novels, as markers of the type of society which puts a premium on easiness derived from TV soaps and cartoons. She argues that:

> It is the substitution of celebrity for heroism that has fed this phenomenon. And it is the leveling effect of cultural studies, which are as interested in hype and popularity as they are in literary merit, which they don't really believe exists.[41]

And indeed, the Harry Potter novels have achieved that magic of turning wishful thinking and repetition (the first volume of the series relies on the mantra-like iteration of the phrase 'he's famous') into actuality, a fact which the epilogue to the very last volume, *Harry Potter and the Deathly Hallows* (2007) humorously registers in Ron's confident understatement that he's 'extremely famous'.[42] The hype surrounding the series has also, in a self-reflexive movement, come to include an academic dimension, the sheer mass of critical studies devoted to Harry Potter bearing ample witness to the fact that, in an ultimate ironic movement, Harry Potter redefines the concept of 'popular literature' in the very circles which started out as – and are still very vocal in – discarding it as unworthy of their attention. It is in that respect very fitting that J. K. Rowling should have chosen to settle down in Edinburgh, this 'other country', this place 'where the old resides so *solidly* in the new, where the music of the place blasts out its ancient lore amid the vague living spaces of the inhabitants'.[43]

This particular genre called the mainstream novel

Certainly J. K. Rowling's novels break the borders between genres, blending public school stories and fantasy, but also borrowing from Bildungsroman, fairy tale, adolescent literature, melodrama, Gothic fiction, or even science fiction. As also the most obvious manifestation of crossover literature – the reading of children's books by adults – Harry Potter gestures towards a redeployment of the neat line drawn between 'serious' or 'adult art' and mere childish fantasy,[44] thereby problematising both its own ontology and its critical reception. Critical neologisms such as 'realistic magicalism' and 'postmodern school stories'[45] certainly reflect on the basic ontological question

repeated throughout the first part of *The Philosopher's Stone*: 'What world?'
And indeed, devices such as forking paths suggest shadow narratives, fictional
worlds that might have been. For example, the first ceremony at Hogwarts,
the sorting hat, gives the reader a furtive glimpse of another story, with a
'small voice' to embody the shadow narrator:

> 'Not Slytherin, eh?' said the small voice. 'Are you sure? You could be great, you
> know, it's all here in your head, and Slytherin will help you on the way to
> greatness, no doubt about that – no? Well, if you're sure – Better be
> GRYFFINDOR!' (p. 91)

The epilogue of *The Deathly Hallows*, with its depiction of Harry's, Ron's, but
also Malfoy's, children's departure for Hogwarts returns to this idea, by suggesting a possible new beginning for the story with different options, as Albus's
anxieties about not being able to avoid being sorted to Slytherin indicates.

Rankin, who by coincidence put an end to Rebus's career the same year
Rowling published the last of the Harry Potter books, also tinkers with
generic boundaries, using pastiche and parody as a sort of farewell gesture to
crime fiction. Indeed, *Exit Music* exhibits an almost self-conscious structure,
with a build-up in the complicated plot involving Russian dissidents and
seedy businessmen, the world of Edinburgh finance and politics, a modest
drug- and a reasonable body-count. But the novel's lack of closure turns it
into a parody of a crime novel, the whole plot turning out to be totally unre-
lated to the murder, a random crime encapsulated by a Poirot-like Rebus in
the stereotypical resolution '*cherchez la femme*'. Following Cafferty's mocking
warning –'sometimes I wish I had your fantasy life, Rebus' (p. 144) – the
whole case collapses as it is revealed to have indeed been a pure product of
Rebus's, or Rankin's, 'fantasy life'. As DI Rebus takes leave of the force, so
does Ian Rankin, revealing in a last stroke of humour, his mastery over the
formulaic aspect of the police procedural.

Iain Banks, in a manner similar to that employed in his mainstream output,
uses his narrators to throw into relief textual and fictional boundaries and
the narrator's fundamental role in setting them up, as well as his power to
break them. Both *The Player of Games* and *The Algebraist* introduce a narrator
whose identity is kept conspicuously mysterious throughout the narrative and
who, in the opening of the latter takes the reader straight to the heart of the
metafictional dilemma:

> I have a story to tell you. It has many beginnings, and perhaps one ending.
> Perhaps not. Beginnings and endings are contingent things anyway; inventions,
> devices. Where does any story really begin? There is always context, always an
> encompassingly greater epic, always something before the described events,
> unless we are to start every story with, 'BANG! *Expand!* Ssss . . .'[46]

While he fittingly confers a mockingly scientific value to the literary notion of parallel worlds, the shadow narrator not only introduces the reader straight into the hidden choices and forks necessary to the construction of a story, but also transfers this ontological hesitation to the characters, by evolving the concept of 'swim' described by Fassin Taak in the following manner:

> 'Swim [. . .] You know; when your head kind of seems to swim because you suddenly think, 'Hey, I'm a human being but I'm twenty thousand light years from home and we're all living in the midst of mad-shit aliens and super-weapons and the whole fucking bizarre insane swirl of galactic history and politics!' That: isn't it *weird*?' (p. 135)

That, indeed, is enough to give Fassin 'swim', as he gets a glimpse of his (science) fictional status, and the reader one of the grinning author behind the narrator's back, incorporating with relish the derogatory definition of science fiction to the novel. Thereby he unveils the shadow narrator's other function, that of taking the reader on a guided tour of the high brow/low brow divide. A very short and affectedly pedantic vatic statement in *The Player* – 'Little textual note for you here (bear with me)' (p. 99) – or a comic intrusion into the thoughts of the characters in *The Algebraist* which contrasts the two stereotypes, leave the readers in little doubt as to where the narrator himself leans: '*And we shall try to pick each other's brains over dinner*, he thought, *My, what highbrow fun. Give me a planet to plunder any day*' (p. 200).

This comment finally reflects upon itself, by dismissing the highbrow, metafictional technique the narrative itself is based on. When Mawhrin Skel is finally revealed to have been the narrator, and admits to making up the parts he did not witness – a crowning irony in a genre which, precisely, is defined as being 'made up'– the reader is led back to *The Algebraist*. There Luseferous contends that 'there was at least a chance that none of it was real' (p. 200). This statement closes the metafictional loop by indicating that life and fiction alike might just be a fictional game, a story told by an 'irascible, ill-mannered little machine' (*The Player of Games*, p. 14). Banks's narrator, who has no qualms about operating from within a sub-genre confers extended validity to the confident statement by the protagonist of *The Algebraist* that 'One day, we'll all be free' (p. 534), Banks himself working to free the novel from 'this particular genre called the mainstream novel'.[47] The fiction – '(sub-)genre'? – produced by such authors as Rankin, Mina, Banks, McDermid, Rowling or McCall Smith, all in their own way, emphatically suggests that the freeing process may well be under way.

CHAPTER SEVENTEEN

Poetry in the Age of Morgan

Donny O'Rourke

In the perennial absence of money, poetic prestige is largely a matter of praise, prizes and professorship, plaudits denied to many who deserve them. By these 'market' criteria the pre-eminent Scottish poets amongst those born since the mid-1950s are easy to identify, most of the *prominenti* having had their work validated in each of the customary ways. Increases in cultural self-confidence and constitutional power notwithstanding, publication in England continues to confer kudos. A sceptic surveying the scene and seeing these successful poets publishing, puffing, promoting and awarding each other prizes might be tempted to look askance at the actual poetry produced. By far the greater part of it, however, would easily survive such scrutiny. Its quality has ensured that the influence of these much-admired writers is felt far beyond Scotland. The attention nowadays paid to contemporary poetry means that in mid-career, these poets born between the mid-1950s and mid-1960s are not just incipiently canonical but already established in school lesson plan and university lecture room, again not merely in their native land. This is extraordinary. But extraordinary too is the strength in depth beyond any possible hyped, self-sustaining élite grouping: not seven but seventy, and then some, with a poetry infrastructure that has helped create, support and further this poetic 'population explosion'.

The point is to try to think outside the canonical 'box'. Yet, if a painter following Sandy Moffat's *Poets Pub did* attempt a significant grouping from the generation and a half whose emergence coincided with the later period of Edwin Morgan's (1920–) work, then the unreliable indicators posited above might suggest a short list of, say, Don Paterson (1963–), Carol Ann Duffy (1955–), John Burnside (1955–), Jackie Kay (1961–), Mick Imlah (1956–2009), Robin Robertson (1955–), W. N. Herbert (1961–), Robert Crawford (1959–), Kate Clanchy (1965–) and Kathleen Jamie (1962–). Only four of these (comparatively) high profile poets live in Scotland and each of the quartet teaches creative writing at the university of St Andrews – Paterson, Burnside, Crawford and Jamie, internationally renowned writers who have been away and returned. Douglas Dunn (1942–), a great poet and esteemed professor who came back to Scotland, has cannily gathered these writers around him. Most informed readers one suspects, and all but their most cur-mudgeonly and paranoid peers, might accept that as a reasonable first eleven, a Scottish team with at least as much élan as its football counterpart, though flawed by lacking any of the fine current Gaelic-writing poets. The sensible course of action would be to get hold of books by these poets and choose your own seven, eight or none. Even better would be to spend time on and with the poets referred to subsequently and others for whom there is a silent salute but no space in this short survey.

Read the poems. Each of these modish, market-friendly poets has produced excellent work. Don Paterson's cool, formal, almost Augustan accomplish-ment eschews the warm and cosy, but his gifts are lavish whether in his slowly ripened, meticulously crafted verses or in the translations he makes his own. Out of the ideas and imagination-crammed cranium of W. N. Herbert pours some of the most energised and energising poetry of the day, in two languages and several forms. A masterly exponent of Scots, adept at deploying images and usages drawn from popular culture, Herbert, whose production is prodigious, sometimes allows quantity to overwhelm quality, but the wit and wizardry almost always redeem him. He is a professor of creative writing at Newcastle University. His sometime collaborator Robert Crawford has also been an exemplar in the brilliance of his poetry in Scots. Crawford's first two books, *A Scottish Assembly* (1990) and *Talkies* (1992), in English mainly, aside from their lyric and satirical merits, were of seminal importance in articulating the idea of the 'new' Scotland to itself. His poetry has not, on the whole, been able to maintain that daunting standard but he remains a crucial thinker and rethinker of Scottish literature. A recent return to something approaching top poetic form, *Full Volume* (2008), augurs well. Some common concerns characterise the tough, taut, often tender poems of Kathleen Jamie, another who has turned Scots adroitly to her purposes but whose writing in English is equally skilled. A feminism rooted in Scottish history finds empowering expression in her work. Robin Robertson made a name for himself in publishing as a shrewd and loyally-liked champion of Scottish writing before his late – after early promise – garnering of plaudits and prizes. His poems are full of vowelly gorgeousness, though perhaps for some, despite this, a little dull and uninvolving. Kate Clanchy, a relatively late starter, has been commended in her poems' chatty, confiding openness, performative power and seeming simplicity for her zeitgeisty, clever, carefully constructed 'competition poems'. Of more immediacy and perhaps emotional substance, Jackie Kay's likeably engaging poetry owes something to that of Liz Lochhead, Glasgow's successor laureate to Edwin Morgan, who, if it does not demean this fine poet and playwright could have been, but for age perhaps, on the substitute's bench of our football team of poets, except that she is published and mostly read and taught in Scotland. Kay's combination of being black and lesbian was the most obvious sign of a welcome and much needed new complexity in Scotland and its poetry. Her former partner Carol Ann Duffy is perhaps the most visible and vaunted of the poets for whom Edwin Morgan was an inspiration. When one of her poems, 'Education for Leisure', was claimed to be 'promoting' knife crime, it was front-page news. Lyrically voluptuous, ironic, paradoxical, excoriatingly ludic, maestra of the sonnet that is also a dramatic monologue, once again, under the influence of Morgan whom she may here even surpass, Duffy 'ticks every box' as the perfect poet to discuss with students or simply to read for the savour and flavour of the times. The worst that can and has been said of her virtuoso productions is that they are 'too perfect', a 'fault' envied by many. Born, like Duffy, in 1955, on the cusp of rock and roll, and like Duffy of Irish Catholic stock, John Burnside is a poet's poet who has found both readers and rewards for his subtle, ruminative and exacting poetry, work less personable and approachable than Carol Ann Duffy's, but meticulously made, quiet, dense, enticingly mysterious without being obscure.

Carol Ann Duffy and John Burnside help us point to several things that have changed since Scotland's poets really could have been gathered round one table in the poets' pub. The presence of women as important poets in their own right and not merely as 'muses' signals progress; and lesbian women at that. Setting aside the psycho-sexual complexities of George Mackay Brown, only Morgan is (discreetly, semi-closetedly) gay in Sandy Moffat's public house pantheon. George Mackay Brown, a convert, is the only Roman Catholic. Beyond the frame of the painting though, the Irish were coming and with Duffy and Burnside they have unquestionably arrived. The Toms, McGrath (1940–) and Leonard (1944–), indispensable champions of working-class Glasgow speech, crucial also as Americanisers of Scottish letters, were generationally disqualified from the salo(o)n but provided progenitorial wit, warmth and informality of a decidedly Hibernian type. Raymond Friel (1963–) whose confiding, relaxed free verse is par excellence the art that conceals art, though much more than simply an Irish Catholic poet, is nonetheless importantly a writer from, and concerned with, that diaspora. His work is 'confessional' in a scholastic, supra Sextonian or Lowellesque way – a poet overlooked and under-rated, running a Catholic sixth form college in southern England, popping up from time to time in the *London Review of Books* to demonstrate that his poems get better and better as he moves attentively through his forties. Better known as a hilarious writer of prose and plays, Des Dillon (1960–) started out publishing, and has recently returned to, poetry, producing haiku of immense laconic acuity as well as looser, more blarney-ish monologues. My own (1959–) poems and perform-ances draw on an Irish heritage – amongst I hope many other things – and may be said to have something of the urban shennachie about them; certainly Irish poets have been the chief influence on my writing alongside American models. Ireland's influence on contemporary Scotland in the professions, political power, the media and cultural production in general is hard to exaggerate and although more obvious in fiction has made its mark on poetry in our period.

It might be objected that there are now more creative writing courses than aspiring poets worthy of the places they are offered on them, their capacity to pay being of more relevance than their ability to create. Of professor-poets, anyhow, there is no dearth, but intelligent poets need not be overtly intellectual or over-concerned with high culture or self-reflexively caught up with poetry as the subject matter for poetry, name-checking, if not name-dropping, influences and role models. Angela McSeveney (1964–) bothers little with any of this, composing instead poems about the – of course, enormous – small things in life. And this is not in any way to damn a superb manipulator of images and ideas with faint praise. A poet completely devoid of the cynical or knowing, McSeveney talks things over, divulges and recounts, never straining to produce poetry with a capital P and thus always telling it like it is, for her and for many, maybe most of us. To be 'full of life' is also to be melancholy, which this wonderful poet often is, when she is not giggling or making the reader laugh out loud at the ever-fascinating everyday.

Although popular culture finds its way into the books of almost all the predecessor poets depicted, it is Edwin Morgan who most relishingly exults in the 'low' admixed with the 'high'. The drastic innovations in television (commercial television arrived in Scotland on 31 August 1957) and recorded music of the mid-1950s have continued to be seen and heard in the poetry published in the *Dream State* (1994) anthology. Another poet whose (post-) modernity is entertainingly diverse and media-derived, Graham Fulton (1959–) does for Paisley what W. N. Herbert has done for Dundee. Since Paisley people are known as 'buddies', perhaps one might style Fulton a Buddy Bukowski. But that label would limit even more than most. True, his street credible loucheries are no more ingratiating than the late Los Angelino's, but in giving us the low-down on the low down, Fulton is his own man. As is the more formally inclined, likeably louche, Roddy Lumsden (1966–), one of whose pop culture suffused books is entitled, *Yeah, Yeah, Yeah* (1997). Lumsden lives in London. None of Moffat's makars did. Carol Ann Duffy and John Burnside left Scotland as children with their prospects-improving parents. Many of those named at the beginning of this essay have thrived in England.

Yet Scotland is a place where poets can be, and are too, with an infrastructure of grants, awards, bursaries, fellowships, public readings and positions teaching creative writing. Three agencies deserve special mention, though there are many more enabling institutions that could be cited. The Scottish Arts Council has done a tremendous amount to get poetry written, performed, translated, disseminated and read. This is the case also with the Scottish Book Trust (1998–), which took over administration of the 'Writers in Public' scheme and initiated several other projects involving mentoring, performance skills, a writers register and much else. And the Scottish Poetry Library (1984–), as guided by its visionary founder Tessa Ransford and her innovative successor Robyn Marsack, has been an extraordinary source of foresight, energy, nurturing and solidarity, devising superb programmes, pub-lishing astutely and building up indispensable holdings for borrowing or refer-ence. One might mention too the many literary festivals, most of which have tried to keep faith with poetry, and Scottish poetry in particular. Libraries have organised individual events and festivals to ever-higher standards and acclaim, several featuring poets of this generation.

Publishers and magazines also play fruitful roles. *The Herald* in Glasgow continues to publish a poem every day. Carcanet, presided over since its inception by Michael Schmidt, now Professor of Poetry at Glasgow University and editor of *PN Review*, a publication critical of the manner in which eager-to-be-canonical poets arrange each other's luck, connects Edwin Morgan and Iain Crichton Smith with the younger Scottish poets presently with the imprint, linking them too to the New York School and other American poets who have had such an influence on this generation. Meanwhile, all of Scotland's magazine editors merit praise for their resilience in maintain-ing outlets for new poems. Especially valuable for this generation have been *Verse* (1984–), *Gairfish* (1990–95) and *The Dark Horse* (1995–). *Verse*, edited by Robert Crawford, David Kinloch and others was published from Scotland and America and found hospitable room for the early work of many of the poets considered here. Gerry Cambridge (1959–), himself an exponent and proponent of formal verse, has made of *The Dark Horse* a fine forum for New Formalist writing. Its widened welcome has come to encompass a range of poetics. And the much-missed *Gairfish*, edited by W. N. Herbert and Richard Price, had daring, dash and dazzle in every issue. And the longer-established *Chapman*, *Lines* and the *Edinburgh Review* have all published significant poetry over this period.

Richard Price (1966–), who after long years of comparative neglect was in 2007 shortlisted for the Whitbread Prize, could at a stretch have been included with the garlanded and influential poets whose merits began this account. He is at least their equal and more accomplished than many of the 'in-group' But, despite his coining of the term 'Informationists' to align himself with some of his co-evals, he has never been part of a scene or 'in' crowd. Indeed it could be argued that his lack of career-minded clubbabil-ity has held him back. Head of Modern British Collections at the British

Library, he has been editor, publisher, collaborator, reviewer, critic, curator and above all creator. These other attainments and generosities must not be allowed to detract from the poetry itself. Now in his early forties, his poetry has a terrific nose for the now-ness of our time, its taste, touch, soundtrack and aroma. And yet there is nothing callow about his evocations, no hint of poetic mutton dressed as lamb, rather a youthful maturity, a seasoned innocence, that beguiles in ballad or open form lyric, in 'edgy' verbal riff or tender lullaby, in translation or love poem or deadpan drollery, across (almost) the range (and what a range!) Edwin Morgan opened up. No-one captures or recaptures childhood better. But the poems refuse to live in the past. Is this celebration of and slight anxiety about the momentousness and momentum of his moment a kind of nostalgia for now? Richard Price, so faltering and even gawky as a performer when he began, is now one of our most compelling readers and reciters. He worked at it. And his oeuvre is *work* that works sublimely on stage as well as page.

Associated with Richard Price in a number of ventures and published like him (and Edwin Morgan and Iain Crichton Smith) by Carcanet, David Kinloch (1959–) co-edited the magazine *Southfields* (1995–2000) with Price and Raymond Friel. Despite prestigious and proto-canonical publishing 'down south', Kinloch has not so far had the attention and acclaim he deserves. In many ways he is the most obvious successor to Edwin Morgan, being both gay and an academic. He teaches creative writing at the University of Strathclyde. Morgan's Cinquevalli is behind Kinloch's dustiefute, the acrobat and tumbler, sawdust on his heels and soles, seeking precarious and entertaining balance. Bravura performances in a street Scots that is also learned and unpreciously arcane and often devastatingly droll, alternate with poems in English that touch and tease and testify to what it is to be a middle-class, homosexual Scot adroit in the literature of France, alert to nuance and frisson in music, sport, painting and life. David Kinloch's cerebral but never solemn Derrida- and Foucault-tinged *grand projet* is amounting, book by beautiful book, to an alternative history of Scotland and of the gay literary sensibility, though it is perhaps time to think of Kinloch less as a gay poet than a master poet *tout court*.

Born in the same year as David Kinloch, Meg Bateman (1959–), a learner of the Gaelic language, attracted early notice for her exquisitely moving poems in that language and despite long fallow spells, she has continued to meditate magnificently on her abiding themes of love and loss. Self-consciously situating herself in relation to the great women bards of the Gàidhealtachd, Bateman teaches at Sabhal Mòr Ostaig, the Gaelic college on Skye, another institution crucial to the expansion of poetic opportunity in Scotland over the last twenty years. Lewis's Anne Frater (1967–) has more recourse to the sardonic astringencies of the verse tradition in Gaelic, but she too can lament her own and her culture's losses. Both of these poets, like ones already mentioned, owe much to 'professor-poets' with whom they studied: Bateman, to Dòmhnall MacAmhlaigh (Professor Donald MacAulay (1930–), who taught her at Aberdeen) and Frater to Ruaraidh MacThòmais (Professor Derick Thomson (1921–), her teacher and supervisor in Glasgow). Although MacAmhlaigh and MacThòmais's most substantial verse dates from earlier decades, both have produced new volumes in the past two years. In the Irishman Rody Gorman's (1960–) wry, sly, often wistful poetry the ancient languages of Ireland and the Scottish Highlands and Islands infuse and inform his mingling of off-beat modernity and timeless bardicism. Long resident on Skye and composing in Scottish Gaelic, Gorman, by entertaining no illusions, entertains us. Equally beguiling and bringing together lessons learned from almost all of the Gaelic poets of the mid-twentieth century, Kevin MacNeil (1972–) has the zaniness of Iain Crichton Smith in Murdo mode and the gravitas of Aonghas MacNeacail (1942–), perhaps, as his mentor, the most evident link in MacNeil's long lyric lineage. In this instance, to describe a bard who has embraced rave culture, rap and rock and roll, Celtic Cool is more than a cliché.

Others have worked at creative distances from Scotland's Central Belt. A writer of surpassing consequence for the far north of Scotland, as dramatist, poet and cultural agitator, is George Gunn (1956–) whose lyric finesse is reinforced by polemical potency and seething satirical skill. Persistently, even obstreperously polemical, Gunn's dialectical rigour and vigour, heightened through his early and formative unliterary labours as an oil-rig worker, make his poetry essential to the burgeoning of the 'new' Scotland and the Highland renaissance. An island satirist with a capacity to excoriate and skewer is the Shetland poet and novelist, Robert Alan Jamieson (1958–), a writer handicapped, as he should not be, by his bravura use of the dialect he grew up speaking. Bleakly comedic, plangent, steeped in lore and custom and yet exhilaratingly up-to-date, there is a skaldic reverberance to the work, combined with an eye and ear for daily detail, whether rendered in old forms or new, even avant-garde ways: a poet who should be better known and more obligingly published. That is true also of Peter McCarey (1956–), head of translation with the World Health Organisation in Geneva and too often out of sight, out of mind, as a poet. Like Jamieson, McCarey, who wrote his doctoral dissertation on MacDiarmid and the Russians, is profoundly au fait with the literature of Scotland, drawing upon it expertly to boldly experimental effect. His almost thrawn determination to 'make it new' never degenerates into the gimmicky search for mere novelty. Perhaps the poet of his generation most seriously interested in the avant-garde, McCarey is equally capable of producing poems of superb and transparent simplicity that can split sides or melt hearts. A collaborator with Peter McCarey and sharing his academic enthusiasm for MacDiarmid, Alan Riach (1957–) has assimilated his Black Mountain and Morganian influences to compelling effect in warm-hearted, cultured poems that are unpretentiously allusive, as full of lived life as they are of art-inflected life. Riach's is usually a broad brush, the impasto generous. Family, its solaces and celebrations as well as its sadnesses, have increasingly figured in this fine poet's work. With this come the temptations, not always resisted, of sentimentality. His perspectives as both a native and an elective Scot, born in Lanarkshire and educated in the south of England, who spent fourteen years teaching and writing in New Zealand, lend Alan Riach's poetry a distinctive allure. Gerrie Fellows (1954–) missed the *Dream State* 'cut-off point' by two years, but this New Zealander, for many years resident in Glasgow, is a first-rate poet never afraid to be difficult or to think big. Meanwhile, Iain Bamforth (1959–), a major figure, works as a doctor in Strasbourg. He has spent his entire career furth of Scotland, a country to which his rich, ravelled poetry almost obsessively returns to worry at and contend with its philosophical and theological obsessions – another superb poet literally too far from the thoughts of the local literati.

Among the great grouping of makars portrayed by Sandy Moffat, Scots was used by most and it continues to distinguish the nation's contemporary poetry. Mathew Fitt (1968–) has come up with poetry of great naturalness, vitality and verve as well as fiction, including science fiction and translations of Roald Dahl. Rab Wilson (1960–), taking on Garioch's mantle, has used an unforced Lallans to write intense sonnets and epic poetry too. William Hershaw (1957–) deploys the relaxed, vivid dialect of his native Fife to marvellous effect and, as with so many of Scotland's poets now, can be warm, witty, wise, poignant and political in his seemingly straightforward poems.

All of the poets mentioned here, even the more restlessly iconoclastic experimenters, could be said to exist in a continuum that stretches from, while having begun long before, that which includes those painted by Sandy Moffat. There are however excellent poets who militantly detest the notion that a poem ought to mean, say, describe, characterise or convey anything. Alexander Hutchison (1943–) bridges the gap between traditional and experimental poetry, as did Gael Turnbull (1928–2004) before him. For texts that aspire to tell us nothing but just to be, a superlative source, if such poems have a 'source', would be Cambridge don Drew Milne (1964–), whose challenging work has affinities with, whilst being distinct from, that of the American L=A=N=G=U=A=G=E poets. Peter Manson (1969–) is another theory-inclined poet suspicious of the defunctly-egotistical lyric and the obsolete pleasures of conventional reminiscence, reflection and epiphany. Theirs is work of high integrity and purpose, highly rewarding (if that is a permissible word) to read. Another author could perfectly plausibly centre an account of present-day Scottish poetry on practice and principle drawn from Modernism as bodied forth in the work of the ongoing avant-garde. The poem as beautiful object, as produced thing, as artefactal sign of what it purports to be – as manifest in concrete poetry or the artist's book along the lines of Ian Hamilton Finlay (1925–2006), Gael Turnbull, Drew Milne or Richard Price – has more to commend it than the 'mass market' poetry favoured by commercial literary culture is economically willing or able to allow.

Although falling outside the remit of the present survey, the output of those poets born just too early for inclusion in the *Dream State* sampling has been copious and of high calibre. Poets born around 1950 have offered instructive example to their immediate successors and they have gone on producing noteworthy books. Tom Pow, Ron Butlin (now Edinburgh's municipal makar), Brian McCabe, Andrew Greig and Frank Kuppner are the best known of these post post-war poets in Scotland. Andrew Greig (1951–), friend of, and soon to be memoirist about, his mentor MacCaig represents a literary and social continuity with the Rose Street writers that the poets born just a few years later cannot boast, although, as in so much else, Edwin Morgan provides the exception, having taught or been befriended by a fair number of younger poets.

It seems unarguable that in terms of quantity, there is a lot more poetry around than in the days when MacDiarmid held sway and court. Many poets have made their débuts since the *Dream State* anthology was published and updated. Taking into account the slams, poetry cafés and exponential rise in the demand for diplomas and degrees in creative writing and the number of *soi-disant* practitioners, I am not aware of a new, youthful scene brimming with publishably exceptional talent and pushing to be anthologised as a dynamic and distinctive peer group. With many more opportunities for spoken word performance and with more accommodating and inclusive ideas as to what a poem is, perhaps contemporary poetry has not died but simply found another place to live, with popular music, film, theatre and conceptual, text-based art.

Some auspicious entries into the field have been noticed, however. Though perhaps even more gifted as a writer of fiction than of verse, Suhayl Saadi (1961–), a Glasgow doctor, has assumed a significant and well-merited role as a writer from, celebrant of and mentor to Scotland's Asian community. Jen Hadfield (1978–), a librarian on Orkney has a T. S. Eliot Prize for Poetry (2009) to add to her already impressive list of poetic credentials. With a recent collection from Carcanet, Gerry McGrath's (1962–) is another promising career newly launched. Jim Carruth's (1963–) commendable efforts to help revivify and transform the Glasgow and Scottish poetry scene have overshadowed his poems somewhat, but he is part of a process that has facilitated the breaking into print and prominence of several younger poets. A. B. Jackson (1965–), Cheryl Follon (1978–) and Andrew Philip (1975–) are poets not merely of promise but of attainment. The Shore Poets in Edinburgh, StAnza in Saint Andrews, St Mungo's Mirrorball and Vital Synz in Glasgow have all done much to provide platforms for emerging talent. Here the vast increase in the publication of pamphlets has played a conducive, perhaps catalytic part. James Robertson with Kettilonia, the Callum Macdonald Memorial Prize and the many new poets brought into print by the trust set up in memory of Tom Wright warrant particular comment in this respect.

Poets writing under the influence of, or at any rate at the same time as, 'late Morgan', have filled teeming shelves with outstanding poetry, poetry more wide-ranging and from more diverse sources, than that produced by the canonical makars of the 1960s and 1970s. Some, maybe much of it, will come to be rated as highly as the great poems of those great poets. Contemporary Scotland takes its place in the world with a literary confidence to match its political and wider cultural confidence. Poets imaginatively inhabiting our time and place may lack the regard and resonance, the éclat and renown of the 'Ulster' poets during the 'Troubles'. The very comparison invites the wrong kind of parochial critique. But Scottish poetry in the new century has achieved new reach and recognition. Its most lustrous exponents remain a small part of the bigger picture. And that is a very crowded canvas indeed.

CHAPTER EIGHTEEN

Entering the Twenty-first Century

Ian Brown

The cliché this chapter seeks to avoid, and well may not, is that the 1999 reconvening of the Scottish Parliament changed the context in which Scottish literature operates entirely, or even, *pace* Yeats, utterly. Yet, the late twentieth and the twenty-first centuries have created and embody a difference. It could hardly be otherwise if the thesis outlined by the editors at the start of this volume's Introduction holds true:

> Literature is an essential way in which people in communities convey to themselves and others their concerns and imaginings.

The twentieth century saw a revisiting of the nature of Scottishness and Scottish literature, of what is mainstream and what liminal, what 'popular' and what 'art'. It also saw the recognition that the imperialist centralising vision of so-called 'EngLit' within which some Scottish writers might be accommodated – though not for Leavis, say, Scott – will not do. New understandings draw on wider considerations. They draw on changed perceptions of what Scotland is, what it is to be Scottish and what the languages and literatures of Scotland are.

In many ways the two major multi-author histories of Scottish literature that straddle the beginning of the millennium, one from Aberdeen University Press, the other from Edinburgh University Press,[1] express and embody those changing perceptions. Both see Scotlands, and so Scottish literatures, that draw on not only the famous definition of Scotland as three-tongued, a formulation to whose potential exclusiveness Michael Gardiner alerts us. Scotland(s) are recognised that have found expression in, besides Gaelic, Scots and English, at least Cumbric languages, Latin, French, Norse and Urdu. And developments and shifts of emphasis and priority between the two Histories exemplify further significant change that continues into the new century. The Aberdeen History has, out of eighty-four chapters, five dealing directly with literature in Gaelic; the Edinburgh out of 104 has nineteen, and more dealing with inter-language issues. Further the *Edinburgh*

History includes significant contextualising chapters on history, geography, languages and international impact that were not included in the Aberdeen History. The necessity for the second after the remarkable achievement of the first was not that the first was, even twenty years later, seen as failing, but that so very much had happened in critical study and wider understanding in those twenty years that the second was essential.

Both result from and reflect the manifold developments in Scottish literature through the twentieth century and into the twenty-first. If one were to suggest one single narrative of these developments for both the nature of Scotland and Scottish literature – and single narratives are dangerously over-simple, of course – it would be of complication and problematisation. Simplicities of empire, English-language primacy in education, 'EngLit' canonicity, high/low art definitions and the separate development, even apartheid, of nineteenth- and early twentieth-century university departments of Celtic and English/Scottish literature have been properly complicated by recognition of the phenomena constituting the nexus of visions and expression called 'Scottish literature'. 'Three-tongued' Scotland is a fine trope as far as it goes. Certainly Scottish writers have produced literatures in Latin, Gaelic, Scots and English that are internationally significant by any standard and the latter three languages are still in active literary and daily use, but, even given this, 'multi-tongued' and 'multivalent' are more apt descriptions of Scottish literature.

It would, nonetheless, be obtuse not to recognise the importance of the twentieth-century ways in which the three languages that are the most frequent current modes of Scottish literary expression have developed in importance. To do so is not to minimise the significance of Scotland's other languages, whether older, but dropped from usage, or newer to its cultural life. In the case of Gaelic, for example, however diminished the native-speaker population has become, estimates of a quarter of a million learners do not suggest a language seen as culturally negligible or uninteresting. The development from Sabhal Mòr Ostaig's 1973 foundation to the current establishment of Gaelic-medium schools in Glasgow, Inverness and Edinburgh – mainly at primary level notwithstanding – underlines the renewed potential to respect Gaelic as a language of learning and scholarship and its importance for the young. The Gaelic Language (Scotland) Act of 2005 and its implementation in the next year, including the launch of Bòrd na Gàidhlig, marks high governmental and institutional priority given to sustaining the language. Whether this initiative is too late, however, to sustain the native-speaking population is yet to be seen. Nonetheless, the Bòrd has robust purposes:

> to promote Gaelic, and [strive] in partnership with the Scottish Government, the people of Scotland and the Gaelic organisations to improve the status of the

language. It is a priority for Bòrd na Gàidhlig to increase the number of Gaelic speakers and users, and that Gaelic and its culture are respected and esteemed throughout Scotland.[2]

The significance of new creative initiatives in Scottish literature in Gaelic has yet to be fully seen, understood and evaluated: only time will help understand their implications. Yet as Michelle Macleod and Moray Watson have demonstrated,[3] the development of the Gaelic novel is fundamentally a twentieth-century phenomenon, and one with an increasing impetus and excellence of achievement in the twenty-first century. Complementing this creativity is the recognition that – whatever the implications of university departmental structures or successive policies since the 1609 Statutes of Iona enforced education of Gaelic-speakers away from speaking Gaelic – Scottish literature is not simply literature in Scots, or in Scots and English, but in many languages. And this recognition offers new challenges to scholars, not least to those who have only one or two of Scotland's three older surviving languages. The attraction of the vitality of Scottish literature in Gaelic is surely not only marked by the work of native speakers, but by the work of such poets as Meg Bateman and Christopher Whyte who, having learned the language, are significant artists in it.

This volume has frequently observed the developing inclusiveness of Scottish literature through the last and present centuries. The constitutional and legislative context in which Scottish writers now work, at least within Scotland, is enhanced by a number of private or semi-private initiatives. These include the foundation of publishers like Itchy Coo (2002) specialising in publication in Scots and the Ùr-sgeul imprint at CLÀR (2003) for Gaelic, referred to earlier, and the continuing, if often fragile ecology of small publishers, which ranges from Canongate founded in 1973 to Two Ravens Press founded as recently as 2007. This diverse institutional development complements the emergence of a whole generation of new Scots which Alastair Niven discusses, at a length not possible here, in an important recent chapter.[4] The work of Jackie Kay, Luke Sutherland, Maud Sulter, Leila Aboulela, Raman Mundair, Maya Chowdhry and Suhayl Saadi is only a representative sample, bringing ever more intercultural perspectives to shape Scottish literature. Saadi's *Psychoraag* (2004) offers new syntheses and hybridities, as Niven comments: 'MacDiarmid, Rushdie and Welsh are linguistic forebears of *Psychoraag*, where the Scots *argot* of the streets of Glasgow combines with Standard English and some Urdu' (p. 328). While the very newest incomers, like East Europeans, have yet to contribute in literature and it will be interesting to see what language(s) they use, the children of a postwar generation of Polish incomers have already contributed substantially. Catherine Czerkawska (1950–) has worked in several genres while Matthew

Zajac (1959–) focuses on drama: his *Tailor of Inverness* (2008), drawing on his father's experience moving from wartime service in the Russian, German and British armies before settling in Scotland, has dialogue in Polish, Russian, Ukrainian and German besides English. Zajac's exploration of his Polish-Ukrainian-Scottish descent – and his father's complex military identities, multiple versions of truth for his children and hidden Polish family, including a rediscovered, previously unknown, half-sister – marks the complexity of both post-war European reality and modern Scottish identity.

A counterpoint to the conception of Scottish literature as such a non-canonically-driven melting pot is the role of Scottish writers in a globalised context. The commodification of the popular novels of Ian Fleming and Alistair MacLean has meant that they are often not seen as Scottish at all. But other authors whose work has been taken up and become part of UK-wide and international 'brands' include A. J. Cronin, M. C. Beaton and Compton Mackenzie, whose *Monarch of the Glen* (1941) became a television phenomenon almost as distant from its source as the James Bond films from theirs. Whether born in Scotland or adoptive, authors like Ian Rankin, Irvine Welsh, Alexander McCall Smith and J. K. Rowling are not only distinguished internationally in their generic fields, but themselves have become globalised brands with a specific Scottish flavour. (Maureen Farrell fascinatingly explicates the elements that locate Rowling's writing within Scottish literary traditions and themes.)[5] Often, of course, television and film have had a role, often problematic, in reflecting and expressing Scottish literature and culture as a generalised brand. Two 1995 films, *Rob Roy*, drawing distantly on Scott's model, but shaped by Alan Sharp's Western-inflected screenplay, and *Braveheart*, drawing very much on Blind Harry's *Wallace*, can be seen to represent the complexities of globalised versions of Scottish topics, even when both draw on Scottish literary classics. Yet it can be argued that any mature culture will be subject to the globalised consumption and institutionalised caricatures such films embody. It is questionable whether the fin-de-siècle *Braveheart* is any more corrupting in its view of Scotland than the mid-century *The Maggie* (1954). Indeed, the point may be that it is the international embeddedness of Scottish literary tropes that allows such usage and that such usage is a badge, if not of honour, of firmly established international reception, something to sustain rather than undermine cultural and literary self-confidence.

The impact of the mass media cannot, however, be understood simply in terms of its representations of Scotland or adaptations of Scottish literature. The grammar of film and, in turn, television has influenced the very structure of literature in Scotland as elsewhere, the shapes in which it is written, the ways it constructs written text. The novel writing of Irvine Welsh, for example, is cinematic in a way that an earlier Edinburgh writer's, Robert Louis

Stevenson's, neither was nor could be. Stevenson builds over longer periods, for example, making less use, if any, of the literary equivalent of the screen's jump cut. This is not to say that all modern Scottish writers are equally influenced by the structures of cinema and television. Iain Banks, while certainly from time to time using techniques drawn from screen grammar, is also interested in the slow build of narrative and visualisation that works through the power of words, rather than the instamatic impact of images.

Arguably, before the impact of mass media, writing did different things. Visualisation in Stevenson, for example, is constructed through accumulation of significant detail rather than televisually by the rapid scanning of suggestive detail. It is not that writing has entirely stopped doing those things; rather, it does them now sometimes, but always in the context of a world on which mass media impinge. Genre-writing held differences, and these differences were not just about the connotations of the subject covered, but in the nature of the ways readers understood and experienced the words read. And writers too have changed ways of writing. Grant Morrison (1960–), for example, has written award-winning plays such as *Red King Rising* (1989), about Alice and Charles Dodgson, and is a musician, but, since the early 1980s, has been better known as an internationally-admired graphic novelist, working on X-MEN and *The Invisibles*. Alan Grant (1949–) brought Batman to Scotland in 1998 where Bruce Wayne boasts that his own ancestors were Scottish (recollecting the fact that Batman's original creator named his character after his own childhood hero, Robert the Bruce). Grant also helped write the cult series *The Bogie Man* in the 1980s and 1990s and has produced pointed political satire in the 'Middenface McNulty' series in the magazine *2000 AD*; and Mark Millar (1969–) has worked on popular comic figures like *Judge Dredd*. As has been noted elsewhere, they are 'fascinated by the exploration and expansion of cross-cultural references and the interaction of popular art, plot, imagery and language across normally perceived boundaries of literature'.[6] The crime-fiction novelist Denise Mina has written graphic novels, introduced by Ian Rankin, in the 'Hellblazer' series set partly in Glasgow and Iona. Meanwhile, the painter-playwright John Byrne brings new visual dimensions to dramatic writing: 'I find that I write in a peculiarly graphic way.'[7] Earlier surreal cartoon experiments should also be remembered here. Both Dudley D. Watkins (1907–69) with *The Broons, Oor Wullie* (both 1936–), *Desperate Dan* (1937–) and *Lord Snooty* (1938–) and Bud Neill (1911–70), whose Sheriff Lobey Dosser of Calton Creek appeared in a series in the Glasgow *Evening News* (1949–56), and in the late 1950s in the *Sunday Mail*, achieved, by mixing genres, bizarre, witty and often hilarious effects. Neill, in particular, explored Glaswegian-Scots language in a manner not far removed from that of more recent poets and novelists, while his characters, transported to the American Wild West, offered sly commentaries on Glaswegian life. Changes in genre and the crossing of older, more rigid, boundaries shift the ways we understand how literature works, what it is and is for.

Playwriting as a specifically dramatic form has naturally been particularly influenced by film and television's grammar. Sometimes this is easy to discern, as in plays like Stephen Greenhorn's *Passing Places* (1997), not only making use of a series of short scenes, often cross-cutting from one to the next, but structurally a road movie for the stage. Like many twentieth-century playwrights, Greenhorn has written for television: he is indeed the creator of the long-running soap, *River City* (2002–). The relationship between Scottish literature and mass media is not then just a matter of the influence of one on the other, whether by adaptation or structural and thematic influence. Many leading Scottish writers, especially since later in the twentieth century, also write for television and film, and not only playwrights: the example of Alan Sharp moving from novel to film was mentioned in an earlier chapter. One has to be cautious in reaching conclusions about the nature of Scottish, or any, literature under the impact of mass media, but one has to recognise that the mass media have transformed the context within and assumptions under which literature is shaped and made. The risk is that mass media's impact sustains globalised visions, the broadly generic rather than the culturally specific, William Wallace in face-paint and antique kilting rather than a member of a Europe-facing military caste.

Certainly, however, there are three countervailing forces at work against globalisation. One is the subversion traded in a variety of genres. Alternative Scottish literary versions of reality exist. They include Christopher Whyte's novels, exploring other modes of perception, and Iain Banks's, constantly varied and unclassifiable. They also include the popular televisual deflation of assumptions of Ford Kiernan and Greg Hemphill's series *Still Game* (2002–). In these, wider visions of reality are explored, rediscovered, revisited and subverted. A second countervailing force is the increasingly wide international reception and impact of Scottish writers who do not engage in international branding. In drama, for example, David Harrower and David Greig have each been translated into more than twenty languages worldwide and received productions across the world, all the time sustaining their quizzical and essentially idiosyncratic dramatic voice and vision. Thirdly, there is a growing recognition of the complex interactions with writers of the wider diaspora. While this volume has considered such diasporic writers as Arthur Conan Doyle, Muriel Spark and Jackie Kay, the relationship of Canadian authors like Alice Munro, Australians like Les Murray, New Zealanders like James Baxter, West Indians like Wilson Harris and South Africans like Roy Campbell to Scottish literature is only beginning to be properly examined. Alan Riach and Iain Wright's pioneering work on this is of particular value.[8]

While it would be wise to avoid any complacency, the narrowing of Scottish literary topics that seemed a threat at the beginning of the twentieth century seems remote from current experience. Two twenty-first century developments in different ways encapsulate this widening of perspective and vision.

In 2004 Edinburgh was nominated the first of the UNESCO Creative Cities Network as World City of Literature. The potential for mocking and self-mocking responses to this form of brand labelling with its hint of commodification is of course unlimited, but the fact is that the nomination was the result of an international vote by an international cultural organisation. Even to suggest that Edinburgh be nominated required an adjustment of self-assertion and security of identity that would have been unthinkable earlier in the last century. At the time of the proposal Scottish literati were to be heard explaining why really Dublin had a better case, only to be astonished, if not reconciled, by the unanimity and swiftness with which the rest of the world thought Edinburgh had an unanswerable one.

And the National Theatre of Scotland was founded in 2006. There had been many failed attempts to establish such an organisation in the twentieth century, carefully and insightfully discussed by Denis Agnew.[9] As early as 1970, for example, a Scottish Arts Council report led to suggestions that a national theatre might be developed out of the major touring group Prospect Theatre Company, which would merge with Edinburgh's Royal Lyceum Company. In 1987 the Advisory Council for the Arts in Scotland (AdCAS) published a working party report arguing that the time had come for a national theatre to be founded, assuming a building-based model. Little seemed to develop until the Federation of Scottish Theatre, representing all the professional theatre companies of Scotland, made the difference and in 1999 marked the imminent new century by arguing for the non-building based co-production-focused model that was finally approved. This model was not only inclusive and forward-looking, it was and is unique, avoiding the dangers of capital-intensive building-based models that the 1970 report and even the AdCAS follow-up did not quite avoid. It is not well known that, at a 1996 Edinburgh lunch hosted by Royal Lyceum Board member Councillor Moira Knox, Lord Lindsay, then a Scottish Office junior minister, offered the company's then-joint chief executives, Kenny Ireland and Nikki Axford, an additional million pounds annual funding to make their company Scotland's building-based national theatre. Ireland and Axford turned this down, seeing it as inappropriate both in terms of national and theatre politics.[10] Possibly this offer was part of John Major's failed campaign to see off devolution, which included the awarding of Scottish (and Welsh) Arts Council independence in 1994: a national theatre offered to deny a national settlement. Undoubtedly it would have been divisive and employed an old-fashioned model. It is a mark of the new confidence of Scottish creativity that the new model could be recommended, adopted and implemented in the progressive way it has. The innovative company's first (February 2006) production was not a single metropolitan/establishment production of a Scottish, or any other, classic, but ten different new productions from Shetland to Dumfries, all entitled *Home* and each adopting specific local/national approaches to that theme. The new settlement in Scotland found an inclusive visionary model for its national theatre.

This movement from nineteenth-century models of singular national expression into broader more inclusive conceptions of multiple national identities is reflected and energised by the actual and symbolic differences between two of Scotland's major poets, productive for most of the period covered by this volume, Hugh MacDiarmid and Edwin Morgan. MacDiarmid, beginning his creative career as new small nations were gaining independence across Europe, can be seen to embody a concern with the profound, even the portentous, and a commitment at various times to differing principles, each at the time held passionately and sincerely, even if later contradicted. He also contributed to twentieth-century Scottish literature a concern that it be seen always in an international context, against international standards. He brought profundity and a concern for self-respect to his art and his concern with others. If at times this made him controversial and even contumaciously carnaptious, then so be it. His art both as poet and polemicist was to controvert the comfortable and challenge versions of Scottish literature that would return it to what he saw as minor modes. Yet when Morgan began to write, MacDiarmid attacked him and his constant innovation. Where MacDiarmid found diversity in profundity, Morgan found profundity in diversity, constantly experimenting, constantly changeable, constantly extending the bounds of what might be expected. If at times MacDiarmid risked pomposity, Morgan at times risked superficiality, the charge of innovation for its own sake. But, he might argue, until one has innovated how can one know for whose or what's sake it is. Experiment must, almost by definition, at times fail. These two offer further polarities among the many that mark twentieth-century Scottish literature and, in a remarkable act of scholarly reconciliation, two years before MacDiarmid died Morgan wrote a sympathetic and insightful 1976 study of his work.[11]

Inclusive, international and even tentatively self-confident, the changes and growth of twentieth-century Scottish literature, and its defeats too, have fed into a quite different literary landscape at the beginning of the twenty-first century. In this version of Scottish literature(s) and of Scotland(s), it is surely significant that one of the major successes of the first decade of the new century was James Robertson's *Joseph Knight* (2003). This novel explores imaginatively Scotland's bloodstained involvement in the slave trade, an involvement about which writers, including historians, had generally previously been very much in denial. Only self-assurance, one avoiding brag-gadocio, could have allowed that honest and transforming book to emerge. Hugh MacDiarmid was for much of the last century a brooding figure, some-times revered, sometimes resisted. But MacDiarmid's commitment to be 'whaur/Extremes meet', where ostensibly irreconcilable elements are – facing, exploring, synthesising and hybridising them – continues as exemplary affirmation of the aspirations and achievements of Scottish writers and the literature they create. And that affirmation is currently being demonstrated in more and more varied ways.

Endnotes

Introduction – Brown and Riach

1. http://en.wikipedia.org/wiki/Joan_Ure, accessed 10 September 2008.
2. See, for example, Ian Brown, 'Celtic Centres, the Fringes and John McGrath', in David Bradby and Susanna Capon (eds), *Freedom's Pioneer: John McGrath's Work in Theatre, Film and Television* (Exeter: University of Exeter Press, 2005), pp. 86–99.
3. For example in Cairns Craig, 'The Study of Scottish Literature', in Ian Brown et al. (eds), *The Edinburgh History of Scottish Literature* (Edinburgh: Edinburgh University Press, 2007), vol. 1, pp. 16–31.
4. Katja Lenz, *Die schottische Sprache im modernen Drama* (Heidelberg: Universitätsverlag C. Winter, 1999), p. 352.
5. Ian Brown, 'Drama and Literature in Scots as an Economic Generator', *Economic Development and Language in Ireland and Scotland*: Conference, Queen's University Belfast, 1 September 2006 (*Proceedings* forthcoming).
6. Joyce McMillan, *The Traverse Theatre Story* (London: Methuen, 1988), p. 77.
7. Michelle Macleod and Moray Watson, 'In the Shadow of the Bard: The Gaelic Short Story, Novel and Drama since the early Twentieth Century', in Ian Brown (ed.), *The Edinburgh History of Scottish Literature*, vol. 3, p. 273.
8. According to http://www.bord-na-gaidhlig.org.uk/about-us/the-gaelic-act.html, accessed 30 July 2008.
9. Ian Brown and Katja Lenz, '"Oh Dearie Me!": Dramatic Rhetoric and Linguistic Subversion in the Scottish Situation Comedy, *The High Life*', in Edgar W. Schneider (ed.), *Englishes Around the World* (Amsterdam and Philadelphia: John Benjamins Publishing Company, 1997), vol. 1, p. 112.
10. Much information drawn on here arises from original research in Denis Agnew, *Contexts and Concepts of a Scottish National Theatre* (unpublished PhD thesis, Queen Margaret University, 2000).
11. Winifred Isaac, *Alfred Wareing: A Biography* (London: Green Bank Press, 1951), p. 34.
12. Richard Butt, 'Literature and the Screen Media since 1908', in Ian Brown et al. (eds), *The Edinburgh History of Scottish Literature*, vol. 3, pp. 53–63.

Chapter 1 – Craig

1. Thomas D. Knowles, *Ideology, Art and Commerce: Aspects of Literary Sociology in late Victorian Scottish Kailyard* (Goteburg: Acta Universitatis Gothoburgensis, 1983), p. 13.

2. Alexander Law, *The Scottish Text Society 1882–1982* (Edinburgh: Scottish Text Society, 1983), p. 2.

3. Quoted from W. C. Dickinson (ed.), *The Court Book of the Barony of Carnwath, 1523–1542*, third series, 1937; http://www.scottishhistorysociety.org/hist1937.htm

4. David Masson, *Essays Biographical and Critical* (Cambridge: Cambridge University Press, 1856).

5. Ibid., p. 24.

6. Ibid., p. 408.

7. Norman Smith, 'The Naturalism of Hume', *Mind* 54, New Series (April, 1905), pp. 149–73.

8. Quoted Crosbie Smith and M. Norton Wise, *Energy and Empire: A Biographical Study of Lord Kelvin* (Cambridge: Cambridge University Press, 1989), pp. 352, 353.

9. Albert Einstein, 'Maxwell and Physical Reality', in *James Clerk Maxwell, A Commemoration Volume 1831–1931* (New York: Macmillan, 1931), p. 71.

10. See C. Smith and M. N. Wise, *Energy and Empire*, pp. 88–9; Basil Mahon, *The Man Who Changed Everything: The Life of James Clerk Maxwell* (Chichester: John Wiley and Sons, 2003), Chap. 3; George E. Davie, *The Democratic Intellect* (Edinburgh: Edinburgh University Press, 1961).

11. Peter Guthrie Tait and Balfour Stewart, *The Unseen Universe or Physical Speculations on a Future State* (London: Macmillan and Co., 1875), p. 82.

12. Glenda Norquay (ed.), *R. L. Stevenson on Fiction: An Anthology of Literary and Critical Essays* (Edinburgh: Edinburgh University Press, 1999), p. 85.

13. Colin Manlove, *Scottish Fantasy Literature* (Edinburgh: Canongate Academic, 1994), p. 83.

14. George MacDonald, *Phantastes: A Faerie Romance for Men and Women* (London: Smith, Elder and Co., 1858), pp. 9–10.

15. Robert Louis Stevenson, *Markheim, Jekyll and the Merry Men* (Edinburgh: Canongate, 1995), p. 247.

16. David Masson, *Recent British Philosophy* (London: Macmillan and Co., [1865] 1867), pp. 151–2; as editor of *Macmillan's Magazine*, Masson had published accounts of the consequences of the energy science by Kelvin and Tait.

17. R. L. Stevenson, *Markheim, Jekyll and the Merry Men*, p. 268.

18. Ibid., p. 292.

19. Ibid.

20. Ibid.

21. See Allen MacDuffie, 'Irreversible Transformations: Robert Louis Stevenson's

Dr Jekyll and Mr. Hyde and Scottish Energy Science', *Representations* 96 (fall 2006), pp. 1–20.

22. See Harvey S. Leff and Andrew F. Rex, *Maxwell's Demon: Entropy, Information, Computing* (Bristol: Adam Hilger, 1990).
23. J. M. Barrie, *Peter Pan* (Harmondsworth: Puffin, [1911] 1967), p. 23.
24. J. M. Barrie, *Peter Pan* (London: Samuel French, [1904] 1928), p. 29.
25. P. G. Tait and B. Stewart, *The Unseen Universe*, p. 156.
26. J. G. Frazer, *The Golden Bough* (Edinburgh: Canongate, [1890] 2004), p. 2.
27. J. G. Frazer, *The Golden Bough* (London: Macmillan, 1922), p. 712.
28. Ibid., p. 56.
29. Ibid.
30. Arthur Conan Doyle, *A Study in Scarlet* (Oxford: Oxford University Press, [1888] 1993), p. 13.
31. Arthur Conan Doyle, *The Hound of the Baskervilles* (London: Pan, [1902] 1975), p. 34.
32. Ibid., p. 173.
33. Fiona Macleod, *The Works of "Fiona Macleod"*, vol. 1, *Pharais*, p. 6.
34. Ibid., p. 164.
35. Ibid., p. 11.
36. She does not appear in the *Edinburgh History of Scottish Literature*.
37. Dickson describes her work as 'so much a product of its time, with its lack of critical engagement with the repressed position of women in nineteenth-century society'; Douglas Gifford and Dorothy McMillan (eds), *A History of Scottish Women's Writing* (Edinburgh: Edinburgh University Press, 1997), p. 345.
38. Ibid., p. 342.
39. Glenda Norquay , 'A Note on Realism', in Glenda Norquay (ed.), *R. L. Stevenson on Fiction*, p. 71.

Chapter 2 – Pittock

1. John Buchan, *Memory Hold-The-Door* (London: Hodder and Stoughton, [1940] 1945), p. 42.
2. Nicola Gordon Bowe and Elizabeth Cumming, *The Arts & Crafts Movements in Dublin & Edinburgh, 1885–1925* (Dublin: Irish Academic Press, 1999), pp. 14, 20, 24–5, 27, 87, 207; see also p. 9. T-GED 8/1/7, 8/1/8, Strathclyde University Archives. A photographic record of the 1904 Celtic Congress is reproduced and annotated in Marion Loffler, *'A Book of Mad Celts'* (Llandysul: Gomer, 2000).
3. Alexander Carmichael, *Carmina Gadelica*, 2 vols ([Edinburgh]: T. and A. Constable, 1900).
4. David Daniell, *The Interpreter's House* (London: Thomas Nelson, 1975) defended Buchan redoubtably against these attacks, but without managing to lay them to rest.
5. Margery Palmer McCulloch (ed.), *Modernism and Nationalism* (Glasgow:

Association for Scottish Literary Studies, 2004), pp. 12, 13, 29–30, 64, 326.

6. D. Daniell, *Interpreter's House*, p. 207.

7. This is misunderstood throughout by Daniell, who describes Leithen, most misleadingly, as 'a very English type' (*Interpreter's House*, p. 158). It is precisely the tension between an international 'English' and a local 'Scottish' identity that Buchan so often investigates.

8. John Buchan, *The Watcher by the Threshold and Other Tales* (Edinburgh and London: William Blackwood, n.d. [1902]), pp. 273–4.

9. *The Best Short Stories of John Buchan*, ed. David Daniell, 2 vols (London: Panther, 1984), vol. 2, p. 60.

10. John Buchan, *Prester John* (London and Edinburgh: Thomas Nelson, [1910] 1922), pp. 10–11, 38, 50, 61, 79, 112, 123, 238.

11. John Buchan, *The Power-House* (Edinburgh and London: William Blackwood, 1912), pp. 64–5.

12. John Buchan, *The Thirty-Nine Steps* (London: Pan, [1914] 1978), pp. 7, 90.

13. John Buchan, *A Prince of the Captivity* (London: Hodder and Stoughton, 1933), pp. 6, 29, 50, 76, 383.

14. John Buchan, *The Island of Sheep* (London, [1936] 1998), p. 11.

15. John Buchan, *Witch Wood*, intr. Christopher Harvie (Edinburgh: Canongate, [1927] 1988), pp. 4, 42, 162–3, 265, 283, 289.

16. All references are to the pagination of *Sick Heart River* in John Buchan, *The Leithen Stories*, ed. Christopher Harvie (Edinburgh: Canongate Classics, 2000).

Chapter 3 – Royle

1. Trevor Royle, *Flowers of the Forest* (Edinburgh: Birlinn, 2006), pp. 12–14.

2. Cairns Craig, 'Introduction', in Cairns Craig (ed.), *History of Scottish Literature: Twentieth Century* (Aberdeen: Aberdeen University Press, 1987), vol. 4, p. 1.

3. Janet Adam Smith, *John Buchan: A Biography* (London: Rupert Hart-Davis, 1965), p. 171.

4. John Buchan, *Poems: Scots and English* (Edinburgh and London: T. C. & E. C. Jack, 1917), p. 7.

5. Colin Milton, 'Modern Poetry in Scots before MacDiarmid', in Cairns Craig (ed.), *History of Scottish Literature*, vol. 4, pp. 11–35.

6. Neil Munro, *The Brave Days: A Chronicle from the North* (Edinburgh: William Blackwood, 1931), pp. 319–20.

7. Neil Munro, *The Poetry of Neil Munro* (Edinburgh: Blackwood, 1931), p. 5.

8. Ibid., p. 59.

9. 'Junior Sub', 'K (1)', *Blackwood's Magazine* (June, 1915), n. p.

10. Ian Hay, *The First Hundred Thousand* (Edinburgh: William Blackwood, 1915), p. 15.

11. Samuel Hynes, *A War Imagined: The First World War and English Culture* (London: Bodley Head, 1990), pp. 48–9.
12. Jean Moorcroft Wilson, *Charles Hamilton Sorley* (London: Woolf, 1985), p. 157.
13. Ibid.
14. Charles Hamilton Sorley, *Marlborough and Other Poems* (Cambridge: University Press, 1916), p. 57.
15. Ibid, p. 68. The poem is dated 12 June 1915.
16. Jean Moorcroft Wilson, *Charles Hamilton Sorley*, p. 214.
17. Alan Ewart Mackintosh, *War, The Liberator and Other Pieces* (London: John Lane, The Bodley Head, 1918), pp. 15–17.
18. Alan Ewart Mackintosh, *A Highland Regiment* (London: John Lane, 1917), pp. 40–2.
19. Alan Ewart Mackintosh, *War, The Liberator and other pieces*, pp. 13–14.
20. Violet Jacob, *More Songs of Angus and Others* (London: Country Life, 1918), pp. 28–9.
21. Mary Symon, *Deveron Days* (Aberdeen: D. Wyllie and Son, 1933), pp. 13–18.
22. James Bell Salmond, *Old Stalker, and Other Verses* (Edinburgh: Moray Press, 1936), pp. 87–8.
23. R. Watson Kerr, *War Daubs* (London: John Lane, 1919), p. 7.
24. Joseph Lee, *Ballads of Battle* (London: John Murray, 1916), p. 21.
25. Derick Thomson, *Introduction to Gaelic Poetry* (London: Gollancz, 1974), pp. 252–4.
26. Dòmhnall Dòmhnallach, *Domhnall Ruadh Choruna: Orain is Dain* (Loch Maddy: Comann Eachdraidh Uibhist a Tuath, 1995), p. 29.
27. Hugh MacDiarmid, *Stony Limits and Other Poems* (London: Gollancz, 1934), pp. 100–3.
28. Catherine Kerrigan, 'MacDiarmid's Early Poetry', in Cairns Craig (ed.), *History of Scottish Literature*, vol. 4, p. 75.

Chapter 4 – Riach

1. Hugh MacDiarmid, *Selected Poetry*, ed. Alan Riach and Michael Grieve (Manchester: Carcanet Press, 2004), p. 157.
2. Harold Bloom, *The Western Canon* (New York: Harcourt Brace and Co., 1994).
3. *Moonstruck: The Songs of F. G. Scott* (Signum Classics: SIGCD096).
4. Cairns Craig, *The Modern Scottish Novel: Narrative and the National Imagination* (Edinburgh: Edinburgh University Press, 1999), p. 31.

Chapter 5 – Smith and Horvat

1. See 'R. F. Pollock and the Arts of Theatre', in [Hugh MacDiarmid,] *Contemporary Scottish Studies*, ed. Alan Riach (Manchester: Carcanet

Press, [1926] 1995), pp. 177–82 (reprinted from *The Scottish Educational Journal*).

2. J. M. Barrie, *Mary Rose* (London: Hodder and Stoughton, 1930), pp. 136–7.

3. See Linda MacKenney (ed.), *Joe Corrie: Plays, Poems and Theatre Writings* (Edinburgh: 7:84 Publications, 1985), pp. 169–74.

4. Ibid., p. 40.

5. This account of Ena Lamont Stewart is indebted to Penelope Cole, *Scotland on Stage: Images of National Identity in the Plays of Joanna Baillie, Ena Lamont, Stewart and Liz Lochhead* (unpublished PhD thesis, University of Colorado, 2007).

6. Ena Lamont Stewart, *Men Should Weep* (Edinburgh: 7:84 Publications, 1983), p. 93.

7. Robert McLellan, *Collected Plays: Volume 1* (London and New York: John Calder, 1981), p. 175.

8. Jan McDonald, '"Is it not Possible to have a Poem made out of Theatre?" – An Assessment of the Dramas and Dramaturgy of Joan Ure', *The International Journal of Scottish Theatre* 3 (1) (June, 2002), n.p., http://www.arts.gla.ac.uk/ScotLit/ASLS/ijost/Volume3_no1/1_mcdonald_j.htm, accessed 23 September 2008.

9. Michael Coveney, 'Playwrights of the North', *Prospect Magazine* 127 (October, 2006), n.p.

Chapter 6 – Watson

1. 'Prefatory Note', *The Evergreen: A Northern Almanac* 2 (autumn, 1895).

2. 'Aims and Ideals', *Rhythm. Art, Music, Literature. Quarterly* 1 (1) (Summer, 1911), p. 36. In this context, one thinks of the Expressionist/Fauvist intensity of MacDiarmid's early Scots lyrics eleven years later.

3. Tom Normand, *The Modern Scot. Modernism and Nationalism in Scottish Art, 1928–1955* (London: Ashgate, 2000).

4. C. M. Grieve, 'Scotland and Belgium' *The Dunfermline Press* (5 August 1922). This was written before he took up the cause of Scots.

5. See Douglas Gifford, 'Re-Mapping Renaissance in Modern Scottish Literature', in Gerard Carruthers et al. (eds), *Beyond Scotland: New Contexts for Twentieth-Century Scottish Literature* (Amsterdam: Rodopi, 2004), pp. 21–3.

6. Edwin Muir, *Scott and Scotland* (Edinburgh: Polygon, 1982), p. 7. Critics have noted how much Muir's case has been drawn from T. S. Eliot's worries about a 'dissociation of sensibility' in English literature.

7. Muir's position reflects the particular rise of English cultural nationalism between 1880 and 1920, with its vision of 'English' literature as an expression of 'the deepest and most serious characteristics of the race': see the brilliant Introduction to Andrew Gibson, *Joyce's Revenge. History, Politics, and Aesthetics in* Ulysses (Oxford: Oxford University Press, 2002), especially p. 11.

8. Edwin Muir, *Scott and Scotland*, p. 4.
9. Cited in Benedict Anderson, *Imagined Communities* (London, New York: Verso, 1991), p. 91. Note that Macaulay 'meant well' too. He was not recommending the total extirpation of Hindu culture (as is often supposed) but saw this 'respectable' class as a relatively small intermediary group between the largely uneducated native population – still close to their roots – and the British imperial presence.
10. Matthew Arnold, *On the study of Celtic Literature* (London, 1867), pp. 11–12.
11. Hugh MacDiarmid, 'English Ascendancy in British Literature', first published in *The Criterion* in 1931, in *Selected Prose*, Alan Riach (ed.), (Manchester: Carcanet, 1992), p. 77.
12. Ibid., p. 61.
13. Cairns Craig, *Out of History. Narrative Paradigms in Scottish and British Culture* (Edinburgh: Polygon, 1996), p. 200.
14. See for example, Cairns Craig, 'Beyond Reason – Hume, Seth, Macmurray and Scotland's Postmodernity', in Eleanor Bell and Gavin Miller (eds), *Scotland in Theory* (Amsterdam: Rodopi, 2004) pp. 249–83; also Randall Stevenson, 'A Postmodern Scotland?', in G. Carruthers et al. (eds), *Beyond Scotland*, 209–28; and Eleanor Bell, *Questioning Scotland: Literature, Nationalism, Postmodernism* (Basingstoke: Palgrave Macmillan, 2004).
15. Note, however, that the title of the collection, as published in 1923, *was* taken from a citation in Smith's book. The original title was to be *Cerebral and Other Studies*.
16. Hugh MacDiarmid, *Annals of the Five Senses and Other Stories, Sketches, and Plays*, ed. Roderick Watson and Alan Riach, with an introduction by Roderick Watson (Manchester: Carcanet Press, 1999).
17. Ibid., 'Introduction'.
18. Ibid., 'In Acknowledgment', p. 4.
19. A frequent phrase of his, from Oliver Wendell Holmes's *Autocrat of the Breakfast Table* where intertextual implications are also present when the author observes that

> We get into a way of thinking as if what we call an 'intellectual man' was, as a matter of course, made up of nine-tenths, or thereabouts, of book-learning, and one-tenth himself. But even if he is actually so compounded, he need not read much. Society is a strong solution of books. It draws the virtue out of what is best worth reading, as hot water draws the strength of tea-leaves.

In *Lucky Poet* MacDiarmid declared his admiration for Holmes's turns of phrase.
20. This issue and MacDiarmid's 'Modernism' is intelligently discussed by John Baglow in *Hugh MacDiarmid: The Poetry of Self* (Kingston: McGill-Queen's University Press, 1987), see especially Chapter 1.
21. Roland Barthes, 'The Death of the Author', Stephen Heath (trans. and ed.), *Image-Music-Text* (London: Fontana, [1967] 1977), p. 146.

22. G. Gregory Smith, *Scottish Literature: Character and Influence* (London: Macmillan and Co., 1919), p. 15, 4.

23. Hugh MacDiarmid, 'The Caledonian Antisyzygy and the Gaelic Idea', first published in two parts in *The Modern Scot* (1931–2), in Duncan Glen (ed.), *Selected Essays of Hugh MacDiarmid* (London: Jonathan Cape, 1969), p. 61.

24. Ibid., p. 68.

25. 'Introduction', in Carol Anderson and Aileen Christianson (eds), *Scottish Women's Fiction, 1920s to 1960s: Journeys into Being* (East Linton: Tuckwell Press, 2000), p. 16. The citation comes from Patricia Waugh, *Feminine Fictions: Revisiting the Postmodern* (London: Routledge, 1989), p. 22.

26. Alison Lumsden, 'Journey into Being: Nan Shepherd's *The Weatherhouse*', in Carol Anderson and Aileen Christianson (eds), *Scottish Women's Fiction*, pp. 59–71.

27. National Library of Scotland, MSS. 27438-274.

28. This is also a central theme in Shepherd's book about the Cairngorms, *The Living Mountain*, written in the mid-1940s but not published until 1977. See Roderick Watson, 'Introduction' to *The Living Mountain*, in Nan Shepherd, *The Grampian Quartet*, ed. Roderick Watson (Edinburgh: Canongate, 1996). All page references within the text are to this edition.

29. Cairns Craig, *The Modern Scottish Novel: Narrative and the National Imagination* (Edinburgh: Edinburgh University Press, 1999), p. 226.

30. Lewis Grassic Gibbon, *Cloud Howe*, in Tom Crawford (ed. and intro.), *A Scots Quair* (Edinburgh: Canongate, 1996), p. 137.

31. Isobel Murray, 'Novelists of the Renaissance', in Cairns Craig (ed.), *The History of Scottish Literature*, vol. 4, p. 109.

32. Douglas Gifford, 'Re-Mapping Renaissance in Modern Scottish Literature', in Gerard Carruthers et al. (eds), *Beyond Scotland*, p. 19.

33. Francis R. Hart, 'Neil Gunn's Drama of the Light', in Cairns Craig (ed.), *The History of Scottish Literature*, vol. 4, p. 92.

34. Neil M. Gunn, *Highland River* (Edinburgh: Canongate, 1991), pp. 103–4. All page references within the text are to this edition.

Chapter 7 – Gifford

1. See Ronald Black/Raghnall MacIlleDuibh (ed.), *An Tuil: Duanaire Gàidhlig an 20mh Ceud /Anthology of Twentieth-Century Scottish Gaelic Verse* (Edinburgh: Polygon, 1999), pp. 150–3; 743–4; also, Bill Innes (ed.), Dòmhnall Ruadh Mac an t-Saoir, *Aeòlus!* (Ochtertyre: Grace Note, 2008).

2. Raymond Ross, *Collected Poems and Songs: Hamish Henderson* (Edinburgh: Curly Snake Publishing, 2000). All citations are from this edition.

3. Somhairle MacGill-Eain/Sorley MacLean, *Dàin do Eimhir/Poems to Eimhir*, ed. Christopher Whyte (Glasgow: Association for Scottish Literary Studies, 2002), pp. 74–5.

4. Michel Byrne (ed.), *Collected Poems and Songs of George Campbell Hay* (Deòrsa Mac Iain Dheòrsa) (Edinburgh: Edinburgh University Press, 2000), p. 161.
5. Edinburgh: Polygon, 1999.
6. See Ronald Black (ed.), *An Tùil*, pp. 254–9; Aonghas Phàdraig Caimbeul, *Suathadh ri Iomadh Rubha* (Glasgow: Gairm, 1973).
7. Robb's discussion is in *ScotLit* 35 (Glasgow: Association for Scottish Literary Studies, 2007), pp. 1–4; see also his biography of Scott, David Robb, *Auld Campaigner: A Life of Alexander Scott* (Edinburgh: Dunedin Academic Press, 2007).
8. This moving poem – to be found in Helena Shire (ed.), *The Wrong Music: The Poems of Olive Fraser 1909–1977* (Edinburgh: Canongate, 1989), p. 65 – has Hitler associate 'guns and butter' instead of Goering's famously bellicose preference for guns over butter.

Chapter 8 – Burgess

1. Douglas Gifford et al. (eds), *Scottish Literature* (Edinburgh: Edinburgh University Press, 2002), p. 725.
2. Such as *The Constant Star* (1945) and *The Westering Sun* (1946). Many others followed, until Blake's death in 1961.
3. Barke's Burns novels are *The Wind that Shakes the Barley* (1946), *The Song in the Green Thorn Tree* (1947), *The Wonder of All the Gay World* (1949), *The Crest of the Broken Wave* (1953) and *The Well of the Silent Harp* (1954), with a posthumously published coda, *Bonnie Jean* (1959).
4. Such as Barke's *Major Operation* (1935) and Blake's *The Shipbuilders* (1936).
5. *Wax Fruit* (1947) was followed by *Aunt Bel* (1949) and *The Hayburn Family* (1952).
6. *The Monarch of the Glen* (1941) and *Hunting the Fairies* (1949) are set in the central Highlands; *Keep the Home Guard Turning* (1943) and *Whisky Galore* (1947) take place on the (fictional) islands of Great and Little Todday, with a less satisfactory sequel in *Rockets Galore* (1957).
7. See Hamish Henderson, 'Folk-Singing in Auld Reekie', in *Alias MacAlias: Writings on Song, Folk and Literature* (Edinburgh: Polygon, 1992), pp. 5–15.
8. In the writer's experience; it is not easy to trace written accounts.
9. *Second Sight* (1940), *The Silver Darlings* (1941), *Young Art and Old Hector* (1942), *The Serpent* (1943), *The Green Isle of the Great Deep* (1944) and *The Key of the Chest* (1945).
10. Gerard Carruthers, 'Introduction', in Gerard Carruthers (ed.), *The Devil to Stage: Five Plays by James Bridie* (Glasgow: Association for Scottish Literary Studies, 2007), p. xvii.
11. Gavin Wallace, 'Mackenzie, Sir (Edward Montague Anthony) Compton

(1883–1972)', *Oxford Dictionary of National Biography* (Oxford: Oxford University Press, 2004).

12. Urquhart published several short story collections in this period: *The Laundry Girl and the Pole* (1955) collects stories from earlier books by then out of print. Novels in this period include *The Ferret was Abraham's Daughter* (1949) and *Jezebel's Dust* (1951).

13. See Sylvia Bryce-Wunder, 'Of Hard Men and Hairies: *No Mean City* and Modern Scottish Urban Fiction', *Scottish Studies Review* 4 (1), (spring 2003), pp. 112–25.

14. See Bill Findlay (ed.), *Scottish People's Theatre: Plays by Glasgow Unity Writers* (Glasgow: Association for Scottish Literary Studies, 2008).

15. 'Introduction', in Maurice Lindsay and Fred Urquhart (eds), *No Scottish Twilight* (Glasgow: William Maclellan, 1947), p. 3.

16. George Blake, *Annals of Scotland 1895–1955* (BBC, 1956) is a pamphlet consisting of a foreword by Edwin Muir, a long essay by Blake, and details of the productions.

17. His plays in this decade are *Mr Gillie* (1950) and *The Baikie Charivari* (1951).

18. *The Big House* (1950) and *Lobsters on the Agenda* (1952); *Travel Light* (1952) and *To the Chapel Perilous* (1955).

19. His only other play, *The Bevellers*, was first produced in 1973.

20. In novels including, in this decade, *The Thistle and the Grail* (1954), *Guests of War* (1956) and *The Changeling* (1958).

21. Such as *The Missionaries* (1957) and *Love is a Fervent Fire* (1959).

22. See Duncan Glen, *In Search of Serif Books [...]* (Kirkcaldy: Akros Publications, 2006).

23. A biography of William Maclellan by Morag MacAlpine is forthcoming from Glasgow publishers Kennedy & Boyd.

24. See David Hutchison, *The Modern Scottish Theatre* (Glasgow: Molendinar Press, 1977), particularly pp. 98–113, covering the 1940s and 1950s.

25. See Helen Murdoch, *Travelling Hopefully: The Story of Molly Urquhart* (Edinburgh: Paul Harris Publishing, 1981).

26. See Bill Findlay (ed.), *Scottish People's Theatre*, particularly the Introduction, pp. xi-xxii.

Chapter 9 – Corbett

1. John Press, *The Chequer'd Shade: Reflections on Obscurity in Poetry* (London: Oxford University Press, 1958), p. 1.

2. Tony Lopez, *The Poetry of W. S. Graham* (Edinburgh: Edinburgh University Press, 1989).

3. Matthew Francis, *Where the People Are: Language and Community in the Poetry of W. S. Graham* (Cambridge: Salt Publishing, 2004).

4. Ralph Pite and Hester Jones (eds), *W. S. Graham: Speaking Towards You* (Liverpool: Liverpool University Press, 2004).

5. Alan Riach, *Hugh MacDiarmid's Epic Poetry* (Edinburgh: Edinburgh University Press, 1991), p. 206n.

6. W. S. Graham, *New Collected Poems*, ed. Matthew Francis; intro. Douglas Dunn (London: Faber and Faber, 2004), p. xvi.

7. Shari Benstock, 'Beyond the Reaches of Feminist Criticism: A Letter from Paris' [1987], reprinted in Michael H. Whitworth (ed.), *Modernism* (Oxford: Blackwell, 2007), p. 226.

8. Matthew Francis, *Where the People Are*, p. 148.

9. John Mullan, 'What are our Poets Writing About?', *The Guardian*, 5 October 2005, http://books.guardian.co.uk/forwardprize2005/story/0,16299,1585250, 00.html, accessed 6 June 2008.

10. John Press, *The Chequer'd Shade: Reflections on Obscurity in Poetry* (London: Oxford University Press, 1958), p. 24.

11. Hugh MacDiarmid, *In Memoriam James Joyce: A Vision of World Language* (Glasgow: William Maclellan, 1955), p. 18.

12. W. S. Graham, *New Collected Poems*, p. 10.

13. Hugh MacDiarmid, *In Memoriam James Joyce*, p. 18.

14. Robert Crawford, *Scotland's Books: The Penguin History of Scottish Literature* (London: Penguin, 2007), p. 553.

15. For example: Kenneth Buthlay, 'The Ablach in the Gold Pavilion', in *Scottish Literary Journal* 15 (2) (1988), pp. 39–57; Alan Riach, *Hugh MacDiarmid's Epic Poetry* (Edinburgh: Edinburgh University Press, 1991).

16. Eloise Knowlton, *Joyce, Joyceans and the Rhetoric of Citation* (Gainesville: University of Florida Press, 1998), p. 10.

17. Christopher Whyte, *Modern Scottish Poetry* (Edinburgh: Edinburgh University Press, 2004), p. 94.

18. Hugh MacDiarmid, *In Memoriam James Joyce*, p. 13.

19. Ibid., p. 14.

20. Ibid., p. 35.

21. Charles Kay Ogden, *Basic English: A General Introduction with Rules and Grammar* (London: Kegan Paul, Trench, Trubner, 1930).

22. I. A. Richards and Christine Gibson, *Learning Basic English: A Practical Handbook for English-Speaking People* (New York: W. W. Norton and Co., 1945).

23. Robert Phillipson, *Linguistic Imperialism* (Oxford: Oxford University Press, 1992).

24. Jennifer Jenkins, *World Englishes* (London: Routledge, 2003).

25. Hugh MacDiarmid, *In Memoriam James Joyce*, pp. 61, 62.

26. Christopher Whyte, *Modern Scottish Poetry*, p. 97.

27. From *The Nightfishing*, in W. S. Graham, *New Collected Poems*, ed. Matthew

Francis; intro. by Douglas Dunn (London: Faber and Faber, 2004), p. 109.

28. Matthew Francis, *Where the People Are*, p. 59.

29. Chris Jones, *Strange Likeness: The Use of Old English in Twentieth Century Poetry* (Oxford: Oxford University Press, 2006), p. 153n; see also Michael and Margaret Snow (eds), *The Nightfisherman: Selected Letters of W. S. Graham* (Manchester: Carcanet, 1999), pp. 104, 117.

30. Ian Sansom, '"Listen": W. S. Graham', in Ralph Pite and Hester Jones (eds), *W. S. Graham: Speaking Towards You* (Liverpool: Liverpool University Press, 2004), p. 16.

31. Matthew Francis, *Where the People Are*, p. 81.

32. Robert Crawford, *Scotland's Books*, p. 617.

33. Matthew Francis, *Where the People Are*, pp. 3–12.

34. Hugh MacDiarmid, *In Memoriam James Joyce*, p. 77.

35. W. S. Graham, *New Collected Poems*, p. 155.

36. See, for example: H. P Grice, 'Logic and Conversation' [1967], reprinted in P. Cole and J. L. Morgan (eds), *Syntax and Semantics 3: Speech Acts* (New York: Academic Press, 1975), pp. 41–58; Mary Louise Pratt, *Towards a Speech Act Theory of Literary Discourse* (Bloomington: Indiana University Press, 1977).

37. Matthew Francis, *Where the People Are*, p. 105.

38. Hugh MacDiarmid, *In Memoriam James Joyce*, p. 123.

Chapter 10 – Sellin

1. Eric Linklater, *Fanfare for a Tin Hat* (London: Macmillan, 1970), p. 67.

2. Robin Jenkins, 'Novelist in Scotland', *Saltire Review* 2 (5) (autumn 1955), p. 7.

3. Trevor Royle, 'Spark and Scotland' in Alan Bold (ed.), *Muriel Spark. An Odd Capacity for Vision* (London: Vision and Barnes and Noble, 1984), p. 148.

4. *The Scotsman*, 6 September 1967, quoted by Trevor Royle, *James and Jim. A Biography of James Kennaway* (Edinburgh: Mainstream, 1983), p. 204.

5. Muriel Spark, 'What Images Return', in Karl Miller, *Memoirs of A Modern Scotland* (London: Faber, 1970), p. 151.

6. Fionn Mac Colla, *The Albannach* (Edinburgh: Reprographia, [1932] 1971), p. 33.

7. Isobel Murray (ed.), *Scottish Writers Talking* (Edinburgh: John Donald, 2006), p. 105.

8. Allan Massie, 'Calvinism and Catholicism in Muriel Spark', in Alan Bold (ed.), *Muriel Spark*, p. 101.

9. Personal interview, 1 September 1983.

10. Muriel Spark, 'What Images Return', in Karl Miller, *Memoirs*, p. 153.

11. Fionn Mac Colla, 'Mein Bumpf', in David Morrison (ed.), *Essays on Fionn Mac Colla* (Thurso: Caithness Books, 1973), p. 11.

12. Isobel Murray (ed.), *Scottish Writers Talking* (2006), p. 128.

13. Manfred Malzahn, 'The Industrial Novel', in Cairns Craig (ed.), *The History of Scottish Literature*, vol. 4, pp. 229–42.
14. The setting of Jenkins's *A Very Scotch Affair* is Glasgow, but it is difficult to get a sense of place. Again the choice is determined by symbolic connotations more than realistic reasons. The hero's name is Mungo, an ironic reference to Glasgow's patron saint.
15. Steven Connor, *The English Novel in History* (London: Routledge, 1996), p. 45.

Chapter 11 – Brown and Nicholson

1. The authors are grateful to Carol Lothian of Publishing Scotland for supplying the foundation date (email correspondence, 6 November 2008).
2. Edwin Morgan, *Essays* (Manchester: Carcanet, 1974), pp. 174–5.
3. Eleanor Bell, 'Old Country, New Dreams: Scottish Poetry since the 1970s', in Ian Brown et al. (eds), *The Edinburgh History of Scottish Literature*, vol. 3, p. 186.
4. Tom Wright and Hugh Rae, 'Burns and the Poets of Today', *Scottish Field*, January 1962, p. 19.
5. Edwin Morgan, 'Poet and Public', *The Scotsman*, 12 March 1962.
6. Hugh MacDiarmid, 'America's Example to Scottish Writers', *Jabberwock: Edinburgh University Students' Magazine* [1959], reprinted in Alan Riach, 'Vitality So Abundant: MacDiarmid and the Americans', *Edinburgh Review* 97 (spring 1997), pp. 102–14.
7. Colin Nicholson, *Edwin Morgan: Inventions of Modernity* (Manchester: Manchester University Press, 2002), pp. 88–9.
8. Alan Bold (ed.), *The Letters of Hugh MacDiarmid* (London: Hamish Hamilton, 1984), p. 814.
9. Kenneth White, *Open World: The Collected Poems 1960–2000* (Edinburgh: Polygon, 2003), p. xxiv.
10. Edwin Morgan, *Essays* (Manchester: Carcanet, 1974), p. 178.
11. 'Robert Garioch', *Writing Scotland*, http://www.BBC.co.uk, accessed 20 March 2008.
12. Ronald Black/Raghnall MacIlleDuibh (ed.), *An Tuil: Duanaire Gàidhlig an 20mh Ceud / Anthology of Twentieth-Century Scottish Gaelic Verse* (Edinburgh: Polygon, 1999), pp. 524–5.
13. Ibid., pp. xlv–lii.
14. *Reothairt is Contraigh / Spring Tide and Neap Tide, Selected Poems 1932–1972* (Edinburgh: Canongate, 1977), pp. 160–1.
15. Ibid., pp. 164–7.
16. Meredith Richard, 'A New Take on "Alice in Wonderland"', *The Ithaca Journal*, http://www.theithacajournal.com/apps/pbcs.dll/article?AID=/20080131/ENTERTAINMENT03/801310318/1082, accessed 13 February 2008.

17. Ian Brown and Colin Nicholson, 'The Border Crossers and Reconfiguration of the Possible: Poet-Playwright-Novelists from the Mid-Twentieth Century on', in Ian Brown et al. (eds), *The Edinburgh History of Scottish Literature*, vol. 3, pp. 262–72.

18. Iain Crichton Smith, 'The Double Man', in R. P. Draper (ed.), *The Literature of Region and Nation* (Basingstoke: Macmillan, 1988), p. 140.

19. Cairns Craig, *The Modern Scottish Novel: Narrative and the National Imagination* (Edinburgh: Edinburgh University Press, 1999), p. 110.

20. Meg Bateman, 'The Autobiography in Scottish Gaelic', in Ian Brown et al. (eds), *The Edinburgh History*, vol. 3, ibid., p. 230.

21. Michelle Macleod and Moray Watson, 'In the Shadow of the Bard: The Gaelic Short Story, Novel and Drama since the early Twentieth Century', in Ian Brown et al. (eds), ibid., p. 278.

22. Richard Butt, 'Literature and the Screen Media since 1908', in Ian Brown et al. (eds), ibid., p. 61.

Chapter 12 – Sassi

1. Scott Michaelsen and David E. Johnson (eds), *Border Theory: The Limits of Cultural Politics* (Minneapolis: University of Minnesota Press, 1997), p. 3.

2. Renato Rosaldo, *Culture and Truth: The Remaking of Social Analysis* (Boston: Beacon Press, 1993), p. 216.

3. Scott Michaelsen and David E. Johnson (eds), *Border Theory*, p. 3.

4. Claudio Magris, 'The Fair of Tolerance', http://www.eurozine.com/articles/2001-12-27-magris-en.html, last accessed 27 August 2008.

5. See for example, among the most recent publications in this field, Richard Robinson, *Narratives of the European Border: A History of Nowhere. Language, Discourse, Society* (Basingstoke: Palgrave Macmillan, 2007).

6. Murray Pittock, *The Road to Independence? Scotland since the Sixties* (London: Reaktion Books, 2008), p. 7.

7. Howard D. Weinbrot, *Britannia's Issue. The Rise of British Literature from Dryden to Ossian* (Cambridge: Cambridge University Press, 1993), p. 479.

8. Lewis Grassic Gibbon, *A Scots Quair* (London: Pan Books, [1932–4] 1978), p. 32.

9. Catherine Carswell, 'Intimations of Mortality, and of Senility', in *Lying Awake* (Edinburgh: Canongate, [1950] 1997), p. 167.

10. Ibid., p. 175.

11. Angus Calder, 'Introduction', in *Scotlands of the Mind* (Edinburgh: Luath, 2002), p. xi.

12. For a recent critical investigation of Scotland's European vocation, see Atsuko Ichijo, *Scottish Nationalism and the Idea of Europe: Concepts of Europe and the Nation. British Politics and Society* (London: Routledge, 2004).

13. See John Corbett, *Written in the Language of the Scottish Nation* (Clevedon: Multilingual Matters, 1999), pp. 126–86.

14. See Cairns Craig, *Out of History: Narrative Paradigms in Scottish and English Culture* (Edinburgh: Polygon, 1996), p. 12.

15. Kurt Wittig, *The Scottish Tradition in Literature* (Edinburgh: Oliver and Boyd, 1958).

16. Francis Russell Hart, *The Scottish Novel: A Critical Survey* (London: Murray, 1978).

17. Such influence has been recently fully acknowledged and convincingly discussed in Eleanor Bell, *Questioning Scotland: Literature, Nationalism, Postmodernism* (Basingstoke: Palgrave Macmillan, 2004).

18. See Berthold Schoene, 'Going Cosmopolitan: Reconstituting "Scottishness" in Post-Devolution Criticism', in Berthold Schoene (ed.), *The Edinburgh Companion to Contemporary Scottish Literature* (Edinburgh: Edinburgh University Press, 2007), pp. 7–16.

19. Cairns Craig, *Out of History*, p. 28.

20. Ibid.

21. Ibid., p. 29.

22. Ibid.

23. Ibid., p. 206.

24. Roderick Watson, 'Postcolonial Subjects? Language, Narrative Authority and Class in Contemporary Scottish Culture', *The European English Messenger* 7 (2) (1998), pp. 21–31.

25. Ibid., p. 30. Quoted from Franz Fanon, 'On National Culture'.

26. Ibid., pp. 30–1.

27. Alan Riach, 'The Presence of Actual Angels: The Fractal Poetics of Wilson Harris', *Callaloo* 18 (1) (1995), p. 36.

28. Christopher Whyte, 'In Search of the Mother Tongue', in James Patrick Mackey (ed.), *The Cultures of Europe, the Irish Contribution* (Belfast: Institute of Irish Studies, Queen's University of Belfast, 1994), p. 157.

29. Ronald D. S. Jack and P. A. T. Rozendaal (eds), *The Mercat Anthology of Early Scottish Literature, 1375–1707* (Edinburgh: Mercat Press, 1997), p. xxx.

30. Glenda Norquay and Gerry Smyth (eds), *Across the Margins: Cultural Identity and Change in the Atlantic Archipelago* (Manchester: Manchester University Press, 2002), pp. 67–82.

31. Ibid., p. 68.

32. In Ian Brown et al. (eds), *The Edinburgh History of Scottish Literature* (Edinburgh: Edinburgh University Press, 2007), vol. 3, p. 262.

33. Tom Scott, *Brand the Builder* (Epping: Ember, 1975).

34. George Mackay Brown, *Greenvoe: A Novel* (London: Hogarth Press, 1972).

35. For an investigation of MacIlvanney and Crichton Smith's 'geography of difference', see Ray Ryan, *Ireland and Scotland: Literature and Culture, State and Nation, 1966–2000* (Oxford: Clarendon Press, 2002).

36. The notion of 'affective community' is adapted from Leela Gandhi, *Affective Communities: Anticolonial Thought, Fin-De-Siècle Radicalism, and the Politics of Friendship. Politics, History, and Culture* (Durham: Duke University Press, 2006).
37. Liz Lochhead, *Mary, Queen of Scots Got Her Head Chopped Off; and, Dracula* (Harmondsworth: Penguin, 1988).
38. The three novellas were collected in Iain Crichton Smith, *Murdo. The Life and Works* (Edinburgh: Birlinn, 2001).
39. Ibid., p. 61.
40. See Carla Sassi, 'Maddening Reason: Bilingualism as Liminality in Iain Crichton Smith's Murdo Novellae', in Michael Kenneally and Rhona Richman Kenneally (eds), *From English Literature to the New Literatures in English: Festschrift in Honour of Wolfgang Zach* (Heidelberg: winter, 2005), pp. 311–21.
41. Ibid. p. 321.
42. Alasdair Gray, *1982 Janine* (Harmondsworth: Penguin, 1984), p. 341.
43. Jackie Kay, *Trumpet* (Picador, London, 1998).
44. Berthold Schoene, 'Going Cosmopolitan', p. 9.
45. Ibid., p. 9.

Chapter 13 – Marsack

1. Christopher Carrell (ed.), *Seven Poets* (Glasgow: Third Eye Centre (Glasgow) Ltd, 1981), interview with Alexander Moffat, pp. 7, 10.
2. George Mackay Brown, 'Poets' Pub: A Personal Tribute', in Joy Hendry and Raymond Ross (eds), *Norman MacCaig: Critical Essays* (Edinburgh: Edinburgh University Press, 1990), pp. 5–6.
3. Murdo Macdonald, *Scottish Art* (London: Thames and Hudson, 2000).
4. Alasdair Gray, *1982, Janine* (London: Jonathan Cape, 1984), p. xx.
5. Hugh MacDiarmid, 'The Dour Drinkers of Glasgow', in *Selected Prose*, Alan Riach (ed.), (Manchester: Carcanet Press, 1992), pp. 194–5, p. 199.
6. Angus Calder, obituary of Callum Macdonald in *The Independent* (4 March 1999).
7. *A Garioch Miscellany*, ed. and sel. by Robin Fulton (Edinburgh: Macdonald Publishers/Lines Review Edition, 1986), p. 37.
8. *Seven Poets*, p. 37.
9. Hugh MacDiarmid, 'The Norman Conquest' [July 1955], in *The Raucle Tongue – Hitherto Uncollected Prose*, ed. Angus Calder, Glen Murray and Alan Riach (Manchester: Carcanet Press, 1998), vol. 3, pp. 346, 347, 349.
10. Hugh MacDiarmid, 'MacDiarmid Replies to Mackenzie' [October 1952], in *The Raucle Tongue*, p. 309.
11. Christopher Whyte, *Modern Scottish Poetry* (Edinburgh: Edinburgh University Press, 2004), pp. 88, 89.

12. *A Garioch Miscellany*, pp. 32–3.
13. Sydney Goodsir Smith, 'Introduction', in Garioch's *Selected Poems* (Edinburgh: M. Macdonald, 1966), p. 7.
14. Maurice Lindsay, *Thank You for Having Me*, quoted by Duncan Glen, in *In search of Serif Books, the Stanley Press & Joseph Mardel* . . . (Kirkcaldy: Akros Publications, 2006), p. 35.
15. *A Garioch Miscellany*, p. 146.
16. Hugh MacDiarmid, 'Sydney', in *For Sydney Goodsir Smith* (Loanhead: M. Macdonald, 1975), p. 43.
17. Norman MacCaig, 'Introductory Note', in ibid., p. 7.
18. Edwin Morgan, 'The Beatnik in the Kailyard' [spring 1962], in *Essays* (Cheadle Hulme: Carcanet New Press Ltd, 1974), p. 174.
19. Angus Calder, 'Unmoved by the Movement: Fifties MacCaig', in Joy Hendry and Raymond Ross (eds), *Norman MacCaig: Critical Essays* (Edinburgh: Edinburgh University Press, 1990), p. 39.
20. Edwin Morgan, 'The Beatnik in the Kailyard', p. 175.
21. Peter Kravitz (ed.), *The Picador Book of Contemporary Scottish Fiction* (London: Picador, 1997), p. xxix.
22. Edwin Morgan, 'Letter 3', in Ross Birrell and Alec Finlay (eds), *Justified Sinners – An Archaeology of Scottish Counter-Culture (1960–2000)* (Edinburgh: pocketbooks, 2002), n.p.
23. Garioch to J. K. Annand, 7 April 1970, in *A Garioch Miscellany*, p. 45. However Morgan notes in his contribution to the *Miscellany* that when the two Roberts came to his flat in Glasgow for editorial meetings, 'how unexpected, and sharp, his comments were, even though he liked to project the image [. . .] of a conservative and distracted person unaccountably brought into the cut-and-thrust of contemporary ideas. Actually he blossomed out and felt happy in that so-called modish decade of the Sixties'. Garioch was excited by Alasdair Gray's *Lanark* – 'extraordinary [. . .] certainly a find: we mustn't let it go' – and was keen to publish D. M. Black and Anne Stevenson, too, in 1968.
24. Tumult included: the anti-Vietnam War Grosvenor Square (London) demonstration (March); the assassinations of Martin Luther King (April) and of Robert Kennedy (June); *les évènements* in Paris, threatening de Gaulle's government (May); and August's Warsaw Pact invasion of Czechoslovakia, suppressing the 'Prague Spring' reforms, and anti-war Chicago Democratic Convention protests, met by, in an official report's words, a 'police riot'.
25. Christopher Whyte, *Modern Scottish Poetry*, p. 59.
26. Hugh MacDiarmid, review 1958–9, *The Raucle Tongue*, vol. 3, p. 388.
27. *The Nightfisherman – Selected Letters of W. S. Graham*, ed. Michael and Margaret Snow (Manchester: Carcanet Press, 1999), 24 September 1969, p. 229.
28. Ibid., undated [1981], p. 368.
29. Neal Ascherson, *Seven Poets*, p. 17. Yet in the interview with Iain Crichton

Smith in the same book, conducted in 1980, he says that he is not a Scottish Nationalist, and sometimes feels that 'there is nothing real in Scotland you can actually operate on to make real poetry', and that on the day of the referendum he had wondered, '"Is it possible to commit yourself to the new, to make the leap into the new?" And I felt – I feel all the time that there isn't enough of this leap. It's just talking about what has gone on in the past.'

30. Norman MacCaig, ibid., p. 38.
31. Edwin Morgan, 'The Beatnik in the Kailyard', p. 175.

Chapter 14 – Macleod

1. Joshua A. Fishman, *Handbook of Language and Ethnic Identity* (Oxford: Oxford University Press, 1999), p. 4.
2. Ibid., p. 154.
3. Michelle Macleod, 'Language and Bilingualism in the Gaelic Poetry of Iain Crichton Smith', *Scottish Studies Review* 2 (2) (autumn, 2001), pp. 105–13.
4. George Campbell Hay, *Collected Poems and Songs of George Campbell Hay*, ed. Michel Byrne (Edinburgh: Edinburgh University Press, 2003), p. 446.
5. Ibid., pp. 324–5.
6. Ibid., p. 152.
7. Ibid., p. 153.
8. Ibid., p. 358.
9. See Michelle NicLeòid, 'Leòdhas agus fànas ann am bàrdachd Ruaraidh MhicThòmais', in Donald Meek (ed.), *Scottish Gaelic Studies* XIX (1999), pp. 59–65.
10. George Campbell Hay, *Collected Poems and Songs*, p. 154.
11. Ibid., p. 290.
12. Ibid., p. 350.
13. Christopher Whyte, *Modern Scottish Poetry* (Edinburgh: Edinburgh University Press, 2004), p. 88.
14. Ibid., p. 81.
15. Derick Thomson, *An Dealbh Briste* (Edinburgh: Serif Books, 1951), p. 37.
16. Ibid., p. 38.
17. Ibid., p. 47.
18. Derick Thomson, *Sùil air Fàire* (Stornoway: Acair, 2007), pp. 18–19.
19. Ibid., pp. 20–1.
20. Ibid., p. 23.
21. Ibid., p. 30.
22. Ibid., p. 134.
23. Michelle Macleod, 'Language and Bilingualism in the Gaelic Poetry of Iain Crichton Smith', *Scottish Studies Review* 2 (2) (autumn 2001).
24. Iain Crichton Smith, *An t-Eilean agus an Cànan* (Glasgow: Glasgow University Celtic Department, 1987), pp. 5, 7, 33.

25. Aonghas MacNeacail, *Oideachadh ceart agus dàin eile* (Edinburgh: Polygon, 1996), p. 72.
26. Christopher Whyte, *Modern Scottish Poetry*, p. 227.
27. Aonghas MacNeacail, *an seachnadh agus dàin eile* (Edinburgh: MacDonald Publishers, 1986), p. 98.
28. Meg Bateman, *Soirbheas* (Edinburgh: Polygon, 2007), p. 22.
29. Christopher Whyte, 'Bho Leabhar-Latha Maria Malibran', *Gairm 175 and 176* (1996), pp. 371–2.
30. Ronald Black (ed.), *An Tuil* (Edinburgh: Polygon, 1999), p. 671.
31. Anne Frater, *Fon t-Slige* (Glasgow: Gairm, 1995), p. 59.
32. Ibid., p. 61.
33. Corinna Krause, 'Gaelic Scotland – A Postcolonial Site? In Search of a Meaningful Theoretical Framework to Assess the Dynamics of Contemporary Scottish Gaelic Verse', *eSharp*, 6 (1) (2005), http://www.gla.ac.uk/media/media_41178_en.pdf, p. 8.
34. Christopher Whyte (ed.), *An Aghaidh na Sìorraidheachd* (Edinburgh: Polygon, 1991).
35. Corinna Krause, 'Gaelic Scotland', p. 9.
36. Nuala Ní Dhómhnaill, 'Why I Choose to Write in Irish, the Corpse that Sits up and Talks Back', in Susan Shaw Sailer (ed.), *Representing Ireland: Gender, Class, Nationality* (Gainesville: University Press of Florida, 1997), p. 48.

Chapter 15 – Gardiner

1. Stuart Hall, 'The Great Moving-Right Show', *Marxism Today* (January 1979), pp. 14–20.
2. Georg Lukacs, *Theory of the Novel: A Historico-Philosophical Essay on the Forms of Great Epic Literature*, trans. Anna Bostock (London: Merlin Press, [1916] 1971).
3. Pat Kane, *The Play Ethic: A Manifesto for a Different Way of Living* (London: Macmillan, [2000] 2004).
4. Riach, Alan, *Representing Scotland in Literature, Popular Culture and Iconography* (Basingstoke: Palgrave Macmillan, 2005).
5. Michelle Macleod and Moray Watson, 'In the Shadow of the Bard: The Gaelic Short Story, Novel and Drama since the early Twentieth Century', in Ian Brown et al. (eds), *The Edinburgh History of Scottish Literature* (Edinburgh: Edinburgh University Press, 2007), vol. 3, pp. 273–82.

Chapter 16 – Pittin-Hédon

1. See Alan Riach, *Representing Scotland in Literature, Popular Culture and Iconography* (Basingstoke: Palgrave Macmillan, 2005), where he gives an

updated definition of popular literature, and develops the concept of 'Scotland's masks', p. 4.

2. Ben Okri, writing in *The New Statesman*, describing a visit to Scotland, as quoted in Alan Riach, ibid., pp. xiv–xv.

3. Kevin MacNeil, *The Stornoway Way* (London: Penguin, 2005), p. 15.

4. Roger Luckhurst, 'Roundtable on SF Criticism', *Science Fiction Studies* 33 (3) 2006, p. 397.

5. See Cairns Craig, *Iain Banks's* Complicity: *A Reader's Guide* (New York and London: Continuum, 2002), on the dialectics of the fearful.

6. See Cairns Craig, 'Player of Games: Iain (M.) Banks, Jean-François Lyotard and Sublime Terror', in James Acheson and Sarah C. E. Ross (eds), *The Contemporary British Novel* (Edinburgh: Edinburgh University Press, 2005), pp. 229–39.

7. Iain (M.) Banks, *Excession* (New York: Bantam, [1996] 1998), p. 185.

8. See Darko Suvin's definition of science fiction in 'On the Poetics of the Science Fiction Genre', in Mark Rose (ed.), *Science Fiction: A Collection of Critical Essays* (Englewood: Prentice Hall, 1976), p. 62.

9. David Horwich, 'Culture Clash: Ambivalent Heroes and the Ambiguous Utopia in the Work of Iain M. Banks', *Strange Horizons* (21 January 2002), http://www.strangehorizons.com/2002/20020121/culture_clash.shtml

10. Gavin Miller, 'Iain (M.) Banks: Utopia, Nationalism and the Posthuman', in Berthold Schoene (ed.), *The Edinburgh Companion to Contemporary Scottish Literature* (Edinburgh: Edinburgh University Press, 2007), p. 203.

11. Ibid., pp. 207–8.

12. Iain (M.) Banks, *The Player of Games* (London: Orbit, [1988] 1989), p. 236.

13. Ian Rankin, 'Foreword' in Barry Forshaw, *The Rough Companion to Crime Fiction* (London: Penguin, 2007), p. vii. In addition, both Rankin's and McDermid's own definitions of 'tartan noir' foreground the link with Hogg and Stevenson.

14. Val McDermid, *The Distant Echo* (London: HarperCollins, 2003), p. 294.

15. Val McDermid, *Beneath the Bleeding* (London: HarperCollins, [2007] 2008), p. 186.

16. Hugh C. Rae, *The Shooting Gallery* (London: Sphere, [1972] 1973), p. 276.

17. Ian Rankin, *Exit Music* (London: Orion, 2007), p. 143.

18. J. K. Rowling, *Harry Potter and the Philosopher's Stone* (London: Bloomsbury, 1997), p. 276.

19. Gill Plain, 'Rankin Revisited: An Interview with Ian Rankin', *Scottish Studies Review* 4 (1) (2003), p. 133.

20. This is revealed in *Harry Potter and the Deathly Hallows*.

21. Louise Welsh, *The Cutting Room* (Edinburgh: Canongate, 2002), p. 214.

22. Ian Rankin, *Knots and Crosses* (New York: St Martin's, [1987] 1995), p. 33.

23. Jennie Renton, 'Death and Literature', *Textualities* (2006) (online magazine), http://textualities.net/writers/features-n-z/welshl01.php

24. Richard Bradford, *The Novel Now* (Oxford: Blackwell, 2007), p. 79.
25. Each of Rankin's books sells 1.5 million copies in the UK; the Mma Ramotswe series of novels sold 5 million copies in 2006. As for the Harry Potter series, it has now sold over 350 million copies worldwide in sixty-five languages.
26. Oline Cogdill, 'Ian Rankin: Inspector Rebus Turns 20', *Mystery Scene* 99 Rankin, however, admitted to trying to shift his own books to the 'Scottish Fiction' shelf when he first realised he'd been classified as a crime writer.
27. Denise Mina, 'The Politics of Writing Crime', http://www.britishcouncil. org/arts-literature-matters-state-mina.htm
28. Barry Forshaw, *The Rough Guide to Crime Fiction* (London: Rough Guides, 2007), p. vi.
29. Ian Rankin, *Set in Darkness* (London: Orion, 2000), p. 119.
30. Denise Mina, *The Dead Hour* (New York: Little Brown, [2006] 2008), p. 76.
31. Barry Forshaw 'The Last Breath, by Denise Mina', *The Independent*, Wednesday, 22 August 2007, http://www.independent.co.uk/arts-entertainment/books/reviews/the-last-breath-by-denise-mina-462563.html
32. Alexander McCall Smith, *The Right Attitude to Rain* (London: Little Brown, 2006), p. 29.
33. Pinkie Mekgwe, '"All That is Fine in the Human Condition": Crafting Words, Creating Ma-Ramotswe', *Research in African Literature* 37(2) (2006) pp. 176–87. (Downloaded at LION database.)
34. Robert Crawford, *Scotland's Books: The Penguin History of Scottish Literature* (Harmondsworth: Penguin, 2007), p. 685.
35. Gill Plain, 'Concepts of Corruption: Crime Fiction and the Scottish "State"', in Berthold Schoene (ed.), *The Edinburgh Companion to Contemporary Scottish Literature*, p. 139.
36. Ibid.
37. LION: author's biography.
38. Alexander McCall Smith, *Friends, Lovers, Chocolate* (London: Abacus, [2005] 2006), p. 2.
39. J. K. Rowling, *Harry Potter and the Deathly Hallows* (London: Bloomsbury, 2007), p. 607.
40. http://www.scottish.parliament.uk/msp/membersPages/index.htm
41. A. S. Byatt, 'Harry Potter and the Childish Adult', *The New York Times*, 7 July, 2003.
42. Iain (M.) Banks, *The Algebraist* (London: Orbit, [2004] 2005), p. 99.
43. Ben Okri, quoted in Alan Riach, *Representing Scotland*, pp. xiv–xv.
44. On this subject, see Rachel Falconer *Crossover Literature: Children's Literature and its Adult Readership* (London: Routledge, 2008).
45. Maureen A. Farrell, 'The Lost Boys and Girls of Scottish Children's Fiction', in Ian Brown et al. (eds), *The Edinburgh History of Scottish Literature* (Edinburgh: Edinburgh University Press, 2007), vol. 3, p. 202.

46. Iain (M.) Banks, *The Player of Games* (London: Orbit, [1988], 1989), p. 1.
47. Andrew Wilson, 'Iain Banks Interview', *Textualities* (1994) (online magazine), http://textualities.net/writers/features-a-g/banksi01.php

Chapter 18 – Brown

1. Cairns Craig (gen. ed.), *The History of Scottish Literature*, 4 vols (Aberdeen: Aberdeen University Press, 1987–8); Ian Brown, Thomas Clancy, Susan Manning and Murray Pittock (eds), *The Edinburgh History of Scottish Literature*, 3 vols (Edinburgh: Edinburgh University Press, 2007).
2. http://www.bord-na-gaidhlig.org.uk/welcome.html, accessed 15 August 2008.
3. Michelle Macleod and Moray Watson, 'In the Shadow of the Bard: The Gaelic Short Story, Novel and Drama since the early Twentieth Century', in Ian Brown (ed.), *The Edinburgh History of Scottish Literature* (Edinburgh: Edinburgh University Press, 2007), vol. 3, pp. 273–82.
4. Alastair Niven, 'New Diversity, Hybridity and Scottishness', in Ian Brown (ed.), ibid., pp. 320–31.
5. Maureen A. Farrell, 'The Lost Boys and Girls of Scottish Children's Fiction', in Ian Brown (ed.), ibid., pp. 201–2.
6. Ian Brown and Colin Nicholson, 'The Border Crossers and Reconfiguration of the Possible: Poet-Playwright-Novelists from the Mid-Twentieth Century On', in Ian Brown (ed.), ibid., p. 271.
7. Quoted in the epigraph of Jennifer Mouat's fascinating essay, 'Slabs and Scripts: John Byrne's "Peculiarly Graphic Way"', *Scottish Studies Review* 9 (1) (spring 2008), pp. 171–85.
8. Alan Riach, 'The Scottish Element in Wilson Harris', *Scottish Literary Journal*, 18.1 (May 1991), pp. 68–81; Iain Wright, 'The Diaspora and its Writers', in Ian Brown (ed.), *The Edinburgh History*, vol. 3, pp. 304–19.
9. Denis Agnew, *Contexts and Concepts of a Scottish National Theatre* (unpublished PhD thesis, Queen Margaret University, 2000).
10. Interview with Nikki Axford, 3 September 2008.
11. Edwin Morgan, *Hugh MacDiarmid* (Harlow: Longman for the British Council, 1976).

Further Reading

Anderson, Carol and Aileen Christianson (eds), *Scottish Women's Fiction, 1920s to 1960s: Journeys into Being* (East Linton: Tuckwell Press, 2000).

Bell, Eleanor, *Questioning Scotland: Literature, Nationalism, Postmodernism* (Basingstoke: Palgrave Macmillan, 2004).

Bell, Eleanor and Gavin Miller (eds), *Scotland in Theory* (Amsterdam: Rodopi, 2004).

Beveridge, Craig and Ronald Turnbull, *The Eclipse of Scottish Culture: Inferiorism and the Intellectuals* (Edinburgh: Polygon, 1989).

Birrell, Ross and Alec Finlay (eds), *Justified Sinners – An Achaeology of Scottish Counter-Culture (1960–2000)* (Edinburgh: pocketbooks, 2002).

Black, Ronald/Raghnall MacIlleDuibh (ed.), *An Tuil: Duanaire Gàidhlig an 20mh Ceud/Anthology of Twentieth-Century Scottish Gaelic Verse* (Edinburgh: Polygon, 1999).

Bold, Alan, *Hugh MacDiarmid: Christopher Murray Grieve: A Critical Biography* (London: John Murray, 1988; rev. edn London: Paladin, Grafton Books, 1990).

Brown, Ian (ed.), *Journey's Beginning: The Gateway Theatre Building and Company 1884–1965* (Bristol: Intellect, 2004).

Brown, Ian, Thomas Owen Clancy, Susan Manning and Murray Pittock (eds), *The Edinburgh History of Scottish Literature*, 3 vols (Edinburgh: Edinburgh University Press, 2007).

Burgess, Moira, *The Glasgow Novel: A Complete Guide*, 3rd edn (Hamilton: Scottish Library Association, 1999).

Burns, John, *A Celebration of the Light: Zen in the Novels of Neil Gunn* (Edinburgh: Canongate, 1988).

Campbell, Donald, *Playing for Scotland: A History of the Scottish Stage 1715–1965* (Edinburgh: Mercat Press, 1996).

Campbell, Ian, *Lewis Grassic Gibbon* (Edinburgh: Scottish Academic Press, 1985).

Carrell, Christopher (ed.), *Seven Poets* (Glasgow: Third Eye Centre, 1981).

Carruthers, Gerard, David Goldie and Alastair Renfrew (eds), *Beyond Scotland: New Contexts for Twentieth-Century Scottish Literature* (Amsterdam: Rodopi, 2004).

Chapman 71, *Peerie Willa Muir* (special issue featuring Willa Muir, winter 1992–3).

Chapman, M., *The Gaelic Vision in Scottish Culture* (Edinburgh: Edinburgh University Press, 1978).

Cheyette, Bryan, *Muriel Spark* (Tavistock: Northcote House, 2000).

Christianson, Aileen and Alison Lumsden (eds), *Contemporary Scottish Women Writers* (Edinburgh: Edinburgh University Press, 2000).

Coveney, Michael, *The Citz: 21 Years of the Glasgow Citizens Theatre* (London: Nick Hern Books, 1990).

Craig, Cairns (gen. ed.), *The History of Scottish Literature*, 4 vols (Aberdeen: Aberdeen University Press, 1987–8).

—, *Out of History: Narrative Paradigms in Scottish and British Culture* (Edinburgh: Polygon, 1996).

—, *The Modern Scottish Novel: Narrative and the National Imagination* (Edinburgh: Edinburgh University Press, 1999).

Crawford, Robert, *Scotland's Books: The Penguin History of Scottish Literature* (Harmondsworth: Penguin Books, 2007).

Crawford, Robert and Hamish Whyte (eds), *About Edwin Morgan* (Edinburgh: Edinburgh University Press, 1990).

— and Thom Nairn (eds), *The Arts of Alasdair Gray* (Edinburgh: Edinburgh University Press, 1991).

— and David Kinloch (eds), *Reading Douglas Dunn* (Edinburgh: Edinburgh University Press, 1992).

— and Anne Varty (eds), *Liz Lochhead's Voices* (Edinburgh: Edinburgh University Press, 1994).

Cuthbertson, Iain et al. (eds), *A Conspectus to Mark the Citizens' 21st Anniversary as a Living Theatre in Gorbals Street Glasgow* (Glasgow: Citizens' Theatre, 1964).

D'Arcy, Julian, *Scottish Skalds and Sagamen: Old Norse Influence on Modern Scottish Literature* (East Linton: Tuckwell Press, 1996).

Edgecombe, Rodney Stenning, *Vocation and Identity in the Fiction of Muriel Spark* (Columbia: University of Missouri Press, 1990).

Fazzini, Marco (ed.), *Alba Literaria: A History of Scottish Literature* (Venezia Mestre: Amos, 2005).

Fergusson, Maggie, *George Mackay Brown. The Life* (London: John Murray, 2007).

Findlay, Bill (ed.), *A History of Scottish Theatre* (Edinburgh: Polygon, 1998).

For Sydney Goodsir Smith (Loanhead: M. Macdonald, 1975).

Francis, Matthew, *Where the People Are: Language and Community in the Poetry of W. S. Graham* (Cambridge: Salt Publishing, 2004).

Fraser, Robert, *The Making of the Golden Bough: The Origins and Growth of an Argument* (Basingstoke: Macmillan/Palgrave, [1990] 2001).

Gardiner, Michael, *From Trocchi to Trainspotting: Scottish Critical Theory since 1960* (Edinburgh: Edinburgh University Press, 2006).

Gifford, Douglas, *Neil M. Gunn and Lewis Grassic Gibbon* (Edinburgh: Oliver and Boyd, 1983).

Gifford, Douglas and Dorothy McMillan (eds), *A History of Scottish Women's Writing* (Edinburgh: Edinburgh University Press, 1997).

—, Sarah Dunnigan and Alan MacGillivray, *Scottish Literature* (Edinburgh: Edinburgh University Press, 2002).

Gish, Nancy K., *Hugh MacDiarmid: The Man and His Work* (London: Macmillan, 1984).

Gow, Carol, *Mirror and Marble: The Poetry of Iain Crichton Smith* (Edinburgh: Lines Review Editions, 1992).

Hagemann, Susanne (ed.), *Studies in Scottish Fiction: 1945 to the Present* (Frankfurt am Main: Peter Lang, 1996).

Hendry, Joy and Raymond Ross (eds), *Norman MacCaig: Critical Essays* (Edinburgh: Edinburgh University Press, 1990).

Hewitt, David (ed.), *Northern Visions: The Literary Identity of Northern Scotland in the Twentieth Century* (East Linton: Tuckwell Press, 1995).

Hewitt, David and Michael Spiller (eds), *Literature of the North* (Aberdeen: Aberdeen University Press, 1983).

Hutchison, David, *The Modern Scottish Theatre* (Glasgow: Molendinar Press, 1977).

Jack, Ronald D. S., *The Road to the Never Land: A Reassessment of J. M. Barrie's Dramatic Art* (Aberdeen: Aberdeen University Press, 1991).

Kövesi, Simon, *James Kelman (Contemporary British Novelists)* (Manchester: Manchester University Press, 2007).

Krause, Corinna, 'Gaelic Scotland – A Postcolonial Site? In Search of a Meaningful Theoretical Framework to Assess the Dynamics of Contemporary Scottish Gaelic Verse', *eSharp* 6 (1) (2005), http://www.gla.ac.uk/media/media_41178_en.pdf

Kravitz, Peter (ed.), *The Picador Book of Contemporary Scottish Fiction* (London: Picador, 1997).

Lindsay, Maurice (ed.), *As I Remember. Ten Scottish Authors Recall How Writing Began For Them* (London: Hale, 1979).

—, *Francis George Scott and the Scottish Renaissance* (Edinburgh: Paul Harris, 1980).

Lopez, Tony, *The Poetry of W. S. Graham* (Edinburgh: Edinburgh University Press, 1989).

Lunan, Lyndsay, Kirsty A. Macdonald and Carla Sassi (eds), *Re-Visioning Scotland. New Readings of the Cultural Canon* (Frankfurt am Main: Peter Lang, 2008).

McClure, J. Derrick, *Language, Poetry and Nationhood: Scots as a Poetic Language from 1878 to the Present* (East Linton: Tuckwell Press, 2000).

McCulloch, Margery Palmer, *The Novels of Neil M. Gunn: A Critical Study* (Edinburgh: Scottish Academic Press, 1987).

—, *Edwin Muir: Poet, Critic and Novelist* (Edinburgh: Edinburgh University Press, 1993).

— (ed.), *Modernism and Nationalism: Literature and Society in Scotland 1918–1939: Source Documents for the Scottish Renaissance* (Glasgow: Association for Scottish Literary Studies, 2004).

McCulloch, Margery Palmer and Sarah M. Dunnigan (eds), *A Flame in the Mearns: Lewis Grassic Gibbon, a Centenary Celebration* (Glasgow: Association for Scottish Literary Studies, 2003).

McDonald, Jan, '"Is it not Possible to have a Poem Made out of Theatre?" – An Assessment of the Dramas and Dramaturgy of Joan Ure', *International Journal of Scottish Theatre*, 3 (1) (June 2002), http://www.arts.gla.ac.uk/ScotLit/ASLS/ijost/Volume3_no1

McGrath, John, *The Bone Won't Break* (London: Methuen, 1990).

—, *Naked Thoughts that Roam About: Reflections on Theatre, 1958–2001*, ed. Nadine Holdsworth (London: Nick Hern, 2002).

MacInnes, John, 'The World through Gaelic-Scots Eyes', *Lines Review* 85 (1983) (on Ruaraidh MacThòmais), pp. 11–20.

Mack, Douglas, *Scottish Fiction and the British Empire* (Edinburgh: Edinburgh University Press, 2006).

MacLachlan, C. J. M. and David S. Robb (eds), *Edwin Muir: Centenary Assessments* (Aberdeen: Association for Scottish Literary Studies, 1990).

Macleod, Donald John, 'Gaelic Prose', *Transactions of the Gaelic Society of Inverness* 49 (1976), pp. 198–230.

McMillan, Dorothy, 'Gender and Creativity in the Fictions of Janice Galloway', in James Acheson and Sarah C. E. Ross (eds), *The Contemporary British Novel* (Edinburgh: Edinburgh University Press, 2005), pp. 154–64.

McMillan, Dorothy and Michel Byrne (eds), *Modern Scottish Women Poets* (Edinburgh: Canongate, 2003).

McMillan, Joyce, *The Traverse Theatre Story* (London: Methuen, 1988).

MacNeil, Kevin and Alec Finlay (eds), *Wish I Was Here: A Scottish Multicultural Anthology* (Edinburgh: Pocketbooks, 2000).

McNeill, Marjory, *Norman MacCaig: A Study of His Life and Work* (Edinburgh: Mercat Press, 1996).

McQuillan, Martin (ed.), *Theorizing Muriel Spark: Gender, Race, Deconstruction* (Basingstoke: Palgrave, 2002).

Manlove, Colin, *Scottish Fantasy Literature* (Edinburgh: Canongate Academic, 1994).

March, Cristie Leigh, *Rewriting Scotland: Welsh, McLean, Warner, Banks, Galloway and Kennedy* (Manchester: Manchester University Press, 2002).

Moffat, Alexander and Alan Riach, *Arts of Resistance: Poets, Portraits and Landscapes of Modern Scotland* (Edinburgh: Cuath Press, 2008).

Monterrey, Tomas (ed.), *Revista Canaria de Estudios Ingleses: Contemporary Scottish Literature, 1970–2000* 41, special issue (November 2000).

Morgan, Edwin, *Crossing the Border: Essays on Scottish Literature* (Manchester: Carcanet, 1990).

Morrison, David (ed.), *Essays on Fionn Mac Colla* (Thurso: Caithness Books, 1973).

Munro, Ian S., *Leslie Mitchell: Lewis Grassic Gibbon* (Edinburgh: Oliver and Boyd, 1966).

Murray, Isobel (ed.), *Scottish Writers Talking: George Mackay Brown, Jessie Kesson, Norman MacCaig, William McIlvanney, David Toulmin* (East Linton: Tuckwell Press, 1996).

—, *Jessie Kesson: Writing Her Life* (Edinburgh: Canongate, 2000).

— (ed.), *Scottish Writers Talking 2: Iain Banks, Bernard MacLaverty, Naomi Mitchison, Iain Crichton Smith, Alan Spence* (East Linton: Tuckwell Press, 2002).

— (ed.), *Scottish Writers Talking 3: Interviews with Janice Galloway, John Herdman, Robin Jenkins, Joan Lingard, Ali Smith* (Edinburgh: John Donald, 2006).

— (ed.), *Scottish Writers Talking 4: Interviews with Jackie Kay, Alan Massie, Ian Rankin, James Robertson, William (Bill) Watson* (Glasgow: Kennedy and Boyd, 2008).

Nash, Andrew, *Kailyard and Scottish Literature* (Amsterdam: Rodopi, 2007).

Neat, Timothy (with John MacInnes), *The Voice of the Bard: Living Poets and Ancient Tradition in the Highlands and Islands of Scotland* (Edinburgh: Canongate, 1999).

—, *Hamish Henderson: A Biography – Vol. 1: The Making of the Poet* (Edinburgh: Polygon, 2007).

Ní Annracháin, M. 'The Force of Tradition in the Poetry of Aonghas MacNeacail', in Colm Ó Baoill and Nancy R. McGuire (eds), *Rannsachadh na Gàidhlig 2000* (Obar Dheathain: An Clò Gaidhealach, 2002), pp. 117–26.

Nicholson, Colin (ed.), *Iain Crichton Smith: Critical Essays* (Edinburgh: Edinburgh University Press, 1992).

—, *Poem, Purpose and Place: Shaping Identity in Contemporary Scottish Verse* (Edinburgh: Polygon, 1992).

—, *Edwin Morgan: Inventions of Modernity* (Manchester: Manchester University Press, 2002).

Normand, Tom, *The Modern Scot: Modernism and Nationalism in Scottish Art, 1928–1955* (London: Ashgate, 2000).

Norquay, Glenda and Gerry Smyth (eds), *Across the Margins: Cultural Identity and Change in the Atlantic Archipelago* (Manchester: Manchester University Press, 2002).

Parnell, Michael, *Eric Linklater: A Critical Biography* (London: John Murray, 1984).

Petrie, Duncan, *Contemporary Scottish Fiction: Film, Television and the Novel* (Edinburgh: Edinburgh University Press, 2004).

Pite, Ralph and Hester Jones (eds), *W. S. Graham: Speaking Towards You* (Liverpool: Liverpool University Press, 2004).

Pittock, Murray G. H., *Celtic Identity and the British Image* (Manchester: Manchester University Press, 1999).

Price, Richard, *The Fabulous Matter of Fact: The Poetics of Neil M. Gunn* (Edinburgh: Edinburgh University Press, 1991).

Randisi, Jennifer Lynn, *On Her Way Rejoicing: The Fiction of Muriel Spark* (Washington: The Catholic University of America Press, 1991).

Riach, Alan, *Hugh MacDiarmid's Epic Poetry* (Edinburgh: Edinburgh University Press, 1991).

—, *The Poetry of Hugh MacDiarmid* (Glasgow: Association for Scottish Literary Studies, 1999).

—, *Representing Scotland in Literature, Popular Culture and Iconography* (Basingstoke: Palgrave Macmillan, 2005).

Ross, Raymond J. and Joy Hendry (eds), *Sorley MacLean: Critical Essays* (Edinburgh: Scottish Academic Press, 1986).

Royle, Trevor, *James and Jim: A Biography of James Kennaway* (Edinburgh: Mainstream, 1983).

— (ed.), *In Flanders Fields: Scottish Poetry and Prose of the First World War* (Edinburgh: Mainstream, 1990).

Saadi, Suhayl, 'Infinite Diversity in New Scottish Writing' (Glasgow: Association for Scottish Literary Studies, 2000), http://www2,arts,gla.ac.uk/ScotLit/ASLS/SSaadi.html

Sassi, Carla, *Why Scottish Literature Matters* (Edinburgh: The Saltire Society, 2005).

Schoene, Berthold (ed.), *The Edinburgh Companion to Contemporary Scottish Literature* (Edinburgh: Edinburgh University Press, 2007).

Schwend, Joachim and Horst W. Drescher (eds), *Studies in Scottish Fiction: Twentieth Century* (Frankfurt am Main: Peter Lang, 1990).

Sellin, Bernard, *The Life and Works of David Lindsay*, trans. Kenneth Gunnell (Cambridge: Cambridge University Press, 1981).

Smith, Janet Adam, *John Buchan: A Biography* (London: Rupert Hart-Davis, 1965).

Sproxton, Judy, *The Women of Muriel Spark* (London: Constable, 1992).

Thomson, Derick, *An Introduction to Gaelic Poetry* (London: Gollancz, 1974).

Stevenson, Randall and Gavin Wallace (eds), *Scottish Theatre since the Seventies* (Edinburgh: Edinburgh University Press, 1996).

Turnbull, Ronald (ed.), Robin Jenkins special issue, *Edinburgh Review* 106 (2001).

Veitch, James, *George Douglas Brown* (London: Herbert Jenkins, 1952).

Walker, Marshall L., *Scottish Literature since 1707* (London: Longman, 1996).

Wallace, Gavin and Randall Stevenson (eds), *The Scottish Novel since the Seventies* (Edinburgh: Edinburgh University Press, 1993).

Watson, Roderick, 'Postcolonial Subjects? Language, Narrative Authority and

Class in Contemporary Scottish Culture', *The European English Messenger* 7 (2) (1998), pp. 21–31.

—, *The Literature of Scotland*, 2nd edn, 2 vols (Basingstoke: Palgrave Macmillan, 2007).

—, '"Death's Proletariat": Scottish Poets of the Second World War', in T. Kendall (ed.), *The Oxford Handbook of British and Irish War Poetry* (Oxford: Oxford University Press, 2007), pp. 315–39.

Whyte, Christopher (ed.), *Gendering the Nation: Studies in Modern Scottish Literature* (Edinburgh: Edinburgh University Press, 1995).

—, *Modern Scottish Poetry* (Edinburgh: Edinburgh University Press, 2004).

Wilson, Jean Moorcroft, *Charles Hamilton Sorley: A Biography* (London: Cecil Woolf, 1985).

Wiseman, Christopher, *Beyond the Labyrinth: A Study of Edwin Muir's Poetry* (British Columbia: Sono Nis, 1978).

Witschi, Beat, *Glasgow Urban Writing and Postmodernism. A Study of Alasdair Gray's Fiction* (Frankfurt am Main: Peter Lang, 1991).

Wittig, Kurt, *The Scottish Tradition in Literature* (London: Oliver and Boyd, 1958).

Notes on Contributors

Ian Brown is a freelance scholar, playwright and poet. He is a visiting professor at the Department of Scottish Literature, University of Glasgow and the Centre for the Study of Media and Culture in Small Nations, University of Glamorgan. He was general editor of *The Edinburgh History of Scottish Literature* (2007).

Moira Burgess is a novelist, short story writer, poet and literary historian. The author of *The Glasgow Novel: A Complete Guide* (1999), she is working on an edition of Naomi Mitchison's collected prose. Her most recent book is *Mitchison's Ghosts: Supernatural Elements in the Scottish Fiction of Naomi Mitchison* (2008).

John Corbett is Professor of Applied Language Studies at Glasgow University and principal investigator of the Scottish Corpus of Texts and Speech and the Corpus of Modern Scottish Writing (1700–1945) (www.scottishcorpus.ac.uk). He works primarily in Scots language studies and intercultural language education.

Cairns Craig is director of the AHRC Centre for Scottish and Irish Studies at the University of Aberdeen. Author of *Out of History* (1996), *The Modern Scottish Novel* (1999) and *Associationism and the Literary Imagination* (2007), he was general editor of Aberdeen University Press's four-volume *History of Scottish Literature* (1987–88).

Michael Gardiner is Assistant Professor in the Department of English and Comparative Literature at the University of Warwick. His publications include *From Trocchi to Trainspotting: Scottish Critical Theory Since 1960* (2006), *The Cultural Roots of British Devolution* (2004), and one book of fiction, *Escalator* (2006).

Douglas Gifford is Emeritus Professor in the Department of Scottish Literature of the University of Glasgow. He has written and edited extensively in nineteenth- and twentieth-century Scottish writing and is honorary librarian of Walter Scott's library at Abbotsford.

Ksenija Horvat is a lecturer in Drama at Queen Margaret University. Her research areas include contemporary Scottish theatre, gender in theatre, dramaturgy and theatre history. She has worked as a playwright, translator, researcher and theatre reviewer.

Michelle Macleod is a lecturer in Gaelic at the University of Aberdeen. Her PhD was on the exile theme in modern Gaelic literature. She has published on Gaelic literature and other areas of modern Gaelic studies.

Robyn Marsack is director of the Scottish Poetry Library. Born in New Zealand, she attended university there before gaining her doctorate from Oxford University, where she did some teaching before joining Carcanet Press. Before taking up her post in 2000 she had been a freelance publishers' editor, reviewer and translator.

Colin Nicholson is Professor of Eighteenth-Century and Modern Literature at Edinburgh University. He is the author of *Poem, Purpose and Place: Shaping Identity in Contemporary Scottish Verse* (1992) and of *Edwin Morgan: Inventions of Modernity* (2002).

Donny O'Rourke is a poet, songwriter, translator, journalist, teacher, filmmaker and editor of *Dream State: The New Scottish Poets* ([1994] 2002).

Marie Odile Pittin-Hédon is a lecturer in contemporary British literature at Avignon University, France, and specialises in Scottish literature. Her most recent publication is *Alasdair Gray: Marges et Effets de Miroirs* (2004).

Murray Pittock is Bradley Professor of English Literature at the University of Glasgow. A fellow of the Royal Society of Edinburgh, the English Association and the Royal Historical Society, his work on Jacobitism and Scottish and Irish Studies in the long eighteenth century is internationally influential.

Alan Riach is Professor of Scottish Literature at Glasgow University, president of the Association for Scottish Literary Studies, general editor of the *Collected Works of Hugh MacDiarmid* (Carcanet) and a poet whose five collections include *First & Last Songs* (1995), *Clearances* (2001) and *Homecoming* (2009).

Trevor Royle is a leading writer and broadcaster on military history and on literature. He is diplomatic and associate editor of *The Sunday Herald* and author of, amongst many other literary and historical volumes, *The Flowers of the Forest: Scotland and the First World War* (2006).

Carla Sassi is Associate Professor of English Literature at the University of Verona. She specialises in Scottish literature and postcolonial studies. Her recent works include *Why Scottish Literature Matters* (2005) and, as co-author, *Caribbean-Scottish Relations* (2007).

Bernard Sellin is Professor of English at the University of Nantes, France. He is the author of *The Life and Works of David Lindsay* (1981) and several articles on modern Scottish fiction.

Donald Smith is director of the Scottish Storytelling Centre, a poet and novelist. He chaired the National Theatre for Scotland Campaign Committee in the 1990s. His publications include *Storytelling Scotland: A Nation in Narrative* (2001) and *God, The Poet and the Devil: Robert Burns and Religion* (2008).

Roderick Watson is a professor at the University of Stirling. General editor of the Canongate Classics since the series began, he is also editor of *The Poetry of Scotland* (1995). His books include *The Literature of Scotland* ([1984] 2007) and a volume of poetry, *Into the Blue Wavelengths* (2004).

Index

The index includes entries for names of persons and organisations; titles of anthologies and significant journals; languages and literary forms. Page numbers suffixed 'n' refer to notes.

Aberdeen, Countess of, 26
Aboulela, Leila, 216
Advisory Council for the Arts in Scotland, 220
Agnew, Denis, 220
Ahead of Its Time (anthology), 188
Aitken, A. J., 5
Aitken, Sadie, 67, 139
Akros (journal), 136–7, 182
Akros Publications, 136
Anderson, Carol, 81–2
Anderson, Dave, 72
Angus, Marion, 39, 109, 164
Annand, J. K., 98, 161
Archer, David, 112–13
Archer, William, 61
Arden, John, 140
Armstrong, Moira, 144
Arnott, Peter, 72, 101–2, 184
Arts Council Scottish Committee, 9, 65, 67, 162; *see also* Scottish Arts Council
Ascherson, Neal, 166
Association for Scottish Literary Studies, 7
Axford, Nikki, 220
Aylife, H. K., 67

Bain, George, 109
Bamforth, Iain, 211
Banks, Iain (M.), 93, 186, 187, 193–4, 202–3, 218, 219
Barbour, John, 3
Barke, James, 59, 104
Barnaby, Paul, 180
Barnes, Grace, 74
Barrie, J. M., 62–3
    Buchan and, 30, 32
    drama, 8, 23, 28, 32, 62–3, 66
    'Kailyard' associations, 15, 27
    Masson and, 23
    novels, 15, 23, 38, 55
    Peter Pan, 19–20, 62
    screen adaptations, 11

Bateman, Meg, 143, 168, 177–8, 191, 209, 210, 216
Baxter, James, 219
Beaton, M. C., 11, 217
Beith, John Hay, 2, 40–1
Bell, Eleanor, 134
Belli, Giuseppe, 137
Benchtours, 70
Benstock, Shari, 113–14
Betjeman, John, 112
Beuys, Joseph, 140
Binnie, John, 73
Birrell, Ross, 163
Black, Ronald, 97, 138
Blackie (publisher), 109
Blackwood, George, 39
Blackwood, William, and Sons, 109, 133
Blackwood's Magazine, 30, 39, 41
Blake, George, 104
Blakemore, Michael, 140
Blind Harry, 217
Bold, Alan, 157
Borderline, 70, 141
Borthwick, Nina, 26
Bowman, Martin, 68
Boyd, Eddie, 69, 144
Boyd, William, 93, 182, 192
Brandane, John, 63
Brandon Thomas Company, 61
Brenton, Howard, 141
Bridie, James
    Citizens Theatre, 8, 9, 67, 110
    Corrie and, 63
    death, 107
    drama, 59, 66–7, 68, 101, 105
    Lindsay's *Ane Satyre of the Thrie Estaitis*, 67
    real name, 2
Brookmyre, Christopher, 189
Brown, George Douglas, 12, 15, 22, 26–7, 38, 57, 77

255

Brown, George Mackay, 157, 158, 160
  border-crossing, 152
  novels, 152, 186
  poetry, 111, 159, 206
  in *Poets' Pub*, 157
  short stories, 144
Brown, Ian, 5, 70, 73, 140, 141, 151
Bruce, George, 105
Bryden, Bill, 4, 69–70, 101, 140, 184
Buchan, Anna *see* Douglas, O.
Buchan, John, 28, 29–36
  criticism of 'Kailyard' school', 38
  Greig's reworking of *John Macnab*, 187
  language, 4, 23, 29, 38
  MacDiarmid and, 29, 52, 57, 116
  Northern Muse anthology, 23, 29, 57
  novels, 21–2, 23, 29, 30–1, 30–6, 57
  poetry, 29, 38, 48, 52
  Scott and, 33
  Scottish Review editor, 38
  short stories, 29–30, 33–4
  Stevenson and, 25, 31, 33
Buchan, Tom, 139–40
Bunting, Lara Jane, 73
Burke, Gregory, 9, 74, 102, 140
Burns, Robert, 7, 15, 54; *see also Honour'd Shade*
  (anthology)
Burnside, John, 204, 206, 207
Buthlay, Kenneth, 116
Butlin, Ron, 187, 212
Butt, Richard, 11
Byatt, George, 144
Byre Theatre, 109, 141
Byrne, John, 71, 140, 183, 218
Byrne, Michel, 96

Cadell, F. C. B., 53
Caimbeul, Maoilios *see* Campbell, Myles
Caimbeul, Tormod *see* Campbell, Norman
Calder, Angus, 148, 159, 163
Calder, John, 133
Caledonia Books, 109
Caledonian Antisyzygy, 10, 76, 77, 79–80
Cambridge, Gerry, 208
Cameron, Norman, 99
Campbell, Donald, 71
Campbell, James, 56
Campbell, Myles, 168, 179–80
Campbell, Norman, 143
Campbell, Roy, 219
Canongate, 133, 216
Carcanet, 208, 209
Carmichael, Alexander, 27
Carruth, Jim, 212
Carswell, Catherine, 7, 54, 147, 148
  novels, 54, 81
Cencrastus (journal), 182
Chambers (publisher), 109
Chapman (journal), 182, 208
Chesney, Marion *see* Beaton, M. C.

Chowdhry, Maya, 216
Christianson, Aileen, 81–2, 151
Christie, Agatha, 29
Citizens Theatre, 59, 68–9, 110, 140
  Bridie and, 8, 67, 110
  Havergal and, 70–1, 141
  Hind and, 142
Civic Theatre Company (at Royal Lyceum), 68,
  140
Clanchy, Kate, 204, 205
Clark, Thomas A., 191
Clifford, John, 72–3
Clocktower Press, 188
Clyde Unity, 70
Cocker, W. D., 46
Collins (publisher), 109, 133
Conan Doyle, Arthur, 21, 28, 219
Conn, Stewart, 6, 9, 69, 70, 74, 140, 141
Connolly, Billy, 140
Constable (publisher), 109
Cording, Alastair, 12
Corrie, Joe, 59, 63–4, 66, 67, 68
Craig, Bill, 143, 144
Craig, Cairns, 3, 38, 58, 78, 142
  Determinations series, 185
  Out of History, 149
  on *The Weatherhouse*, 83
Crawford, Robert, 116, 120, 190, 200, 204, 205,
  208
Crockett, S. R., 26, 27, 38
Cronin, A. J., 11, 57, 143–4, 217
Crozier, Andrew, 50
Cruikshank, Helen, 164
Cullen, Mike, 74
Cummings, Alan, 5, 6
Cuthbertson, Iain, 140
Cutler, Ivor, 136
Czerkawska, Catherine Lucy, 74, 216

Daiches, David, 52
Dark Horse, The (journal), 208
Davie, Elspeth, 185–6
Davie, George E., 15, 164, 183
Demarco, Richard, 140, 163
di Mambro, Ann Marie, 72, 73
Dickson, Beth, 23
Dillon, Des, 206
Dishonour'd Shade (anthology), 162
Dòmhnall Ruadh Chorùna *see* MacDonald,
  Donald (Dòmhnall Ruadh Chorùna)
Dòmhnall Ruadh Mac an t-Saoir *see* MacIntyre,
  Donald
Douglas, O., 23
Downie, Anne, 74
drama, 4, 7–9, 61–74, 219
  1920s and 1930s, 58–9
  1940s and 1950s, 104, 105, 106, 107, 108,
    109–10
  1960s and 1970s, 133–4, 139–41, 143–4
  1980s and 1990s, 183–4, 189–90

World War Two, 100–2
see also Gaelic drama; National Theatre of
  Scotland
Dream State (anthology), 207, 211, 212
Duffy, Carol Ann, 204, 206, 207
Duncan, John, 25
Dundee Repertory Theatre, 8, 109
Dunlop, Bill, 68
Dunn, Douglas, 78, 113, 137, 164, 190, 204–5
Dunne, J. W., 55

Edinburgh Review (journal), 163, 182, 208
Edwards, Owen Dudley, 185
Eliot, T. S.
  Cairns Craig and, 149
  collage technique, 116
  Graham and, 120, 165
  MacDiarmid and, 49, 51, 115
  rejection of Lallans collection, 161
  on Smith's *Scottish Literature*, 3, 14, 38
  The Waste Land, 51
Elphinstone, Margaret, 185, 186
Emslie, Gordon, 9, 74, 141
English language, 4, 5, 6, 12, 58, 118, 161
Evaristi, Marcella, 72
Eveling, Stanley, 69, 134
Evergreen, The (journal), 22, 25
Ewart, Gavin, 99
Eyre, Richard, 140

Farrell, Maureen, 217
Featherstone, Vicky, 74
Federation of Scottish Theatre, 220
Fellows, Gerrie, 211
Ferguson, J. A., 61
Fergusson, J. D., 53, 75–6, 116, 117–18
Ferrier, Susan, 146
fiction *see* novels; short stories
Findlater, Jane, 15, 54
Findlater, Mary, 15, 54
Findlay, Bill, 68
Finlay, Alec, 163
Finlay, Ian Hamilton, 163, 190
  border-crossing, 140
  Glasgow Beasts, 136, 137
  Little Sparta, 136, 164
  MacDiarmid and, 135–6, 164
  Morgan on, 162
  poetry, 134, 135, 212
  Poor. Old. Tired. Horse, 135, 190
  Wild Hawthorn Press, 135
Finney, Albert, 140
Fisher, Gregor, 143
Fishman, Joshua, 167
Fitt, Matthew, 4, 13, 211
Fleming, Ian, 11, 23, 28, 143, 217
Fleming, Tom, 140
Follon, Cheryl, 212–13
Ford, James Allan, 89
Forsyth, Bill, 189

Fox, James, 141
Frame, Ronald, 187
Francis, Matthew, 114, 119, 120, 122
Fraser, G. S., 98, 115
Fraser, George Macdonald, 93
Fraser, Olive, 98–9
Frater, Anne, 168, 178–9, 209–10
Frazer, J. G., 20–1
Friel, George, 13, 76, 111, 130, 142, 142–3,
  143
Friel, Raymond, 206, 209
Fulton, Graham, 207
Fulton, Robin, 137

Gaelic drama, 192
Gaelic language, 2, 4–5, 6, 152–4, 171–80,
  215–16
Gaelic novels, 22, 192, 216
Gaelic poetry, 167–80, 209–10
  1930s, 58
  1960s and 1970s, 137–9
  1980s and 1990s, 191–2
  F. G. Scott and, 57
  'Seven Poets' generation, 160–1
  World War One, 47–8
  World War Two, 95–7
Gairfish (journal), 190, 208
Gairm (journal), 108, 111, 138, 160, 161, 186
Gaitens, Edward, 60, 105–6
Gallacher, Tom, 70, 92, 140
Galloway, Janice, 93, 185, 188
Gardiner, Michael, 214
Garioch, Robert, 7, 159–60, 239n
  language, 137, 161
  poetry, 97–8, 109, 137, 159, 160, 161
  in *Poets' Pub*, 157
  Scottish International board member, 164
  Wilson and, 211
Garnett, Edward, 57
Gateway Theatre Company, 8, 65, 67, 68, 110,
  140
Gavin, Catherine, 89
Geddes, Patrick
  The Evergreen, 22, 25
  'Scottish Renascence', 1, 8, 15, 22, 25, 26, 27,
    35, 53, 75
Gibbon, Lewis Grassic, 54–5, 86, 129
  border-crossing, 147, 148
  Cloud Howe, 84
  Duncan McLean compared to, 188
  Grey Granite, 13, 27, 55–6
  Hood compared to, 186
  Muir's *Scott and Scotland*, 10
  A Scots Quair, 12–13, 27, 28, 54, 77, 82,
    84–5, 154
  short stories, 54, 55, 144
  Stained Radiance, 13, 54
  Sunset Song, 12, 27, 50, 84, 144, 147, 152
Gifford, Douglas, 76–7, 85
Gillies, William, 54, 191

Glasgow Repertory Company, 8, 61
Glen, Duncan, 136–7, 182
Glover, Sue, 72, 73, 183–4
Gorman, Rody, 210
Graham, R. B. Cunninghame, 57
Graham, W. S., 108, 109, 112–16, 119–22, 165
Grant, Alan, 218
Gray, Alasdair
    1982, Janine, 154, 158, 182
    Banks and, 186
    drama, 72
    Friel and, 143
    Gunn and Grassic Gibbon and, 13
    Lanark, 93, 131, 182–3, 187, 239n
    in Lean Tales, 185
    in 'Magnetic North', 188
    Meek compared to, 188
    novels, 56, 60, 142, 182–3
Gray, Canon John, 28
Greenhorn, Stephen, 74, 189, 219
Gregory, André, 240
Greig, Andrew, 88, 92–3, 100, 187, 212
Greig, David, 68, 73, 74, 189, 219
Grice, Paul, 121–2
Grieve, Christopher see MacDiarmid, Hugh
Grieve, Dorian, 99
Grotowski, Jerzy, 139, 140
Gunn, George, 210
Gunn, Neil M., 6–7, 27, 57, 90, 105, 129
    The Atom of Delight, 108
    Buchan and, 30, 35
    Butcher's Broom, 27, 28
    Gibbon and, 13
    Highland River, 27, 35, 59, 77, 85–7, 90
    Scots Magazine contributions, 110
    Shepherd and, 82, 86
    The Silver Darlings, 27, 103, 105
Guthrie, Allan, 189
Guthrie, Tyrone, 67

Hadfield, Jen, 212
Hall, Stuart, 182
Hanlin, Tom, 106, 107, 110
Hannan, Chris, 72, 73
Hardie, Sean, 72
Hare, David, 141
Harris, Wilson, 150
Harris, Zinnie, 73–4
Harrower, David, 74, 219
Hart, Francis R., 85, 149
Havergal, Giles, 70, 141
Hay, George Campbell, 58, 95, 160, 167, 168–71, 191
    Frater compared to, 179
    Fuaran Sleibh, 104
    MacNeacail compared to, 176
    Mokhtar and Dougall, 94–5, 169, 191
    in Nua-Bhàrdachd Ghàidhlig, 138
    O Na Ceithir Airdean, 159

poems set to music, 57
war poetry, 96–7, 99, 100
Hay, Ian see Beith, John Hay
Hay, John MacDougall, 15, 38
Haynes, Dorothy K., 106
Haynes, Jim, 134
Heggie, Iain, 73
Henderson, Hamish, 94–5, 100, 104, 106, 152
Henderson, Meg, 92
Hendry, J. F., 99, 104, 115
Hendry, Joy, 182, 191
Henley, W. E., 25
Herbert, W. N., 190, 204, 205, 207, 208
Hershaw, William, 211
Hind, Archie, 110, 130, 142
Hird, Laura, 188
Hogg, James, 25, 29–30, 35, 78, 129, 143
Honour'd Shade (anthology), 162–3, 165
Hood, Stuart, 89, 92, 186
Hulme, Keri, 219
Hume, David, 16–17, 134
Hunter, George Leslie, 53
Hutchison, Alexander, 211
Hyde, Douglas, 26

Imlah, Mick, 204
Imrie, Marilyn, 74
Innes, Neil, 136
Ireland, Kenny, 220
Itchy Coo, 5, 216

Jack, R. D. S., 23, 150–1
Jackson, A. B., 212–13
Jackson, Barry, 67
Jacob, Violet, 15, 28, 39, 45, 48, 164
Jamie, Kathleen, 93, 100, 190, 204, 205
Jamieson, Robert Alan, 210
Jenkins, Jennifer, 118
Jenkins, Robin, 123, 130, 141–2, 186, 192
    The Changeling, 128, 130
    The Cone-Gatherers, 90, 108, 125
    Fergus Lamont, 91, 125, 128, 130, 131, 141, 186
    Guests of War, 90, 125, 130
    Happy for the Child, 108, 131
    Just Duffy, 131, 186
    nationalism, 130
    pessimism, 76, 131
    religion, 128
    Scotland and, 125, 126, 129, 130, 132
    So Gaily Sings the Lark, 108, 130
    Spark and, 128, 129
    A Toast to the Lord, 128, 129
    A Very Scotch Affair, 128, 130
    war and, 90–1, 124–5
    A Would-be Saint, 90–1, 124–5, 128
Johnstone, William, 53–4
Jones, Chris, 120
Jouvet, Louis, 133

Joyce, James, 184
  collage technique, 116
  Finnegan's Wake, 60, 114, 117
  Goodsir Smith compared to, 162
  Graham and, 114
  A Portrait of the Artist as a Young Man, 55
  Scottish Renaissance and, 2, 10, 51
  Ulysses, 51
  see also MacDiarmid, Hugh, *In Memoriam James Joyce*

Kane, Pat, 183
Kantor, Tadeusz, 140
Kay, Ada F., 68, 69
Kay, Jackie, 155, 204, 205, 206, 216, 219
Kelman, James
  drama, 72
  Gunn and Grassic Gibbon and, 13
  language, 78
  in *Lean Tales*, 185
  McCall Smith compared to, 200
  in 'Magnetic North', 188
  novels, 13, 56, 142, 152, 184
  short stories, 189
Kemp, Robert, 67–8, 68, 101, 110, 133, 139
Kennaway, James, 123, 126, 127, 129, 130–1, 132
  Tunes of Glory, 125, 126
Kennedy, A. L., 88, 93, 100, 188–9, 192
Kerr, Roderick Watson, 46, 47, 48
Kerrigan, Catherine, 49
Kesson, Jessie, 92, 108
Kettilonia, 213
Killick, Jenny, 72
Kincaid, John, 109
Kinloch, David, 190, 208, 209
Kinninmont, Tom, 74
Knight, Joan, 141
Knowlton, Eloise, 117
Knox, Moira, 220
Krause, Corinna, 180
Kravitz, Peter, 163, 164
Kuppner, Frank, 212

Laing, R. D., 141, 163, 183, 185, 190
Lang, Andrew, 23
language, 2–3, 3–6, 9–10, 12, 13, 72, 184, 215;
  see also English language; Gaelic language; Scots language; *Scott and Scotland*
Lean Tales (anthology), 185
Leavis, F. R., 3, 183, 214
Lee, Joseph, 46, 47, 48
Lenz, Katja, 4, 5
Leonard, Tom
  drama, 72
  Graham and, 165
  language, 4, 78, 137, 164, 184
  Lochhead and, 165
  in 'Magnetic North', 188
  poetry, 13, 137, 164, 206

Lichtenfels, Peter, 72
Lindsay, Lord, 220
Lindsay, David, 55
Lindsay, Sir David, 67, 139
Lindsay, Maurice, 99, 106, 109, 135, 159, 161
Lines Review, 111, 137, 139, 159, 191, 208
Linklater, Eric
  autobiography, 124, 125
  drama, 100–1
  Juan in America, 55, 126–7
  Magnus Merriman, 56, 88
  novels, 88–9, 123, 124, 125, 126–7
  Position at Noon, 131
  Private Angelo, 88–9, 106, 124, 127
  Scotland and, 125, 126–7, 129, 132
  short stories, 104, 106
Lochhead, Liz
  border-crossing, 153
  drama, 68, 72, 102, 153, 184, 189
  Gunn and Grassic Gibbon and, 13
  language, 4, 13, 72, 78, 137
  Morgan and, 165, 184
  poetry, 137, 165, 205–6
Locke, John, 183
Long, H. Kingsley, 11, 56, 105
Lorimer, R. L. C., 68
Lowell, Robert, 120
Lukacs, Georg, 182
Lumsden, Alison, 82
Lumsden, Roddy, 207

Mac a' Ghobhainn, Iain *see* Smith, Iain Crichton
Mac an t-Saoir, Dòmhnall Ruadh *see* MacIntyre, Donald
Mac Colla, Fionn, 27, 55, 105, 123, 127–8, 129–30, 132
Mac Iain Dheòrsa, Deòrsa *see* Hay, George Campbell
MacAmhlaigh, Dòmhnall *see* MacAulay, Prof. Donald
MacArthur, Alexander, 11, 56, 105
MacAsgaill, A. I., 47
MacAulay, Lord, 77–8
MacAulay, Prof. Donald, 138, 191, 210
Macbeth, George, 100
McCabe, Brian, 212
MacCaig, Norman, 157
  on Goodsir Smith, 162
  Andrew Greig and, 212
  Honour'd Shade editor, 162
  language, 3, 5, 134
  MacDiarmid and, 160, 165
  Callum MacDonald and, 159
  poetry, 108, 115, 116, 134, 159, 164
  in *Poets' Pub*, 157
  Scottishness, 166
  teacher, 7, 159
MacCance, William, 53
McCarey, Peter, 210

McCartney, Nicola, 73
MacCormaic, Iain see MacCormick, John
MacCormick, John, 22
McCrone, Guy, 104
McDermid, Val, 193, 194–6, 197, 198, 199, 203
MacDhonnchaidh, Aonghas see Robertson, Angus
MacDiarmid, Hugh, 7, 51–4, 58, 107, 112–22, 222
    Annals of the Five Senses, 52, 79–80, 81
    at Albert Hall, 134
    border-crossing, 147, 148
    Buchan and, 29, 52, 57, 116
    Callum MacDonald and, 159
    Collected Poems, 134, 159
    Contemporary Scottish Studies, 49, 52
    de-authorising/plagiarism, 116–17, 183
    'The Dour Drinkers of Glasgow', 158–9
    on drama, 61–2
    'A Drunk Man Looks at the Thistle', 3, 81, 184
    Finlay and, 135–6, 164
    The Golden Treasury of Scottish Poetry, 10, 58
    on Goodsir Smith, 162
    on Graham, 165
    Gunn and, 86
    In Memoriam James Joyce, 76, 103, 108, 109, 112, 113, 114, 115, 116–19, 121, 122, 159
    influence on later poets, 156, 157
    on Jacob and Angus, 164
    A Kist of Whistles, 104
    language, 6, 116, 118, 121, 162
    in Linklater's Magnus Merriman, 56
    MacCaig and, 160, 165
    McCarey and, 210
    MacLean and, 138, 160
    Morgan and, 135, 137, 162, 164, 221
    Muir's Scott and Scotland, 10, 58, 77–8, 81, 107
    'Nisbet: An Interlude in Post-War Glasgow', 50
    Northern Numbers, 32, 48, 52
    parliamentary candidate, 159
    in Poetry Scotland series, 109
    in Poets' Pub, 157, 158
    politics, 49, 51, 58, 159
    Saadi and, 216
    Scottish Chapbook, 49
    Scottish International and, 164
    Scottish Literary Renaissance, 1, 2, 6, 15, 48–9, 75, 76, 77–81, 106
    Three Hymns to Lenin, 108, 159
    'Towards a New Scotland', 48
    Trocchi and, 133, 135, 163
    war and, 48, 49, 99
MacDonald, Callum, 137, 159–60, 162
MacDonald, Donald (Dòmhnall Ruadh Chorùna), 47–8
Macdonald, Frances, 75
MacDonald, George, 17–18

McDonald, Jan, 69
MacDonald, Margaret, 75
Macdonald, Murdo, 157
MacDonald, Robert David, 70–1, 141
Macdonald, Sharman, 69, 73
MacDonald, Stephen, 69, 140
MacDonald, Tom see Mac Colla, Fionn
McDougall, Peter, 144
McEwan, John Blackwood, 56
McGibbon, David, 26
MacGill-Eain, Somhairle see MacLean, Sorley
MacGillivray, Ina, 8
MacGillivray, James Pittendrigh, 8, 40
McGrath, Gerry, 212
McGrath, John, 68, 70, 101, 144, 184
McGrath, Tom, 68, 70, 140, 184
    poetry, 134, 206
McGuffie, Jessie, 135
MacIlleDuibh, Raghnall see Black, Ronald
McIlvanney, William, 130, 132, 142, 152, 189
MacIntyre, Donald, 94
McKay, George, 189
Mackay, Shena, 182
Mackenzie, Compton, 11, 104, 105, 108, 217
Mackintosh, Charles Rennie, 53, 75
Mackintosh, Ewart Alan, 41, 43–5
Maclaren, Ian, 26, 27, 38
Maclaren, Pharic, 144
MacLean, Alistair, 11, 93, 143, 217
McLean, Duncan, 73, 188
MacLean, Sorley, 2, 157, 158, 159
    criticism by, 191
    Dàin do Eimhir, 10, 58, 95–6, 97, 100, 137, 138, 160
    death, 191–2
    essays on, 191
    Garioch on, 164
    'Hallaig', 108, 160
    MacDiarmid and, 138, 160
    Callum MacDonald and, 159
    MacNeacail contrasted with, 176
    poetry, 138–9, 160, 191
    in Poets' Pub, 157, 160
McLeish, Robert, 106, 110
McLellan, Robert, 59, 65–6, 68, 101, 110
    Jamie the Saxt, 59, 65, 69
    language, 4, 5
Maclellan, William, 105, 109
McLennan, Dave, 72
MacLennan, Elizabeth, 70
MacLeod, Alistair, 219
Macleod, Finlay J., 111
MacLeod, Fiona see Sharp, William
MacLeod, Iain F., 74
Macleod, James, 22
McLeod, Joseph, 99
MacLeod, Ken, 187
Macleod, Michelle, 5, 143, 192, 216

MacLeòid, Seumas *see* Macleod, James
MacMillan, Hector, 70, 140, 141, 184
McMillan, Joyce, 4
McMillan, Roddy, 68, 70, 108, 140, 143, 144, 184
Macmurray, John, 183
MacNeacail, Aonghas, 6, 153, 168, 176–7, 191, 210
MacNeil, Kevin, 192, 193, 210
McNeill, F. Marian, 109
McNeillie, John, 59
Macrae, Duncan, 143
McSeveney, Angela, 207
MacTaggart, James, 144
McTaggart, William, 53, 54
MacThòmais, Ruaraidh *see* Thomson, Derick
McWilliam, Candia, 187
'Magnetic North', 188
Magris, Claudio, 145–6
Mambro, Ann Marie di, 72, 73
Manlove, Colin, 17
Manson, John, 99
Manson, Peter, 211
Mardel, Joseph, 159
Marsack, Robyn, 208
Marshall, Bruce, 89, 105
Martin, J. S., 116
Massie, Allan, 91–2, 182
Masson, David, 16, 18, 23
Masson, Forbes, 5, 6
Maxwell, Douglas, 74
Maxwell, James Clerk, 16, 18–19, 20
Meacham, Michael, 140
Meek, James, 188
Merry Mac Fun Company, 188
Millar, J. H., 38
Millar, James Hepburn, 16
Millar, Mark, 218
Miller, Gavin, 194
Milne, Drew, 190, 211, 212
Mina, Denise, 189, 193, 194, 197–8, 199, 203, 218
Mitchell, James Leslie *see* Gibbon, Lewis Grassic
Mitchell, Robert, 64
Mitchison, Naomi, 54, 98, 104, 107–8, 109, 110
Modern Scottish Gaelic Poems, 138, 191
Moffat, Alexander, 156–66, 204, 206, 211
Moffat, Graham, 68
Moireach, Murchadh *see* Murray, Murdo
Montgomerie, William, 98, 165
Montgomery, Mary, 168, 175–6
Morgan, Edwin, 166, 204, 206
  'The Beatnik in the Kailyard', 135, 162–3
  drama, 68, 184, 189
  on Finlay, 162
  'Glasgow Sonnets', 185
  Goodsir Smith and, 162
  Graham and, 165

influence on later poets, 156, 184, 206, 209, 212, 213
  in *Justified Sinners*, 163–4
  language, 6, 134, 137, 162
  Lochhead and, 165, 184, 205
  MacDiarmid and, 135, 137, 162, 164, 221
  poetry, 13, 98, 108, 134, 135, 183, 184, 190, 204, 207, 208, 209
  in *Poets' Pub*, 156, 157
  Scottish International board member, 164
  Scottish Literary Renaissance, 7
  The Second Life, 98, 164
  Sonnets from Scotland, 185
Morrison, Grant, 218
Muir, Edwin
  autobiography, 108
  Buchan's *Witch Wood* and, 34
  poetry, 56, 58, 90, 94, 98, 106, 106–7, 108
  Poor Tom, 55
  'Scotland 1941', 76
  Scott and Scotland, 10, 58, 77–9, 81, 182
  Scottish Journey, 56, 189
  Soutar and, 93
Muir, Willa, 54, 81
Mullan, John, 114
Mulrine, Stephen, 68
Mundair, Ramon, 216
Munro, Alice, 219
Munro, George, 68
Munro, John, 47
Munro, Neil, 39–40, 48, 57, 61, 143
Munro, Rona, 72, 73
Murray, Charles, 15, 28, 39, 48
Murray, Isobel, 85
Murray, Les, 219
Murray, Murdo, 47

National Theatre of Scotland, 9, 70, 71, 220–1
Neill, Bud, 218–19
Neilson, Anthony, 13
Nelson (publisher), 109, 133
Niall, Ian *see* McNeillie, John
Nichol, John, 16
Nichols, Peter, 140
Nicholson, Colin, 151
Niven, Alastair, 216
Normand, Tom, 76
Northern Muse, The (anthology), 23, 29, 57
Northern Numbers (anthology), 48, 52
novels, 10–13, 17–18, 21–3, 26–8
  1920s and 1930s, 54–6, 57, 59–60
  1940s and 1950s, 104, 105, 106, 108, 109, 111
  1960s and 1970s, 141–4
  1980s and 1990s, 182–3, 184, 185–9
  popular and genre fiction, 11, 23, 104, 186–7, 189, 193–203, 217
  post-war, 123–32
  Scottish Renaissance, 81–7

novels (*cont.*)
  World War One, 37–8
  World War Two 88–93
  see also Gaelic novels

Object Permanence (journal), 190
Ogden, C. K., 118
O'Hagan, Andrew, 189
Oliver and Boyd, 109, 133, 159
O'Rourke, Donny, 206–7
Owens, Agnes, 185, 188

Park Theatre, 109
Parr, Chris, 4, 140
Paterson, Don, 190, 204, 205
Paton, Alan, 219
Peel, John, 136
Peploe, Samuel, 53, 76
Perry, Clive, 69, 140
Perth Theatre, 8, 109, 141
Philip, Andrew, 212–13
Phillipson, Robert, 118
Pitlochry Festival Theatre, 8, 110, 141
plays *see* drama
PN Review, 208
poetry, 28, 204–13
  1920s and 1930s, 9–10, 58
  1940s and 1950s, 104, 105, 106–7, 108, 109, 111
  1960s and 1970s, 134–9
  1980s and 1990s, 190–2
  'Seven Poets' generation, 156–66
  World War One, 28, 37, 38–48
  World War Two, 93–100
Poetry Scotland, 109, 111
Poets' Pub, 156–66, 204, 206, 211
Pollock, R. F., 61–2
Polygon (publisher), 133, 185, 188
Poor. Old. Tired. Horse (journal), 135, 190
Pound, Ezra, 2, 49, 51, 116, 120, 122, 157
Pow, Tom, 212
Press, John, 112, 114, 115, 117, 119
Price, Richard, 190, 208–9, 212
Prospect Theatre Company, 220
Prowse, Philip, 141
Prynne, J. H, 114
publishers, 108–9, 133, 159, 208, 213, 216; *see also* Akros Publications; MacDonald, Callum; Maclellan, William; Wild Hawthorn Press
Purves, David, 68
Purves, Robin, 190

Rae, Hugh C., 135, 195
Ramsay, Allan, 25
Rankin, Ian, 189, 193, 194, 195, 196, 198, 202, 203
  on 'high' and 'low' art, 197, 198
  Mina and, 218
  Rowling and, 196, 202

Scottish branding, 11, 217
Spark's influence, 185, 189
Ransford, Tessa, 208
Rayner, Patrick, 74
Rebel Inc, 188
Reid, Alastair, 136
Reid, Alexander, 68, 110
Reid, Thomas, 16
Riach, Alan
  on Harris, 150
  on MacDiarmid, 99, 113, 114, 116
  'Magnetic North' and, 188
  poetry, 190, 211
Richards, I. A., 118
Riddell, Alan, 159
Riffaterre, Michael, 119
Robb, David, 97
Roberts, William, 157, 158
Robertson, Angus, 22
Robertson, James, 213, 221–2
Robertson, Robin, 204, 205
Ronconi, Luca, 139
Ronder, Jack, 144
Rorie, David, 39
Rose, Dilys, 185
Ross, John Merry, 16
Ross, Raymond, 94, 191
Rossiter, Leonard, 140
Rothach, Iain *see* Munro, John
Rowling, J. K., 193, 196, 197, 201–2, 203, 217
Royal Lyceum Theatre Company, 8, 68, 69, 140, 144, 220
Royle, Trevor, 28, 126
Rutherglen Repertory Theatre, 62, 109

Saadi, Suhayl, 212, 216
St Mungo's Mirrorball, 213
Salmond, James Bell, 46–7
Saltire Society, 7, 59
Sansom, Ian, 120
Schmidt, Michael, 208
Scoop Books, 109
Scotland, James, 68
Scots language, 4–5, 6, 58, 151
  Buchan and, 38
  drama, 4, 9, 59, 63–6, 68, 71
  novels, 12
  poetry, 38–40, 45–6, 137, 152, 161–2, 211
Scots Magazine, 46, 110
Scott, Alexander, 97, 108, 109, 159
Scott, Douglas, 93
Scott, F. G., 53, 56–7, 106, 107
Scott and Scotland (Muir), 10, 58, 77–8, 77–9, 81, 107, 182
Scott, Tom, 99–100, 152, 159, 163
Scott, W. R., 16
Scott, Sir Walter, 3, 15
  adaptations of novels, 7, 11, 61, 71, 217
  border-crossing, 146
  Buchan and, 33, 34, 35

language, 12
  Stevenson and, 25
  Waverley, 182
Scottish Arts Council, 208, 220; *see also* Arts
  Council Scottish Committee
Scottish Book Trust, 208
Scottish International (journal), 138, 164
Scottish Literary Renaissance, 1–2, 6–7, 27,
  75–87, 103, 106–7, 161
  Ascherson on *Poets' Pub* and, 166
  Morgan on, 162
  second wave, 103, 123, 181, 185
  Soutar and, 58
Scottish National Players, 8, 61, 63, 67
Scottish National Repertory Theatre, 8
Scottish Playgoers *see* Glasgow Repertory
  Company
Scottish Poetry Library, 159, 164, 185, 208
Scottish Society of Playwrights, 7, 65
Scottish Text Society, 15
Scottish Theatre Company, 9
Searle, John, 121
Serif Books, 109, 159, 164
Seth, Andrew, 16
7:84 (Scotland) Theatre Company, 65, 68, 70,
  110, 141, 144, 184
Seven Poets, 166
Sharp, Alan, 142, 219
Sharp, William, 22, 26–7, 61
Shepherd, Nan, 54, 77, 81, 82–4, 86
Shore Poets, 213
short stories, 110
  Buchan, 29–30, 33–4
  Crichton Smith, 186
  Gaitens, 105–6
  Grassic Gibbon, 54, 55, 144
  Hanlin, 106
  Haynes, 106
  Kelman, 189
  Kennedy, 189
  Linklater, 104, 106
  Mackay Brown, 144
  Rose, 185
  Urquhart, 91
  see also MacDiarmid, Hugh, *Annals of the Five
    Senses*
Sim, Alastair, 67
Skene, W. F., 26
Smith, Adam, 16–17
Smith, Alexander McCall, 11, 193, 197, 199–
  201, 203, 217
Smith, Gregory, 3, 10, 76, 79, 80
Smith, Iain Crichton, 157, 159
  border-crossing, 152, 153–4
  death, 192
  language, 2, 6, 141, 168, 175
  Mac Colla and, 127
  on MacLean and MacDiarmid, 95
  MacLean's *Dàin do Eimhir*, 138, 160
  nationalism, 166, 239–40n

novels, 13, 134, 153–4, 164, 186
  poetry, 134, 137–8, 159, 162, 168, 175, 186,
    208, 209: Hay's contrasted with, 169;
    MacNeacail's compared to, 176; MacNeil
    compared to, 210; Scottish Parliament
    opening, 192
  in *Poets' Pub*, 157, 160
  short stories, 186
Smith, Norman Kemp, 16
Smith, Sydney Goodsir, 7
  Carotid Cornucopius, 104
  on Garioch, 161
  language, 5, 162
  Omens, 159
  poetry, 103, 106, 109, 159, 161
  in *Poets' Pub*, 156, 157, 158
  The Wallace, 162
Smith, W. Gordon, 101, 102
Smith, William Robertson, 20, 21
Sorley, Charles Hamilton, 15, 41–3
Soutar, William, 58, 93–4, 108
Southfields (journal), 209
Spark, Muriel, 123, 127, 128–9, 131, 141, 185
  The Ballad of Peckham Rye, 126, 128, 141
  The Girls of Slender Means, 126, 131
  The Hothouse by the East River, 126, 185
  language, 3, 5
  on MacDiarmid, 99
  Memento Mori, 111
  poetry, 164
  The Prime of Miss Jean Brodie, 129, 130, 131,
    141, 187
  Rankin compared to, 189
  religion, 128
  Scotland and, 125, 126, 128, 129, 132, 192
  Symposium, 131, 185
Spence, Alan, 187
StAnza, 190, 213
Stevenson, Robert Louis
  border-crossing, 146
  Buchan and, 28, 31, 33
  Conan Doyle and, 28
  death, 15, 25, 37
  'Humble Remonstrance', 17
  influence, 25
  Kennaway and, 126
  language, 12
  The Master of Ballantrae, 21, 25, 36
  Munro and, 39
  on realism, 17, 23–4
  screen adaptations, 11
  Strange Case of Jekyll and Hyde, 11, 18, 25, 28,
    78, 187
  Welsh compared to, 217–18
Stewart, Balfour, 20
Stewart, Ena Lamont, 66, 67, 68, 69, 101
  Men Should Weep, 64–5, 104, 110
  Starched Aprons, 64, 110
Stewart, John, 109–10
Sulter, Maud, 216

Sutherland, Luke, 216
Swan, Annie S., 23
Sweeney, William, 191
Symon, Mary, 39, 45–6, 48

Tait, Bob, 164
Tait, Peter Guthrie, 16, 18, 19, 20
Taylor, C. P., 69, 71, 101, 140
Tennant, Emma, 187
Theatre Hebrides, 102
Thomas, Dylan, 112, 115
Thompson, Alice, 187
Thomson, Derick
  border-crossing, 153
  Gairm magazine, 111, 138, 161
  language, 2, 171, 172–3, 174–5, 177
  on MacDonald, Donald (Dòmhnall Ruadh
    Chorùna)'s poetry, 48
  poetry, 99, 108, 137–8, 159, 160–1, 167,
    171–5, 210: Bateman compared to, 177;
    Creachadh na Clàrsaich, 171, 191; Frater
    and, 178, 179, 210; Hay's and, 169, 171;
    MacNeacail's compared to, 176
  translation of John Munro's poetry, 47
Thomson, James, 47
Thomson, William (Lord Kelvin), 16, 18, 19
Tiffany, John, 9, 140
Tonge, John, 158
Torrington, Jeff, 185
Tosg (theatre company), 102
Tranter, Nigel, 182
Traquair, Phoebe, 26
Traverse Theatre, 69, 72, 139, 140
  foundation, 7, 9, 134
  'Points of Departure' season, 185
  Scottish plays, 4
  writing workshops, 72
Trocchi, Alexander, 134, 183, 185, 190
  MacDiarmid and, 133, 135, 163
  Welsh compared to, 187
Turnbull, Gael, 135, 211, 212
Two Ravens Press, 216
Tynan, Kenneth, 133

Ùr-sgeul, 5, 192, 216
Unity Theatre, 59, 108, 110
  closure, 9, 65, 67, 110
  foundation, 8–9, 110
  Lamont Stewart and, 64, 65, 104, 110
  McLeish's The Gorbals Story, 106, 110
Ure, Joan (Betty Clark), 2, 69
Urquhart, Fred, 91, 105, 106
Urquhart, Molly S., 109

Verse (journal), 208
Vital Synz, 213

Walker, Hugh, 16
Walker, Marshall, 166
Wareing, Alfred, 8, 61
Warner, Alan, 188, 189
Watkins, Dudley D., 218
Watson, John see Maclaren, Ian
Watson, Moray, 5, 143, 192, 216
Watson, Roderick, 149–50, 190
Watson, T. M., 68
Watts, Arthur, 43
Waugh, Patricia, 82
Wells, H. G., 55
Welsh, Irvine, 56, 187–8, 216, 217
  McKay's DIY Culture and, 189
  Marabou Stork Nightmares, 186, 187–8
  Rankin and, 198
  Saadi and, 216
  Trainspotting, 187, 188, 190
Welsh, Louise, 189, 193, 196–7, 198–9
White, Kenneth, 136, 164, 190
White, T. H., 116
Whyte, Christopher
  border-crossing, 150, 151
  on Gaelic poets' readership, 161
  on Hay, 170–1
  In the Face of Eternity, 191
  language, 6, 150
  on MacDiarmid, 113, 117, 119
  MacLean's Dàin do Eimhir, 160
  on MacNeacail, 176
  Modern Scottish Poetry, 113
  novels, 6, 219
  poetry, 6, 168, 178, 191, 216
  on women poets, 164–5
Wilcox, Michael, 140
Wild Hawthorn Press, 135
Wildridge, Ella, 68
Williams, Gordon M., 77, 130, 142
Williamson, Kevin, 188
Wilson Barrett Company, 8, 61
Wilson, Rab, 211
Wittig, Kurt, 149, 165
Wright, Iain, 219
Wright, Tom, 135, 144, 213

Yeats, Elizabeth Corbet, 26
Yeats, W. B., 2, 10, 26, 49, 51, 117
Young, Douglas, 58, 96, 109, 161

Zajac, Matthew, 216–17